To MARRY An ENGLISH LORD

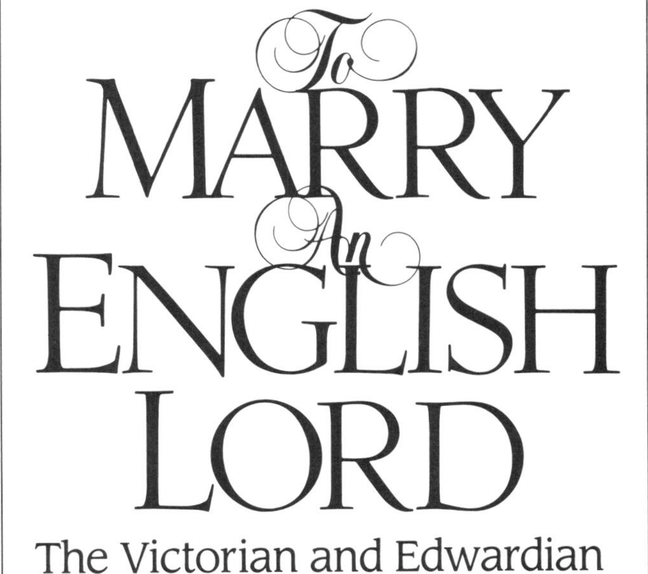

The Victorian and Edwardian Experience

Gail MacColl and Carol McD. Wallace

Sidgwick & Jackson
London

First published in Great Britain in 1989 by Sidgwick & Jackson Limited

Originally published in the United States of America by Workman Publishing Company, New York

ISBN 0-283-99972-1

Printed in the United States of America

for Sidgwick & Jackson Limited
1 Tavistock Chambers, Bloomsbury Way
London WC1A 2SG

Cover and book design by Kathleen Herlihy-Paoli with Lisa Hollander and Lori S. Malkin

Illustrations by David Cain

Cover marble by Paula Poleschner

Cover details from *The Marlborough Family* by John Singer Sargent. Reprinted by kind permission of His Grace the Duke of Marlborough, J.P., D.L.

For Peter Jarrett,
my very own English husband,
with love and thanks.
G.L.M.

With affectionate respect
to the memories of
Mrs. Wharton and Mr. James.
C.McD.W.

ACKNOWLEDGMENTS

Our heartfelt thanks to:

Lynn Seligman, who always believed it was possible to place this book with a publisher who would understand it,

that publisher, Peter Workman,

and his amazing staff, including Sally Kovalchick, who made sense of it all; Charles Kreloff, who helped inspire us years ago; Kathy Herlihy-Paoli for the beautiful design; Rona Beame for the imaginative and thorough picture research; Lynn St. C. Strong who sorted out our transatlantic inconsistencies, and Bob Gilbert, who was unfailingly patient about logistics.

We also gratefully received editorial advice, research assistance, reminiscences and hospitality from the following in Britain and America: Barbara and David Clague; the Countess of Craven; Mrs. John R. Drexel; Christian Lady Hesketh; Lord Hesketh; Hilary Hinzmann; Libby and Jonathan Isham; Lord Leigh; Victor Montagu; the Hon. Mrs. Charles Pepys; Gemma Nesbit; the Duke of Roxburghe; Sir Michael Culme-Seymour; and Liz Thurber.

The staffs of the following institutions were remarkably helpful: the British Library; the Huntington Library, especially Mary Wright; the New York Public Library; the New York Society Library; the Newport Historical Society; the Newport Preservation Society; and the Redwood Library in Newport.

And finally we thank our husbands, Rick Hamlin and Peter Jarrett, who provided in-house editorial advice and years of moral support.

CONTENTS

Jennie Jerome, Lady Randolph Churchill

CHAPTER 3

AMERICAN HEIRESSES: WHAT WILL YOU BID?

Consuelo Vanderbilt, Duchess of Marlborough

CHAPTER 4

MARRIED HEIRESSES

Cornelia Martin, Countess of Craven

CHAPTER 5

THE NEW HEIRESSES

Elizabeth French, Lady Cheylesmore

AN AMERICAN HEIRESS DIRECTORY

PROLOGUE

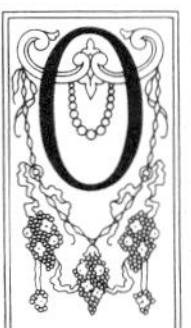

On a bright fall day in 1860, three hundred thousand people, nearly half the population of New York City, stood jostling each other and craning their necks on either side of Broadway. They were waiting to catch a glimpse of the latest distinguished visitor to their metropolis, a slender, fair-haired nineteen-year-old who had captured the imagination of the populace. He was Albert Edward, Prince of Wales, and as his open barouche bowled down the street, the crowds cheered and waved their welcome.

That was his greeting from the democratic masses. The upper-class welcome was fancier, though no less hysterical. A banquet had been proposed, but this idea was dimly received by the Prince's suite. His Royal Highness had just left Canada, where he had

The Prince of Wales is introduced to "Cousin Columbia" by "Lord Punch" in a cartoon published at the time of his American visit.

Yes, dance with him, Lady,
and bright as they are,
Believe us he's worthy those sunshiny smiles,
Wave for him the flag of the Stripe and the Star,
And gladden the heart of the Queen of the Isles.

We thank you for all that has welcomed him—most
For the sign of true love that you bear the Old Land:
Proud Heiress of all that his ancestor lost,
You restore it, in giving that warm, loving hand.

Punch (1860)

> *“Before the century is out, these clever and pretty women from New York will pull the strings in half the chanceries in Europe.”*
>
> LORD PALMERSTON, British prime minister

been to so many banquets. He was awfully fond of dancing. Could there not be a ball to welcome him to New York?

So a ball there was. The select planning committee faced the invidious task of deciding just who in New York society was worthy of meeting the Prince of Wales. Never had there been such groveling, such angling, such pleading for invitations. And when, on

HARPER'S WEEKLY.
A JOURNAL OF CIVILIZATION.

Vol. IV.—No. 197.] NEW YORK, SATURDAY, OCTOBER 6, 1860. [Price Five Cents.

Entered according to Act of Congress, in the Year 1860, by Harper & Brothers, in the Clerk's Office of the District Court for the Southern District of New York.

The face that launched a thousand daydreams. Every socialite in Manhattan wanted to say she'd danced with the Prince of Wales.

The Academy of Music transformed into a vast ballroom. Right: The Prince portrayed by famous Civil War photographer Mathew Brady; an extremely valuable piece of pasteboard.

the night of October 12, the four thousand chosen people succeeded in fitting themselves into the Academy of Music, another thousand un-chosen succeeded in joining them. The floor promptly collapsed, just as His Royal Highness was about to make his entrance, so the guests had to spend two hours milling around, examining each other's *toilettes* (the Rhinelander emeralds, Mrs. Gardiner's silver-and-coral dress from Worth, the new Paris dressmaker) as a swarm of carpenters made an ungodly racket hammering beneath them. The floor was repaired, the ball began, and though his dancing partners had been carefully chosen in advance, the Prince was mobbed by women—prim, well-bred Victorian ladies who would not let him alone. (''Not in strict accordance with good breeding,'' sniffed the Duke of Newcastle, H.R.H.'s chaperon.) The Prince did not seem to mind.

It was the Prince's first exposure to American women. His enthusiasm for them—and their reciprocal feelings for him—would have a profound effect on English society for the next fifty years.

CHAPTER 1

THE BUCCANEERS

Old New York

❖

Rule Britannia

❖

Pushy Mamas

❖

The First Marriages

OLD NEW YORK

The dozen years that passed after the Prince of Wales' visit to New York brought the Civil War and profound changes in the economy of America. But New York's social patterns remained unruffled. For most of the nineteenth century, the city's society was simple, comprising the families that had been there forever. They were known as "Knickerbockers," after the knee-length trousers worn by early Dutch settlers from whom many of them were descended. In fact, New York's social leaders could—with the sole addition of large neck-ruffs—have posed convincingly for portraits of seventeenth-century burghers. Conservatism, thrift, hard work and modesty ruled the day.

The men were bankers, or lawyers, or heirs to mercantile concerns. Some of them had tidy fortunes produced by increasingly valuable Manhattan real estate. But however rich they might be, Knickerbocker families were never showy. The rows of brownstones between Washington Square and Gramercy Park were virtually uniform, with square

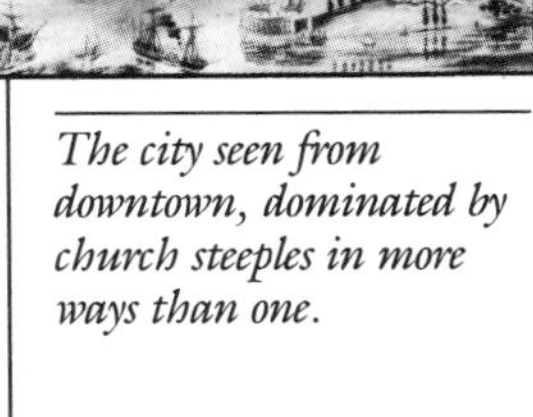

The city seen from downtown, dominated by church steeples in more ways than one.

One of New York's endless rows of brownstones—pleasantly uniform or stiflingly monotonous, depending on one's attitude.

COMME IL FAUT
Dinner at seven is followed by after-dinner calls among old-fashioned New Yorkers.

parlors and suites of rosewood furniture and three sets of curtains at each window. On the dining room table was family silver, thin and worn from generations of use, and Chinese export porcelain. A maid would serve dinner and dust the knickknacks, a cook would manage the unadorned roasts, and a coachman, with a single horse, would convey the family to the opera.

THE KNICKERBOCKER WAY OF LIFE

Social occasions were also simple. Weddings often took place at home, followed by a "wedding break-

On New Year's Day, Knickerbocker males went from house to house calling on ladies of their acquaintance, who stayed put, looked pretty and poured punch.

fast." A young girl's début—when she was formally presented to society, i.e., to her parents' friends—involved little more than donning a white dress, putting up her hair and receiving guests at a tea. Later she could accompany her parents to evening parties, where the entertainment included parlor games for the young people and cards for the grownups, with a bowl of punch and some shredded ham to punctuate the festivities. Dances meant rugs rolled back, furniture pushed to the wall, and a willing spinster pounding away on the piano. Ballrooms, in those days, were unheard of.

It was a stable way of life, and a secure one. The débutante, daydreaming in the dark parlor, could easily envision her future: two or three seasons of paying calls with Mama, looking at albums of Venice with young men at parties, blushingly sharing a hymnal at church, having her hand pressed meaningfully on the dance floor. A proposal, and marriage to an upstanding young banker or lawyer. Her own brownstone on a side street, and managing the house and children. Being a matron, and wearing elegant dark colors, perhaps even (if she'd chosen the right young banker) dresses from Paris, though they would have to lie unworn in trunks for a season or two to be right for New York—a Knickerbocker woman should not be *too* fashionable. A box for the opera at the Academy of Music; possibly a summer cottage; and, in time, a débutante daughter of her own, looking at albums of Venice with her best friend's son.

If life in Old New York was dull and predictable, the Knickerbocker families liked it that way. But this Eden of the bourgeoisie couldn't last. In the 1860s, a whole new group of people began making money in industry—in armaments, in railroads, in preserved meats to feed the soldiers, in harvesters that freed workers from the fields. These enterprises made a lot of men very rich, very fast. And when they got rich, they came to New York.

Some respectable Old New York families didn't even bother to keep a horse and carriage, renting instead from a livery stable as the need arose.

Because it was considered vulgar to be "en avant de la mode," *ladies in Old New York either had their Paris dresses altered by their maids or stored them for a season or two before putting them on.*

"A fortune of only a million is respectable poverty."
WARD MCALLISTER

WORLDS IN COLLISION

That New York was the social citadel, nobody doubted. Boston had evolved its own peculiar intellectual and sumptuary restrictions that took all the fun out of the high society game. Philadelphia had been left behind by commerce, and commercial money provided the new blood that kept the competition sharp. Washington, ever since the early, emphatic separation of politics from society (America was the only country in the world where having been born in a log cabin could be construed as a political advantage), was a backwater.

So, wherever money was made and social aspiration followed, New York was the acknowledged Great Good Place. And though New Yorkers had known this for generations, they were taken aback by the sudden mass-market appeal of their hitherto quiet city. Suddenly, there were new carriages on the drives

THE CUT DIRECT

Definition: A social technique designed to express disapproval, reinforce superiority, demonstrate exclusivity; a very public snubbing. ("For reasons that you and I and everyone watching us comprehend, I do not choose to acknowledge your existence, despite our having met at tea/gone to finishing school together/ been bridesmaids at each other's weddings.")

The Victims: Outsiders, either unsavory social climbers or former insiders who have let down the side.

The Technique: Choose the most public place available—a ballroom, the opera house or Fifth Avenue. Make sure your intended victim sees you; establish eye contact if possible. Wait for a sign of acknowledgment—a nod, a raised hand, a smile. (This is important; if the victim ignores you, she may feel she has been the cuttor and you the cuttee.) Approach—and sail past, stony-faced, as if the individual were not there. Do not look back to revel in discomfiture. That would be rude.

AT HOME ON WASHINGTON SQUARE

❖

Intended for family life, the New York brownstone is neat, cozy and decorous. The young lady's bedroom has an adjoining bath, of course, and "improving" pictures on the wall. In the parlor, a new set of carved rosewood furniture and a vase of pampas grass, with a marble statuette for a conversation piece. Many curtains at each window; many patterns in each room.

Mrs. Astor's house at 34th and Fifth had one of the few private ballrooms in New York. It held just four hundred people; hence, "the Four Hundred."

in Central Park. New faces appeared in the stalls at the Academy of Music (but not in the boxes, for these were handed from one generation to another). New names were heard on husbands' lips, in connection with business downtown.

Naturally enough, these new people thought they might like to take part in the social life of New York. If the Knickerbocker menfolk could do business with the husbands, couldn't the Knickerbocker ladies call on the wives? The answer was: Absolutely not. And nothing could make them. For New York society was run by women, and they were implacable in their distaste for new people. These *arrivistes* had no business upsetting the quiet, dignified, family-oriented city of prewar days. And they were so *showy*. Their womenfolk, for instance, were capable of wearing Paris dresses the instant the trunks from Worth cleared Customs. These people, with their new money still gritty from the mines or tacky with shoe polish, knew nothing of culture or manners, and certainly nothing of restraint. Why, August Belmont, who had married the perfectly respectable Caroline Perry, owned a gold-plated dinner service! Wasn't china good enough? And what was the use of all that fancy French cooking when a brace of canvasback duck had kept gentlemen happy for decades?

Clearly, something had to be done before these *nouveaux riches* achieved a critical mass and the sedate refinements of Old New York were lost forever in a welter of ostentation.

In black festooned with diamonds, Mrs. Astor receives her carefully selected guests. Her annual ball on a Monday in January defined the limits of New York's élite.

NOBS VS. SWELLS

At this time Knickerbocker society was led by Mrs. William Backhouse Astor, widely known as *the* Mrs. Astor, and she was seconded in her task of keeping

THE MRS. ASTOR

Ward McAllister may have done the actual work of drawing up lists, scrutinizing the merits of débutantes and leading cotillions, but he was just an eager worker bee carrying out the commands of his queen, Mrs. Astor. Born Caroline Schermerhorn, of an old shipping family, Mrs. Astor was uniquely suited to the task of running New York. Her husband was the wealthy William Backhouse Astor, Jr. (she made him drop his middle name because it was vulgar), whose money was some fifty years older than Bouncer money and thus acceptable. In addition, she had the pride and strength of purpose to keep society pure of newcomers. Tall, dark-haired and commanding, she breezed through the city's social rituals with the confidence of a woman who had rarely, in her forty years, been crossed.

The crucial question in New York was whether or not Mrs. Astor "knew" you. Had she spoken to you at a tea party? Had she paid a call? (It was always up to a social superior to make the first visit.) Most important, had she invited you to her annual ball? If not, you'd best leave town or sit at home in the dark lest anyone know of your shame. Even among those who did gain entrée to the sacred precinct, favorites were singled out still further. The queen of society had a throne, a red velvet divan set upon a dais, from which she watched the dancing; the truly chosen were fetched to sit with her for a few breathless moments, and everyone knew them as the elect.

The lady who kept New York safe for the Knickerbocracy; her husband, who bankrolled her mission; and his yacht, where he escaped from it.

> *"There are only about four hundred people in fashionable New York society. If you go outside that number, you strike people who are either not at ease in a ballroom or else make other people not at ease."*
> WARD McALLISTER

Ward McAllister, the brains behind Mrs. Astor's brawn.

order by a self-important Southerner named Ward McAllister. A man to whom social nuance was the very bread of life, McAllister came up with a grand idea for coping with the onslaught of new people. He organized a group called the Patriarchs, twenty-five New Yorkers who would give three balls each season beginning in the winter of 1872. Each Patriarch could invite four ladies and five gentlemen as his guests, vouching for their social acceptability. The goal was to redefine society, so that anyone consistently invited to the balls would be clearly In.

The brilliance of the plan lay in McAllister's selection of the Patriarchs. They were carefully chosen to form a new social élite, representing not only the "Nobs" (the old oligarchy) but the "Swells" (the high-living possessors of new money). This coalition would, McAllister thought, create an unchallenged and unchallengeable hierarchy. He expected that once they were assimilated into the chosen people, the Swells would hasten to align themselves against their former fellows and step on the hands of the climbers just below them on the ladder.

McAllister's calculations left out, however, a distinctive feature of American society: there is always new money. Even the apparent codification of New York society in the Partriarchs' Balls couldn't solve the problem of the *nouveaux riches* forever. They kept coming to Manhattan, richer and richer, and more and more insistent on social recognition. So, to strengthen their defenses, the anointed demanded the "correct" ways of doing things, from leaving calling cards to marrying off a daughter. They made lists: guest lists, visiting lists, members' lists. And New York society, by the mid-1870s, was more self-consciously exclusive and compulsively regimented than ever.

RULE BRITANNIA

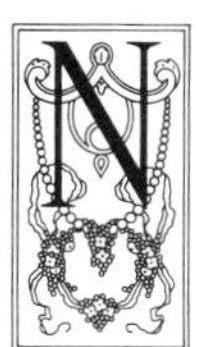

New money and new faces, the same forces that were convulsing Old New York, were finding a far different reception in London. Society here was not threatened by newcomers; instead, it welcomed the glamour and opulence the newcomers could bring. This reception had much to do with the fact that London society's commander in chief was not a persnickety matron but a party-loving playboy who happened to be next in line for the British throne.

Though christened Albert Edward, the Prince of Wales would be known throughout his life by the jaunty nickname "Bertie."

WRETCHED HIGHBORN BEINGS

The party-loving playboy was, of course, Albert Edward, Prince of Wales. In 1861, a year after the Prince's tour of North America, his father had died, leaving his mother the Queen quite inconsolable. Victoria had depended on her husband not only as head of the family (they had nine children) but as her

London's Piccadilly boasted both architectural and social variety that put New York to shame.

English society was defined as those who were eligible for presentation at court. Her Majesty received her splendidly dressed subjects at several Levées and Drawing Rooms during the season.

The very picture of a deferential Victorian wife: Queen Victoria, looking up to her husband, Prince Albert.

The Lord Chamberlain is
commanded by Their Majesties
to invite

to a Court at Buckingham Palace
on __________ 19__ at __ o'clock
Full Dress
Ladies Court Dress with Feathers and Trains

It is my desire to attend the Levée on
on which occasion I propose to present the following Gentleman
for whom I am personally responsible.—

Profession ______
Address ______
I have already been presented at a Levée.
(Signature of Presenter) ______

The Lord Chamberlain's office issued the invitations.

chief, most reliable adviser on affairs of state. In fact, her entire existence had centered on her straight-backed, right-thinking consort. "My *life* as a *happy* one is *ended*!" she mourned. "The world is gone for *me*!"

For her eldest son, however, life was just beginning. In the spring of 1863, Bertie married a pretty eighteen-year-old Danish princess named Alexandra. For taking this step into responsible adulthood, he was rewarded with Marlborough House, his own London residence. Soon afterward he bought Sandringham, a country estate in Norfolk. Now the twenty-two-year-old Prince could entertain whom he pleased, as he pleased. So he chose to entertain people like Louisa, Duchess of Manchester, who, Victoria warned Alexandra, *"is not a fit companion for you."* And the Duke and Duchess of Sutherland, she being, according to Victoria, "a foolish, injudicious little woman" whose husband did "not live as a *Duke* ought."

Bertie and Alix had fallen in with the "fashionable set." And the fashionable set, so long denied royal favor, was delighted to have them. While Albert was alive, sobriety, simplicity, domesticity and respect for the hard-working lower orders had been the hallmarks of royal style. Queen Victoria and Albert could never really be bothered with events of the social season such as Ascot or Derby Day. Their view of fashionable society was not far different from that of

Princess Alexandra of Denmark, aged eighteen, a few months before her marriage to the Prince of Wales. She was as sweet-natured as she was beautiful, but matrimony even with this paragon couldn't tame Bertie's high spirits.

Marlborough House, the Prince of Wales' London residence, which gave its name to his fashionable set of friends.

the Knickerbocker crowd in New York, who tended to consider "aristocratic" a synonym for "decadent." In fact, the royal pair had nothing but disdain for the free-living nobility—"the wretched, ignorant, high-born beings," as Victoria described them, "who live only to kill time."

BERTIE TAKES OFF

Though grief-stricken, Queen Victoria continued to keep a firm grip on the reins of power. And, despite her own ministers' advice that she give her son something serious to occupy his mind, she denied him any responsible occupation—even something as innocuous as the presidency of the Society of Arts. The Prince of Wales, a restless, energetic, enthusiastic young man who liked nothing so much as a diary crammed full of engagements, was thus left with little else to do in life but have fun.

The Prince of Wales in 1871, a year after the Mordaunt scandal. He is costumed as Lord of the Isles.

In pursuit of this goal he quite naturally began to emulate those masters of purposeful leisure, the English aristocracy. He took up horse racing, hunting, shooting. He played cards for money until early in the morning; he gambled at casinos when he went abroad. He attended balls and teas. He went to Ascot, not just on opening day, but every day, driving onto the course with his friends in a glittering carriage procession. He also went to music halls, and after the theater he went to Rules or the Café Royal or Kettner's, restaurants that provided not only meals but private rooms with settees for postprandial sex.

Moreover, as all England eventually came to know, the Prince did not confine his extramarital lust to showgirls in the upstairs rooms of restaurants. The first big scandal of his career broke in 1870 when Sir Charles Mordaunt sued his young wife for divorce. (Harriet Mordaunt's solicitor countersued, claiming she was not of sound mind.) A packet of letters from the Prince to Harriet was entered as evidence, and he was subpoenaed to give testimony. So, for the first time in English history, a Prince of Wales entered the witness box at a public trial. Bertie acquitted himself well—he managed to sound convincing as he denied that he had committed no "improper familiarity or criminal act"—but the damage was done. The Prince was clearly not the paragon of domestic virtue his parents had raised him to be.

AT HOME ON BERKELEY SQUARE

❖

Domesticity is not the point here; the house is meant to *impress*. Huge hall where footmen waste time, grand stair for receiving streams of visitors, splendid ballroom used perhaps six times a year. Milady's boudoir features many photographs of aristocratic friends, and desk for endless English letter-writing; her bedroom is elegant but small. Servants' quarters are an afterthought.

The young Prince of Wales clad, mid-nineteenth-century style, in a dress.

OUTSIDE IN

There was irony in this, for Bertie's entire upbringing had been meticulously designed by his father to produce an exemplar of the modern monarchy. Albert was farsighted enough to realize that monarchs at the end of the nineteenth century would not be allowed to get away with the kind of behavior that had distinguished the Regency years. The threat of revolution was not to be taken lightly; republican sentiments were being voiced loudly and regularly. The licentious behavior of monarchs and their noble friends in other European countries had already cost them their heads. Albert wanted to make sure that the Prince kept his.

To this end, young Bertie had been allowed as little contact with the English aristocracy as his father could politely manage. The "corrupting influence of British patrician frivolity" must not spread to the boy. So the Prince was presented with carefully chosen companions, vetted and approved by Albert. He spent his youth surrounded by older men and tutors, who were supposed to report back regularly to his father. He was always being watched, expected to be reading and studying, rarely allowed to play. He was

Domestic bliss: England's Royal Family in 1843. The Prince is learning to recognize the letter "W," no doubt for "Wales."

not allowed to attend Eton, and while he followed some courses at Oxford, he was forbidden to have any part in undergraduate life there.

Although Albert's plan was bound to backfire, Bertie's childhood seclusion had at least one beneficial result. Having been raised outside the traditional English system, he was without some of the traditional English prejudices. He himself wasn't altogether English (his father was German, he had three German grandparents, and there was a distinct Germanic flavor in his pronunciation of certain English words), so why should he mind if some of his friends weren't classic English aristocrats? If a wealthy, amusing man like Alfred Rothschild was willing to host the Prince and his entourage, the Prince was willing to give him social entrée. "All manner of strange, wild millionaires were wandering round London then," recalled Christopher Sykes, "and the Prince, perhaps recognizing natural Devil-mates, yearned to make these men his friends." In other words, the Prince of Wales willingly counted among his companions the very sort of recently rich, big-spending industrialists who were giving Old New York an upset stomach.

His Royal Highness would popularize many fashions in his lifetime, but perhaps none as persistent as the sailor suit he wore as a small boy.

THE ROCK OF ENGLAND

The Prince's taste for expensive entertainment, his enthusiasm for the social round, and his willingness to call in from the social wilderness those previously without hope (as long as they were amusing and could pay their way) converged with London's growing position as the center of a far-flung empire. By the 1870s, social climbers not merely from the rest of England but from all over the world had begun to arrive in London. But London's society matrons, unlike their New York counterparts, were not coming unglued at the prospect. Revolutions they worried about; social climbers they could deal with, without needing recourse to McAllister's lists and Patriarchs' Balls. They already had an ancient and noble system

THEIR NOBLE LORDSHIPS

Without an up-to-date Peerage, listing all titled Britons and their families, the task of sorting out the nobility was next to impossible. Adding to the difficulty was the fact that the upper ranks of the English aristocracy often had several titles, of which they would use only the highest. The ranks, in descending order, are as follows.

DUKE: A great catch; only twenty-seven in existence at any time. The duke's wife is a duchess, and both are referred to formally as "Your Grace." Their eldest son uses one of the duke's subsidiary titles, and *his* eldest son uses a different subsidiary title. (The Duke of Manchester's son, for example, is called Viscount Mandeville, and the Viscount's son is called Lord Kimbolton.) Other children use the honorary title "Lord" or "Lady" in front of their Christian names.

MARQUESS: A great leap down into the body of the peerage, who are always referred to informally and addressed as "Lord So-and-So." The marquess's wife, a marchioness, is "Lady So-and-So," and the children's titles are the same as those of a duke's children.

EARL: The bread-and-butter of the peerage, numbering in the hundreds. The earl's wife is a countess, and their eldest son uses a subsidiary title. Other sons are merely "Honourable"; daughters are "Lady" before Christian name.

VISCOUNT: Often a newer title, awarded for success in politics. The viscount's wife is a viscountess. The eldest son uses a subsidiary title, if any; other children are "Honourables."

BARON: Always referred to and addressed as "Lord"; "Baron" is rarely used. His wife is a baroness; all children are "Honourables." There are no subsidiary titles, since no lower rank exists.

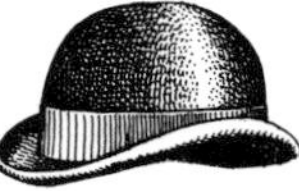
MERE SIRS: The baronet and the knight. The former is hereditary; the latter, a lifetime honorific. In each case, men are addressed as "Sir" (as in "Sir William Gordon-Cumming," known as "Sir William," never "Sir Gordon-Cumming") while the wives are "Lady" ("Lady Gordon-Cumming"). Their children have no titles.

for keeping people sorted out, for deciding who, ultimately, was socially acceptable. They had the British peerage.

And, unlike the nobility of the fallen European monarchies, the British peerage was still in fighting trim. For one thing, it hadn't lost control of Parliament; the peers themselves sat in the House of Lords, while their sons and untitled friends sat in the House of Commons. For another, thanks to the policy of primogeniture, the titles and estates of the British peers had remained more or less intact. Primogeniture meant that the eldest son in a noble family got everything—the land, the houses, the paintings, the jewels, the titles. This way, the title proliferation that afflicted the French and Italian aristocracies was not a problem in England. In France there might be several comtes de Castellane running around at any one time; in England there were only twenty-seven dukes, and a duke had to die before his son could take his place. Linked with primogeniture was the policy of entail, a means of tying up estates in trust so that they were not broken up into ever smaller plots of land but passed whole from one generation to the next. Ruthless, but wise. This system, though hard on the daughters and younger sons who lost by it, gave the English titles and consequently the entire English aristocracy a certain irrevocable cachet.

The badge of the Prince of Wales consists of three ostrich plumes, a coronet, and the motto Ich dien, *which means "I serve." It was not particularly appropriate for Bertie.*

Because England's social structure was so explicit and because it was agreed on by everyone, non-aristocrats included, society could be more relaxed. Status had already been determined by title and family history, and little short of outright scandal could alter it. While New York, in its effort to be exclusive, was becoming ever duller, London was on its way to becoming the most brilliant social capital of the era. And, fortunately for American heiresses, this capital's social leader was the Prince of Wales—a man who had already proved that he had an open mind as far as outsiders were concerned and a more than keen eye for the ladies.

THE LONDON SEASON

The great houses in Mayfair and Belgravia, shuttered and somber most of the year, have suddenly turned gay. There are striped awnings and flowerboxes at all the windows. The royal standard flies over Buckingham Palace; the Widow Queen is in town. It must be the season—Hyde Park is packed. Spectators have gathered to watch the parade of elegant riders in Rotten Row, the long strip of reddish brown earth beside the green of the park. Suddenly, chairs are pushed back, voices are lowered—the Prince of Wales and his wife have been spotted at the Marble Arch entrance.

It's just after Easter, and England's aristocrats have come up to London to attend Parliament. The city churns with political gossip. There are great parliamentary debates to listen to, speeches to be read in the morning papers. Issues of import are settled, careers made or broken. And while the Empire is ruled, the great hostesses hold their political receptions. Piccadilly is clogged with carriages, their doors emblazoned with coats of arms, as noble guests arrive at one of the great houses. A strip of carpet leads up to the front door beneath an awning, lined on either side by a phalanx of footmen, policemen and spectators. Inside, the grand staircase sags beneath the weight of guests making their way to the top. There they are greeted by the host and hostess, she in the biggest, heaviest, shiniest tiara the family arsenal can provide. In the upstairs reception

Left: Royal Ascot, pictured here in 1900, has long been as famous for the millinery on view as for the actual races. Below: Park Lane, the very grand address of, among others, the Earl of Dudley, the Marquess of Londonderry, and the Duke of Westminster.

Above: Her Majesty the Queen, the Prince and Princess of Wales, and the Houses of Parliament, where the business of the nation was carried on between social events. Left: The race meeting at Goodwood, which finished the season. Below: The courtyard of Lansdowne House, one of London's few private mansions with its own gardens.

rooms, a band plays from behind a screen of potted azaleas. Downstairs, the rooms are crammed with little tables and a buffet supper for 600.

In the June fortnight between the Derby and Ascot, the season reaches its peak. Invitations lie in stacks on silver salvers just inside every front door. More dinners, parties, balls, concerts, teas, breakfasts even, than anyone can possibly attend. The aristocracy socializes morning, noon and night, going without sleep for the sake of another dance or one last hand of "baccy."

The end of July looms. The sailing has begun at Cowes; in another few weeks, there will be shooting in Scotland. Parliament must recess. The town houses are closed up again; all the great families scurry back to the country. And their friends, those without country houses of their own, go with them. Because everyone knows: better dead than seen alive in London in August.

Clara Jerome as a young bride. Her family, the Halls, attributed their black hair and high cheekbones to their grandmother's reputed rape by an Iroquois. The "Indian" look got stronger as Clara got older.

PUSHY MAMAS

Leonard Jerome once claimed that Wall Street was "a jungle where men tear and claw." But that was nothing compared to what the womenfolk were doing up on Fifth Avenue. The New York Stock Exchange was a far less forbidding environment than the New York drawing room. Social climbing grew ever more difficult. Any aspirant who deviated from the standards laid down by Mrs. Astor and Ward McAllister was doomed. A big house, tasteful parties, fine horses, a reasonably presentable husband guaranteed nothing. If Mrs. Astor refused to know you, you might as well be living in Cleveland.

This was a sad fact of life for many wives of social upstarts, and one they might have been willing to accept had it not been for their daughters. For while sons of *arrivistes* were frequently deemed acceptable to the Astor set, the young ladies hadn't a chance. And since ambitious parents always hope their children will outshine them, this bleak outlook for their daughters acted, for three New York matrons, as the last straw.

Even as a little girl, Jennie (shown here with her mother) was strikingly beautiful.

EXIT CLARA

For every pleasure in her marriage, Clara Jerome could point to a corresponding unpleasantness. On the one hand, for instance, there was the house. As soon as he'd made enough money, Leonard Jerome had built a mansion in Madison Square. Big and showy, it was the first of New York's private palaces, a great strawberry shortcake amid blocks of dull brown townhouses. It was lovely for Clara to be able to move out of Brooklyn and have her own house, which she decorated all in red and gold. But attached

The mansion on Madison Square was a distressingly far cry from New York's standard-issue brownstones.

Jennie, little Clara and Leonie Jerome would come to be known as "the Beautiful," "the Good" and "the Witty."

to the house was a small private theater. Her husband, it seemed, liked opera. And opera singers. Unbeknownst to Clara, he had named their second daughter Jennie after Jenny Lind, the Swedish soprano. He launched the century's great diva, Adelina Patti, in America. Minnie Hauk, another beloved prima donna of the era, also began her career at the Jerome opera house. Unlike Patti, Hauk was included in family life, being much the same age as Jerome's three daughters—in fact, she was generally thought to be a fourth daughter. Years later, an acquaintance wrote to one of Jerome's legitimate offspring: "I remember my first opera. I went in 1866 to the début of Minnie Hauk. Your father educated her voice and her morals I believe?"

This kind of thing might have amused Jerome's fellow stockbrokers, but it did not go down well with their wives. (It was always easier to be one of the boys than to get in with Mrs. Astor.) Clara's situation grew even less palatable when Leonard took up with Fanny Ronalds. A society matron *manquée,* Fanny had decided to trade in her husband for a career on the stage. In the eyes of other matrons, her divorce and her theatrical aspirations disqualified her from society.

"It was not the custom in Old New York drawing rooms for a lady to get up and walk away from one gentleman in order to seek the company of another."

EDITH WHARTON, *The Age of Innocence*

Dark-eyed Jerome protégée Minnie Hauk and dark-eyed Jerome daughter Jennie: New Yorkers drew nasty conclusions.

She was certainly not suitable company for young girls. But Jerome encouraged his daughters to go ice-skating with her, to ride up Fifth Avenue in her carriage, to visit her little house for tea and gooey cakes. She gave them singing lessons, and they attended her concerts at the private theater on Madison Square.

If Clara Jerome, proper, boring Clara, ever had a hope of being accepted by New York society, Fanny Ronalds demolished it. Clara sat in her mansion, knowing that the best invitations for the most exclusive dinners and dances would never come her way. And if they didn't come to her, they surely weren't going to come to young Clara or Jennie or little Leonie. A new strategy was in order. So, in 1867, she informed Leonard that she wasn't feeling well and required an apartment for herself and the girls on the Boulevard Malesherbes in Paris. He could visit as often as he liked and would please pay the bills.

With his drooping mustaches and extravagant personality, Leonard Jerome was very attractive to women of a certain type—not, however, to the women who ran New York.

EXIT ELLEN

Clara was not alone in trading New York for Paris. Ellen Yznaga also took her daughters from heartless New York to the more welcoming City of Light. Like Clara, she had received the cold shoulder from the captious social arbiters of Fifth Avenue. While it was true that there was a perfectly respectable plantation in Louisiana, her husband Antonio sprang from Cuban stock. And while it was true that Ellen Yznaga was a very handsome woman, from a New England family, she was also thought to be "fast" by prudish New Yorkers. The merits didn't outweigh the demerits, and Mrs. Yznaga took her daughters Natica, Consuelo and Emily to Paris. There, in the late 1860s, she and the girls were frequently seen at the musical parties at the Imperial Palace of the Tuileries, singing duets with great refinement.

Consuelo, the future Duchess of Manchester.

Antonio Yznaga with his wife Ellen (left) and daughter Consuelo. A potent laissez-faire charm ran in the family.

The worldly glitter of the French capital under Emperor Napoleon III held enormous allure. Empress Eugénie mandated brand-new dresses and plenty of diamonds at court fêtes, and didn't care if these were worn by American women. Least of all did she care what rung of New York's social ladder these women once occupied as long as they had charm, beauty and plenty of money. The Empress thoroughly understood that a sparkling court was not possible if it received only the out-at-elbows *ancien noblesse*, so the Yznaga women (sparkling to a fault) were made welcome.

EXIT MARIETTA

Clara Jerome and Ellen Yznaga gave up without really trying to conquer New York society, but Marietta Stevens was made of sterner stuff. Furthermore, she had what might, in some circles, have been considered an advantage: her husband, Paran Stevens, ran the famous Fifth Avenue Hotel. So Marietta was not only rich but also had some advanced ideas about hospitality.

She began by giving musicales, featuring some of the city's noted performers. Cleverly, she scheduled these for Sunday evenings, which until then had been

The Fifth Avenue Hotel proved an inadequate launching pad for the aspirations of Marietta Stevens, shown at left in her Queen Elizabeth costume.

WORDS FOR THOSE ON THE OUTSIDE WANTING IN

Le monde snob was the American heiress's home turf. A woman was always caught up in the process of getting the cold shoulder and then, at the first available opportunity, giving it. The point of getting in, after all, was to keep everyone else out. Those with one foot in the door were known as:

1. *Arrivistes*
2. Bouncers (so called for their bumptious demeanor)
3. Climbers
4. Comers
5. Detrimentals (defined by Rev. C.W. de Lyon Nicholls, author of *The Ultra Fashionable Peerage of America,* as persons "of however excellent moral character or ability, who do not blend well with either the conservative Knickerbocker element, or the ultra-fashionables")
6. New people
7. *Nouveaux riches*
8. Outlanders
9. *Parvenus*
10. Shoddees
11. Swells (as opposed to Nobs in the social system concocted by Ward McAllister)
12. Upstarts
13. Vulgarians

MARCH OF ANGLOMANIA
In the 1870s, Tiffany & Co. added a special heraldry department to attend to "blazoning, marshalling, and designing of arms."

devoted to sober readings in the bosom of the family. Even more cleverly, she dared to flout precedent by serving champagne. The men of Old New York soon began to find that on Sunday nights they were called out of the house and would somehow end up at Mrs. Stevens'. Their wives, respectable matrons observing the Sabbath, stayed home.

But this was only success of a sort. Mrs. Stevens' hospitality backfired–she so angered the ladies that they resolutely refused to follow where their husbands so eagerly led. For herself, perhaps, Marietta Stevens could have accepted a partial triumph, trusting to time to bury the vicious rumors that she'd been a chambermaid in her husband's hotel. (In fact, she was a grocer's daughter from Lowell, Massachusetts.) Time, however, was just what her daughter Minnie didn't have. Minnie was eighteen in 1871, of

THE AGE OF REVENGE

The first blow was landed in 1869 by Mary Mason Jones, powerful dowager of a *very* Old New York family, after the completion of her grand new house on Fifth Avenue. She called it Marble Row, and she dedicated it with the words: "There is one house Mrs. Stevens will never enter."

Mrs. Stevens took the punch and bided her time for a dozen years. Then her son Harry fell in love with a relative of Mary Mason Jones, a handsome young redhead named Edith. This gave Marietta Stevens, the social-climbing newcomer, a chance to give Old New York a taste of humiliation. Harry received his instructions, and Miss Jones was unceremoniously dropped.

In the fullness of time, Mrs. Stevens' revenge appeared complete. Mary Mason Jones died, and Mrs. Stevens bought the forbidden premises—Marble Row was now one house Mrs. Stevens entered as often as she liked. But the Joneses had the last word. Edith recovered from her broken engagement, married someone else and wrote novels about the New York of her youth. To this day, Mrs. Stevens lives unhappily on as Mrs. Lemuel Struthers of the "bold feathers and brazen wig" in Edith Wharton's *The Age of Innocence*.

The mansard-roofed Marble Row. Insets: Teddy Wharton and his bride-to-be, Edith Jones.

an age to be presented to society. She was very pretty, slender and green-eyed and charming, but society clearly wanted no part of her. So Mrs. Stevens, ever practical, closed up her house and took her daughter off to the greener, nobler pastures of Europe.

COMME IL FAUT
Unlike Americans, who always introduce themselves, the English wait for a formal introduction—which very often is not forthcoming.

AT HOME ABROAD

In abandoning a lost cause, the ladies Jerome, Yznaga and Stevens were only doing the sensible thing. Little did they think that in packing their trunks and hopping on a steamer for the Old World, they were setting a pattern for hundreds of American women over the next half-century.

It wasn't that American women had never before sailed to Europe. It was that they'd never before had fun when they got there. The Knickerbocker families went abroad to look at ruins, cathedrals, pictures or scenery. They did not go to parties or make friends; they did not break into society in Paris or Florence or Geneva. Old New Yorkers were not interested in the approval of Europeans.

This was because Europeans and their culture were not to be trusted. For years, Old New York lived in dread of what it considered "dubious foreign influences." It was acceptable to return from abroad with French academic paintings but not with a hint, a whisper, a trace of Old World manners and customs. When, for instance, Ellen Olenska returns to New York to recover from an unhappy Continental marriage in Edith Wharton's *The Age of Innocence*, she is greeted by her family with worry and doubt. Can they persuade the rest of Old New York to allow the tainted lamb back into the fold? Can they train her back to their simple ways, make her forget the attractions of perfumed boudoirs, powdered bosoms, witty conversation?

The answer, of course, is no. As Henry James also found, some New Yorkers, having once "bitten deep into the apple of Europe," were loath to let go. The Pushy Mamas never looked back.

WALL STREET FATHER NO. 1: THE SPORTING MAN

While the *parvenu* wife found New York too lonely, too humiliating and most of all too dull to be borne, her husband might well be having the time of his life. This newly, hugely rich Wall Street speculator, who wanted to *enjoy* his wealth, turned to England for inspiration. And England, that country where the social season was just a break squeezed in between the end of hunting and the start of shooting, gave him sport.

The Sporting Man type of Wall Street Father was, first, last and always, a gentleman. He didn't cheat at cards, he always paid his debts, and he never discussed business on a boat; he was kind to horses and almost as kind to his mistresses.

The archetypal Sporting Man was Leonard Jerome. With his confrères August Belmont and William Travers, Jerome thought horse racing (which had fallen into disrepute, being too much associated with rowdy types) should be elevated to British standards. So he built the Jerome Park Race Track and, to get there, a sweeping new boulevard called Jerome Avenue. And in April 1866 he met with Travers and Belmont in his Wall Street office to found the American Jockey Club. Modeled after the English Jockey Club, it would have a membership of only fifty at any one time; no matter how socially prominent, a horse fancier had to wait for death or disaster to make room for him.

Horses also pull carriages, so Jerome naturally became an early enthusiast of amateur coaching. His friend William Jay imported a coach from England, and together they introduced fellow Sporting Men to the intricacies of driving

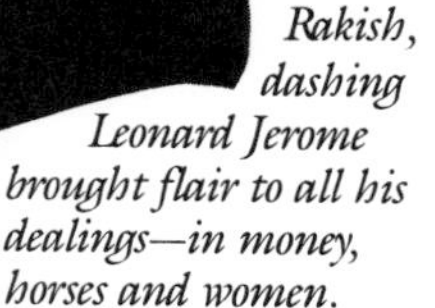

Rakish, dashing Leonard Jerome brought flair to all his dealings—in money, horses and women.

Above: Fanny Ronalds, who managed to keep Leonard Jerome and August Belmont simultaneously fascinated. The Four-in-Hand Club dashing off to the races at Jerome Park in 1875. Right: One of America's first polo matches, played at Jerome Park in 1876.

a stagecoach behind four horses in the proper manner. The sport was meticulously regulated (each horse must have artificial flowers attached to its throat-latch, for instance) and a prime source of Anglomania.

Like all true Sporting Men, Jerome, Travers and Belmont also raced boats. Jerome and his brother Lawrence proposed the first international yacht race across the Atlantic, with the victory celebration to be held at the Royal Yacht Squadron in Cowes. The American yacht *Henrietta*, owned by James Gordon Bennett, Jr., and heavily backed by Jerome, won the race and the $90,000 stake.

Jerome exhibited another Sporting Man trait: the grand gesture. When the Atlantic cable broke, he offered his yacht to take an engineer to repair it. And he personally got behind a breech-loading machine gun when a mob threatened the *Times* building (he was part owner of the newspaper) in the Draft Riots of 1863. In his grandest gesture, upon hearing at dinner that his fortune had been lost, he announced to his guests: "Gentlemen, I am a ruined man. But don't worry—your dinner is paid for."

On one occasion, Jerome, Travers and Belmont competed to see which man could host the most perfect supper. (At Jerome's dinner, each female guest opened her napkin to find a souvenir of the *Henrietta*'s victory in the form of a gold bracelet.) The competition ended in a draw—not altogether surprising since Lorenzo Delmonico produced all three meals. It is fitting, then, that the most succinct accolade to the Sporting Man type of Wall Street Father is August Belmont's tribute to his lifelong rival. "One rode better, sailed better, banquetted better," said Belmont, "when Mr. Jerome was of the party."

"For richer, for poorer..."

THE FIRST MARRIAGES

Mrs. Jerome's eldest daughter, Clara, made her début in Paris. Her suitors were French noblemen, whom she and her mother were adept at assessing—and discarding, since French titles were a particularly unreliable guide to material inheritance and social status. Nevertheless, Mrs. Jerome began to dream of an alliance with a significant French family, her daughter a marquise de Breteuil or duchesse de Noailles.

The invasion of Paris by the Prussian army in 1870–71 put a halt to such plans. The Second Empire fell. Everyone associated with it fled Paris. Leonard Jerome was summoned from New York to rescue his family from the Germans and find them suitable shelter in London. In no time at all, the gallant husband had installed his wife and daughters at Brown's Hotel—in rooms with a piano so that Clara and younger sister Jennie might continue to practice their duets—and returned alone to New York. Already in London were the Yznaga women, and Mrs. Stevens and Minnie.

ON TO ALBION

Now the Pushy Mamas were truly breaking new ground. If Continental society was disapproved of by Old New York, English society was beyond redemption. England represented, after all, the hand of tyranny cast off. It was not so many generations back that the Republic had earned its independence from the perfidies of the English monarchy. The subsequent War of 1812 had dashed any notions of forgiveness from American hearts. Each side continued to form and file plans for the invasion and final subjugation of the other. New York society was also well aware that the sympathies of the English aristocracy (and therefore the English government) had been with the South during the American Civil War. In the period directly after that conflict, relations between Albion and her former colonies were as strained as ever they were at the height of the Revolution. A third Anglo-American war was not thought to be out of the question.

This Anglophobia was most fiercely felt toward the English aristocracy, who were perceived as a decadent, hypocritical, conniving, ill-mannered bunch of snobs incapable of understanding the higher principles of democracy and freedom. It was anathema to the republican heart to consider bowing down before English titles; rather, it had been for years the tradition in Old New York to ignore them. If, in Knickerbocker eyes, the seductive gaieties of Paris and Rome could tarnish a woman, then dirty old London could turn her black.

What the Jeromes and Yznagas and Stevenses found, however, was that London, dirty as it was, did not ignore them. London society did not refuse to attend their dinner parties or make lists that excluded their names. London society, the Pushy Mamas discovered, was more stimulating and more permissive, more leisurely and more sophisticated than Old New York. Best of all, London society had the Prince of Wales. Bertie took one look at the green-eyed Minnie Stevens, the luscious Consuelo Yznaga, the entrancing Jerome girls—and all doors opened before them.

H.R.H. the Prince of Wales in a casual mood. The increasing girth of middle age didn't interfere with his appreciation of women—or with their appreciation of him.

“Last night at the circus, someone told me that Jennie would marry the second son of the Duke of Marlborough—a Good Thing tho’ he is *a younger son.”*
LEONIE JEROME, in her diary

LOVE AT FIRST SIGHT

Certainly, when dark-haired Jennie Jerome made her début in 1872, there was no problem about invitations. Jennie spent her nineteenth summer with her mother and two sisters at Cowes on the Isle of Wight. In August she attended a ball on board the cruise ship H.M.S. *Ariadne* in honor of the Prince and Princess of Wales and the Prince’s aunt and uncle, the Czarevich and Czarevna of Russia. At this dance, she was introduced to Lord Randolph Churchill, the brilliant, unruly second son of the seventh Duke and Duchess of Marlborough. He was a bit of a dandy, popeyed and slender, but charismatic—not much of a dancer, but as a talker, hard to resist. Three days later he proposed to the American girl and was accepted.

When, four days after that, Mrs. Jerome was informed, she was aghast. In the first place, neither pair of parents had been consulted, and in the 1870s it was customary for a suitor to reveal his intentions to a girl’s parents or guardians as well as his own before making any firm commitments. For Jennie to plight herself to Randolph before he’d spoken to her mother was rash, if not unbecomingly bold.

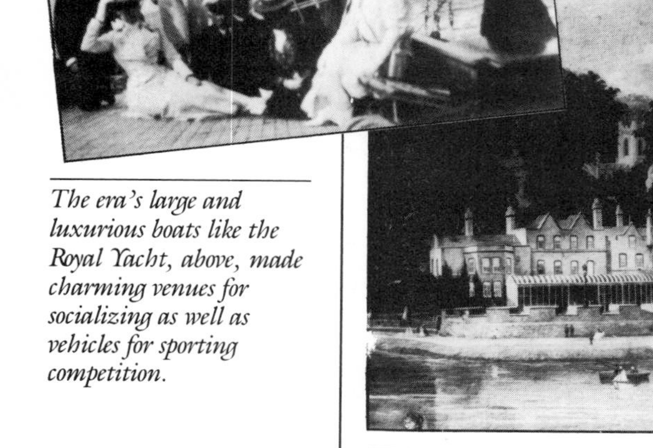

The era’s large and luxurious boats like the Royal Yacht, above, made charming venues for socializing as well as vehicles for sporting competition.

Social life at Cowes centered on the Royal Yacht Squadron, which hosted a famous annual regatta.

Then there was his position. Clara Jerome had been in Europe long enough to know that Lord Randolph, a mere second son, was not in line to inherit his father's dukedom.

The Duke and Duchess of Marlborough were equally disapproving. That their son should marry an American about whom they knew nothing was in itself a shock. They moved swiftly to find out more about Leonard Jerome from New York correspondents, and learned nothing they liked. "[T]his Mr. J. seems to be a sporting, and I should think vulgar kind of man," wrote the Duke to Randolph. "I hear he drives about six and eight horses in New York (one may take this as a kind of indication of what the man is)." Continuing in this vein, the Duke called Jerome a connection "which no man in his senses could think respectable."

Headstrong fiancés, Jennie Jerome and Lord Randolph Churchill. A meeker couple would have yielded to their parents' objections.

But the force of history was not on the side of the Jerome and Marlborough parents. The Prince of Wales took up Jennie's cause, informing Their Graces that he, who knew something about American society in general and this family in particular, could see nothing at all objectionable in the match. In fact, Bertie told them, he positively endorsed it. The Marlboroughs then decided to put their faith in Randolph's renowned fickleness. They would not allow their son to marry Jennie—or even to see her again—until he had gained a seat in the House of Commons. Fortuitously, Parliament was promptly dissolved, a new election called, and Randolph voted in by the people of his home village of Woodstock.

Finally the engagement was accepted—and then nearly foundered on the financial negotiations. Randolph could bring little to the marriage (even though his father would pay his debts beforehand and increase his allowance to £1,100 a year), so the young couple would have to live on the marriage settlement. After all, an illustrious Churchill was marrying a nobody; her family would gain immense prestige from this connection, which meant the dowry had to

" . . . both Mr. Jerome and myself have too high an opinion of our daughter, too much love ever to permit her to marry any Man without the cordial consent of his family. "

MRS. LEONARD JEROME, to Lord Randolph Churchill

be generous. Jerome came up with £50,000, which would produce £2,000 of income annually, but insisted on making Jennie an allowance of £1,000 for her personal use. This outraged Lord Randolph's lawyers, one of whom wrote to him: "The Duke says that such a settlement cannot as far as you are personally concerned be considered as any settlement at all, for. . . Miss Jerome would be made quite independent of you in a pecuniary point of view, which in my experience is most unusual. . . . Although in America, a married woman's property may be absolutely and entirely her own, I would remark that upon marrying an Englishman, she loses her American nationality and becomes an Englishwoman so that I think that the settlement should be according to the law and

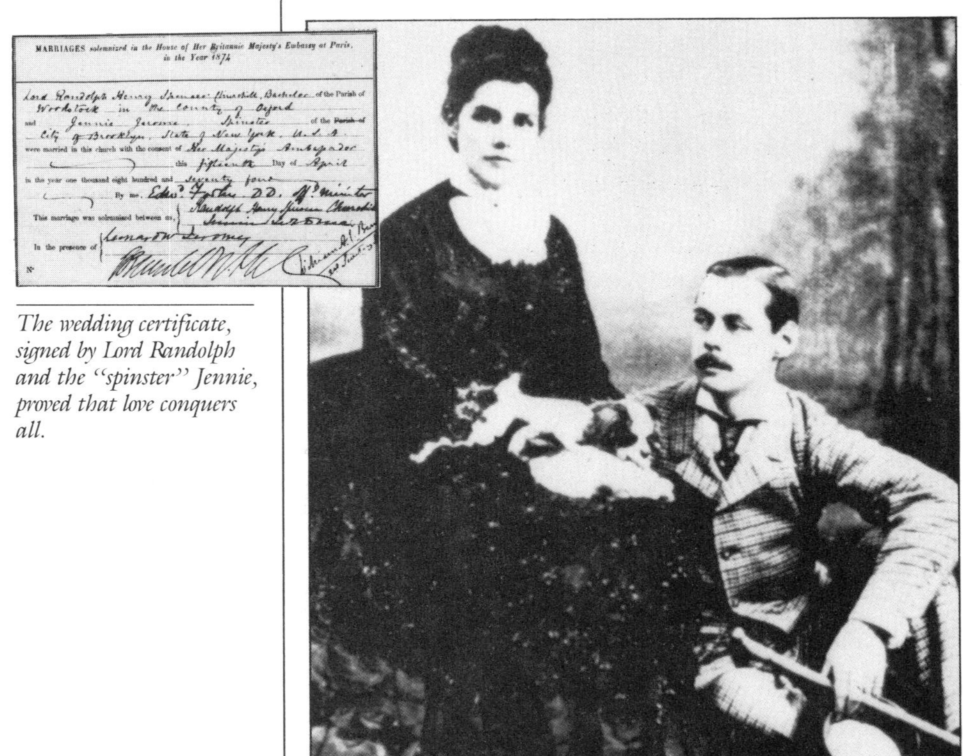

MARRIAGES solemnized in the House of Her Britannic Majesty's Embassy at Paris, in the Year 1874

Lord Randolph Henry Spencer Churchill, Bachelor of the Parish of Woodstock in the County of Oxford
and Jennie Jerome, Spinster of the ~~Parish of~~ City of Brooklyn, State of New York, U.S.A.
were married in this church with the consent of Her Majesty's Ambassador this fifteenth Day of April
in the year one thousand eight hundred and seventy four
By me, Edwd. Forbes DD. Off. Minister
This marriage was solemnized between us, Randolph Henry Spencer Churchill, Jennie Jerome
In the presence of Leonard W. Jerome

Nº

The wedding certificate, signed by Lord Randolph and the "spinster" Jennie, proved that love conquers all.

The triumphant young couple. Jennie lost no time in becoming pregnant with Winston.

THE WILSON FAMILY SCORECARD #1 May & Ogden

Among the families arriving in New York after the Civil War were the R.T. Wilsons, a classic example of what the Knickerbockers found so distasteful. Wilson, who stood six and a half feet tall, had an ambition that matched his size. Born the son of a Scottish tanner in Georgia, he began his career as a traveling salesman. The Civil War meant opportunity for a man of his stamp, and he advanced to be commissary general of the Confederate Army. He found it expedient, however, to move his family to London in 1864, and at war's end the Wilsons returned and settled at 812 Fifth Avenue.

The mother of the "marrying Wilsons," known as the most successful matchmaker of her day.

Wilson brought with him his wife Melissa, sons Marshall Orme and Richard Thornton, Jr., daughters May, Belle and Grace—and $500,000. No one knew where the money had come from, but Old New York assumed he'd been selling Confederate supplies to foreign governments while in London. He set about increasing his fortune and was highly successful in banking and southern railroads (as well, some sources say, as the widely fraudulent public franchising of Detroit).

But the Wilsons remained social outcasts in New York until 1877, when eldest daughter May married Ogden Goelet. The Goelets were Old New York denizens, deriving their genteel income from New York real estate. To be sure, Ogden's income wasn't immense, but his connections were impeccable. Suddenly the Wilsons were related by marriage to some of New York's stuffiest families. Wilson settled $75,000 on the newlyweds. Then Peter Goelet died, leaving his nephew Ogden as much as $25 million. Now the respectable match looked like a brilliant one, and the Wilson family strategy against New York society was set: if you can't beat them, join them—in holy matrimony.

Baby May Goelet and her mother, née May Wilson.

A "Spy" caricature of the 8th Duke of Manchester (1853–1892) when he was still Viscount Mandeville but already a reprobate.

custom here." Jerome saw it differently: "I can but think that your English custom of making the wife so entirely dependent upon the husband, is most unwise."

Young love eventually got its way. In April of 1874, in the modest manner quite typical of the era, Jennie Jerome and Lord Randolph Churchill were married at the British embassy in Paris. Lord Randolph's parents did not attend (noble parents were not expected to drag themselves across the Channel simply because a child was getting married), but the Prince of Wales sent a representative, indicating not only his friendship for Randolph but also his admiration for Jennie.

Emerging from the wedding breakfast into the spring sunlight, Jennie stepped into an open carriage and waited for her husband to join her. As he settled himself beside her, she opened the gold-and-tortoiseshell-handled parasol that had been a gift from her father and turned with one last smile for her mother and sisters. Then they were off. The new Lady Randolph Churchill could expect to go directly from her honeymoon in France to the center of English society. Reports had reached Paris that a more than usually brilliant London season was about to get underway (the wedding had in fact been pushed forward for this reason), and Jennie had every intention of being part of it.

A NOBLE RAKE

A terse, single-sentence announcement in *The New York Times* informed the Four Hundred that Jennie Jerome, protégée of the scandalous Fanny Ronalds, was now an English aristocrat. (Fanny already knew, since she'd taken a cue from the younger girls and moved to London herself.) Consuelo Yznaga was not so discreet.

If the Jeromes' reputation was dubious, the Yznagas' was worse, and Consuelo's careless behavior had something to do with this. Blond, pretty, with a merry, easy manner, she was completely uninhibited in an era when bending down to buckle a slipper was considered unladylike. Consuelo thought nothing of picking up a banjo and singing minstrel songs in a Mayfair drawing room, behavior that rather intrigued London's fashionable set.

One of the dominant women in this circle was the Duchess of Manchester, the former German princess of great beauty and high spirits whose reputation was such that Queen Victoria had demanded the Prince of Wales shun her. The Prince ignored his mother. Louisa Manchester was too charming, her entertainments too amusing to forgo. People played cards for money after her dinner parties; married women flirted and carried on with men not their husbands. The Duchess of Manchester was the sort of woman who went to a music hall with the Prince and danced a cancan.

Consuelo Yznaga costumed as Beauty of "Beauty and the Beast," all too appropriate considering her marital fate.

Her eldest son, Viscount Mandeville, himself fell somewhat short of respectable behavior, and he was charmed by the irrepressible Consuelo when they met at the Grand Union Hotel in Saratoga, New York. The story has it that he later visited the Yznagas at a country home (in Louisiana according to one source, New Jersey according to another), where Consuelo nursed him through a bout of typhoid fever. By the time he was well, they were engaged.

The seventh Duke and Duchess of Manchester were as ill-pleased by this engagement as the Duke and Duchess of Marlborough had been by Randolph's. Mandeville, after all, was going to be a duke himself, and the prospect of an American duchess (particularly a banjo-playing one) seemed unthinkable. But a woman who danced the cancan could not disapprove too successfully of one who played the banjo. Furthermore, Mandeville's profligate behavior had already spoiled his chances for a respectable English match.

Louisa, Duchess of Manchester, considered a great beauty in her youth. By middle age, her looks had set into a kind of fearsome grandeur.

Where Jennie Jerome's wedding, announced from Paris, had warranted a single sentence, Consuelo Yznaga's, a local affair, required headlines in the New York newspapers. It was one of the most elaborate weddings the city had yet seen, with the carriages of the 1,200 guests creating a traffic jam along Broadway outside Grace Church. At the bride's request, there was a special musical arrangement of the English hunting tune "John Peel." *The New York Times* was forced to cover the May 1876 ceremony as a news event, although a social snub was nevertheless administered in the article's headline: "Lord Mandeville Married." The bride, in other words, was not someone whose name New York was expected, or even asked, to recognize.

"A GREAT HEIRESS"

Mrs. Paran Stevens' name, in contrast, was practically a byword in New York society, and daughter Minnie soon gained a renown of her own. The Stevens women arrived in Europe in 1872, and Minnie naturally charmed the Prince of Wales. She charmed a few others as well and began to receive proposals of marriage, which were promptly turned down as not being impressive enough. The rejects included Lord William Hay and Lord Newry as well as Captain Arthur Paget, a boon companion (and reputed bookmaker) of the Prince. But Minnie was apparently intent on making a really spectacular match, and Paget didn't qualify.

As Mrs. Stevens trolled her daughter through the social shoals of England and the Continent, Minnie came to be known as "a Great Heiress." She was the first—if not, as it later transpired, the most deserving—American girl to earn the label. Finally, she (and her mother, it must be assumed) accepted the offer of the French Duc de Guiche. As a son of the Duc de Gramont, his pedigree was unassailable. The Duc, however, was cautious, and he sent a man

Despite the bouquet, this photograph of Minnie Stevens Paget was not taken at her wedding. Her dress, hair and jewelry would have been far more elaborate.

"I must say I think this business very cruel, but at the same time I can't help thinking she deserved a snubbing as she told me she had £20,000 a year and would have more and she told me that sum in dollars as well, so there is no mistaking the amount."

LADY WALDEGRAVE to Lady Strachey, on the Stevens/Gramont debacle

of business to New York to investigate the Stevens family finances. His offer was subsequently retracted. The Stevens women had, it seemed, inflated Minnie's net worth.

The chagrined and now somewhat desperate Minnie (she was twenty-five, practically a confirmed spinster by the standards of the era) decided to go with the sure thing. If he wasn't actually titled, Captain Paget was certainly well connected, son of General Lord Alfred Paget, grandson of the Marquess of Anglesey, member of a family prominent in court life for several generations. Mrs. Stevens promptly booked the ceremony for July 27, 1878, at St. Peter's Eaton Square, scene of many fashionable English weddings.

The real moment of triumph, however, came

COMME IL FAUT
A bride may wear her wedding dress for formal occasions in the first year of her marriage.

the day before the wedding, when the Prince of Wales "condescended to pay a visit" (as the press reports phrased it) to offer congratulations and best wishes. Marietta Stevens could gloat, as she fell asleep that night, over just how tough to swallow New York would find that little nugget of news. Queen Victoria's son calling on the hotelkeeper's wife—it was a scene that didn't bear contemplating.

But it was contemplated a great deal over the next few decades. The irony was that this suddenly

THE LAST WORD

Edith Wharton's last novel was published posthumously in its unfinished state in 1938. Called *The Buccaneers*, it traces the marital careers of a band of American girls who landed in London in the 1870s. As she did in many of her novels, the author based her characters to some extent on people she knew.

Lovely, lazy, guitar-playing Conchita Closson clearly resembles Consuelo Yznaga. She marries improvident Lord Richard Marable in circumstances similar to those surrounding the courtship of Consuelo and Lord Mandeville. Mrs. Wharton also creates a pair of sisters reminiscent of the socially successful Yznagas and Jeromes. The pretty and high-spirited St. George girls have a father who is a Southerner, like R.T. Wilson, and an inconsistently successful stock speculator, like Leonard Jerome. One marries the Earl of Seadown; the other, the Duke of Tintagel. Finally, Lizzy Elmsworth, a dark-haired beauty resembling Jennie Jerome, marries Hector Robinson, a rising M.P. in the Randolph Churchill mold. The focus of the novel was to be Nan St. George, Duchess of Tintagel (based on Consuelo Vanderbilt, an heiress of the 1890s), who would eventually run away from her husband.

Near the end of the fragment, Mrs. Wharton sets the scene not only for the rest of her story but for the rest of the century. "The free and easy Americanism of this little band of invaders had taken the world of fashion by storm.... 'Wherever the men are amused, fashion is bound to follow' was one of Lizzy's axioms; and certainly, from their future sovereign to his most newly knighted subject, the men *were* amused in Mayfair's American drawing rooms."

Capt. Arthur Paget, costumed as Edward the Black Prince, an earlier, more famous military man.

In the 1870s, the splashy wedding was the exception rather than the rule. The reception, or "breakfast," was short and far from lavish. Nevertheless, the aesthetics of the era mandated incredibly ornate wedding cakes.

wealthy woman, snubbed by Mrs. Astor, was considered quite good enough for the future king of England. Many years later that future king would turn at a dinner party and say to Jennie's grown son, Winston Churchill, "You know, you wouldn't be here if it weren't for me." It was a statement Bertie might have extended to include many of Winston's contemporaries, the entire generation of half-American English aristocrats that he, more than anyone else, made possible.

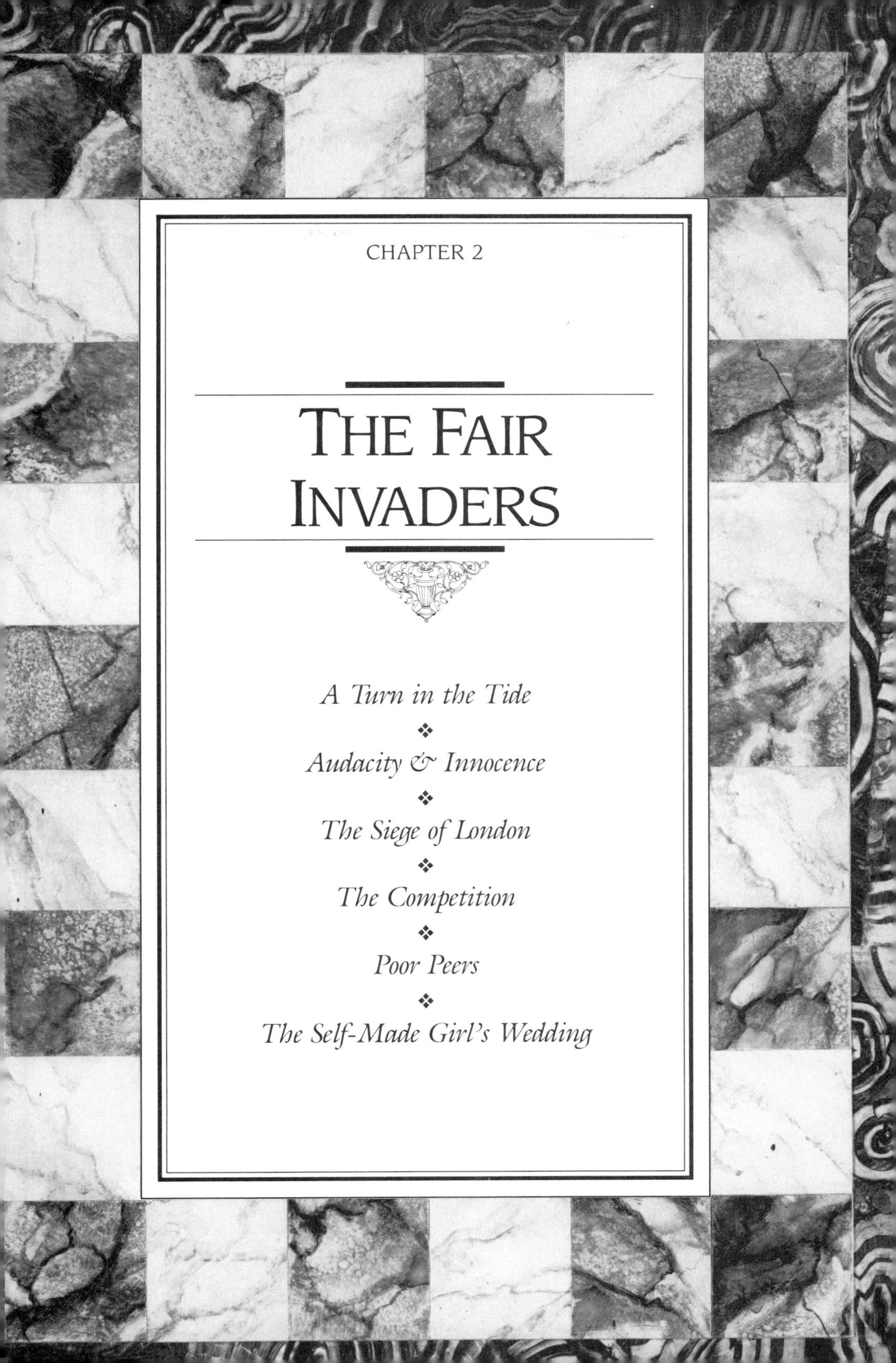

CHAPTER 2

THE FAIR INVADERS

A Turn in the Tide

❖

Audacity & Innocence

❖

The Siege of London

❖

The Competition

❖

Poor Peers

❖

The Self-Made Girl's Wedding

A TURN IN THE TIDE

As the 1870s moved into the 1880s, the Buccaneers became fashionable young matrons and key players in the English social scene. Clearly, abandoning the fiercely competitive New York social scene had paid off for them. But even in the stuffy mansions of Fifth Avenue, times were changing. The sovereign power of *the* Mrs. Astor was coming under assault by Alva Vanderbilt—a childhood friend of Minnie Stevens and Consuelo Yznaga. In fact, Alva was a Buccaneer in her own right, but a Buccaneer who stayed home.

THE BUCCANEER IN NEW YORK

Like Jennie and Minnie and Consuelo, Alva could not call herself an Old New Yorker; her father, Murray Forbes Smith, had brought his family to New York from Mobile, Alabama, in the 1850s. Also like the

A sketch of the Smith house in Mobile, showing its crenellated roofline. There is a story about Mrs. Smith's giving a ball to which le tout *Mobile did not come; if true, it would account for some of her daughter's ambition.*

Alva, in mourning for her grandfather-in-law Cornelius Vanderbilt, with her children William K. Jr., Harold and Consuelo.

other Buccaneers, Alva had gone to school in France, returning at the end of the Civil War. Smith, however, did not prosper in business, and there are tales of the Smith home being turned into a boarding house during the 1870s. Whether or not things got that bad, the Smith family was not wealthy by the standard of the times. So when Consuelo Yznaga introduced her to William K. Vanderbilt at a party in the early seventies, Alva may well have seen a way out of genteel poverty.

William K. Vanderbilt was the grandson of the famous Commodore, who had founded the Vanderbilt railroad fortune. The Commodore's son, William H., doubled the family's worth, and it was this estate

William K. Vanderbilt, a gentleman to his very marrow, was a match for Alva only in the marital sense.

Alva never looked like anything but what she was: pushy, pugnacious and determined.

of some $200 million that Willie K., as he was known, would eventually share with his sisters and his brother Cornelius. But while they had money, the Vanderbilts had no social standing in the New York of the 1870s. The Commodore was never better than uncouth, swearing like a longshoreman to his dying day. His son William H. was more civilized (he amassed a large collection of French academic paintings, for example) but lacked any ambition to be received by the Astor set.

Enter Alva. Whereas the difficulties of New York social climbing had defeated her Buccaneer friends, Alva was magnificently equipped for the fight. Marriage to Willie K. had given her the money, and God had given her the temperament. She was aggressive, determined and ambitious. She was impervious to insults. And she had a strategy. America was just waking up to its native cultural insufficiencies. Europe, formerly the source of "dubious foreign influences," was now being hailed as the fount of all that was refined. So Alva Vanderbilt chose to make her assault on New York society backed by nothing less than the weight of European civilization.

ALVA & ANGLOMANIA

Already, European ways were making their mark on New York. Where a parlormaid in a neat apron had sufficed for years, suddenly servants in livery appeared. Though the Ladies' Mile of shops on Broadway was no less safe, suddenly young ladies couldn't go out to buy a bonnet without a chaperone. Men's clubs on the English model sprang up and multiplied. Dresses from Worth no longer needed to mellow for a season in the attic before they were worn. Above all, fashionable American houses began to be furnished with the spoils of European travels. Italian sculpture, portraits by French painters, Sèvres vases, Gobelins

By the early 1880s, the homespun coachman in his own coat had given way to smart fellows in top hats and the family livery. The Astors, in a preemptive strike, chose the shade of blue used by the Royal Family at Windsor.

tapestries appeared in the cluttered interiors of Fifth Avenue mansions. Possession of these objects connoted connoisseurship on the part of the owners, and connoisseurship rapidly became a gambit in New York's ongoing social wars.

Another of Alva Vanderbilt's great gifts was timing. She didn't make the error of a grand gesture too soon after her 1875 marriage, but threw herself into being a rich man's wife. She produced children, two sons and a daughter, whom she named for her close friend Consuelo Yznaga, now Lady Mandeville. She ran the huge Long Island house, Idlehour, which was built shortly after she married Willie K. When the Commodore finally died in 1877, the living reminder of the Vanderbilts' unsavory beginnings was removed. It was time to start her push.

THE HOUSE THAT ALVA BUILT

Within months of the old man's death, William H. Vanderbilt and both his sons filed plans for new houses with New York City's Buildings Department. Following in the old traditions of New York domestic architecture, William H.'s double mansion on the west side of Fifth Avenue was built entirely of brownstone and massed in two blocky shapes. The Willie K. Vanderbilt mansion, however, was something else again. To begin with, it was clad in pale limestone, a startling departure from the brownstone norm. And then, it looked nothing like a *house*; what it looked like, quite frankly, was a château. It had a steeply pitched roof with copper cresting, elaborate dormers, balustrades, flying buttresses, and a slender tourelle decorated with fleurs-de-lis.

Naturally, the building of such a house provoked a great deal of curiosity. As dozens of workmen carved and painted and gilded, as carpets and tapestries and stained glass were carried into the house, New Yorkers longed to see the final result. And in the

Idlehour, the country house built on Long Island by Richard Morris Hunt for the young Vanderbilts. It burned down in 1899, and Hunt's son built a new house on the site for William K. Jr.

The château at 660 Fifth Avenue, Hunt's first venture into the style that would prove so gratifying to his clients (and lucrative to him). Soon châteaux by Hunt and his imitators would line the avenue.

winter of 1883, Alva Vanderbilt let it be known that they would soon be satisfied. Her dear friend Lady Mandeville would be paying a visit to New York. (Lord Mandeville, having other fish to fry, wouldn't be coming.) By then the house would be finished, so a party in honor of Consuelo seemed appropriate.

With the classic Alva combination of timing and nerve, the party was scheduled for March 26. Timing, because that was the Monday after Easter; New York still observed a somewhat somber Lent, so the Vanderbilts' housewarming would be the first big social event in six weeks. And nerve because Alva chose to give a costume ball, a form of merriment that had long been frowned upon in Old New York as encouraging loose behavior. Finally, Monday was the night when Mrs. Astor was traditionally at home to receive guests. In giving her ball on that day of the week, Alva was flinging down the gauntlet.

Alva's Louis XV salon, with its Boucher tapestries. Decorating with antiques, particularly those of one period, was a new idea in the early 1880s.

Calling-Card Protocol

he censorious Thorstein Veblen may have referred to paying calls as "purposeless leisure," but the call of ceremony was the basic unit of social intercourse. It was how a lady made acquaintances, who in turn became friends. At its most purely ceremonial, it was something to get dressed up for.

The call itself was a formal visit of fifteen minutes. The caller, togged out in hat and veil and gloves and parasol, didn't remove any of these. She perched on a chair, made small talk and then departed, leaving, on her way out, her card and two of her husband's (one each for the hostess and host; a woman could not, however, leave a card for a man).

A card could substitute for a call. If, upon entering the house, the caller was told the lady was Not at Home, she left a card to signal that she had called. The lady might very well be up-

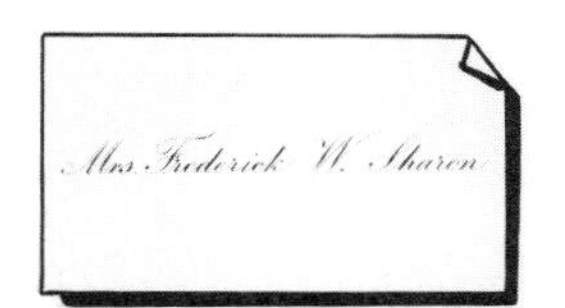

Card with top-right corner folded down: calling to pay respects.

stairs reading French novels, but the pleasant fiction allowed the caller to discharge her social duty and be on her way. A code of folded corners would let the unseen lady know the reason for the call.

The occasions on which this duty was decreed were numerous. Strictly speaking, a call should be returned within ten days. That was the basic, cutlet-for-cutlet reciprocation that kept an acquaintanceship cordial. Then there was the "party call," a visit to one's hostess within a week of being entertained.

The most important call was the "first call," always made by a social superior. It was considered terribly forward for newcomers to make "first calls" on people they didn't know; they had to wait to be noticed.

It was also necessary to make farewell calls when leaving town, or at least drop off "P.P.C." cards (*"pour prendre congé"*). However, P.P.C. cards could be mailed to all one's acquaintances without giving offense.

Of course, this many required calls could get burdensome, and the rules relaxed somewhat over time. Mrs. William Collins Whitney, when her husband was secretary of the navy, invented a "professional visitor"—a young woman who distributed Mrs. Whitney's cards to the right people. It became acceptable to send one's carriage and footman around leaving cards, though a woman had to be seen sitting in the carriage (usually one's lady's maid was deputed for the job). By 1910, one lady simply left her calling list with her stationers, who printed the cards and delivered them for her twice yearly, saving her—or her lady's maid—the trouble of ever having to make another call.

THE WILSON FAMILY SCORECARD #2
Orme & Carrie

Marshall Orme Wilson, painted in 1894 by Léon Bonnat; his intended, Carrie Astor, in her Star Quadrille costume.

Though Caroline Astor was implacable in her mission to keep society pure, her soft spot was her concern for her children. And in 1884, a year after Alva's ball, daughter Carrie again put it to the test. This time, she wanted to marry Orme Wilson. Mrs. Astor hesitated—giving the Vanderbilts the nod was one thing, but becoming related to the Wilsons was something else entirely. The Astors set a condition: that the Wilsons match Carrie's $500,000 dowry. Though his fortune had receded from its multimillion high-water mark to a scant million, R.T. scraped together the fee. Astor in-laws, after all, would be a matchless asset in New York society.

This gold-plated calling-card receiver was named "Hilarity" by its manufacturer. It cost a mere $10.

ALVA STRIKES BACK

Needless to say, the Vanderbilt ball was the talk of the city. While Alva was ransacking novels and history books to come up with her costume and decorating details, 140 dressmakers labored day and night for weeks to finish the outfits commissioned by the guests. (A fancy-dress costume was an extravagance, but this event demanded nothing less from the *invi-*

tées.) Press coverage commenced well before party night: each course to be served at the 6:00 A.M. breakfast, the names of the various kinds of roses used by the thousands for decorating, every detail of the hostess's costume—these and more particulars were doled out to a hungry public. Everyone wanted to go, and more than a thousand people were blessed with invitations.

A line had to be drawn somewhere, of course, and Alva, in the boldest stroke yet, drew the line at Mrs. Astor. After all, Alva knew her place in New York; as a newcomer, she must wait for Mrs. Astor to call on *her*. A reversal of the procedure would have been pushy. But, as it happened, Mrs. Astor had a débutante daughter named Carrie who, with a group of her friends, had whiled away the tedious weeks of Lent by practicing a little dance called the Star Quadrille to be performed at the Vanderbilt ball. The girls would present themselves as pairs of stars, costumed in yellow, blue, mauve and white, each with an electric light in her hair.

Perry Belmont, of the banking Belmonts, costumed as a Ruritanian hussar for the ball. He later had a distinguished career in New York politics.

The invitation to Alva's ball was delivered to the Astors' genteel four-story brownstone (center) with the pedimented door. The more imposing mansion to its right belonged to department-store magnate A. T. Stewart.

Word of Miss Astor's rehearsals came to Alva's ear. She let it be known that she was surprised: how could Miss Astor come to her ball when Miss Astor's mother had never officially recognized the existence of Mr. and Mrs. William K. Vanderbilt? It was blackmail, certainly, but Mrs. Astor could not let New York's social purity outweigh her daughter's happiness. A footman in blue livery delivered an Astor calling card at 660 Fifth Avenue, and shortly afterward a footman in maroon livery delivered an invitation at the Astor house at 350 Fifth Avenue.

Mrs. Cornelius (Alice Gwynne) Vanderbilt, holding high her electrified torch. Though her husband was senior to Willie K. and just as rich, Alice was content to cede social honors to her sister-in-law.

THE GREAT VANDERBILT BALL

On the night of March 26, a crowd gathered at Fifth Avenue and 52nd Street to catch glimpses of the élite hurrying along the red carpet to the door. Inside, Alva (costumed by Worth as a Venetian princess), her husband (impersonating the Duc de Guise, in yellow tights) and Consuelo Mandeville (a French princess) stationed themselves by the grand stairway to receive the guests. Upstairs, maids costumed as French peasants waited to replace hairpins and stitch up torn trains. Footmen in powdered wigs patrolled the salon ready to fetch the champagne. By eleven o'clock, the immense front hall was full of New Yorkers trying hard not to stare at what Alva had wrought.

First, there was the interior of the house. The rooms were crammed with references to Greek mythology and French kings, paneled with wainscoting ripped from a Loire Valley château, hung with Boucher tapestries, stocked with Boulle cabinets; here a pair of Renaissance mantelpieces, there a Rembrandt portrait, and in the corner a set of Gouthière bronzes commissioned by Marie Antoinette. Polite *sang-froid* forbade gaping, but really, New York had seen nothing like it. (Polite *sang-froid* also forbade obvious efforts at pricing, but close to three million dollars had been spent on the interior of the house, and nearly a quarter of a million on the party.)

COMME IL FAUT
A girl is always accompanied to and from a ball by her mother, a chaperone or, at the very least, a maid.

And then there were the New Yorkers themselves, done up as they had never seen each other. Willie's older brother, Cornelius Jr., had roused himself from his usual sobriety to appear as Louis XVI, while his plain wife Alice had decided to come as "the Electric Light"—in a costume that inspired Worth to install gas jets in the folds of pale yellow satin trimmed with diamonds so that his client could, periodically, light up. Mrs. Paran Stevens, back from her European wanderings, was costumed as Queen Elizabeth, so laden with jewels it was a wonder she could walk. Mrs. Bradley Martin gave Mrs. Stevens some competition in the jewel department, for across her impos-

Alva, prepared for her moment of glory. The doves were a conceit of the photographer and had nothing to do with her costume.

The Leslie paper sent sketch artists to the Vanderbilt ball, the first of the era's highly publicized social events. Right: Bradley Martin made a convincingly foppish-looking Louis XV.

ing bosom was draped a triple strand of pearls, punctuated with five diamond brooches and a diamond cluster pendant. Mrs. Martin (alias Mary Stuart for the evening) watched the proceedings with a measuring eye, for she too had social ambitions and longed to make her mark.

The evening was a triumph. For Consuelo Mandeville, there was immense pleasure in the warm greeting of a New York that had been in no hurry to know her as a débutante. For Alva, there was the satisfaction of having successfully launched the Vanderbilt family onto the high seas of social acceptability. And for New York society, a new orientation had been imposed. Quaint republican simplicities be damned: Alva's ball, with its European extravagances and pretensions, was New York's first heady dose of Anglomania.

THE BIG SHOWDOWNS

The early 1880s saw a critical shift in New York's balance of social power, as marked by the fates of a pair of cultural institutions. For a number of years, the New-York Historical Society had been the city's preeminent museum of fine arts. Then, in 1872, a league of artists and art connoisseurs founded the Metropolitan Museum of Art. Initially they had proposed an amalgamation with the Historical Society, but were turned down, theoretically because Knickerbocker Nicholas Fish found the Metropolitan's committee socially unacceptable. By 1880, in contrast to the socially correct but languishing Historical Society, the new museum had outgrown its downtown quarters and moved to Central Park at 80th Street.

It took a single season for the Academy of Music, another bastion of Old New York, to fall by the wayside. The Academy made the mistake of rejecting men like William H. Vanderbilt, whose offer of $30,000 for a box was turned down, and soon faced opposition in the form of a brand-new theater. The opening night of the Metropolitan Opera House, as it was called, coincided with the seasonal opening of the Academy of Music on October 22, 1883. The house was splendid, all crystal chandeliers and

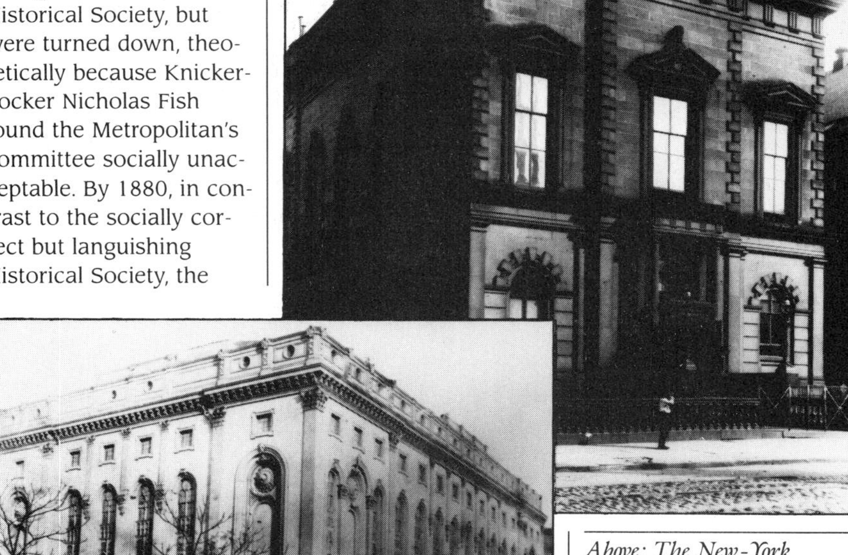

Above: The New-York Historical Society was headquartered on lower Second Avenue, a neighborhood long popular with Knickerbockers. Left: The Academy of Music, Old New York's clubhouse.

The best feature of the Metropolitan Opera House was the seating; it had terrible acoustics and minimal storage space for sets and costumes. The first tier (inset) was known as "the Diamond Horseshoe" after the occupants' jewels.

rosewood and gold plush. The singing (though hardly the point) was fine. Most important, boxes had been taken not only by *nouveaux riches* such as the Vanderbilts, but also by the Astors and Goelets and Iselins. And though Mrs. Astor went to the Academy of Music that night (and Mrs. Paran Stevens, hedging her bet, went to both, seeing a bit of Gounod, a bit of Wagner and a great deal of Broadway), it was clear that the Metropolitan Opera would be a success. By the 1885 season the Academy of Music had gone out of business—and its demise can be taken, for all intents and purposes, as the demise of Old New York itself.

W.H. Vanderbilt donated much of his collection to the new Metropolitan Museum of Art.

Everyone thought the new museum building ugly but predicted that soon it would be hidden by new additions.

AUDACITY & INNOCENCE

If New York society was so crazy about all things European, the social climbers figured they might as well head for Europe. And, more specifically, England. The Buccaneers had already proven that London society could be a good deal easier to crack than New York society. Ambitious heiresses everywhere took heart. No need to either flail against the cliffs of New York indifference or slink home to remain a big fish in a small midwestern pond. They could follow the formula laid out for them by their predecessors in social high adventure—the Stevenses, the Yznagas, the Jeromes. Success, relatively pain-free success, could still be theirs.

THE SELF-MADE GIRL

But if these new heiresses intended to copy the Buccaneers, they were yet very different from them. For one thing their fathers were richer, sometimes very much richer, than Leonard Jerome or Paran Stevens. And they were American in a way that the Buccaneers with their Paris débuts and European experience were not. These American heiresses had no Pushy Mamas to wheedle invitations on their behalf or to teach them how to fold their napkins properly, much less how to put on an evening's entertainment following all Mrs. Astor's tricky rules about white sauces and brown sauces and the correct flavoring for the Roman punch (maraschino or amaretto, *not* rum). Nor had they the benefit of a Sporting Man type of Wall Street Father, who could at least teach them how to handle a horse.

A trade card for a steamship line. Fortunately for ambitious Americans, the age of the sail was over and passage to Europe was safe and reliable.

As naïve Americans discovered Europe in increasing numbers, cartoonists and other commentators (among them Mark Twain, in Innocents Abroad*) chuckled.*

They were, in the phrase of the day, "self-made girls," whose social successes would be entirely their own doing, built by each on her own charms, her own merits, her own unceasing efforts. Each would raise herself from the depths, would transform herself from American nobody to English aristocrat by what Henry James called "the simple lever of her own personality."

> *"Thirty years ago, in England as well as on the Continent, the American woman was looked upon as a strange and abnormal creature, with habits and manners something between a Red Indian and a Gaiety Girl."*
>
> LADY RANDOLPH CHURCHILL (1910)

COMME IL FAUT
In England a young girl must not walk alone in London, take a hansom cab, travel in an unreserved train compartment, sit in a stall at the theater or visit a music hall.

AMERICAN GODDESSES

That personality was indeed something to be reckoned with, as the English were shortly to discover. It was nurtured on adulation, clothed in admiring words and appreciative gazes. Heiresses were the deities of America's new communities, where the raw civilization's worship of the vitality and promise of youth and the virtues of womanhood combined to

Cleveland's Jeannie Chamberlain was a classic American beauty.

turn young girls into cherished goddesses. A pretty girl with a rich father was automatically a treasured being, a social star, a "belle." What she wore and what she said, where she went and whom she saw, were of intense interest to the rest of her hometown. Her belledom constituted a matter of civic pride. She and her rich, pretty sisters were, as French writer Paul Bourget put it, "the delegates to luxury in this utilitarian civilization," elegant antidotes to the pragmatic business of nation building. In their apparent

"American youths are pale and precocious, or sallow and supercilious, but American girls are pretty and charming—little oases of pretty unreasonableness in a vast desert of practical commonsense."
OSCAR WILDE

idleness and frivolity, they were living proof of just how hard their fathers, and everyone else, worked.

But the Self-Made Girl was working, too. Not to make money, but to make herself into a grand lady. Being American, she believed that anything could be accomplished by an act of will and plenty of effort. So, from her power base as a belle, she set out on that most American of paths: a campaign of self-improvement. She went to singing lessons and dancing lessons and drawing lessons. A great believer in book learning, she read constantly. She studied history, and foreign languages, and the "society pages."

If she decided she needed to attend Miss Brown's School for Young Ladies in New York, she sent herself to New York. If she decided she needed to become more sophisticated, to see museums and galleries and old churches, then she purchased Baedeker Guides to various foreign capitals, recruited her parents (or at least her mother) and set off on a step-by-step tour of Europe. And when she decided she was ready, this girl from the American Midwest went to London. Husband-hunting. Simple as that.

THE MORNING GLORY

The exemplar of the Self-Made type of girl was Jeannie Chamberlain, originally of Cleveland, Ohio. Spectacular-looking in a way that was already recognized as characteristically American, she had honey-blond hair, dark blue eyes with long dark lashes, full lips and a tall, slender, graceful figure. Her sweetly dazzling appearance first created a storm in 1883 when she went to New York, and her photograph appeared in shop windows along with those of other, less respectable beauties such as actress Lillie Langtry. The result was a front-page article in the *Times*, announcing that her father was prepared to prosecute any photographers caught selling her picture, and more notoriety for Miss Jeannie Chamberlain.

Jeannie's parents, the classic anonymous Ameri-

PROFESSIONAL BEAUTIES

In the 1880s, competition for the Prince's favor became so fierce that certain society women had themselves photographed professionally and then allowed their pictures to be placed on sale in the shop windows of London. The general public, who, according to novelist Gertrude Atherton, stood on penny chairs in Hyde Park "to see the objects of current worship drive by," went mad for the photographs. So great was Victorian reverence for physical beauty that these "professional beauties," as they came to be called, suffered little loss of dignity. After all, perfectly respectable society women had been known to stand on the gilt chairs of ballrooms in order not to miss the entrance of Lillie Langtry, a leading professional beauty of the day.

> *My Transatlantic friends are always welcome; they have what I call 'the three f's': figures, francs, and faith! That is why I like dressing the Americans.*
> CHARLES WORTH

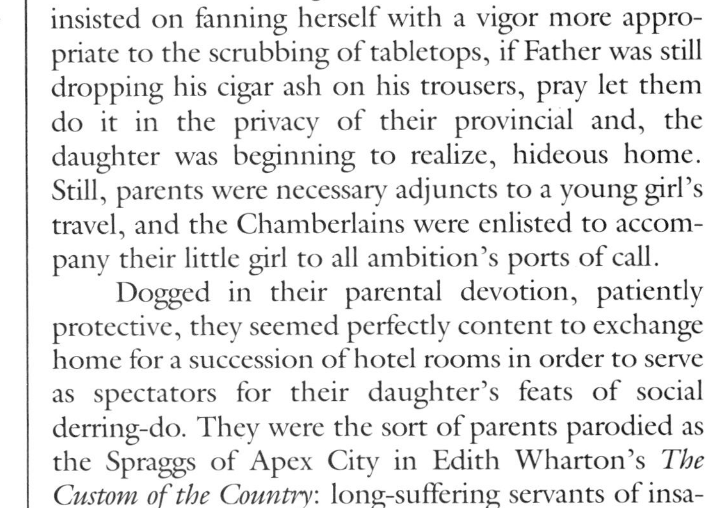

can duo, saw their sole function in life as facilitating their daughter's rise to stardom. Sometimes the Self-Made Girl might want to shuffle the ignominious authors of her being off to one side. If Mother insisted on fanning herself with a vigor more appropriate to the scrubbing of tabletops, if Father was still dropping his cigar ash on his trousers, pray let them do it in the privacy of their provincial and, the daughter was beginning to realize, hideous home. Still, parents were necessary adjuncts to a young girl's travel, and the Chamberlains were enlisted to accompany their little girl to all ambition's ports of call.

Dogged in their parental devotion, patiently protective, they seemed perfectly content to exchange home for a succession of hotel rooms in order to serve as spectators for their daughter's feats of social derring-do. They were the sort of parents parodied as the Spraggs of Apex City in Edith Wharton's *The Custom of the Country*: long-suffering servants of insatiable youth and beauty, only barely grasping the daughter's purpose but too fascinated by her progress to do anything but keep watching—and paying.

A TRIP TO THE RUE DE LA PAIX

Once in Europe, Jeannie captivated the two men crucial to the success of American girls: Charles Worth, the founding father of *haute couture*, and Albert Edward, Prince of Wales.

Many women who wore Worth dresses examined the models, dealt with a vendeuse and a fitter, but never merited the great man's personal attention. This he saved for his best clients, many of whom were American.

Worth, an expatriate English dressmaker who had set up shop in Paris' rue de la Paix, was delighted to have Jeannie among his clientele. American women were braver than the staid Englishwomen and considerably more profligate than the Parisiennes, who were liable to choose three exquisite costumes and make them last a season or more—true elegance, but not about to make Worth a rich man. Americans like Jeannie never stopped at three dresses; they were hard put to stop at eighty or ninety.

And the Americans had such a sense of occa-

An invitation to stay at Sandringham, the Prince's country house, would ensure any lucky heiress's social success in England.

Although he had no power to govern, the Prince had supreme social power, and he wielded it a bit impulsively for his mother's taste.

sion. They seemed instinctively to understand the shades of significance in different bodices or tailoring, this or that amount of lace, a lighter velvet or a heavier brocade. They would never humiliate a reception gown, for instance, by wearing it to the theater. And they didn't waste the designer's time. When Charles Worth deigned to dress a woman, she must mind him to the last piece of lace. He didn't want to pour out his genius on some woman who went home and had her maid lengthen the sleeves and add a ridge of jet to the shoulders. Americans, fortunately, were too loyal, too respectful, to consider such philistinism. They knew one didn't fiddle with a work of art.

And that's what a wardrobe by Worth was. He looked a girl over, turned her round, and with a few sweeping gestures conjured up a season's worth of dresses especially for her. The result was inevitably magnificent. Thus Jeannie Chamberlain left Paris a changed woman, her natural vitality refined by Worth's sublime tailoring as she set out for the spas. Her all-American body now presented itself in cream silk moiré, her corn-fed good looks framed in taffeta shawls with *diamante* insets. She positively glowed.

THE GENIUS OF CLOTHES

Worth considered himself an artist and dressed accordingly. His headquarters on the rue de la Paix featured a specially lit chamber for choosing ball gowns.

Being perfectly turned out, from kid slippers to lace parasol, including pearl-embroidered petticoats and the third new pair of gloves that day, was the exclusive province of the American woman. More, it was her patriotic duty. The daughters of dukes could indulge in loose-waisted "pre-Raphaelite" dresses, but Americans had to look like aristocrats. Enter Worth, the genius of clothes.

There were other dressmakers, to be sure, on both sides of the Atlantic, but Charles Worth had the monopoly on the American market. However temperamental and autocratic he might be, he had brilliant insight into his customers' personalities and a wonderful logic lay behind his designs. He knew what colors would revive a fading complexion. He made fashionable clothes for mourning and pregnancy, those inevitable inconveniences of a lady's life. And Worth was *it* for wedding gowns: "Was ever an American girl who could afford it," que-

Clothes by Worth were instantly recognized, even without the label sewn into each waistband.

ried the English magazine *Orange Blossoms,* "married in a gown built by any other man?"

Thus, quite happily, the American heiress made the twice-yearly pilgrimage to Paris, undergoing weeks of strenuous fittings and, in between, shopping for the proper accessories to complete each outfit. For an entire season's wardrobe, she might pay as much as $20,000 (over $500,000 in today's dollars) and then half again the cost in duty when the clothes were shipped back to New York—exquisitely packed in yards of tissue paper, resting on networks of tape so as not to crush the layers of dresses beneath. Of course, to the heiress, price was no object. Worth gowns were one of the necessities of life.

Above: A Worth display of mannequins called "Going to the Drawing Room" showcased a court dress with its long train.

Right: The Comtesse Greffuhle, one of Proust's models for the Duchesse de Guermantes, in a pearl-trimmed gown by Worth.

Far right: Mary Leiter (Lady Curzon) in Worth's beaded "Peacock Dress"; the center of each peacock's eye was an iridescent green beetle shell.

THE CHASE IS ON

Inevitably this apparition attracted the attention of the Prince of Wales, also on the Continent for his annual R&R at Baden-Baden. The Prince, veteran of so many love affairs, had never met a girl like Jeannie Chamberlain. European girls were held close to the bosom of the family, sheltered from society, from books, from boys. European girls stayed home. And European girls were virginal in a pronounced, emphatic way. They wore white with high collars and low heels and pastel ribbons in their hair.

The social rules were relaxed a bit at the German spas, where the Prince went to recover after a year of overeating. A girl might even meet him on a stroll through the grounds.

Jeannie's open, easy, flirtatious manner, as much as her well-dressed beauty, entranced the Prince. He was unaccustomed to finding such audacity in usually unapproachable virgins, such innocence in a woman of fashion. But Self-Made Girls knew the value of the hunt, and Jeannie was careful not to be too accommodating. The Prince was forced to follow Cleveland's one-and-only from resort to resort, and *never* permitted to see her alone. The press, who had labeled Jeannie "the American Beauty" and "the Morning Glory," kept pace with his pursuit. Journalists interviewed the beauty's doughty progenitors, as affable and unassuming as ever, and quoted them as finding the Prince to be "a homely man" and "the most agreeable gentleman" they had ever met.

The Prince must have been truly smitten: he not only put up with the ubiquitous parents but allowed Jeannie to address him as "Prince Tum-tum" and "Jumbo." (In retaliation, the Princess of Wales was known to refer to Jeannie as "Miss Chamberpots.") By the time she arrived in London for the season, Jeannie had snagged the all-important invitation to stay with the Prince at Norfolk.

"Every American girl is entitled to have twelve young men devoted to her. They remain her slaves and she rules them with charming nonchalance."
OSCAR WILDE

Whom the Prince of Wales invited, all of London wanted to entertain, so Jeannie's success was assured. A belle must finally select among her suitors, and Jeannie chose one of the Prince's friends, a Captain Herbert Naylor-Leyland of the Grenadier Guards. The pair married and moved into Hyde Park House in London, and Jeannie was finally able to send her devoted parents packing.

LA BELLE AMÉRICAINE

Jeannie Chamberlain's story was by no means unique. There were lots of American girls traipsing around Europe, seeking knowledge, invitations, proposals of marriage. In the 1880s they were as superabundant, in European eyes, as the huge quantities of cheap American wheat that was ruining agriculture on the Continent and in England. To the English in particular, American heiresses were an alien horde, more and more of them confidently jumping off every steamer that docked from across the pond, heading straight for London and the season and the men.

As a group, these girls were serving a larger purpose than each girl's desire to marry well. Just as it was up to the American father to make America rich and powerful, it was up to the American heiress to make America respectable. That was what New York and the rest of American society were after—respect.

Because she was young and rich and pretty, and because her father and brothers were too busy making money to take on the job, the American heiress was the New World's ambassador to the Old. She presented, in her perfect little person, America's coming of age. If the English gentleman was the emblem of his civilization, its fondest creation and most identifiable representative, so *la belle Américaine* was fast becoming the emblem of hers. She had it in mind to be the best-dressed, best-educated, most refined and utterly acceptable woman those foreigners had ever seen. She would show them. She would prove that Americans were just as good at being aristocratic as anyone else. And possibly better.

The staff of the Harvard Lampoon *in 1885. Compared to European men, Americans were earnest, boyish and, above all, dull.*

WALL STREET FATHER NO. 2: THE SILENT PARTNER

Above: Ticker tape was to the menfolk what Burke's Peerage *was to the ladies. Left: Sooty, urgent and noisy, America's railroads paid for Worth dresses but were not drawing-room material.*

In 1861, America had a mere handful of millionaires. By 1900, there would be four thousand of them. Not all the new millionaires could pass on a legacy of wealth and style, anecdote and accomplishment that would make their names recognizable generations after their death. While the Sporting Men left behind tales of dinner parties and yacht races, the Silent Partners left behind railroads. Or they were men like Frank Leggett, stepfather to the future Countess of Sandwich, who ran a wholesale grocery business in New York City. Or Anson Stager, father of the future Marchioness of Ormonde, whose obituary was subheaded "The Busy Career of the Prominent Electrician." More concrete, but less memorable.

The Silent Partner may have been a titan of industry, but he was a social pygmy. Passion, personal style, ambition—these were entirely the province of his wife and daughter. It was for him to stay out of focus,

The Silent Partner's gear was a far cry from the Sporting Man's buggy whip.

somewhere in the background, the black-suited, ashen-faced figure a few exhausted steps behind his superbly outfitted ladies. To Elizabeth Drexel Lehr, later Lady Decies, he and his fellow Wall Street warriors were "too nerve-racked by the strain of building a fortune to be able to relax. They were prepared to spend their last cent in gratifying the whims of their womenfolk, but they were incapable of amusing themselves."

Rendered unsuitable for the drawing rooms of Europe by his ceaseless, conversation-killing attention to business, the Silent Partner was sooner or later banished from the side of his insatiable loved ones. It was his fate to become but the faceless name that followed "daughter of" in *Burke's Peerage*: "W.S. Chamberlain of Ohio" or, more vaguely still, "H. Gordon Lister, USA." While his daughter lived it up in the Old World—waltzed with the Prince of Wales, stood in the Royal Enclosure at Ascot, kissed the hand of the Queen—he was left behind in the New, sleeping in a hotel or boarding house, taking meals at his club.

The Silent Partner's only communication with wife and daughter was by cable and on the subject of "drawing" (getting more money out of the bank), his only required response permission in the form of the single word "Draw." "Your letter and draft for £2,000 came today with the kindest message," wrote Mrs. Leggett, wife of the wholesale grocer. "You have blessed manners. I almost expected an impatient reply to my letter or complaint, and so hoped it wouldn't come and it hasn't; just *sweetness* and a *cheque*."

The old New York Stock Exchange. At left are the offices of Drexel, Morgan—names that would soon be familiar to the British peerage.

THE TOP DOLLARS

In the land of opportunity, where nobody's past was held against him, where hard work was the norm and the vast scale of the country produced similar-size profits, there were innumerable ways to get rich. And portions of some of these fortunes subsidized the aristocratic leisure of a daughter's English husband. The men who struck it rich (and the daughters, in most cases, on whose behalf their money went to England) are listed here.

NELSON BECKWITH *(Helene, Lady Leigh):* import-export; estate valued at $1 million.

CHARLES BONYNGE *(Virginia, Viscountess Deerhurst):* San Francisco landscape gardener turned stockbroker; Comstock Lode millionaire.

WILLIAM BORDEN *(Mary, Lady Spears):* dairy products.

WILLIAM L. BREESE *(Anna, Lady Alastair Innes-Ker; Eloise, Countess of Ancaster):* Wall Street broker.

WALTER BURNS *(Mary, Viscountess Harcourt):* J.P. Morgan's son-in-law.

SEN. J. DONALD CAMERON *(Martha, Hon. Mrs. Ronald Lindsay):* banking, railroads; worth $4 million at death.

HORACE CARPENTIER *("unofficial niece" Maud Burke, Lady Cunard, who was also rumored to be daughter of William O'Brien of Comstock Lode):* San Francisco real estate.

SAMUEL COLGATE *(widow Cora, Countess of Strafford):* industrial manufacturer.

DANIEL CORBIN *(Louise, Countess of Orford):* railroads, among them Spokane Falls & Northern Railroad.

JOHN H. DAVIS *(Flora, Marchioness of Dufferin):* banker.

Marshall Field, of department store fame, at age twenty-four.

ANTHONY J. DREXEL *(Margaretta, Countess of Winchilsea and Nottingham):* banking, investments; Philadelphia real estate.

MARSHALL FIELD *(Ethel, Countess Beatty):* Chicago department store tycoon.

HAMILTON FISH *(Edith, Hon. Mrs. Hugh Northcote):* lawyer; New York real estate (his mother inherited Stuyvesant farm, 10th to 23rd streets east of Third Avenue).

WILLIAM J. FITZGERALD *(Caroline, Lady Fitzmaurice):* husband of co-heiress of White real estate fortune on New York's Fifth Avenue and Upper West Side.

WILLIAM GARNER *(Florence, Lady Gordon-Cumming):* fabric mills in upstate New York.

WILLIAM GARRISON *(Martha, Hon. Mrs. Charles Ramsay):* son of San Francisco bank founder; Missouri Pacific Railroad and urban elevated railroads.

OGDEN GOELET
(May, Duchess of Roxburghe; dowry reckoned as high as $8 million): New York real estate (family owned land on both sides of Fifth Avenue from 46th Street to Union Square).

WILLIAM W. GORDON
(Mabel, Hon. Mrs. Rowland Leigh): Savannah-Macon Railroad.

George Jay Gould, slightly more respectable son of swashbuckling financier Jay Gould.

GEORGE GOULD
(Vivien, Lady Decies): son of Jay Gould, quintessential robber baron whose worth was assessed at $82 million when he died; large Western Union interests.

JOHN W. GRACE
(Olive, Lady Greville): brother of W.R. Grace, founder of steamship line (and first Catholic mayor of New York).

MICHAEL P. GRACE
(Elena, Countess of Donoughmore; Elisa, Hon. Mrs. Hubert Beaumont): another brother of W.R. Grace; in charge of Peruvian arrangements when company was in shipping and mining. (Among his partners was Donoughmore, Elena's future father-in-law.)

LOUIS HAMMERSLEY
(widow Lily, Duchess of Marlborough): New York merchant who invested wisely.

HIRAM E. HOWARD
(Hannah, Hon. Mrs. Octavius Lambart): banker in Buffalo; managing officer of Marine Bank.

LEONARD JEROME
(Clara, Mrs. Frewen; Jennie, Lady Randolph Churchill; Leonie, Lady Leslie): stock speculator.

Frank Leggett, wholesale grocer.

CHISWELL LANGHORNE
(Nancy, Lady Astor): Virginia real estate; worth over $1 million despite protestations of poverty.

WILLIAM TRACY LEE
(Lucy, Mrs. Ernest Beckett): New York banker.

FRANK LEGGETT
(Frances, Viscountess Margesson; stepdaughter Alberta Sturges, Countess of Sandwich): wholesale grocery business.

LEVI Z. LEITER
(Daisy, Countess of Suffolk; Mary, Lady Curzon): Marshall Field's original partner; Chicago real estate speculator.

Pierre Lorillard, tobacco magnate.

PIERRE LORILLARD
(Maude, Lady Revelstoke): heir to tobacco fortune begun by grandfather; developer of Tuxedo Park.

William H. McVickar *(Katharine, Lady Grantley):* stockbroker.

Bradley Martin *(Cornelia, Countess of Craven):* son-in-law of Isaac Hull Sherman, who made a fortune from lumbering interests in upstate New York.

Henry May *(Lily, Lady Bagot):* Baltimore lawyer.

John Meiggs *(Helen, Lady M'Grigor):* partner in Michael P. Grace's Peruvian railroads.

Henry Phipps, associate of Andrew Carnegie in iron and steel.

Ogden Mills *(Beatrice, Countess of Granard):* son of Darius O. Mills, successful California merchant, president of Bank of California and later a New York-based investor in eastern banking and industry.

Charles Pfizer *(Helen, Lady Duncan):* founder of the chemical fortune.

Henry Phipps *(Amy, Hon. Mrs. Frederick Guest):* Andrew Carnegie's best friend and business partner in iron and steel; fortune estimated at $50 million.

Henry Huttleston Rogers, mastermind of the oil pipeline.

James W. Pinchot *(Antoinette, Hon. Mrs. Alan Johnstone):* prominent New York merchant.

Frederick G. Potter *(Clara, Lady Green-Price):* New York banker and lawyer.

Whitelaw Reid *(Jean, Lady Ward):* son-in-law of Darius Mills; journalist, editor of New York *Tribune;* co-developer of Mergenthaler linotype machine.

Henry Huttleston Rogers *(Cora, Lady Fairhaven):* Standard Oil executive, partner of William Rockefeller; interests in gas, banking, railroads; a director of U.S. Steel and associated with Anaconda Amalgamated Copper; business manager of Mark Twain, whose work he admired.

Benjamin A. Sands *(May, Hon. Mrs. Hugh Howard):* lawyer; trustee and director of many banks and of Columbia University.

William Sharon, senator from Nevada and mining millionaire.

William Holt Secor *(Rosalind, Lady Chetwynd):* New York lawyer.

William Sharon *(Flora, Lady Fermor-Hesketh):* crooked senator from Nevada; Bank of California's representative at Comstock Lode, with controlling stock in many mines.

William Watts Sherman *(Mildred, Lady Camoys):* husband of Rhode Island heiress Anne Wetmore, then of Sophia Brown, whose father founded Brown University.

George S. ("Chicago") Smith
(niece Mary, Lady Cooper): stock speculator; bequeathed $20 million to Mary in will.

Anson Stager
(Ellen, Marchioness of Ormonde): Western Union executive, also involved with Vanderbilt interests; president, Western Electric and Western Edison.

Paran Stevens
(Minnie, Lady Paget): hotels (notably Fifth Avenue Hotel, where Prince of Wales stayed when in New York).

Anson Phelps Stokes, real estate investor and clock manufacturer.

Anson Phelps Stokes
(Sarah, Baroness Halkett of Hanover): Phelps, Dodge executive; founder of two realty companies; official of Ansonia (Conn.) Clock Co.; brother of William Stokes, who developed the Ansonia Hotel on Broadway at 74th Street.

William Thaw
(Alice, Countess of Yarmouth): coal mining interests; major shareholder in Pennsylvania Railroad.

William A. Tucker
(Ethel, Countess of Lindsay): Boston banker; founder of Tucker, Anthony & Co.

Lawrence Turnure, Jr.
(widow Romaine, Lady Monson): New York banker and stockbroker; director of National City Bank.

William K. Vanderbilt
(Consuelo, Duchess of Marlborough): president, New York Central Railroad and its subsidiaries; chairman, Lake Shore & Michigan Southern Railroad.

Gen. James Samuel Wadsworth
(Elizabeth, Lady Barrymore): rental income from huge land holdings in upstate New York, managed in near feudal arrangement.

William Fitzhugh Whitehouse *(Lily, Hon. Mrs. Charles Coventry):* Chicago and New York lawyer; director, Louisville & Nashville railroad.

William Collins Whitney *(Pauline, Lady Queenborough):* developer of New York City's trolley monopoly, later consolidated into Metropolitan Transit; realized personal profit of $40 million in five years.

Richard T. Wilson
(Belle, Lady Herbert): Georgia merchant who served as commissary general for Confederate Army; later, New York banker and railroad investor.

Frank Work
(Frances, Hon. Mrs. James Burke-Roche): stockbroker for Vanderbilts; Wall Street speculator.

Antonio Yznaga
(Consuelo, Duchess of Manchester; Natica, Lady Lister-Kaye): Spanish owner of Louisiana plantation and merchant in Natchez, Mississippi.

Eugene Zimmerman, petroleum millionaire.

Eugene Zimmerman
(Helena, Duchess of Manchester): early investor in petroleum; major stockholder in Standard Oil, with additional railroad and mining interests.

THE SIEGE OF LONDON

The year after Jeannie Chamberlain's wedding, Mary Leiter was among the Americans invading London. Another classic Self-Made Girl, she was the daughter of Levi Leiter, Marshall Field's original partner, who made a fortune in Chicago real estate. The family moved to Washington, where Mary (despite her mother's astounding vulgarity) became an habitué of the White House and a bosom friend of the young Mrs. Cleveland.

Her début in Washington was followed by successes in New York and Newport. "Miss Leiter represents exactly the sort of girl," proclaimed the Boston *Herald,* "whom we should send over to England with pardonable pride." But Mary's triumph did not, initially, travel well. She and her family went to Europe several times in the late 1880s. They stayed at

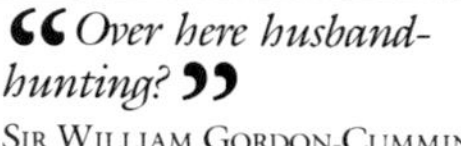

"Over here husband-hunting?"
SIR WILLIAM GORDON-CUMMING to Leonie Jerome, on her arrival in London

"It's been the worst season I can remember, Sir James! All the men seem to have got married, and none of the girls!"—Cartoon published in 1884, commenting on the real purpose of the London season.

An 1889 miniature of Mary Leiter painted for New York bachelor Peter Marié, who collected miniatures of the prettiest women of his day.

hotels with names like the Palace and the Metropole, thumbed their Baedekers and met no one. In June of 1890, Mary and her mother and sister were guests at Claridge's in London and again felt themselves to be mere tourists. "I think London wonderfully delightful," wrote Mary to her father, "although I know so little of its people. Everything is in full swing, and we read long accounts of balls we don't go to!"

THE BERTIE FACTOR

And then, overnight, everything changed. Mary had a letter of introduction to Sir Lyon Playfair, an M.P. who was married to the former Edith Russell of Boston. On July 10, Sir Lyon took Mary to a formal

COMME IL FAUT
Lavish, American-style tipping is considered vulgar in England.

"American girls are livelier, better educated, and less hampered by etiquette. They are not as squeamish as their English sisters and they are better able to take care of themselves."
THE PRINCE OF WALES

luncheon at the Board of Admiralty in Greenwich. Among the guests was the Prince of Wales, to whom Mary was presented by the Duchess of St. Albans. That very evening the Duchess took her to Parliament, where she was introduced to Gladstone. She had wakened in her Claridge's bedroom just another American tourist; by the time she went to bed that night, she had met a duchess, a former prime minister and the Prince of Wales.

She was invited to Parliament again, then to a fashionable wedding, then to visit Oxford with Sir William Harcourt and his American wife. And then, on July 17, Mary went to the Duchess of Westminster's ball at Grosvenor House. It was the peak of the season. The reception rooms were brightly lit (the Duke was an early fan of electricity) and the ballroom already crowded when she arrived. The dancing was about to begin. As she entered the room, a stat-

Young ladies waiting for partners at a ball: the initiative was entirely in the men's hands.

Like the wistful subject of "The Morning After the Ball," Mary Leiter could only read about parties until the Prince took her under his wing.

uesque beauty in a stupendous Worth gown, the Prince approached her. He wanted to open the quadrille with Mary as his partner. She agreed, and they took the floor.

Mary's career, from that moment, was made. She was taken into the inner circle of London society, admired, applauded and, most important, invited everywhere. All because the Prince of Wales approved of her. Like Jeannie Chamberlain, like all American heiresses, Mary owed her success to the inclinations and influence of that one popeyed, rather paunchy, all-powerful man.

By the mid-1880s the Prince was beginning to deserve the nickname "Jumbo," given him by Jeannie Chamberlain.

THE MARLBOROUGH HOUSE SET

The division of royal duties that had begun in the 1860s was now complete. While Queen Victoria, in her remote and brilliant way, ruled the British Empire, the Prince of Wales ruled British society. After training him in the ways of pleasure, the fashionable set now took his lead. In fact, it had been renamed the "Marlborough House Set" after the Prince's London residence. When the Prince showed a preference for dinners lasting only an hour, rather than the usual four, short dinners became the vogue; when his wife had a stiff knee, society women took to walking with "the Alexandra limp." When the Prince allowed cigarettes after dinner, in place of cigars, the traditional after-dinner port was abandoned in favor of brandy, which better suited the taste of cigarettes. Society men copied the Prince's beard, his hats, his suits—to the extent that the streets of London swarmed, it seemed to some observers, with imitation Berties. And when the trend-setting Prince took up American heiresses, American heiresses became all the rage. Their spirit, irreverence and flirtatiousness appealed to him. They dressed well, and the Prince took particular pleasure in pretty girls in pretty dresses, going so far as to request that society women always wear new dresses to dine at Marlborough House.

"It is you, sir, who will be the greatest show on earth."

P.T. BARNUM, to the Prince of Wales

The Flip Side: Queen Victoria's Court

Queen Victoria in 1886, aged sixty-seven. She had been Queen for forty-nine years and a widow for twenty-five.

While the aristocrats around the Prince of Wales were having a gay time, the Queen's circle was terminally dull. The Queen was a stickler for the correct forms of showing grief, and in her forty years of widowhood her mourning never lightened. She insisted that her court formally mourn the death of any of her numerous relatives or other heads of state. A lady-in-waiting had to consider, when replenishing her wardrobe, the healthy odds that the court would be plunged into black during her attendance. Evening clothes were always black, white, gray, purple and mauve, the colors of half-mourning.

The Queen was also a stickler for her own consequence. She might not have enjoyed her position, but she took it very seriously and even admitted in a letter to one of her children that she felt she could never be truly intimate with someone who wasn't of royal blood. When Prince Albert died in 1861, she is supposed to have said: "There is no one left to call me Victoria now."

She would never dream of relaxing protocol. It is the traditional privilege of aristocrats to serve their rulers, and the Queen would not accept personal service from mere menials except at table. If a door was to be opened, a blanket placed over her knees, a walking-stick brought, a letter written, a courtier must be called. Duchesses carried her umbrella; countesses and marchionesses stood behind her chair after dinner. No one was allowed to sit in her presence unless specially invited to, and the ladies-in-waiting habitually bought shoes a size too big since their feet swelled so badly. (Some also suffered chronically from hemorrhoids, the result of so much standing.)

This was a far cry from the opulent gaiety of the Marlborough House Set. Jennie Churchill, after a "dine and sleep" at Windsor, lamented the stilted conversation at dinner and described how, "when the Queen spoke, even the whispers ceased. If she addressed a remark to you, the answer was given while the whole company listened." Another American heiress, who underwent this ordeal twice, characterized dinner as "a most depressing function." Conversation afterward, in a "narrow and somber passage," was no better: "We were, in turn, conducted to where the Queen sat and she addressed a few words to each of us. I found it most embarrassing to stand in front of her while everyone listened to her kind inquiries to my reaction to my adopted country. . . ."

Though she had a very sweet smile, the Queen would more likely greet new acquaintances with an uneasy laugh; on top of it all, she was shy and hated meeting strangers. She abhorred novelty (in marked contrast to her restless son) but cherished continuity, especially in families. That was one reason so many of her courtiers in the 1880s and '90s were the sons and daughters of equerries and ladies-in-waiting from the 1840s and '50s.

It also explained why Americans, however high they might rise in the Prince of Wales' circle, would never be accepted by the Queen. Everything they represented, the liveliness, the frivolity, the taste for luxury, the informality, were characteristics that made Her Majesty nervous. And for their part, the Americans found the Queen's set dull and dowdy and boring. Which was precisely what they had said about the most exclusive sets of Americans back home.

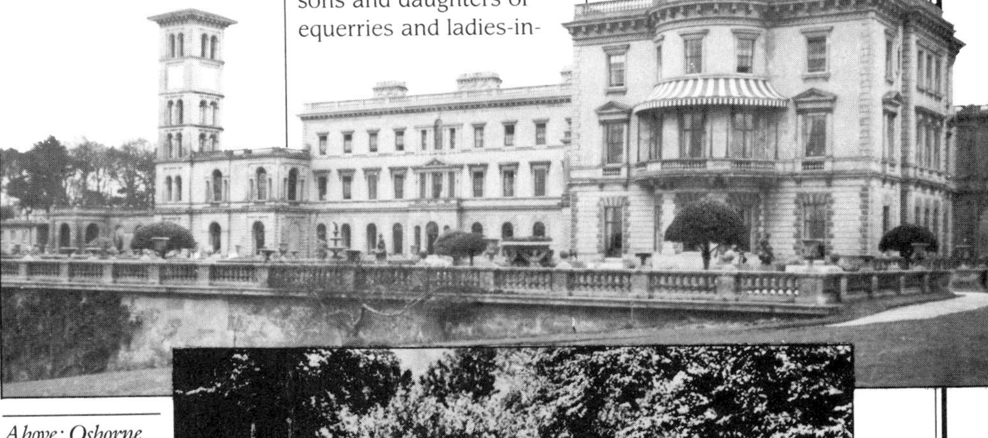

Above: Osborne House, the Queen's private refuge on the Isle of Wight.
Right: Three generations of the Royal Family. To Victoria's right are George V and Edward VIII.

According to the Prince, American girls "could tell a good story and were born card players"—and he should know, having spent a lot of time listening to stories and playing cards. They were also new, and the Prince, boredom ever nipping at his heels, craved novelty.

By the end of the 1880s, boredom was the Prince's biggest problem. And if it was his problem, it was society's problem. It was up to the Set to make sure the Prince was supplied with an endless round of parties to go to, food to eat, birds to shoot, girls to flirt with. Since royalty traditionally designates not only the time and place and guest list of any party but also the host, the Prince was in a position to be a tyrant-guest, an *invité* who gave orders. His favorites were permanently on call, sometimes given as little as twenty-four hours' notice of the Prince's intention to be entertained at their home. Nevertheless, the Set's hostesses competed with each other for his love and approval. They lived for the sound of his satisfied purr and would stop at nothing to keep the thick royal fingers from drumming testily on the tabletop. And if this meant entertaining upstart American females, they would do just that—no matter how galling the sight of their future king smiling contentedly under the spell of some showy little savage.

The ever restless Prince of Wales founded his own gentlemen's club, the Marlborough, and in 1870 presented this silver snuffbox to its members.

BY ROYAL DESIRE

Right at the center of the Set were the Buccaneers: the former Consuelo Yznaga Mandeville, now Duchess of Manchester (Mandeville succeeded to the title in 1890), Lady Randolph Churchill and Minnie Paget. Their marriages had been blessed by the Prince, their welcome in English society facilitated by him. For instance, the season often featured charity concerts of classical music performed by aristocratic amateur musicians. In the 1883 and 1885 seasons, these concerts featured, "by royal desire," performers taken exclusively from the circle of American ladies in

The Buccaneers as English ladies: Consuelo, now an American duchess; Minnie Paget (in a 1900 photograph); and Lady Randolph Churchill, dressed for the hunt.

London. The American ladies returned the favor by joining in the task of keeping the Prince happy.

The Prince hated to be alone. So if he was off for a month's shooting in Austria, Jennie must drop everything and go with him. When he was in London over the deadly quiet Easter week, Consuelo would scamper up to town and organize a party or two. Minnie always took a house in Cowes during the sailing season, simply to ensure that the Prince had a hostess there whom he could count on.

> *“Whenever I ask Consuelo, Duchess of Manchester, about an American lady I am invariably told, ‘Oh, sir, she has no position at home; out there she would be just dirt under our feet.’”*
>
> THE PRINCE OF WALES, to Alice Rothschild

A private theatrical at Chatsworth, the Devonshires' country estate. The bearded gentleman in the foreground is the Duke; the Prince of Wales is visible midway down the row.

The Prince had two lives: a formal public, ceremonial one, and the informal, private, occasionally rather naughty one. So it was with the parties of the Set. There were the huge receptions to which everyone who was anyone was invited, and there were the "small evenings," dinner parties seldom graced by the presence of the Princess of Wales that went on till dawn. It was the latter particularly that the Prince enjoyed and the American women excelled at giving. They created intimacy by seating guests at small, round tables rather than the conventional great long ones; they created excitement by paying the Prince's favorite soprano to chuck a concert in Paris and come sing privately for an evening. And they had good cooks. The Prince was a gourmet in a country where much food served in even the best houses was simply execrable, so for the meals alone he adored them.

COMME IL FAUT
Friendly American curiosity—"How many brothers do you have? Do you know many people in New York?"—is considered rudely intrusive in England.

THE TRANSATLANTIC PIPELINE

All their efforts on the Prince's behalf gave the Buccaneers considerable leverage in London society. Who better to supply the Prince with the season's allotment of American heiresses? Across the ocean were a score of sisters, mothers and friends with whom they established a transatlantic pipeline, a delivery system that pumped the audacious and innocent from Fifth Avenue right into the heart of Mayfair.

Let's say an heiress débuted in New York. All the matrons there got a chance to look her over, while she got a chance to charm one or two of them. When the heiress announced she was going to England, one of the matrons offered to write a letter of introduction for her. If it was Mrs. Stevens, she could send the heiress to daughter Minnie. If it was Alva Vanderbilt, the girl would be sent on to best friend Consuelo Manchester. Fifth Avenue hostess Mrs. Ogden Mills could send an heiress she liked to her twin sister Elizabeth, married to a socially prominent M.P. named George Cavendish-Bentinck.

Upon arriving in England, the heiress would present her letter of introduction. If she sought out Consuelo Manchester, for instance, and met with her approval, a tea would be arranged and she would be introduced to other notable Americans in London. Consuelo could then ask her sister Natica, married to a great friend of the Prince named Sir John Lister-Kaye, to have the heiress round to dinner when she was entertaining H.R.H. If Bertie liked her, other hostesses would soon find out and she'd be well on her way.

For those heiresses not connected by blood or friendship to the transatlantic pipeline operators, all was not lost. It was possible to engage the services of one of the "social godmothers," as they were known, much as one hired a carriage for the season—by paying with a check. Or with some stock tips or an emerald brooch. Some of the first-generation fortunes were running dry. Consuelo Manchester's husband had been declared a bankrupt when he succeeded to the ducal title. Leonard Jerome's finances had taken a turn for the worse in the mid-seventies, and he had long since curtailed the amount of money he sent to his three daughters. And Minnie Paget still had to

"*The almighty dollar*
will buy, you bet
A superior class of coronet;
That's why I've come
from over the way,
From New York City of
U.S.A."

From *The American Girl*, a musical comedy

Natica Yznaga, Lady Lister-Kaye, costumed as the French Duchesse de Guise for an 1890s ball.

FIFTH AVENUE MEETS THE PEERAGE

❖

The British essayist and newspaper columnist known as Juvenal stated that "New Yorkers are beginning to regard themselves as a sort of annexed wing of the British nobility." Well, the New Yorkers weren't far wrong—at least not at the turn of the century.

BRADLEY MARTIN
20-22 West 20 Street

EARL OF CRAVEN
Cornelia Martin, Countess of Craven

PARAN STEVENS
244 Fifth Avenue

PAGET FAMILY
Minnie Stevens, Lady Paget

OGDEN GOELET
608 Fifth Avenue

DUKE OF ROXBURGHE
May Goelet, Duchess of Roxburghe

W.K. VANDERBILT
660 Fifth Avenue

DUKE OF MARLBOROUGH
Consuelo Vanderbilt, Duchess of Marlborough

WILLIAM WATTS SHERMAN
838 Fifth Avenue

LORD CAMOYS
Mildred Sherman, Lady Camoys

HENRY PHIPPS
1 East 87 Street

GUEST FAMILY
Amy Phipps, the Hon. Mrs. Frederick Guest

WILLIAM C. WHITNEY
871 Fifth Avenue

PAGET FAMILY
Pauline Whitney, Lady Queenborough

ANTHONY J. DREXEL
1015 Fifth Avenue

EARL OF WINCHILSEA & NOTTINGHAM
Margaretta Drexel, Countess of Winchilsea & Nottingham

GEORGE J. GOULD
857 Fifth Avenue

LORD DECIES
Vivien Gould, Lady Decies

THE WILSON FAMILY SCORECARD #3 Belle & Mungo

One of Worth's great success stories was Belle Wilson, second daughter of the increasingly well-connected R.T. Taken to Worth before her début, Belle was completely transformed from a quite ordinary girl into a striking young woman. It was in this guise that she fascinated the Hon. Michael Herbert, a secretary in the British legation in Washington. Her older siblings had married into powerful New York families, but Belle did them one better. Herbert, known affectionately as "Mungo" by such friends as the Prince of Wales, was the younger brother of the Earl of Pembroke. Thus, when Belle was wed in 1888, the Wilson web of matrimonial alliances reached into the very heart of the British aristocracy.

The Hon. Michael Herbert, aristocratic English gentleman par excellence.

COMME IL FAUT
A girl must never dance more than twice with a young man at a ball. Strict mothers do not even permit girls to "sit out" with young men.

share her father's money with her mother. The American hostesses in London, and some of their English counterparts, paid their dressmakers' bills with the money received for engineering the husband-hunting campaigns of on-the-make American heiresses.

THE MATING SEASON

The sponsors were aided in their scheming by the very nature of the London season, which, despite all the festivities, was at bottom just a marriage market. English girls were hauled up from the country for three months of carefully chaperoned but more or less constant exposure to men roped in for dinner parties and dances and house-party weekends. The girls at the balls, clacking open their plumed ivory fans, dance cards dangling from their wrists, were really mere goods on display, the men stepping into the ballrooms doing up the last buttons on their dance gloves just shoppers—wary of being cheated, eager to make a deal, or pleased to be able to afford the best.

Because the end of the season was always in sight, a sense of urgency prevailed. Eager English mothers and canny social godmothers aimed to secure the men's proposals and the girls' acceptances by the end of July, after which everyone could go back to the country where they belonged and not have to think about the entire business for another nine months. This cattle-drive approach to courtship worked in the newcomer's favor. In the clamor and thrill of swirling skirts and flickering candles, the pallid, serene womanliness of the English girl was no match for the "snap" and "go" of the American heiress.

The requirements of limited access and quick decisions also meant that the young English lord got to see just enough of the strange, forward child to become infatuated. And he liked being infatuated. The English aristocracy are, as Henry James pointed out, the most romantic people in the world, entirely

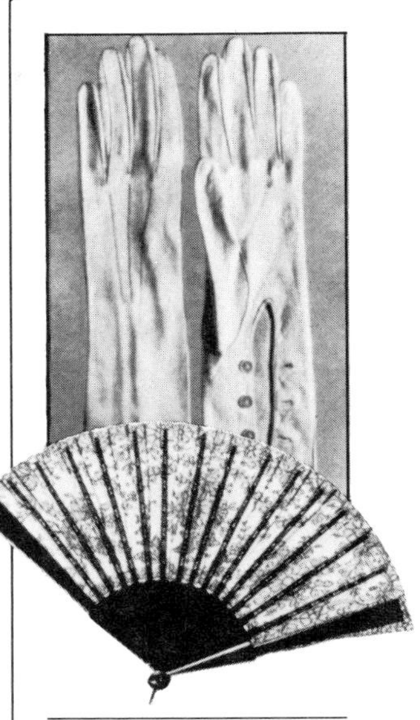

Ladies and gentlemen both wore gloves on the dance floor; flesh never touched flesh. Kid gloves were supposed to fit so tightly that the outline of the fingernails was visible; they lasted for only one wearing. Fans were essential for more than flirtation, as crowded ballrooms often got very hot.

The heiresses' goal: a coronet. This one is an earl's, alternating strawberry leaves and raised gold balls. The "cap of maintenance" is crimson velvet; the fur is ermine.

"The Hypnotist and His Easy Subject," a cartoon from the American magazine Life. *The exodus of American girls to Europe was increasingly fodder for cartoonists.*

capable of marrying their cooks and their coachmen. This romantic tendency, this thirst for novelty and rebellion, was just another factor that worked to the advantage of the fiercely midwestern American heiress. The more resemblance she bore to Annie Oakley of the Wild West Show, the better. If the English aristocrat wanted to be modern, to be fashionable, to take a chance, annoy his parents, flatter the Prince of Wales, he got himself engaged to some little American. One evening, in the lantern-lit garden of a great London house, the young lord would listen to the American heiress's chatter and let himself get carried away.

And the little American, who seemed such a child, saw that the thing was sealed as quickly as it was agreed with the obligatory announcement in the very next edition of the *Morning Post.* She had got what she came for and only smiled to see the flurry of distress her maneuvering caused her English rivals. Too bad for them. She had played the game, snared her victim, gained critical ground in her quest for class. She was the victor. Or was she?

ANOTHER SIDE OF THE STORY

By the time American heiresses were beginning their siege of London, the Marlborough House Set had put twenty years into amusing the Prince of Wales. He was increasingly petulant—and some of them were going broke trying to keep up. The most famous sacrificial lamb was Christopher Sykes, of whom the Prince took merciless advantage until the poor man was wrung dry and ruined from party-giving. There were others, such as Daisy Warwick, Lord Hardwick and Lord Dupplin, who managed to avoid complete ruin but nevertheless spent their family fortunes on entertaining the heir to the throne.

For them, the American heiress was more than a mere novelty, more than just spice to be added to the endless round of dinner parties, house parties, receptions and teas. To them, she was salvation. They intended to get their hands on all that American money and see that it was spent right there in London. It would be a waste for the heiresses to go back home and marry Americans. They were pretty, they were accomplished, they were rich. Properly married off, they could take their turn at entertaining the Prince of Wales, and most of the Set along with him.

So an heiress who had won their approval would be put in the way of a man they thought could make use of her, regardless of their own views of his merits as a husband. They might know things about him—the size of his debts, the state of his property, the level of his drinking, the number of his mistresses—which did not recommend him. But they kept these things to themselves. And the social godmother's protection did not extend this far. She had social debts, social responsibilities of her own. As far as she was concerned, if the Set wanted an heiress they could have her. As far as the Set were concerned, American heiresses—so good at distracting the Prince, so capable of taking up the burden of the bills—could invade London anytime they liked.

Christopher Sykes, whose only reaction to his Prince's excessive commands was "As His Royal Highness pleases." Ultimately, this passivity bankrupted him.

MISS DAISY MILLER

The American reading public loved Daisy Miller from the moment she appeared, smoothing her bows and ribbons, gazing unappreciatively upon the Swiss landscape and declaring to a complete stranger that she had "always had a great deal of gentlemen's society."

She hadn't any idea what a gentleman was, of course, but that was just the point. For *Daisy Miller: A Study* was intended to portray the great difference in the American and European way of looking at things, right down to the differing use of the same words. To Daisy a gentleman was any nice young man; to a European, of course, the word could be applied only to a man from a particular class. Likewise, to Daisy "gentlemen's society" meant picnics and tea dances and nice little chats walking home from church; to the European ear, the phrasing suggested something just short of prostitution.

Henry James' American publisher rejected the story—perhaps, the eventual English publisher conjectured, because it was "an outrage on American girlhood." But only an Englishman could see it that way. Daisy's woeful ignorance of social standards made her all the more appealing to Americans. In the eyes of her countrymen she wasn't a vulgar little ignoramus, but a wonderful example of the freshness and vitality of American youth refusing to give way before stodgy old Europe. *Daisy Miller* was a huge hit—the only really big popular success of Henry James' literary career. Daisy Miller hats appeared at the milliners', and Daisy Miller's behavior was discussed in great detail in the etiquette books. As far as the

The frontispiece of Harper Brothers' 1892 edition included a mock coat of arms with two bleeding hearts and an arrow.

American public was concerned, James had not created "a piece of pure poetry," as he later claimed, but simply reproduced, straight from life, a typical American girl.

Daisy was full of contrasts, the very contrasts that were driving European men crazy. She had "the *tournure* of a princess" and the manner of a flirt. She dressed with "extreme elegance," while her conversation was all "a charming, innocent prattle." She was "dying to be exclusive" but would not for a moment consider abandoning her inappropriate Italian on the main thoroughfare of Roman society just for the sake of appearances.

Her characteristic mix of naïveté and self-confidence, celebrated by James as "an inscrutable combination of audacity and innocence," was precisely what it was about American heiresses that so perplexed the Europeans, so astounded the English. Was the American girl sophisticated or simple-minded, a calculating woman or an unself-conscious child? Daisy said such naughty things—claiming to have spent so much time with men, for example—in so straightforward a manner. Didn't she know she was being brazen? Or didn't she care? They never could figure it out.

Henry James thought he, perhaps, had. After Daisy's death (from Roman fever, naturally) Winterbourne, a Europeanized American like James himself, chides her Italian suitor for having taken her into the Colosseum at night. He should have known it would expose her to serious illness. But the Italian, while conceding to the danger, can only shrug his shoulders and say, "She did what she liked!"

That statement was added to the story thirty years after it was first published, when James was preparing a uniform edition of his collected works. It came after nearly three decades of writing fiction about American women abroad in foreign society and was practically a single-sentence elegy on the lives of all the American heiresses. These girls weren't just innocent or ignorant. They were also, in an unsupervised, ill-informed way, free. No one told American girls what to do; no one knew better than they. They hadn't a clue, but they intended to sweep all before them. "Il faut vous preparer d'une vie de sacrifices with me, my dear," eighteen-year-old Jennie Jerome had warned Lord Randolph Churchill. "I won't marry you if you don't let me do *exactly* as I like." Or as Daisy Miller's brother could have told him, along with the rest of the English aristocracy, "She's an American girl, you bet!"

ON BEHALF OF THE HEIRESS

"It's very well for Europe to have a few phrases that will do for any girl," says a society matron in James' "Pandora." "The American girl isn't any girl; she's a remarkable specimen in a remarkable species." James himself found the right words to do her justice in the following literary portraits.

The Golden Bowl, Daisy Miller: A Study, Portrait of a Lady, The Reverberator, Wings of the Dove, A London Life

"An International Episode," "Lady Barbarina," "Lord Beaupré," "Miss Gunton of Poughkeepsie," "Mrs. Medwin," "Pandora," "The Pension Beaurepas," "The Siege of London"

Sargent's portrait of Henry James.

THE COMPETITION

English girls and their English mamas cast fearful glances southward. Just who would be on the next train from Atlantic ports of call? Noble husband-hunting was hard enough, thank you very much. Foreigners need not apply. Unfortunately, their English brothers and sons seemed not to agree. American girls. What did men see in them?

A NATURAL APPEAL

First and foremost, American girls were pretty. Always. They seemed never to have the bad teeth or long noses or excessive height of English girls. True, they lacked the porcelain complexion and drooping lids considered the crowning glories of aristocratic good looks, but the average American girl was handsomer, more elegant than her English counterpart. And her natural beauty was, of course, clothed to perfection. Her parents were willing to spend more than the English girl's parents, who could seldom afford to bring out their daughters in a succession of new gowns—much less new gowns from Worth. The American girl also had a superior clothes sense, while the English girl, for reasons never fully made clear, clung to the national tradition of dowdiness. "The general consensus of opinion," wrote Lady Randolph Churchill, no impartial observer, "is that she [the American girl] is perhaps the best dressed woman in the world."

The great thing about English girls was their regal carriage, their quiet, simple *hauteur*, but even this feature was offset by their tendency to efface themselves unto evaporation. Their detachment was noble, but it could also be deathly dull. No one

"*If you could only see what sticks English women are and how badly most of them dress. . . .*"
CLARA JEROME, in a letter to her mother

looked better perched sidesaddle on her horse in Hyde Park, straight-backed and serene, than the English girl, but one would, perhaps, rather take the American girl down to dinner.

Jeannie Chamberlain, the blooming American beauty in person, captured by fashionable portraitist Edward Hughes.

THE AMERICAN BEAUTY ROSE

Right from its 1885 launching by a nursery in Washington, D.C., the American Beauty Rose was society's favorite flower. No dinner, ball or wedding was properly decorated without hundreds of the red blooms, covering tables, walls and latticed arches. Part of their appeal was the expense (everyone knew they brought $2 a stem) and part was their showy look (so much more luxuriant than the tea roses they replaced), but undoubtedly the greatest draw was their name. There were better roses in the United States and in Europe—hardier, easier to grow, longer lasting once they were cut. But the American Beauty has remained the florists' best seller because, 100 years ago, an astute nurseryman decided that his customers wouldn't buy a rose called "Madame Ferdinand Jamin" and renamed it for the prettiest girls he knew.

THE LIFE OF THE PARTY

The American girl was animated. She moved. She asserted herself. She liked to have fun. The Englishman was always amazed, according to Oscar Wilde, at her "extraordinary vivacity, her electrical quickness of repartee, her inexhaustible store of curious catchwords." On going down to dinner for the first time, the English débutante might also be expected to talk to adults for the first time; naturally, since these adults were not only friends and relations but Cabinet ministers and peers of the realm, she might find herself tongue-tied. Not so the American heiress. Encouraged from the earliest age to express herself, and fully confident that herself was an entirely worthwhile thing to express, she would be utterly unfazed by finding the Chancellor of the Exchequer on her left. She'd had a number of "experiences" she was willing to recount in a burbling, gushing fashion that could, despite her atrocious accent, entrance her otherwise jaded dinner partner.

The American girl might be too familiar, what in English eyes amounted to being "pert," but she was so innocent it hardly seemed an affront. While the English girl was trained, according to Daisy, Princess of Pless, to greet introductions with "eyes demurely fixed on the ground," the American girl strode across the room to shake a man's hand in a way that was pleasing from a young matron, delightfully shocking from a fifteen-year-old.

Lafayette was London's society photographer. Good friends might exchange signed photographs, which would sit, silver-framed, on a drawing-room table. Photographs of the "Professional Beauties" (Jennie Churchill and Lillie Langtry among them) could actually be bought in shops.

"THE COURAGE TO BE HERSELF"

The American girl enjoyed a freedom of movement and association reserved in Europe solely for married women. She was neither as sheltered nor as ignored as the English girl, who had always to concede first place to her noble brother. While American girls were getting French lessons and history lessons and music lessons from the best possible tutors, the English girl was being educated by "a more or less incompetent governess" in the third-floor schoolroom of the country seat. While the American girl was tripping through the capitals of Europe, looking at pictures, listening to lectures, examining monuments of civilization, the English girl was traveling between the nursery and the stableyard.

"The New York woman has the courage to be herself," asserted Mary MacDonald Brown, an Englishwoman. "The English society woman is trained from her cradle in the art of pleasing and charming." In the process her individuality is apt to be obliterated." In England it was unthinkable to allow an unmarried girl to ride alone in a carriage, to cross a street without her maid, to attend a dance unchaperoned. Her parents' surveillance extended to the people she mixed with, her correspondence, the books she read, the thoughts she tried to express. Consuelo Vanderbilt, Duchess of Marlborough, pitied "the limited outlook" produced by such a restricted upbringing.

Lady Sarah Wilson, Lord Randolph Churchill's sister. With her deep-set eyes and long nose, she typified the English style of good looks.

In America, on the other hand, girls and boys went on picnics together, had their own little dinner parties, went walking or sailing or riding. It was entirely possible for a young American couple to be left sitting innocently alone in an American drawing room. American girls did not approach the altar, as Daisy Pless swears English girls did, with the expectation of "for the first time in our virginal lives actually touching the elbow of a man." Unhampered by constant parental surveillance and suspicion, they could launch themselves into the London season with a confidence that simply could not be shared by their shy, inexperienced English sisters.

POINTS IN HER CAMPAIGN

Acquiring sponsorship and putting together a wardrobe by Worth were only the first steps in preparation for the American heiress's campaign. Other ploys were required to ensure unqualified success in gaining an English title of the first magnitude.

THE RIGHT ADDRESS

The accommodations, of course, were crucial: Claridge's or Brown's, or a rented house in Mayfair if one was absolutely confident in one's—or one's mother's—abilities as a hostess. Sponsors knew which families were not coming up to town for the season, and who might be willing to unload their large house on wealthy Americans while they rented some other, smaller house. One most wanted something discreet yet impressive, with a good staircase for making grand entrances. In the 1870s and '80s, a house off Berkeley Square, in Bruton Street or Hill Street or Curzon Street, was ideal; by the turn of the century, Portland Place and Grosvenor Square were addresses of choice.

Above: Brown's Hotel, the American heiress's home away from home. Left: The grand houses on Carlton House Terrace, an admirable setting for many an heiress's charms.

A PRIVATE YACHT

A surefire way to the Prince of Wales' heart was through his sailing competition with Kaiser Wilhelm II, the nephew whom he strove to prevent from becoming "the boss of Cowes." Since Americans were increasingly the owners of the world's most luxurious yachts, and since they tended to keep them in England to avoid American registry and higher crew salaries, the Prince found himself consorting with persons whom, yachtless, he would have ignored. Royal racing circles were the cream of European nobility, and inclusion meant a regular exchange of shipboard dinner invitations as well as a chance to socialize with the Prince when he was at his most relaxed and friendly.

THE OFF-SEASON

Though it was widely conceded that one should never be seen in London in August, it was possible to make use of the less crowded field of the off-season. There was, for instance, the "little season," when Parliament met in December, as well as the preseason in late winter/early spring. There would be no large political receptions or major balls, but in general the social corset was laced less tightly—a circumstance always advantageous to the newcomer. Mrs. Leggett saw the off-season, "when the butterflies are in Egypt, Cannes, and Rome and the solid men at work in Westminster," as an opportunity for her daughter Alberta to meet "men of brain and position."

Left: The Prince of Wales, combining his two favorite pastimes—yachting and flirting.

Below: Marlborough House, the ultimate goal.

MEDIA COVERAGE

It was always a good idea to get one's name about—in the same paragraphs, preferably, with other, more well-known names. If necessary, the free-lance journalist covering a social event could be paid to include an heiress's name in the list of preeminent attendees. If the heiress was generous, he might expend himself on a description of her glowing appearance. In the 1870s and '80s, frequent mention in the *Morning Post* ("seen riding in the Row," "seen in her magnificent carriage") would do; in the '90s, a paragraph in the *World* set the standard. After the turn of the century, publication in the *Tatler* of a photograph by Alice Hughes or Lafayette (one preferred a caption such as "Another American Beauty" to "A Welcome American Invader") was a good promotional ploy.

WHEN TO SAY NO

No doubt about it, to be shown the ancestral pile was to have the inside track—a chance to show how well one fit with the turrets, Van Dycks and broad acres of the intended setting. But the heiress must weigh her response to the marriage proposal that often accompanied her visit: one didn't want to jump too fast, nor did one wish to alienate the family. Nancy Langhorne Shaw's apparent lack of interest in a titled suitor provoked an acquaintance to warn: "I think you should realize, Mrs. Shaw, that it is a very serious matter to refuse a peer." And Belle Wilson Herbert, in a letter to her sister Grace, noted that "the men get so *nasty* when they are refused over here." The heiress must walk a tightrope, with no letup of caution, lest she end up without her English lord.

POOR PEERS

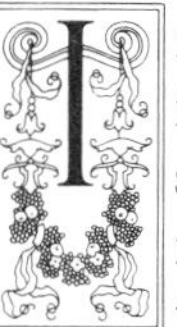

In many ways, money had always been a factor in aristocratic marriages. There was a long-standing tradition in England of noblemen marrying heiresses to refresh the family coffers. It was the only choice they had. All the manners and impeccable tailoring and aristocratic connections of London's bachelors effectively hid the harsh truth that many of these men had no money and no way of getting any. In England, gentlemen didn't work. The custom was a hangover from the palmy days of English agricultural society, when the great landowning families lived on their estates, collected rents from tenant farmers and ran the country. The land yielded sufficient income to live well, some-

LORD TUFFNUTT: *"You have nothing to grumble at; you were a rich American girl, I am an impoverished English nobleman with a proud title. You bought me with your wealth. I was what you call, in shopping, a bargain!"*
LADY TUFFNUTT: *"Pardon me! Not a bargain—a remnant."*

Early in the twentieth century it was possible to live comfortably in London with two servants, eating five meals a day, for £400 a year.

times splendidly; and it was part of the landowner's duty to contribute his time to local or national government by serving as a justice of the peace or taking a seat in Parliament.

The growing industrialization of Britain and the swelling wealthy middle class, however, had put pressure on the aristocracy. The new bourgeoisie, adopting the manners and habits of the upper classes, were sending their sons to public schools and studying the etiquette books to puzzle out the use of calling cards. The crucial distance separating the upper class from the upper-middle was shrinking. Unemployment was the last true distinction.

MARCH OF ANGLOMANIA
American huntsmen often imported packs of foxhounds from England.

HARD TIMES

The concomitant of aristocratic unemployment was aristocratic poverty. A younger son (or, for that matter, an elder son who had not yet inherited) was forced to live on whatever allowance the family estates could muster. To be sure, he might go into the army; but army officers had only recently begun to receive pay, and in a fashionable regiment that would have to be supplemented by as much as £500 per year just to keep up with his messmates in terms of champagne drunk and polo ponies ruined. Politics was an option for, perhaps, the younger son of a great family who could wield age-old influence to obtain a seat in Parliament (as in the case of Lord Randolph Churchill). Political campaigns were expensive, however, and members of Parliament were not paid.

A typical American college graduate, viewing education as a means to getting ahead in the world. For the aristocratic Englishman, education was merely gilding the lily.

Dispiriting as these prospects were, they were exacerbated by economic conditions, for England had fallen into an agricultural depression. Beginning around 1873, the income from farms began to slide. The influx of imported foodstuffs, especially refrigerated meat from the Antipodes, Dutch margarine and, worst of all, American wheat drove down prices on native products. Landlords had to permit rent rollbacks or lose their tenants; and there were no new

Tandragee, the Duke of Manchester's estate in Ireland. It produced £25,000 a year in rents before the agricultural depression, £14,000 a year afterward.

tenants moving onto the land. It became impossible to improve, let alone maintain, agricultural estates. The land was no longer cultivated. Landlords who wished to sell found no buyers, since the return on investment for land had dropped so radically.

By the early 1880s, when the Self-Made Girls began emerging from their schoolrooms, a number of families across the ocean had been very hard hit. Not only were younger sons' allowances cut back, but even an eldest son who had inherited might have urgent needs (a new roof, for example) not covered by his income. English heiresses were always scarce, owing to primogeniture. If they had brothers, they wouldn't be heiresses. And now, if a young lady's family fortunes were agriculturally based, her financial expectations were considerably diminished.

"Try one of the Leiter girls."

Advice from a London dowager to the impecunious Earl of Suffolk, future husband of Miss Daisy Leiter

But America's Founding Fathers had thought primogeniture a barbaric system, so they made certain that citizens of the new country would be free from such customs. In America a man could dispose of his fortune however he liked, splitting it equally among all his children or leaving a larger portion to an elder son (some families did cling to this tradition) while still providing for the others—even the girls.

A MOST SUPERIOR PERSON

By 1890 the advantages of the transatlantic match were plain to the dimmest of English gentlemen, and the Honourable George Curzon was anything but

Curzon (left) vacationing in Scotland. His bad back exempted him from the pressure to play games at Eton, so, unlike many students, he actually studied.

The Hon. George Curzon, one of the most brilliant men of his generation. His ambitions matched his intelligence.

ESTATE DRAINS

❖

To Americans, the height of English glamour was country-house life, because nothing was more alien. But for the English, nothing was more expensive. A hundred years earlier, a country estate had been a going concern; now, with the pressure of industrialization and a bitter agricultural depression, the income from the estate had dwindled while the cost of upkeep was resulting in negative balance-sheets.

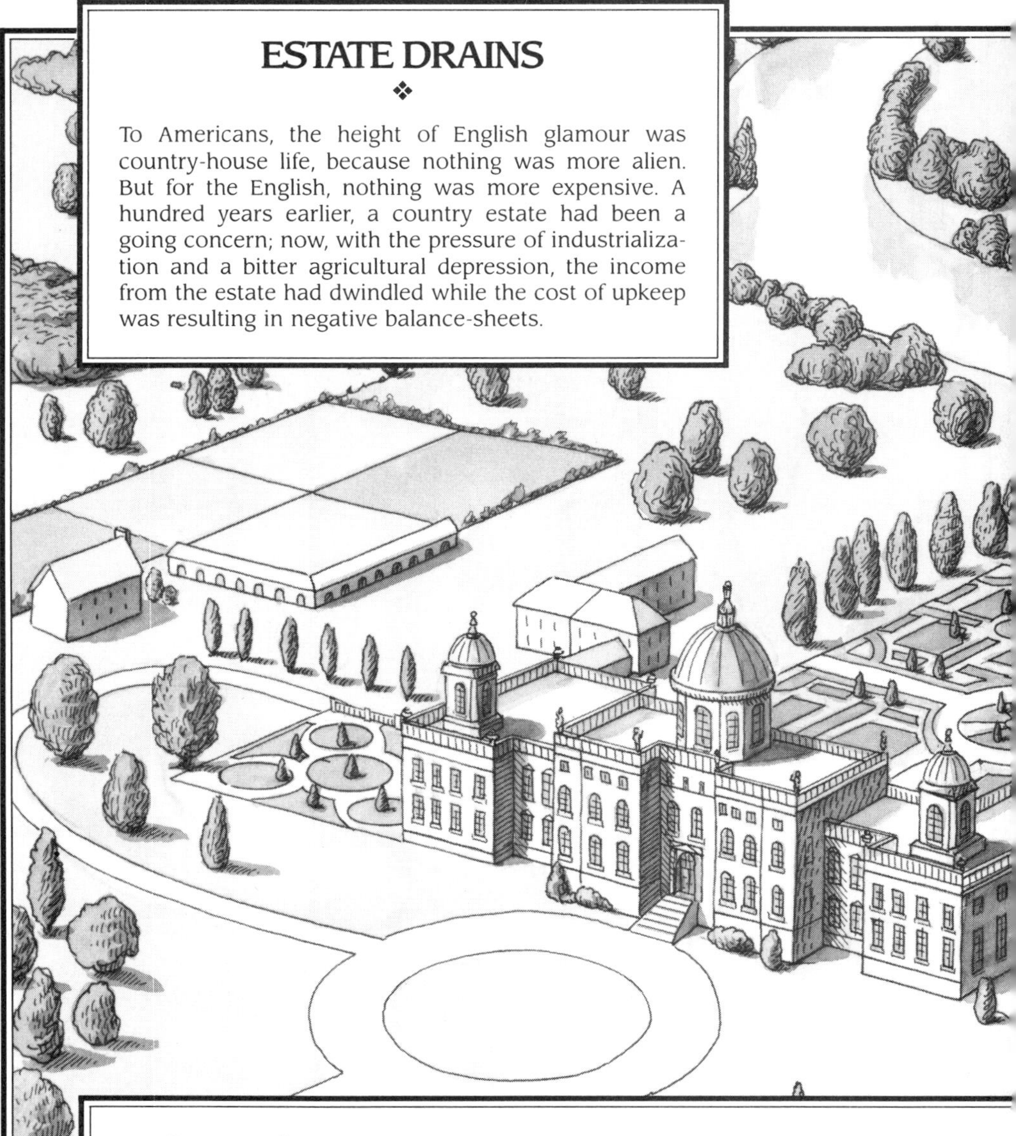

Operating Expenses

❖

- Allowance to Dowager in Dower House: £2,000 per annum (to include servants' salaries and household costs).
- Allowance to Aunt Agatha, still living upstairs in the Norman Room: £60 p.a. Ditto to Uncle Augustus in Marrakech (£650) to stay there.
- Repair of church steeple: £600.
- Teacher's salary, coal, books for village school: £250.
- Pension to old Briggs, ex-gamekeeper: £10 p.a. and rent-free cottage. Ditto to Wood, Dotry, Nobb and Jeffries (£40 total) and to old Nanny, living in West Wing (£15).
- Salary for land agent to collect rents, administer estate: £1,000 p.a..
- Two carriage horses, and three hunters for His Lordship: £135.
- Fodder, grooms' salaries, stable repairs, carriage upkeep: £300.
- Leaving fields uncultivated to provide cover for pheasants, partridges, grouse; winter feed for game; salaries for gamekeepers: £2,250 p.a.
- Pruning trees, shrubs, seeding lawn, dredging ornamental pond, clearing thickets, regraveling paths: £600 p.a.
- "Pin money" (clothing and charity allowances) for unmarried daughters Lady Agatha, Lady Maude and Lady Enid: £200 each.
- Household staples ordered from London (candles, soap, brooms, buckets, etc.): £800.
- Coal for 25 fireplaces (lit only at night in bedrooms): £75.
- Salaries of carpenters, tilers, brickmakers in building yard: £1,500 p.a.

- Household salaries: six housemaids (£18 p.a. each); governess (£25); schoolroom maid (£15); four footmen (£40 each); hall-boy (£10); French chef (£100); three kitchen maids (£15 each); scullery maid (£8); housekeeper (£50); His Lordship's valet (£65); butler (£80).
- Allowances to Hon. Cedric and Hon. Marmaduke £1,000 p.a. each.
- His Lordship's personal expenses: £4,500 (includes club dues, tailor, debts of honor, entertaining in town).
- House party entertaining: meals for 12 guests with their 12 servants five times a day for three days, six house parties: £600. Plus: writing paper in all guests' bedrooms, renewed daily (£15 per house party); bill for claret and champagne (£875) for year; cost of transporting Blue Hungarian Band to play at each house party (£600 total).

TOTAL EXPENSES: £20, 216

INCOME on estate:	£12,500	rent from tenants (on 43,000 acres, 35,000 under cultivation)
	£1,000	sale of timber
	£300	dividends from other investments
	£55	sale of Lady Agatha, Lady Maude and Lady Enid's hunters
TOTAL:	£13,855	
SHORTFALL:	£6,361	

Scale: £1 = $5; 5 × 33 = today's dollar
Total income: $2,286,075.00
Total expenses: $3,335,640.00

Ironically, Kedleston was used as the model for Government House in Calcutta, the home of India's British viceroy.

After his stunning career at Eton, where he won the most prizes in the history of the school, Curzon (center) went on to win the Arnold and Lothian prizes at Oxford.

dim. He was the eldest son of the fourth Baron Scarsdale, and had been brought up with his nine siblings at Kedleston, the Scarsdale seat in Derbyshire. An eighteenth-century predecessor, Sir Nathaniel Curzon, had greatly expanded and improved Kedleston, hiring Robert Adam to design staterooms in the new neo-Classical taste. (Samuel Johnson thought the house "would do excellently well as a town hall.") Sir Nathaniel, a Tory, was making a bid for political supremacy over the Whig Cavendishes, the local magnificos. Though Kedleston soon rivaled Chatsworth (the Cavendish seat) in size, the Curzon fortune wasn't up to supporting such a large house. Property in London had to be sold, and by the 1880s the Curzon family was drastically, if grandly, overhoused. The estate, about 10,000 acres, brought in £18,000 a year, of which the house ate up a great deal. The Baron could afford to pay George an allowance of only about £1,000 a year.

For a young bachelor, that sufficed, and George supplemented his allowance with £400–500 a year from journalism. His position as M.P. paid nothing. But Curzon was no less ambitious than his forebear who had expanded Kedleston. He had inordinate talents (he swept the academic prizes at Eton and

Oxford, and was elected a Fellow of All Souls at the age of twenty-four) and knew it. In 1888 he went abroad. But Curzon was no adventurous dilettante, knocking around the world with a pair of Purdey shotguns looking for sport. His itinerary took him to Samarkand, where he watched and listened and made notes on the politics of the area, and upon returning to England he published *Russia in Central Asia*.

Curzon went abroad again in 1889, this time traveling on horseback through the remotest areas of Persia and sending articles back to *The Times* to pay for his trip. Because his health was poor (he suffered from chronic back pain, frequently resorting to an iron brace), the primitive travel methods were grueling, but Curzon would always push himself beyond human endurance. His goal was a lofty one: he wanted nothing less than to be viceroy of India, and his voyages of discovery (for he penetrated areas where white men had never gone) were intended to make him England's expert on Eastern politics.

AMBITIOUS LOVE

He could not, however, become viceroy on a mere £1,500 a year. His father was young and healthy, so there was no hope of inheriting soon. It occurred to him to marry money, and to this end he strenuously courted Lady Grosvenor, the wealthy widow of the Duke of Westminster's heir. She turned him down in 1887, but by 1890 his heart (and self-esteem) were whole again when he returned from Persia to the flurry of the London season. His charm, intelligence, looks and breeding guaranteed a place in the most fashionable circles; his achievements made him much sought after. On July 17, at the peak of the season, he went to the Duchess of Westminster's ball at Grosvenor House and watched Mary Leiter dance with the Prince of Wales.

Curzon later wrote that he "never loved Mary Leiter more than at the moment when he first saw her

Lord Terence Temple-Blackwood, second son of the 1st Marquess of Dufferin and Ava. Like Curzon and other younger sons, he had to make his own way in the world; he chose the Foreign Office, rising as high as Second Secretary at the British embassy in New York before his older brother was killed in the Boer War. He married New Yorker Flora Davis in 1893.

RATING A MATE

The task of the Self-Made girl was to differentiate among all the attractive, well-bred Englishmen who sought her favor. This was where her social sponsor (or the unusually astute mama) came in, weighing the family history, youthful peccadilloes and financial circumstances of society's bachelors.

THE PEER would make a girl a peeress. This meant wearing ermine and velvet at coronations and having a place of honor at dinner, a crest on one's writing paper and a coronet on one's sheets. It also probably meant inheriting an ancestral home full of creaky ancestral machinery: shooting parties for which the guest list hadn't changed in three generations; family jewels that could not be reset no matter how ugly they were; family religion, family politics, family traditions. Marrying a peer turned the heiress into an institution, incessantly compared to the last woman who'd held the job and, because she was American, frequently found wanting. It would be her dollars that made her acceptable, if she spent them on restoring the glory of the family name. And if she conformed, with time she might even be loved.

May Goelet, Duchess of Roxburghe, is still spoken of at Floors Castle, the family seat, with fond respect.

THE MEMBER OF PARLIAMENT offered stature of a different sort. No indolent aristocrat (though frequently aristocratic), the M.P. needed the American energy to achieve his ambitions. He might need American money, too: campaigning was expensive, and M.P.s were paid a pittance. His wife could give receptions in the mansion her father's dollars bought; she could charm key members of both parties. A remarkable number of Cabinet-level statesmen chose American wives: Joseph Chamberlain, Sir William Harcourt, Lord Randolph Churchill, George Curzon, Viscount Harcourt.

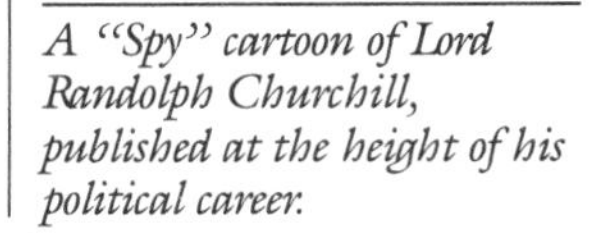

A "Spy" cartoon of Lord Randolph Churchill, published at the height of his political career.

The courtier was in effect a servant of the Royal Family. (Queen Victoria had once proven to a skeptic that she could not travel with fewer than 100 courtiers and servants, while her son needed a similar retinue.) Principal characteristics were discretion and a generations-old loyalty to the Crown; courtiers were naturally drawn from the oldest aristocratic families. A courtier would travel with H.R.H. (duties rotated week by week), so a courtier's wife could expect to spend weeks alone. The advantages were probable royal presence at the wedding and royal godparents to the children. And a woman whose husband had served long and well might ultimately be made a member of the Order of British Empire, which gave her a medal to wear with her evening dresses.

The younger son was always the sideshow, never the main event. If he was the second son and his older brother died without children, he would get the title. If he was the fifth son, he'd have to make his own way; since he had no position to keep up, however, he didn't need as rich a wife. But it was a hard life—especially if one had an American sister-in-law whose superior firepower had brought down a superior quarry. To stay in England, sentenced to sitting below the salt and sleeping in the eighth-best bedroom, just because your husband had been born fourth in the family, would be a constant irritant to the American heiress's pride.

Lord Kitchener, the Empire's man on the spot in South Africa, was an example of how far the ambitious military man could go.

The military man appeared at balls in full-dress uniform, all red twill and gold braid and (for a cavalryman) black boots to above the knees. Ah, men in uniform! In peacetime the soldier's life was pleasant enough: guard duty at Windsor, perhaps, or at the Curragh in Ireland, with plenty of time for hunting and polo. It was less glorious when the regiment was in South Africa or the Sudan, under fire. But if all went well the military husband might, like the naval hero David Beatty (married to Marshall Field's daughter Ethel), be made a peer for his exploits.

The black sheep looked as charming as the other men, perhaps even more so, but was actually a disgrace to the family name. He might have enormous debts. He might have made an effort to go on the stage. Or there might simply be rumors of unspecified indiscretions on faraway shores. An English mama appreciated the gravity of these flaws, but Americans, overly optimistic or simply uninformed, frequently sailed straight into them.

Curzon (seated, center) en route to Afghanistan. He sent home many articles for the Times, but his fiancée went for months without a letter.

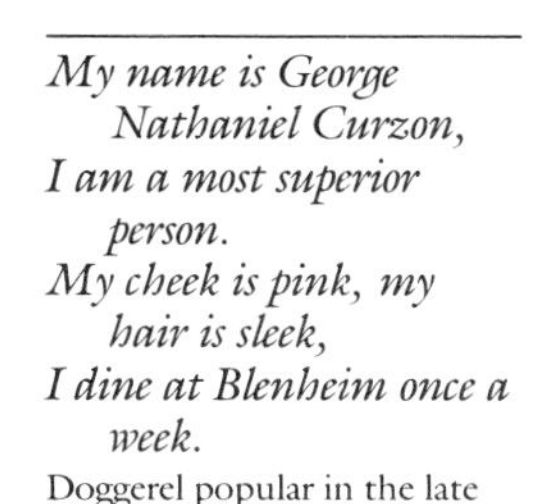

My name is George
Nathaniel Curzon,
I am a most superior
person.
My cheek is pink, my
hair is sleek,
I dine at Blenheim once a
week.

Doggerel popular in the late '80s

walk into that great assembly." Perhaps, yet within days he had written to a friend in Washington to ask about the Leiters' background and had heard back that she was very rich but lacked social standing. There is no record that they danced together that night, but George and Mary met again at a house party. A short time later, before returning to America, Mary sent George a pearl from her necklace, made into a gold tie pin. This was a forward gesture, even for an American. He wasn't to know it yet, but Mary found him "the most wonderful, the most charming, the most handsome, the most clever of all the men I have met. I almost died when he touched my hand."

For his part, George had made known his opinion of Americans: he found them "the least attractive species of the human genus." Though Mary wrote to him faithfully from America, his responses were few and measured. For one thing, he could not be seen marrying for money in such an obvious fashion; Sibell Grosvenor was one thing, Mary Leiter something else entirely. He was afraid of what his father would say.

And besides, he had his agenda. In 1891 Lord Salisbury asked him to accept a Cabinet position as undersecretary of state for India. His scheme of becoming England's foremost expert on Eastern politics would require more traveling.

"I WILL HAVE HIM..."

Meanwhile, Mary wrote to a friend: "I will have him, because I believe he needs me. I have no shame." She was back in London—chaperoned as ever by her mother—for the 1891 season. She was presented at court, helped Jennie Churchill arrange a *tableau* for the Marchioness of Londonderry's ball, stayed at Hatfield with the Salisburys and at Wilton with the Pembrokes. George saw her almost daily but somehow managed to keep their relationship on a completely ambiguous footing. Though Mary would have been his at a word, by the end of July, when the season was over, he still hadn't let her know whether his interest was romantic or merely friendly.

Traveling through the Far East, Curzon (right) still hadn't made up his mind about Mary.

George's intentions may have seemed clearer once Mary went back to America, for in the next eighteen months he wrote to her barely half a dozen times. And when he went around the world in 1892, actually passing through Washington, he made no effort to see her. The Leiters went abroad themselves at the end of 1892, to Italy and Egypt; again, though George was in Cairo just a day before the Leiters, on the last leg of his trip, they did not meet.

Then, on March 3, 1893, after dining with the Leiters in Paris, George asked Mary to marry him. "I had entered the hotel without the slightest anticipation that this would be the issue," he later wrote. "She told me her story. How she had waited for nearly three years since the time when we first met, rejecting countless suitors and always waiting for me." This account was somewhat disingenuous on George's part. While he may not have known that Mary was waiting for him, he was well aware that she

DARLING DAISY

Occasionally, England produced an heiress of her own. Frances Evelyn Maynard, the Essex heiress known as Daisy, married Lord Brooke, heir of the 4th Earl of Warwick, in "the most splendid wedding of a dozen seasons." Beautiful and intelligent, with an unrestrained enthusiasm for living, she soon became one of the great hostesses of her day. Weekend guests were brought by private train to Easton Lodge, the family estate, where Daisy's unique extravagance was evident at every turn. Elephants, hyenas, giraffes and pet marmosets joined the deer and pheasant in the park, and guests could expect to have their meals enlivened by the vision of a goat eating from the plate of their magnificently gowned and jeweled hostess. There were fresh flowers every morning on each guest's dressing table, a spray of gardenias for each female guest in the evening.

Daisy Warwick in the 1880s: she was not a typical aristocrat, but for all her passion and energy, she was completely of her time.

Women in the Marlborough House Set must have love affairs, so Daisy dallied with such Set stalwarts as Lord Charles Beresford, Lord Randolph Churchill and, inevitably, the Prince of Wales himself, on whom she practiced her German. But she also had great feeling for those less fortunate. She spent years and much of her fortune on working-girl education projects such as Lady Warwick's Agricultural Scheme for Women. And in 1895 she joined the most radical branch of the Socialist party in England; having spent an evening at her London townhouse singing the *Internationale* with "fellow travellers," she would attend next day's State Opening of Parliament—in emeralds to match her eyes.

Inevitably, Daisy's fortune collapsed. She tried to sell her love letters from the Prince, but succeeded only in precipitating a blackmail scandal. She went on a lecture tour of the States to talk about society's ills, but all her listeners wanted to hear was the latest gossip from London. She showed visitors through Easton Lodge, in almost every room of which were photographs of the late king. And she wrote her memoirs several times over, as full of contradiction in ink as she was in life, forty years of socialism having done nothing to dim her pride: "When I came out," she declared in *Life's Ebb and Flow*, "social prestige meant something."

During George's long silences, Mary was reduced to sending him reminders of how many other men would be happy to marry her.

was an heiress. And that fact, though unrecorded in his reminiscences, must have weighed heavily in his decision. He certainly doesn't record that he fell in love with Mary when faced with her patient devotion. He merely took advantage of it. Mary Leiter solved several of his problems: he hadn't much time for courting, and he had almost no money; she was hopelessly in love with him, and she had pots of money. So George proposed. And then, perhaps regretting his precipitous move, insisted the engagement be kept secret. He went off on another trip, this time to Afghanistan, while Mary went back to politely fending off suitors and watching her mother wonder why she wasn't engaged yet.

COMME IL FAUT
Any man who reverses (changes the direction in which he's spinning his partner during a waltz) is a cad.

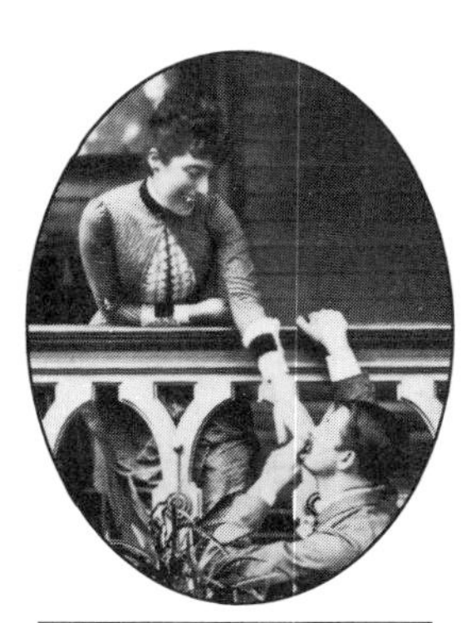

Leonie Jerome and her fiancé, John Leslie. His parents disapproved of the Jerome family almost as strongly as the Churchills had, but it was a happy match.

THE SABINE WOMEN

Nearly two years after proposing to Mary, George came around to telling his father and speaking to hers. He could wait no longer; in order to realize his ambitions, he needed to be married and he needed to be rich. Any misgivings he had had about marrying an American were overcome by Mary's charms; the financial arrangements were all that he had hoped for. Mary might have been disappointed when Mr. Leiter came up with only £6,000 annually, but by English standards that was exceedingly generous. Leiter compounded George's pleasure by agreeing to buy the young couple a London house, 1 Carlton House Terrace, in the row so popular with American heiresses and their English husbands. Finally, he settled a large sum (rumored at both $1 million and, more modestly, $700,000) on Mary and set aside an additional amount for any children she and George might have.

The engagement, announced simultaneously in London and Washington on March 4, 1895, just six weeks before the wedding, prompted an immediate response on both sides of the Atlantic. In England, there was shock that the proud George Curzon was stooping to marry an American—however lovely—of no background. In America, there was dismay that still another of the native belles was being lost to England.

Though the participants couldn't know it, George and Mary's wedding marked the beginning of a new era in the transatlantic marriage. More money, grander titles, greater publicity were the rule from then on. In fact, social historian Dixon Wecter dubbed 1895 the *annus mirabilis*, or "year of miracles," for the Anglo-American match and claimed that it was the beginning of "the great invasion of titled bankrupts in search of American heiresses, than which nothing more sweeping had been known since the rape of the Sabine women."

"Why couldn't she have married a normal American and lived in my Country!"

LEONARD JEROME on the marriage of Leonie, his third daughter to wed an Englishman

THE SELF-MADE GIRL'S WEDDING

"For richer, for poorer. . ."

If the waning modesty of the mid-nineteenth century influenced the weddings of the Buccaneers, it was the vulgarity of new money that colored the wedding of the Self-Made Girl. A new desire for pomp and circumstance resulted in certain fixtures of American heiress weddings: the wedding march from *Lohengrin*, the white satin gown from Worth, the crowds, the newspaper coverage. In New York, Grace Church was the fashionable spot, and Rev. (later Bishop) Henry Potter the fashionable pastor, who officiated at Clara Jerome's wedding in 1881.

Outside the city, minus the restraining Knickerbocker influence, the participants' delusions of grandeur might run riot. Mrs. Leiter's choice of a lavishly beaded purple dress was a bit ostentatious for a mother of the bride, while every feature of Flora Sharon's wedding was larger than life. Flora was married in San Francisco, and afterward a special train took 800 guests to her father's house just outside the city. The reception was held principally in the sixty-eight-foot-long music room, which was lined with mirrors. Floral decorations, executed in camellias, tuberoses and smilax, included festoons on chandeliers, horns of plenty, a marriage bell, and a shield with the letters "H" and "S" in blue and white violets. Supper was served, followed by dancing—a far cry from the modest Eastern "wedding breakfast" of the previous decade.

In America, the land of religious freedom, socialites were always Episcopalians and romantic-looking churches like New York's Grace Church were the favored venues for worship and weddings.

CHAPTER 3

AMERICAN HEIRESSES: WHAT WILL YOU BID?

He Stoops to Conquer

❖

The Plutocrats' Daughters

❖

The Match of the Century

❖

She Is Now a Duchess

❖

The American Aristocrat's Wedding

HE STOOPS TO CONQUER

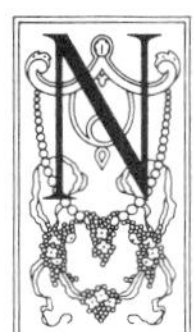ot all impecunious Englishmen waited, like George Curzon, for American heiresses to come to them. A certain variety of Poor Peer bypassed the formalities of the London season and took the steamer to New York, hoping his bad reputation didn't follow him. Men whom even the most jaded of the English social godmothers had rejected might find, in America, the heiress of their dreams—utterly naïve, or completely jaded herself.

THE CASTLE & THE PALACE

At first Englishmen came to the United States hunting game, not heiresses. One hunting party, in 1878, included Irish landowner John Adair, his American wife Cornelia (née Wadsworth, of upstate New York) and Moreton Frewen, second son of an old Sussex family. Frewen was back in 1879 with another hunt-

Moreton Frewen met with disapproval from Jennie Jerome as a husband for her sister Clara, partly because he'd been one of Lillie Langtry's most assiduous suitors only a year earlier—going so far as to give Lillie a horse named Redskin.

Frewen's Wyoming house was known as "the Castle" for the high level of civilization it brought to the wilderness.

Clara Frewen was enough of a Jerome to insist on taking her French maid along to rural Wyoming.

ing party, this one including the Honourable James Burke-Roche (soon to marry New Yorker Frances Work) and the Honourable Gilbert Leigh of Stoneleigh Abbey (whose brother would marry New Yorker Helene Beckwith). This time, Frewen bought a ranch on the Powder River in Wyoming and built a house that would come to be known as "the Castle."

The Castle soon featured a female occupant—the former Clara Jerome, whom Frewen had married in New York in the summer of 1881. (Ranching was not so arduous that he couldn't go home to woo and win a wife.) After losing her first baby, Clara was sent back east in the Deadwood Coach, a feature of Buffalo Bill's Wild West Show, while Moreton stayed to take care of business. Business was, inevitably, bad, and the Frewens were soon back in London.

Sir Thomas Fermor-Hesketh was another wandering Englishman. In 1879 he had set off from England in his yacht, the *Lancashire Witch,* to see what he could see. He looped around Africa, disembarking to help fight in the Zulu War, then setting sail again for points east. Several months and a tour of the Orient later, he put into San Francisco Harbor. Here his fate awaited him, in the form of Flora Sharon.

San Francisco abounded in colorful characters, one of whom was William Sharon, Flora's father. He was a U.S. Senator from the state of Nevada, where he had been the Bank of California's representative at the immensely rich silver mine known as the Comstock Lode. Sharon was as ruthless and possibly dishonest as any of the "desperadoes" Englishmen loved to meet; it was even said that he'd driven a business partner to suicide, then bought and moved into his partner's home. He was the owner of the ostentatious Palace Hotel in San Francisco when Fermor-Hesketh arrived in town, and it was here that the young baronet was reported to have met Miss Sharon. She was invited to a dinner on board the *Lancashire Witch,* one thing followed another, and they were soon engaged.

The Palace Hotel's famous courtyard featured a glass roof. Horses and carriages could drive right in and circle the fountain.

LAND-POOR

The more or less coincidental marital successes of Frewen, Burke-Roche and Fermor-Hesketh inspired their fellow aristocrats. Englishmen began to visit America with a purpose more serious than sightseeing or sport. A trip across the Atlantic—and a few months in the new country's provincial drawing rooms—did not seem such a high price to pay for a lifetime free from financial worry.

That worry was often substantial. Take, for instance, the situation faced by Blandford, eighth Duke of Marlborough. Blandford's father, the seventh Duke, had been unable to make ends meet. There were six plain but aristocratic Churchill daughters to dower, and the Blenheim estate yielded only £37,000 a year. First he sold land: in 1874 Baron Ferdinand de Rothschild bought the estates of Wichendon and Waddesdon. Then in 1875 it was the Marlborough Gems, which fetched £10,000 at Christie's. In 1882–83 the Sunderland Library was dispersed for £60,000, and in 1883 the Blenheim Enamels brought in £73,000. Despite the gradual stripping of Blenheim's splendors, the seventh Duke's will was proved at a mere £7,000.

The fact was that Blenheim, the only non-royal palace in Britain, drank money. John Vanbrugh had designed it in the early eighteenth century, in honor of the first Duke of Marlborough's military achievements, with "Beauty, Magnificence, and Duration" in mind. It took one man a year to wash all the windows, and when he finished he went round again. There were fourteen acres of roof that

During the agricultural depression, the income from the Duke of Manchester's estates dropped from £95,000 a year to an annual deficit of £2,000.

Lord Randolph Churchill's brother, still known to his family as Blandford after he became 8th Duke of Marlborough.

Her Majesty Queen Anne contributed £240,000 toward the construction of Blenheim. It took its name from the battle in 1704 where the 1st Duke of Marlborough defeated the French army.

needed to be releaded, over and above daily concerns such as feeding and paying the scores of servants required to keep the place running.

When the eighth Duke inherited, more treasures were sold. Eighteen canvases by Rubens, additional Van Dycks, two Titians, two Rembrandts, and paintings by Claude Lorrain, Poussin and Watteau brought £400,000. It still wasn't enough. So, in the spring of 1888, prompted perhaps by the financial security Jennie Jerome had brought his brother Randolph, the new Duke set sail for New York.

Raphael's Ansidae Madonna *fetched £70,000 for the Marlboroughs (and ended up in England's National Gallery) but still didn't make a dent in their debts.*

A NOBLE RAKE

Blandford had every reason to expect a fulsome reception. By now, Anglomania had gained a real foothold in New York. Visiting English peers were welcomed effusively by eager hostesses and their daughters. (This enthusiasm did not go unnoticed in the press: when the Marquess of Stafford visited the United States, the New York *World* marked his arrival with the headline "Attention, American heiresses, what will you bid?") But indiscriminate as they usually were toward noble Britons, the ladies of New York couldn't bring themselves to welcome Blandford. He might be a duke, he might be lord of Blenheim Palace, who cared if he was bankrupt—but he was not a nice man. As one newspaper acerbically put it, "Everything His Grace of Marlborough brought with him was clean, except his reputation."

The Duke, as Marquess of Blandford, had married the eminently respectable daughter of the first Duke of Abercorn. He always had an eye for a pretty woman, and caused some uncomfortable ripples in the family when he gave sister-in-law Jennie Churchill a ring that belonged to his wife. That was smoothed over soon enough, but his next peccadillo was not, for he was very indiscreet about his affair with the Countess of Aylesford.

In 1876, the Earl of Aylesford heard from his wife Edith that she intended to elope with Blandford. So Joe Aylesford threatened to divorce her. Divorce meant public knowledge of the affair and a major society scandal. The Prince of Wales attempted to intervene, castigating Blandford for taking advantage of the husband's absence—while on a trip to India with the Prince—to woo the wife. He asked Blandford to give up any notion of running away with Edith. Blandford responded by brandishing before the Princess of Wales a packet of rather indiscreet letters H.R.H. had himself once written to Edith Aylesford.

The Prince did not take kindly to being blackmailed. He refused to attend any social function at which he might be faced with either Blandford or his brother Randolph. The Churchill brothers—in fact, the entire family—were for all practical purposes exiled from London society. This, despite the fact that by now Joe Aylesford had calmed down and agreed not to try to divorce his wife. However, Lady Blandford had had quite enough—she moved out of Blenheim and, in 1883, successfully sued her husband, recently become the eighth Duke of Marlborough, for divorce. She was not received in society thereafter. The final twist in the affair came some years later when Joe

COMME IL FAUT
Port is passed round the table counterclockwise. If a gentleman changes his mind and decides to fill his glass once the decanter has passed him, he must wait till it goes all the way round before reaching him again. The decanter is never lifted, but slid. The first toast in England is "Gentlemen, the Queen."

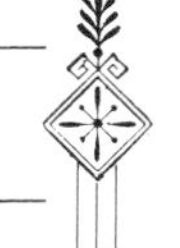

THE OTHER ASTORS

At Cliveden (above), William Waldorf Astor added the famous Borghese balustrade to Charles Barry's 1850 house; to Hever Castle (right), a dilapidated farm when he bought it, he brought Ann Boleyn's bedposts, Queen Elizabeth's clothes-brushes and Martin Luther's Bible.

While a handful of Englishmen were crossing the ocean to America in the 1880s and '90s, one notable American crossed the other way. He was William Waldorf Astor, son of John Jacob Astor III and nephew of William and Caroline, and he took his family to England because his native land was not, he felt, "a fit place for a gentleman to live."

Astor had suffered a series of blows to his ego, including failure in his U.S. Senate campaign and, the ultimate insult, his aunt Caroline's refusal to step down and allow his wife Mamie to become simply "Mrs. Astor"—her proper designation after he became head of the family. (He'd even been compelled to inform the Newport post office, in the summer of 1890, that any mail addressed to "Mrs. Astor" should be delivered not to Caroline but to his wife.) Once in England, however, he made little headway in his quest to be accepted by society. Indulging his mania for security, he installed a special system in his London

estate office that allowed him to lock all the interior doors from a button on his desk, and he built a huge wall around Cliveden on the Thames after discovering its attractiveness to boating parties. (The latter effort earned him the nickname "Walled-Off Astor.") Then, in July 1892, the New York papers reported his death of pneumonia and heaped on the praise in long obituaries; Willie himself read the obituaries with relish, for he was alive and well—and probably the source of the hoax.

Becoming a naturalized Briton in 1899, Astor bought Hever Castle in Kent and promptly spent some $10 million on restorations. He even went so far as to erect a complete "Tudor Village," adjacent to the castle, to house his guests. His aspirations were now plain, and he made them plainer. In 1911 he appeared at a fancy-dress ball in a peer's robes of state and a coronet. Not until 1916, however, after massive contributions to the Red Cross and other causes during World War I, was he finally ennobled. (In 1917 his title was upgraded, for no very clear reason, from Baron Astor of Hever to Viscount Astor.)

Willie Astor's long-awaited recognition was by no means welcome news to his son Waldorf, who was appalled at the implications for his own future. Raised as an English boy, attending Eton and Oxford, he had married the bewitching, outspoken Virginian Nancy Langhorne Shaw, and the pair had devoted themselves to his career as Tory M.P. from Plymouth. Elevation to the House of Lords would, he feared, finish his further political aims. But in 1919, after Willie Astor's death, the new Lady Astor was able to fill Waldorf's vacant seat since British women had been given the vote and the opportunity to stand for Parliament the year before.

Thus, she became the first woman to actually sit in Parliament. Over the years, her quick wit and vitality earned her a fame that eclipsed that of her father-in-law—and perhaps even that of *the* Mrs. Astor of New York.

Nancy and Waldorf Astor, shortly after their 1906 marriage. Nancy, one of three Langhorne sisters legendary for their beauty, could take her pick among her English suitors.

Aylesford, living on a ranch in Texas, fell in love with someone else and asked permission to divorce the troublesome Edith. The Queen's Proctor stopped the case—although Edith had already borne Blandford an illegitimate son.

LILIAN (RHYMES WITH MILLION)

Much as New York loved English aristocrats, loose aristocratic morals were entirely unacceptable. While the Aylesford scandal was by now ancient history in London (the Churchills were back to being bosom friends of the Prince), Americans found it appalling.

Lilian Hammersley paid for the grand organ in the library at Blenheim. The inscription reads:

In memory of happy days
and as a tribute
to this glorious home
we leave thy voice
to speak within these walls
in years to come
when ours are still
LM and MM
1891

Not, however, Marietta Stevens. Minnie's indefatigable mother was back in New York and as ambitious as ever. The eighth Duke of Marlborough was a friend of her daughter. Furthermore, Mrs. Stevens subscribed to the more sophisticated English view of his old indiscretions. She, at least, was happy to entertain him.

So was Leonard Jerome, still every inch the Sporting Man though less of a power on Wall Street. Jerome, knowing full well the reason behind the Duke's visit, had someone he wanted him to meet. She was Lily Hammersley, a rich, attractive, thirty-four-year-old widow. Born Lilian Price of Troy, New York, she had married Louis Hammersley of New York City, noted for his large fortune and his large head. She changed her name from Lilian to Lily, it was said, to avoid the unfortunate rhyme with "million." Although Jennie Churchill would later write snide letters about her new sister-in-law's weight and mustache, Lily was widely remembered as a beauty who usually wore white to set off her rose-gold coloring. She was also known for having her entire opera box hung with orchids.

"I hope the marriage will come off," Leonard wrote to his wife, "as there is no doubt she has lots of tin." Although Hammersley's will was under dispute at the time of the Duke's visit, it was rumored that

Randolph Churchill wrote to his mother, the Duchess of Marlborough, that Lily's "mustache and beard are becoming serious," but other men considered her strikingly handsome.

"The Duke has gone off this morning with Lawrence [Jerome] and a party to the Adirondacks trout fishing, to be gone a week. I rather think he will marry the Hammersley. Don't you fear any responsibility on my part. Mrs. H. is quite capable of taking care of herself. Besides I have never laid eyes on the lady but once."

LEONARD JEROME, in a letter

Lily had $100,000 a year as well as $1 million of her own. By the end of June, a "friend" of Mrs. Hammersley had told *The New York Times*: "The Duke is very fond of money and I know for some time that he was making inquiries as to Mrs. Hammersley's for-

THE PRINCESS DIANA CONNECTION

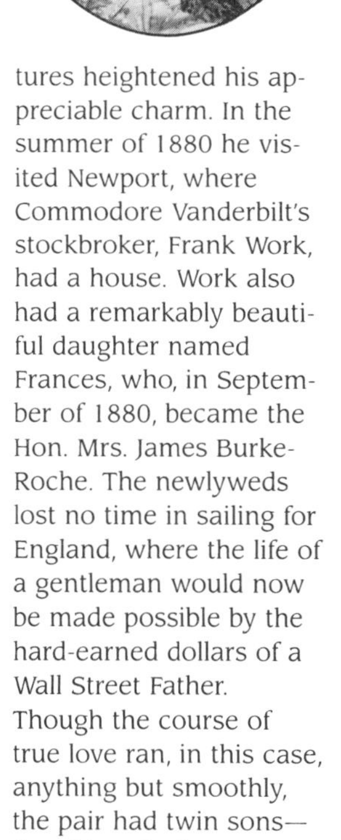

Regal reflections: Mrs. Burke-Roche (left) and Diana, Princess of Wales, whose middle name is Frances after her mother and her American great-grandmother.

The Hon. James Burke-Roche, younger brother of an Irish baron named Lord Fermoy, was a classic example of the broke aristocrat. The title, just a generation old, carried with it only some 16,000 acres in County Cork and County Waterford, land that brought in roughly £7,000 a year. The family seat, Trabolgan, was a long Georgian house facing the sea near Cork Harbor. Its mile-long drive passed under a triumphal arch, but the effect was somewhat spoiled: in a southeast gale, it was impossible to open the front door against the wind. After around 1880, this was no longer the Fermoys' problem, since Trabolgan was then sold by Burke-Roche's elder brother.

An income of £7,000 would not go far. It would certainly rule out a lavish allowance to a younger brother. What, then, was the younger brother to do? Being a gentleman of an enterprising nature, he did the logical thing. He left England. His good looks and good manners, his little bit of money and plenty of address, would be worth a lot more off British soil. Always adventurous, he wound up in Wyoming with aristocratic younger son Moreton Frewen, attempting to raise cattle and enjoying the occasional tussle with hostile Indians.

After that, Burke-Roche found his way to New York, where the glamour of his adventures heightened his appreciable charm. In the summer of 1880 he visited Newport, where Commodore Vanderbilt's stockbroker, Frank Work, had a house. Work also had a remarkably beautiful daughter named Frances, who, in September of 1880, became the Hon. Mrs. James Burke-Roche. The newlyweds lost no time in sailing for England, where the life of a gentleman would now be made possible by the hard-earned dollars of a Wall Street Father. Though the course of true love ran, in this case, anything but smoothly, the pair had twin sons—the elder of whom was the maternal grandfather of Diana, Princess of Wales.

tune. . . . I am only sorry that Mrs. Hammersley is not better acquainted with the Duke's little affairs in England than she is."

On June 29, it was all over. Leonard Jerome got into a cab with the Duke at his hotel, and they drove down to City Hall at 1 P.M. In the anteroom of Mayor Hewitt's office were some forty friends, including Ward McAllister (who later took credit for making the match). Mrs. Hammersley, in écru cashmere with *passementerie* trim, impressed the *Times* reporter "simply as a magnificent woman." After a long wait (while the contracts were drawn up), the mayor finally performed the ceremony and the little group dispersed—only to gather again, a few hours later, at the Tabernacle Baptist Church on Second Avenue. Because no Episcopal minister would marry a divorcé, the Duke had prevailed on the Baptist minister to read the Episcopal wedding service. Lily wore a shot-taffeta street dress for the ceremony, and a broad gold band was added to the small solitaire diamond used in the first service.

Following a dinner for a dozen people at Delmonico's, the Duchess retired to her house at 257 Fifth Avenue while the Duke returned to his hotel. They embarked the next morning for England, and by way of valediction the *Times* stated: "It has been generally understood that Mrs. Hammersley married the Duke for a title and that the Duke married her for her money." (The Duke, in fact, was so anxious to make the marriage stick that he insisted on a third ceremony in England, at the registry office on Mount Street in Mayfair.)

It was a pretty cynical performance, and it would have its repercussions. Another bankrupt duke was soon to descend on New York, and everyone would remember his father's wooing of Lily Hammersley.

"*Well, Blandford is married! I went with him to the Mayor's office in the City Hall at one o'clock to-day and witnessed the ceremony. The bride was looking very well and all passed off quickly. I took charge of his cable to the Duchess, also sent one of my own to Jennie. I dine with them at Delmonico's this evening; a dinner given by Mr. and Mrs. Clews to the Duke and his friends. I shall go down to the* Aurania *in the morning to see them off. They had great difficulty in arranging the religious marriage. The clergy refused, he being a divorced man. . . .*"

Leonard Jerome, in a letter

Delmonico's, on Fifth Avenue at Twenty-sixth Street, was society's watering-hole in the 1890s.

DUKE'S PROGRESS: THE ENGLISH LORD'S AMERICAN JOURNEY

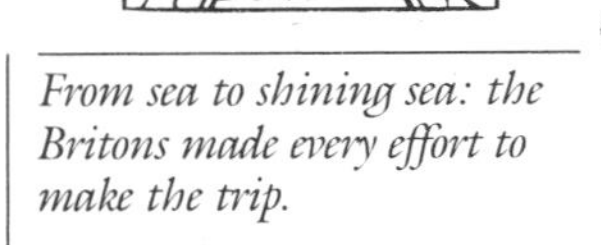

Gallons of ice water. Great gusts of suffocating steam heat. The heiress-hunting Englishman was always being buffeted by extremes in America. Take, for instance, the hotels: so wonderfully luxurious, yet so deeply uncomfortable. The elaborate meals were poorly served, and wine was not a matter of course with dinner. The elegant bedrooms were heated to the point of boiling, the enormous, shiny bathrooms overrun with complex, unmanageable systems of faucets. There were bells, buttons and switches everywhere—but no one

From sea to shining sea: the Britons made every effort to make the trip.

Above: The American taste for luxury (if not outright vulgarity) was evident in plush-upholstered railroad cars. Right: George Pullman's leather-tufted private parlor car.

Charles Dana Gibson captioned this drawing: "$ $ $ $ $."

to look after His Lordship *personally*, to meet his own little idiosyncratic needs. And topping it all was the demeaning practice of signing the guest book, where any plebeian might thereafter finger his noble name.

No less confounding were the young American ladies. Never before had the English lord found himself in such unrestricted contact with unmarried females, hurrying here and there, from one social or sporting activity to the next, with no evidence of adult supervision. It was not the least bit necessary for the Englishman to exercise any rituals of courtship formalities until the very last moment. Although he might perpetually expect the red-faced, indignant parent to appear on the horizon of his lovemaking, none ever materialized. The indignity was, in fact, all his own and from another quarter: he soon discovered that he was only one among many, that the girl in question had a veritable horde of equally favored "admirers."

The question of the girls aside, the English lord found that civilized America bored him. True, the famous American openness was preferable to the stilted formalities back home—no one was kept standing in the States, and everyone was free to speak his or her mind. But this very freedom produced a certain blandness. Only occasionally could one enjoy an excited discussion of corruption in government, and there was almost no gossip—no little scandalous stories, no intrigues to titillate and amuse. Of much greater interest was primitive America. "Though one can dine in New York," wrote Oscar Wilde, "one could not dwell there. Better the far West with its grizzly bears and its untamed cowboys." (Indeed, the West was so full of aristocratic Englishmen that the famous Antlers Hotel in Colorado Springs had become known as "little London.") Thus the wife-hunting English lord, after a patient review of American heiress strongholds along the Atlantic coast (where he might or might not attend to the business at hand), would head happily west to points wild and unknown.

LORD HEAVYDEBTS: "I have got to do something, by jove! And your tin is needful, you know. I hate your beastly loud voice and manners, but, er. . . let's marry, you know."
MISS DOUBLEDOLLAR: "I like somebody else better, but just think of the syle I could put on . . . well, I am your girl."

"HAVING A GRAND TIME . . ."

Rustic Maine.

BAR HARBOR. Newport, round two, minus the Marble Age. Here were set-pieces of American relaxation—perpetual dressing, dining, dancing, and that horror of horrors, according to Lady Randolph Churchill, the leaving of cards. Decided pluses: the wraparound porches, the spectacle of men and women swimming together.

BOSTON. Vaguely frightening, somehow, even to Americans. The finicky denizens of Beacon Street, who had an overdeveloped sense of their role in the Revolution and its attendant responsibilities, displayed a mannered reserve and distaste for opulence that should have pleased the English but only underscored the pointlessness of being there at all. If the town took itself seriously, the girls were worse; they took a perverse pleasure in hewing to some arch intellectual line that got on everyone's nerves and ensured that proposals of marriage would not be forthcoming.

Boston Common.

Eastern hospitality.

NIAGARA FALLS. One of the better opportunities for the Englishman's preferred travel mien: admiration doused in complaint. The falls were magnificent, but the trinkets, the distractions, the buying and selling and building all round obligingly prevented unrestrained awe.

U.S. DOLLAR. Although the exchange rate on the pound was favorable, the cost of luxury American-style was deucedly high. To maintain the standards of a man of leisure, the Englishman would have to part with twice the amount he was used to spending in London.

THOMAS ALVA EDISON. Every Englishman's favorite American. The 8th Duke of Marlborough's most treasured moment may have been his meeting with the Wizard of Menlo Park (which he squeezed in while working on Lily Hammersley), who then wrote Moreton Frewen: "I thought the English Duke was a fool with a crown on his head. But this one knows a great deal which I do not intend inventing until next fall."

The Wizard of Menlo Park.

POSTCARD

Washington, D.C. A few comments here about the general blandness, architecturally and socially; a tour of the Capitol building, which was remarkably (or grossly, depending on the Englishman in question) free of guards, uniforms, any figures of authority or hierarchy; plenty of five o'clock teas where one had not the slightest chance of meeting members of Congress or in fact anyone to do with government, all of whom up to and including the President were considered by local matrons to be too gauche for words.

Symbol of the surprising gulf between government and society.

An American curiosity.

Spittoon. "America," declared Oscar Wilde, "is one long expectoration." Quite foreign and therefore quite apt to be noticed, a constant in the background of the Englishman's U.S. travels was the sound of tobacco being spit and then landing, splat, in the ubiquitous cuspidor.

The South. Virginia a joy, with the cult of the horse in full flower. Obvious similarities to English country life, and shared sympathies over the outcome of the Civil War, meant the Englishman felt right at home; however, selfsame similarities and Civil War meant he was going nowhere with Southern girls (as poor as English girls) or Southern mamas (like English ones, not about to let their daughters marry away from home).

Languor at White Sulphur Springs.

Sitting Bull himself, with Buffalo Bill.

The Wild West. Ranches, and ore mines, and lots and lots of buffalo. The West had danger, heathens, horses, big game—in short, the romance of adventure. The romance of romance was necessarily absent, since Western daughters went east the minute they became heiresses. The Englishman would have better luck meeting Wild West millions at his mother's house in London.

San Francisco. The second leading supplier, after New York, of heiresses to the English nobility. The wet, fertile land was nicely reminiscent of home, but there was a lamentable lack of scent in the flowers and the gorgeous-looking fruit was tasteless. Dinner was liable to be served not in courses but in lots of little dishes, laid on the table all at once. Oyster cocktails and Monterey were, however, considered worth the trip.

Western hospitality.

Cattle. Nowhere near as rewarding as young ladies with large dowries. Younger sons who plumped for cattle ranching would soon realize their mistake. In the 1880s, Englishmen lost £10 million ($50 million) on American cows.

MARCH OF ANGLOMANIA
Robert W. Garrett, former railroad president and Newport resident, convinced himself that he was the Prince of Wales. His house was altered to resemble the Court of St. James, his servants wore British livery, and his wife made believe she was the Princess of Wales.

THE PLUTOCRATS' DAUGHTERS

The English aristocrats, by the 1890s, had finally learned what to expect of the American heiress. She wouldn't pack a pistol, throw tomahawks or dance the cancan. Her voice would be loud, her dresses showy, her parents preposterous and her dowry large. But then along came a new, improved model of American heiress, retooled at great expense for the European market. This version of the heiress was the American Aristocrat, and she would marry a nobleman not on a whim, not because she needed the social boost, but because it was her *right*.

Halcyon days in Newport, where boys and girls could picnic innocently together. Consuelo Vanderbilt is shown above (center of photo) with spiky flowers on her hat; the girl on her left, in the scallop-brimmed hat, is May Goelet.

THE GILDED AGE

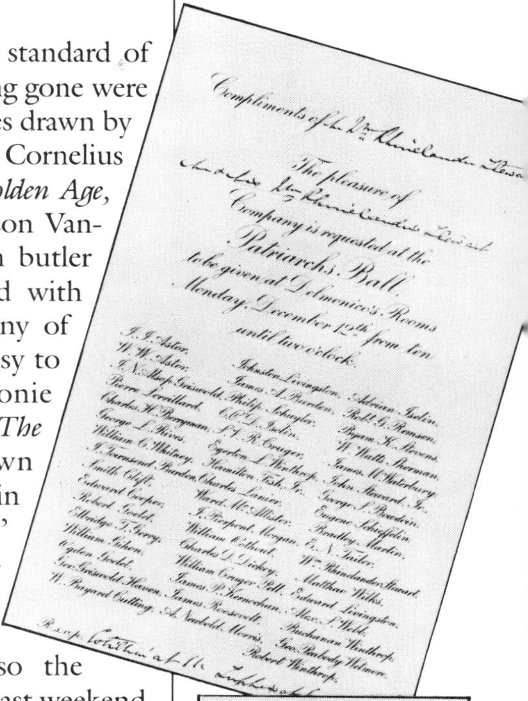

By the 1890s, Old New York's modest standard of living had become a quaint memory. Long gone were the poky brownstone parlors, the carriages drawn by one horse, the frugal evening parties. Cornelius Vanderbilt IV boasted in *Queen of the Golden Age*, his biography of his mother, Grace Wilson Vanderbilt, how "our hard-pressed English butler often complained that our family lived with more pomp and circumstance than many of the crowned heads of Europe." It was easy to believe. Seymour Leslie, son of Leonie Jerome and Sir John Leslie, writes in *The Jerome Connection* about being shown around Frederick Vanderbilt's house in Hyde Park: "These are Watteau panels," Vanderbilt's wife Lulu told him breathlessly. "This whole house was copied for us by Stanford White. . . . Fred's bedroom, early Italian Renaissance. . . . Also the guest bedrooms, why we had a man here last weekend who said the chairs were so valuable he just had to sit on the floor." Rugs were always Aubusson, chairs always Louis XVI crusted with ormolu, paintings always Old Masters. If there was anything American-made in the house, it would be a magnificent version of something European, such as Alva Vanderbilt's stained-glass window (in the banquet hall at 660 Fifth Avenue) depicting the battle of the Field of the Cloth of Gold. The only frankly American features would be the plumbing and the kitchen.

It was also increasingly likely, in the 1890s, that the leaders of American society would have friends abroad. The phenomenon of the raw tourist gaping with his Baedeker was still around, but the plutocrats no longer fit the pattern. Their trips to Europe now included, along with pilgrimages to Worth and expensive sessions with art dealers such as Duveen, a satisfying measure of social life. Gone were the days

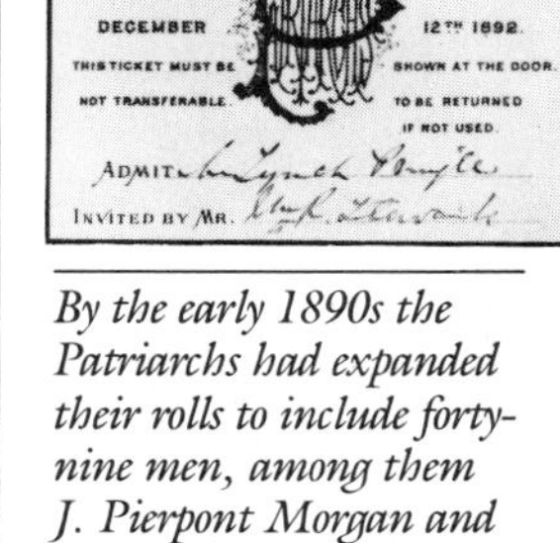
PATRIARCH BALL
DECEMBER 12TH 1892.
THIS TICKET MUST BE SHOWN AT THE DOOR.
NOT TRANSFERABLE. TO BE RETURNED IF NOT USED.
ADMIT
INVITED BY MR.

By the early 1890s the Patriarchs had expanded their rolls to include forty-nine men, among them J. Pierpont Morgan and Bradley Martin.

On a cruise up the Nile, c.1882: Oliver Belmont, seated at left, with Willie K. Vanderbilt and Consuelo next to him and Alva lounging in a hammock at far right.

Cornelia Martin, raised as much in England as in New York.

when New Yorkers considered it bad form to force themselves on the notice of acquaintances in foreign countries. Quite the contrary. They now eagerly sought out acquaintances, taking London by a slow accumulation of introductions in Rome, Monte Carlo, Paris. This was easy now: there were so many Americans living abroad, delegates from New York society, so that travelers had friends, or at least letters of introduction, in every port. Mrs. Ogden Goelet (née May Wilson), for example, lived mostly on her yacht, the *White Ladye,* cruising from harbor to harbor as the seasons dictated and earning the sobriquet "Steamboat Mary." With her was young daughter May, who was gaining a very cosmopolitan view of the world.

The Bradley Martins, another extreme case of the expatriate rich, had a perfectly nice double house off Fifth Avenue but rarely spent more than the winter season in New York. They preferred the estate in Scotland and the luxurious London house, where they entertained extensively. A number of Anglo-American couples, New Yorker Helene Beckwith and Lord Leigh among them, were introduced under Mrs. Martin's hospitable roof. The Martins' daughter Cornelia, with a million dollars of her own and only a nodding acquaintance with her native land, seemed inevitably destined for the British peerage.

Their growing exposure to Europe led the American rich to emulate the European aristocratic life. The ideal of the territorial nobility, dimly grasped, resulted in the erection of enormous country houses clumped together in acceptable-to-the-plutocracy locales such as Tuxedo Park and Newport. Especially Newport. The aristocratic fantasy, the plutocrats' personal myth, took its most concrete form on the cliffs overlooking Rhode Island Sound.

The 4th Earl of Craven stayed with the Martins at Balmaccaan, the house they rented in Scotland. Cornelia was engaged to him before she reached her seventeenth birthday.

THE KINGDOM BY THE SEA

For some of America's wealthiest citizens, the year was divided into international social seasons: Lenox in early fall, New York for the winter, an interlude in Paris to purchase a new wardrobe, London in late spring. But in the summer, wherever else they might have been during the year, America's socialites went to Newport.

Newport resembled London in that it was a national rather than local social center. New York, Philadelphia, Chicago and Washington were all represented in Newport by their foremost citizens. Amer-

The gate at Tuxedo Park, the lakeside community planned by Pierre Lorillard. The Tuxedo season reached its zenith in the early autumn, after Newport's was over.

Bailey's Beach, the sanctum sanctorum, was America's most exclusive strip of sand.

The Newport Casino, built by James Gordon Bennett, Jr., to Stanford White's design. Newport's principal daytime gathering place, it featured grass tennis courts as well as the shops that faced Bellevue Avenue.

ican society, quite simply, made a wholesale annual migration to Aquidneck Island. In the summer of 1895, for instance, the entire British embassy (headed by Sir Michael Herbert, husband of American heiress Belle Wilson) closed up shop in Washington and moved to Bellevue Avenue.

Newport had not always enjoyed such social eminence. In the early 1870s it was still an unpretentious resort town favored by Southerners, who took the long train ride north to savor the cool evenings, the crisp shadows under copper beeches, the brilliant sun and the constant pulse of the waves, steady as a heartbeat. It was a town of pleasant, rambling wooden houses with wide verandas, where doors and windows were kept open and sea breezes blew letters off writing tables; donkey carts and picnics and vivid blue hydrangeas were the order of the day. Then the town changed. By the mid-nineties, the air and the beeches and the glittering sea were still there, but the informality had been buried. Newport had entered the Marble Age. Cheek by jowl the houses loomed along Bellevue Avenue, many of them designed by Richard Morris Hunt, most of them evoking some European model. Palazzo nestled next to hunting lodge (land in Newport was scarce, so the houses were

Coaching in Newport reached new heights of elaboration. Here, Mrs. August Belmont prepares to go for a drive with her four matched horses, two liveried postilions, and two coachmen behind the carriage.

"The Emperor Caesar Augustus 'found Rome a city of brick and left it a city of marble.' Richard Morris Hunt might well have said, 'I found Newport a town of wood and I left it a town of marble.'"

Maud Howe Elliott

awfully close together), château next to manor.

It was supposed to be country life, but it wasn't; it was resort life, with all the artificiality and homogeneity that this implies. Country life, in the European aristocratic sense, meant retiring to one's ancestral acres surrounded by dependents, tenants and other social inferiors. That wasn't what Newport was about at all. In America, that kind of country life wasn't even possible for the élite since the peak of the social pyramid was reached—and retained—only through constant social effort. Where would Mrs. Astor be if she retired to the country for six months? Forgotten, and nobody would save her place for her. So American society stuck together. Not only could no one afford to be absent; the truth was, to exist at all, society had to raise a quorum. In America, rank was only relative: it had to be measured against someone else's. Thus the wholesale move, come June, to Bellevue Avenue. No one with real social ambitions could afford to miss the action.

"Such clothes! How they swished and rustled! Petticoats of satin, of lace, of taffeta; petticoats embellished with elaborate designs of plump cupids playing gilded lyres, true-love-knots interspersed with doves embellished in seed pearls. Parasols to match every dress, enormous flopping feather hats assorted to every costume. White gloves to the elbow, three or four new pairs every day, priceless lace ruffles at throat and wrists, yards of lace flouncing on underskirts, thousands of dollars worth dragged over the Casino terrace. Different dresses for each occasion, eighty or ninety in a season, worn once or twice and put aside."

ELIZABETH DREXEL LEHR

THE EXCLUSIVITY GAME

The schedule was rigorous and utterly inflexible. One did not drive in the morning or visit the Casino in the afternoon. Furthermore, the prescribed costume must be worn for each activity, and fashionable women wore a new dress for every occasion, with matching hats and parasols and four or five pairs of new kid gloves a day. The Philadelphia *Times* even commented that "you will see at a reception at Newport more Worth dresses than anywhere else in America, except in New York during the height of the season."

What you would see even more of in Newport than in New York was rigid etiquette enforced with unremitting vehemence. A self-conscious passion for correct behavior reassured the plutocratic class in a way that even their furniture with its royal provenances and their houses by Richard Morris Hunt could not quite do. For beneath the opulence and the

THE LOUIS FIXATION

The Petit Trianon at Versailles. If they'd had their way, the plutocrats would have shipped it to Newport, block by block.

Having surfaced from the project of amassing more money, the *nouveaux riches* looked around them and decided that a bit of grandeur would be appropriate in their housing, their dress, their entertainments. And what would be most becoming for a plutocrat? Gilding, by all means. Elaborate furniture, yes, and of course expensive. What's more, it should *look* expensive. Eighteenth-century French furniture and decoration satisfied all these conditions. Hence, the Louis fixation.

An aura of courtliness, of indolent aristocracy that was the very antithesis of industrial magnates, the whiff of Versailles and minuets and *droit de seigneur*—these became the robber baron's goal. Marble House allowed the William K. Vanderbilts to dwell in their own, graceful Petit Trianon. A Grand Trianon at Rosecliff lent Francophile splendor to the shipping/Comstock Lode combine of the Hermann Oelrichs family. The coal-mining Berwinds based The Elms on a smaller Mansart château called Asnières. The houses that harked back to other eras, like the stupefying Breakers in the Medici mode, contained their Louis rooms. Even funny old Château-sur-Mer, with its quaint Eastlake paneling, boasted a grand Louis XV salon.

This *nostalgie de la cour* also surfaced, less permanently but more explicitly, in the grand set-piece entertainment of the era: the costume ball. Wearing fancy dress per-

Marble House, featuring paired medallions of Mansart (the architect of Versailles) and Richard Morris Hunt (the architect of Marble House). Top right: Its ballroom, with enough mirrors and gilding to stun the Sun King himself.

Stanford White's Rosecliff. Tessie Oelrichs, a California girl, used the urns for shooting practice.

mitted the expression of fantasy. It also allowed women to wear all their jewels at once, no small advantage when sumptuary laws, though vestigial, did exert some restraint. And—a small but valid point—the silhouette of eighteenth-century dresses, with snug busts and full skirts, conformed to the nineteenth-century ideal of fashion. Why dress as Empress Josephine for a costume ball if it meant wearing one of those ugly, skimpy muslin dresses? Much better to go as a French king's mistress in satin with gold embroidery and an eight-inch diamond stomacher pinned to one's boned bodice.

For some, the identification was closer still than merely dressing and living in the Louis manner. Grace Wilson Vanderbilt once said to her son, "Poor dear Marie Antoinette. I'm sure if we had a revolution, I'd be the first to go!"

Left: A royal-looking bust on a marble-topped table ennobled The Elms.

Right: Paneling from a French château graced the walls of the W.C. Whitneys' ballroom in New York.

THE LOUIS LOOK: WARNING SIGNS

- Iron banister with bronze hand-rail, usually paired with marble stairs; gilding optional.
- Anything curved that could be straight. (Louis XV or rococo.)
- Marquetry, or elaborate inlays of different-color woods.
- Louis XVI staff. (Adele Grant's bridesmaids received jeweled staffs.)
- Portrait of any Louis, by any painter.
- Theme ball. (Mrs. Bradley Martin wins the prize: at her costume ball in 1897, she wore the same ruby necklace that had hung on the neck of Marie Antoinette herself.)

Guests at a Louis XV ball included Stanford White (fourth from the right) and Mrs. Stuyvesant Fish (far right).

Newport was proud of the tall, graceful elms shading its streets. Most of them are now long gone.

pretensions to grandeur lurked a tenacious insecurity. Americans had been mocked for their gaucheries too long ever to be quite comfortable about their taste or their manners. Where once had been a spontaneous, informal style appropriate to a democratic country, there was now a peculiar version of what Americans supposed English manners to be. The salient feature, in the American view, was stiffness. So stiffness was adopted as the mode of social intercourse.

This rigid etiquette also served to winnow the élite from the aspirants. The unyielding, complex code of behavior baffled the uninitiated and kept them at a distance. For the real fun at Newport had nothing to do with fresh, salty air and glorious sun—or even the company of congenial friends. The real sport was Exclusivity. As the Newport *Mercury* put it in 1889, "The plutocrats have gradually more and more given up trying to pretend that they liked equality, and the give-and-take of democratic hotel life, and have drawn off into their cottages—villas they call them now—and taken a good deal of satisfaction in the reserve and withdrawal from the vulgar herd of resorters."

An important factor in Exclusivity was that Newport was run by women. In the city, they might have to defer to their husbands' wishes and entertain business-connected undesirables. But most New York businessmen visited Newport only on the weekends, taking the Fall River boat up and then, on Sunday nights, leaving dinner parties before dessert to head back to the city. The women took their social life very seriously; it was, after all, their fiefdom, and they could be implacable. At Newport you were In, in which case you went to the Casino and Bailey's Beach and to Beechwood and The Breakers; or you were Out, in which case you could drive on Bellevue Avenue and see Mrs. Astor and Mrs. Mills and Mrs. Goelet (you could also be sure they knew exactly who you were and were probably betting on how long you'd last) but be ignored. Blanche Oelrichs, writing

DAUGHTER: "We no sooner learn a little about one subject, mamma, than we stop and turn to another."
MOTHER: "You must remember, dear, that I am fitting you to enter society."

as Michael Strange, describes how "one morning shortly after breakfast I found a lady actually crumpled up on the stairs outside Mama's door, weeping bitterly because my good-natured mother had failed to procure for her an invitation to somebody's ball." Manuals for social climbers suggested they attempt the assault on Newport in stages, beginning with a visit in a yacht, to see how one "took." The process of getting In could take five years, but as *Munsey's Magazine* pointed out, acceptance was "a hallmark of approval recognized all over the Continent."

In Newport, moreover, society was the only game in town. No culture, no business, no philanthropic activities distracted attention from the matter at hand. That was the way the socialites liked it; they wouldn't be tainted by any social inferiors. Equally to the point, neither would their débutante daughters. These perfect gems, newly released onto the marriage market, could go to polo matches and dinner parties all summer long, casting their well-polished lures with no danger of fishing up something nasty. The pool had been purged of ineligibles.

MARCH OF ANGLOMANIA
The first international polo match was played at Newport in 1886, when England's Hurlingham team beat the Westchester Polo club.

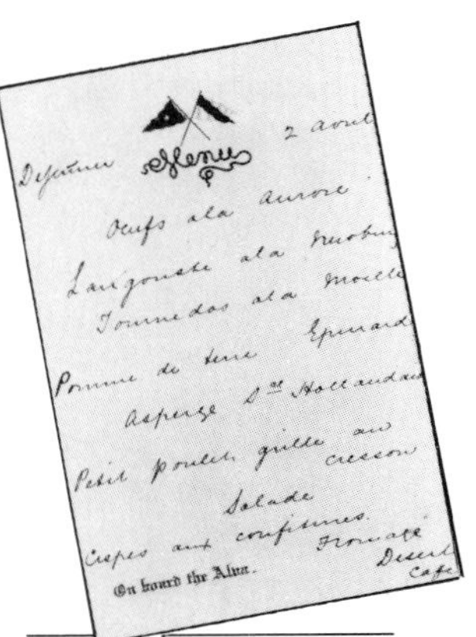
Déjeuner Menu 2 avril
Oeufs a la aurore
Langouste a la Newburg
Tournedos a la moelle
Pomme de terre Epinard
Asperge Sce Hollandaise
Petit poulet grillé au cresson
Salade
Crepes aux confitures. Fromage
Dessert
Café
On board the Alva.

Menu for a spring luncheon on board the Vanderbilts' first yacht, the Alva: *eggs, lobster Newburg, tournedos with marrow, potatoes, spinach, and asparagus with hollandaise; chicken with watercress, salad, crepes, dessert and cheese.*

"I know of no profession, art or trade that women are working in today as taxing on mental resource as being a leader of Society."
MRS. WILLIAM K. VANDERBILT

THE PUSHIEST MAMA

Newport's most exquisitely displayed débutante of the 1890s was, naturally, Consuelo Vanderbilt. Alva had seen her best friend (and her daughter's godmother), Consuelo Yznaga, marry the heir to a dukedom and take an important place in English society despite undistinguished breeding and decidedly unconventional manners. Surely a girl with a Vanderbilt fortune and faultless manners could do better, not only in the marriage market but in her performance of a duchess's duties. So Alva trained her daughter, from the cradle, to be a duchess. As Consuelo reflected of her mother, "it was her wish to produce me as a finished specimen framed in a perfect setting."

Alva's role in all this (as per the European child-rearing model) was largely executive. Consuelo was placed in the hands of governesses, who supervised her daily education. Alva would see her every day, for lunch, and on Saturday she would have her recite the week's lessons. She also sent for the Oxford and Cambridge entrance examinations, and had them administered to Consuelo, who passed with flying colors.

Consuelo, who did her lessons wearing an iron brace to improve her posture, had separate governesses to teach her French and German.

Scholarly pursuits, however, were not the main event, and there was never any chance that Consuelo would be permitted to go to university. Alva's plans for her daughter were revealed in a portrait she commissioned from the French painter Émile Carolus-Duran. Though he preferred to pose his sitters against a dark background, Alva insisted that Consuelo be painted in a white dress, descending the steps of a terrace set in a vaguely classical landscape. The finished picture would thus fit in with the row of family portraits by Lely, Kneller, Gainsborough and Romney in the stately English home that Consuelo was being groomed to occupy.

Whatever stately home it eventually was, Consuelo would do it justice, as would any of the American Aristocrat heiresses. They wouldn't be troubled

In the Carolus-Duran portrait commissioned by Alva, the pale draperies of Consuelo's dress added to the "classical" effect.

by the task of writing out menu cards in French; they would know exactly which fork should be used for the ortolans; they would never stare at frescoed twenty-foot ceilings. They had been brought up to these things. They had been scolded and chaperoned and drilled and dressed so that, when they made their débuts, they were refined little specimens indeed. No awkwardness about how to dance a quadrille, no hesitation when pouring tea, no clumsy handling of a train would mar the picture. When they came to Newport for their first summers "out," these daughters of the American aristocracy were magnificent.

MARCH OF ANGLOMANIA
Cornelius Vanderbilt, Jr., was taught to speak with an English accent; when he was sent to boarding school, his fellow students called him "Limey."

WALL STREET FATHER NO. 3: THE COLLECTOR

In the era of the American Aristocrat, a new sort of Wall Street Father came to the fore: a captain of commerce who was also a captain of culture. This father, best represented by Anthony J. Drexel, Michael P. Grace, J.P. Morgan and William Whitney, did not stay quietly behind while his wife and daughter roamed Europe; rather, he led the way, with his wife and daughter bobbing along in his wake. His was the dominating social ambition.

Having used up the challenge of the New World, this Wall Street Father was now prepared to take on the Old. He became a London resident, bought a country house, traveled widely on the European circuit. J.P. Morgan went so far as to dress his Scottish retainer in a spurious Morgan tartan. Obsessed with the surface of aristocracy, he oversaw his family's wardrobe selections in the rue de la Paix and was one of the few clients ever allowed the privilege of visiting Worth

William Collins Whitney, one of the most voracious collectors of his era; below, his house in New York.

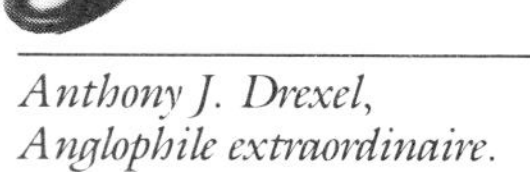

Anthony J. Drexel, Anglophile extraordinaire.

"If we go to Europe, Cynthia, I don't want you to marry any of them counts or dukes. You just wait until we run across some king in reduced circumstances."

Shipping magnate Michael P. Grace bought and restored Battle Abbey, built by William the Conqueror after the Battle of Hastings.

at his country home in Suresnes. He was said to have sobbed openly at the news of Worth's death in 1895.

But, more than anything else, this father was a plunderer, a top client of art dealers Duveen and Wertheimer, forever sifting through the detritus of the fallen French or Italian aristocracy for more paintings, wall panelings, priceless tapestries, anything that was older than the republic to which he belonged. He wanted to buy history, to purchase a past—not a little piece of the past but as much of it as he could get his hands on. (Consuelo Vanderbilt's father had to construct his own wharf and warehouse at Newport to accommodate all the marble furniture and statuary being shipped from Europe for his new house on Bellevue Avenue.)

The Collector, having somehow made his pot, hadn't the faintest intention of letting anyone else—the womenfolk, for instance, spend it. His entire mission was to propel himself, in one great leap, onto the narrow social ledge occupied by the cultivated sons of England's oldest families, and it was therefore of the very first importance that his daughter marry an English aristocrat. Without a title, she not only compromised his social successes but also denied him that final item to round out his collection. He needed one crucial other acquisition to display along with the Savonnerie carpets, the Boulle desks, the settees by William Kent, the embroidered pillows once owned by Marie Antoinette, the Tintoretto ceilings, the medieval manuscripts and Renaissance miniatures. The Collector's daughter must fetch for him the *pièce de résistance* of his collection—the noble English son-in-law.

THE MATCH OF THE CENTURY

In the fall of 1893, Consuelo Vanderbilt joined her parents and younger brother Harold on a cruise to India. Also aboard the 312-foot family yacht the *Valiant,* along with the governess, tutor, doctor, and 72 members of the crew, were Oliver H.P. Belmont and Winthrop Rutherfurd. Belmont and Consuelo's father, Willie K., were best friends; they were both sons of rich men, both horse lovers, both clients of Richard Morris Hunt. If Belmont's attentions to Alva had been rather pointed recently, Willie seemed willing to ignore it. Rutherfurd, a young attorney of impeccable lineage (his mother was a direct descendant of Peter Stuyvesant, the last Dutch governor of New York), shared the sporting interests of the other two men.

By the time she was eighteen, Consuelo was the "finished specimen" her mother had groomed her to be.

THE FIRST HINT OF TROUBLE

The Vanderbilts saw India as scheduled, but upon reaching Paris in the spring, Alva announced that she and Willie K. were parting company. Unperturbedly, she shopped and planned Consuelo's coming-out ball while Cornelius, Willie K.'s elder brother and head of the family, hustled across the ocean to try to patch things up. Alva, as he should have expected, was implacable. Willie was keeping mistresses; rumor had it that a certain not-quite-lady in Paris had dressed her servants in Vanderbilt livery. Alva was not one to toe the society line, turning a blind eye to her husband's errant attentions. He was committing adultery, and she would divorce him for it.

Consuelo's Paris début went well. Her mother's rigorous child-rearing program had produced an exquisite girl. Tall and slender, she had beautiful posture (apparently the iron brace had paid off), a cloud of dark hair and a gloriously long neck. A number of aristocratic Frenchmen took note of her many attractions and approached Alva for permission to pay court to her daughter. They were turned down. Alva had her plans, and they did not include a Continental *parti*. She took Consuelo on to London.

THE HUNT BEGINS

The first stop was Minnie Paget's pretty house on Belgrave Square, where Consuelo later remembered being assessed by "a pair of hard green eyes." "If I am to bring her out," said Minnie, "she must be able to compete at least as far as clothes are concerned with far better-looking girls." So, as Consuelo wrote in her memoirs, "Tulle must give way to satin, the baby décolletage to a more generous display of neck and

In Paris a distinction was made between the bal blanc, *where the only ladies present were débutantes and their chaperones, and the infinitesimally racier* bal rose, *to which the young married ladies were invited.*

In Minnie Paget's Mayfair boudoir, the young Consuelo got the first inkling of her fate.

Comme il Faut
Gentlemen do not wear gloves to a dinner. Gentlemen do wear gloves to a dance.

arms, naïveté to sophistication." The clothes were achieved, and a little dinner was arranged with the Duke of Marlborough as the principal guest. This was not the eccentric roué snubbed by most of New York eight years earlier—Blandford had died in 1892—but his twenty-four-year-old son, Sunny. That evening Lady Paget placed the slender, mustached Duke at her right hand and seated Consuelo on his right. It wasn't subtle, but then it didn't have to be.

Sunny (so called for his childhood title, Lord Sunderland) needed to marry an heiress. His late father's efforts in heiress-hunting had made a small dent in the grim Blenheim financial situation; Lily Hammersley's money got the place reroofed and built a laboratory for her husband's electrical experiments. But there was more to do, and Sunny burned to do it. Proud, shy, fastidious, he had been deeply wounded by his parents' divorce. Blenheim alone seemed to offer consolation. No sacrifice would be too great if he could restore some of its baroque glories and ensure a more stable future.

As Sunny's fiscal burden was oversize, so was his pride. If a mere younger son like Moreton Frewen couldn't work for a living, even less could a duke who bore one of the most glorious names in English history. His statement years later, informing a visitor to the chapel at Blenheim (where the first Duke's tomb far outshines the altar) that "The Marlboroughs are worshipped here," wasn't in the least bit facetious. Family pride was the cornerstone of Sunny's faith. To do justice to Blenheim and the Marlborough name was his absorbing goal, and his task, in 1894, was to find a suitable wife. She would have to be enormously rich. She must also be worthy of the title Duchess of Marlborough.

ALVA A VANDERBILT NO MORE

Consuelo and the Duke (whom she found "good-looking and intelligent") saw each other only once

In Paris, where she made her début, Consuelo was known as "la belle Mlle. Vanderbilt au long cou" for her swanlike neck.

that season. In August, Alva withdrew from London to a rented house on the Thames and concentrated on her divorce. Her counsel was Joseph Choate, the attorney who would later be America's first ambassador to the Court of St. James. He advised her against taking legal action, as did all her friends, but Alva's mind was made up. She would divorce her husband, and she would do it in New York State, where the only ground for divorce was adultery.

She and Consuelo were back at 660 Fifth Avenue for the winter season, and though Willie K. was not allowed in the house, Alva's social standing was sufficiently strong for Consuelo's New York début to be successful. She chaperoned Consuelo very carefully all that winter; then on March 6, 1895, the Vander-

At Newport's fashionable Trinity Church, the prominent families had their boxes upholstered in the same color as their servants' livery.

Oliver Belmont was always considered feckless by his family, particularly after his disastrous four-month marriage to Sarah Swan Whiting of Newport. A dozen years later, he seemed ready to give matrimony another try.

bilt divorce was announced as a *fait accompli.*

Choate had done a very good job. The case was heard *in camera,* and the records were sealed. The necessary witnesses to Willie K.'s adultery (carried out *pro forma* with one Nellie Neustretter of Nevada) had been whisked over from Paris and whisked back. Alva got sole custody of the children, $100,000 a year and the Newport mansion, as well as a capital sum rumored to be as much as $10 million. Willie K. had offered her 660 Fifth Avenue, but she declined it because the upkeep was too expensive.

Shortly after the divorce was announced, Alva and Consuelo sailed for Europe and so escaped the inevitable rumors. Would Willie K. now marry the widowed Consuelo, Duchess of Manchester? Was Alva planning to marry Willie's best friend, Oliver Belmont? Alva, however, was willing to shelve her relationship with Oliver until Consuelo had been properly married off. The difficulty was that Consuelo, the most biddable of girls, was proving stubborn about her nuptial fate.

CONSUELO BALKS

The Valiant *replaced the* Alva, *which sank after a collision off Martha's Vineyard. Built in England, she crossed the Atlantic in a mere seven and a half days. Monthly salaries for her crew of seventy-two (including a French chef) came to $10,000.*

The trouble dated back to the cruise on the *Valiant,* when Consuelo had fallen madly in love with Winthrop Rutherfurd. It was easy to see why. Not only was he a dashing sportsman like her father; he was also handsome, with "really breathtaking good looks," as a lady later said of him. But, at twenty-nine, his age was against him. Consuelo was a very sheltered sixteen, and Alva had seen enough of life to consider a youthful crush on a glamorous older man a poor foundation for a lifelong relationship.

The careful chaperoning of the previous winter had been aimed at keeping Consuelo and Win apart, but they had snatched a few moments together in March just after the divorce was announced. While bicycling (the new rage of society) on Riverside Drive, they had escaped their party of friends. Win had proposed marriage. Consuelo had accepted. Then Alva, pedaling furiously, had caught up with them. The next day, the Vanderbilt ladies left for Europe.

They stayed abroad for five months. Rutherfurd followed them to Paris, but Alva was ruthless. He was never allowed to see Consuelo, and his letters to her were confiscated. Consuelo went to balls, went to the Louvre, went to Worth, always chaperoned. Alva went to Worth as well, for a little private business of her own. June saw them in London, where they went to a ball at Stafford House, home of the Duke of Sutherland. Sunny was there, and he danced with Consuelo several times, still trying to assess her duchess potential. She must have appeared promising, for he invited Alva and Consuelo to Blenheim. He would have to see her in the actual setting.

The setting impressed Consuelo with its grandeur, though no doubt Alva rejoiced to find that the aristocratic splendors of Blenheim were more than matched by those of Marble House. The dining room

In July of 1895, Marble House was known in Newport as "Marble Heart," for Alva's treatment of Consuelo.

Above left: Louis Laguerre's inventive trompe l'oeil frescoes in Blenheim's dining room. Right: Marble House's marble dining room.

LIKE FATHER, LIKE SON

The Marlboroughs were not the only father-son pair of dukes to seek American wives. The son of the 8th Duke of Manchester and Consuelo Yznaga had succeeded to his title in 1892, at the age of fifteen. Finances were already an issue: his father had declared bankruptcy three years earlier. The Yznaga dollars hadn't offset the results of the agricultural depression on the Manchester estates. But, whereas his father had married his helpful dollars by chance, "Kim" (for his childhood title, Lord Kimbolton) set out methodically to find himself an heiress. By the time he was twenty, he was an acknowledged fortune hunter, and reporters quoted him as saying that he needed an Astor or Vanderbilt to save him. In 1897, in a bold attempt to stave off his creditors, he announced publicly that he had become engaged to the American heiress of the moment, May Goelet. Worse, he didn't even allow her family time to deny his statement but retracted it himself.

Kim's fondness for newspapermen and his need for an American heiress may have been behind his next outlandish move: in 1899 Randolph Hearst paid him $1,000 in advance, in a single banknote, to join the staff of the New York *Journal* as a reporter. He spent more time giving interviews than seeking them, however, and the *Journal* dispensed with his services.

Consuelo, Duchess of Manchester, upon learning of her son's secret marriage to Helena Zimmerman, was appalled that he'd chosen an American nobody—perhaps foregetting her own past status.

Returning to London, he was lucky enough to find and charm the aunt (and guardian) of an innocent American heiress named Helena Zimmerman, daughter of a Cincinnati millionaire. He then won over the niece as well, and on November 14, 1900, shortly after being declared bankrupt with debts amounting to $135,000, he put his financial problems to rest with a secret wedding ceremony at Marylebone Parish Church. Dignity, once again, was conspicuously absent from the proceedings. A newspaper photo showed Kim surrounded by portraits of the twenty-two women to whom he had supposedly been engaged, and Helena's maid was bribed into providing Kim's underclothes to be photographed for the papers and captioned "Wedding Trousseau of a Duke."

at Blenheim, after all, was only *trompe l'oeil* marble; *her* dining room was paneled with genuine deep-pink Numidian marble, the most expensive variety in the world. On Saturday night, Marlborough and his guests sat in the Long Library and listened to a concert on the organ that heiress Lily Hammersley had paid for. On Sunday, Sunny took Consuelo for a drive around the estate. When Alva invited him to visit them at Newport in August, he accepted. It could only mean one thing. If he went to Newport, he knew what was expected of him.

ANOTHER SHOWDOWN FOR ALVA

Throughout the summer of 1895, the little town by the sea was convulsed with Vanderbilt gossip. Alva was planning a big ball for August, but who would go to it? Certainly not the Vanderbilts or their friends. *Town Topics* ran weekly bulletins about Alva's plans, Willie's plans, the reaction of the Cornelius Vanderbilts, whose new house, The Breakers, was opened in July.

In the event, everyone behaved disappointingly well. Willie K. was in Newport, living on the *Valiant,* when Alva and Consuelo arrived. He took a party to watch the America's Cup trials, took Consuelo driving, then went off to Bar Harbor. Oliver Belmont stayed out of sight, busy with his horses. The one moment of drama the situation offered was the spectacle of Alva and Cornelius Vanderbilt coming face to face at the door of the Country Club. Nothing happened. Clearly the Great Vanderbilt Wars were a wash.

Society, however, managed to keep its best stories to itself that summer. No reporter saw Consuelo snatch a dance with Win Rutherfurd at a ball. Certainly no reporter saw the great showdown between Alva and Consuelo immediately afterward, when the halls of Marble House echoed late into the night. Alva shouted and raged, Consuelo later wrote, and

The Cornelius Vanderbilts' Newport "cottage," designed by Richard Morris Hunt and called The Breakers, was completed in the summer of 1895—in time for daughter Gertrude's début.

THE NEWPORT SCHEDULE

A group of Newport residents, photographed in 1892 in all their summer finery.

THE TIME: July and August **THE PLACE:** Newport, Rhode Island

BASIC REQUIREMENTS.

AMERICAN HEIRESS: 80–90 new dresses; entertaining budget for mother of $150,000 to $300,000; substantial mansion, preferably designed by Richard Morris Hunt, on Bellevue Avenue or the cliffs; Casino membership; cabana at Bailey's Beach.

HEIRESS-HUNTING ENGLISHMAN: A title, a few introductions, stamina.

THE DAILY ROUTINE

A.M.

8:00–9:00

Large breakfast *à l'anglaise* (eggs, sausage, oatmeal, kidneys); change into riding habit.

9:00–11:00

Morning ride; change to day dress and drive in phaeton (preferred carriage because low sides allow maximum exposure of costume) behind matched pair to Casino to visit Worth boutique, watch tennis, discuss last night's party; return home, change for trip to the beach.

11:00–12:00

Ladies' "swimming" at Bailey's Beach (widely considered the worst beach on the eastern seaboard owing to rocks and red algae). Swimming means bobbing in chest-deep water, fully clad, with big hat for protection from sun. At noon, a flag is run up to announce the gentlemen's turn; the ladies disappear.

Newport's beaches were not its real attraction.

P.M.

12:00–2:00

Luncheon on steam yacht in harbor. (Jewels permitted for matrons: "At noon they will have at their waists turquoises as big as almonds, pearls as large as filberts at their throats, rubies and diamonds as large as their fingernails."—Paul Bourget) Or *fête champêtre* on local farm, complete with tent, linen, crystal, silver, footmen, champagne, and rented sheep to add rustic touch.

Tea, tennis and gossip were the principal activities at the Casino.

2:00–3:00

Drive to Polo Field to watch a few chukkers of polo match from carriage.

3:00–5:00

Afternoon promenade begins as every gate on Bellevue opens to release the family carriage, with all female members inside and footman behind; cards left at friends' houses by footman. *Protocol:* Never overtake the carriage of a social superior; nod when passing the carriage of an acquaintance for the first time, smile the second time, look away the third.

Where the rich vacation, they also shop. Even Worth had a boutique on Bellevue Avenue.

5:00–8:00

Tea on the lawn or terrace; change for dinner.

8:00–10:00

Dinner on steam yacht, similar to luncheon though dresses are more *décolleté*. Or "light" (five-course?) supper before weekly Casino dance, to which $1 tickets are sold to spectators. Or formal dinner, 8–12 courses, 20–200 guests; cadets recruited from local navy post on Sunday nights to fill in for businessmen.

10:00–DAWN

Housewarming or débutante dances; cultural offerings, including performances by theatrical troupes hired away from Broadway for the night; theme balls, with a second supper at midnight, strolling on well-lit grounds, and breakfast as dawn breaks over Sakonnet Point.

Balls were so commonplace in Newport that often themes were chosen for decorations and attire.

told her that Win was in love with a married woman and wanted her only for her money. She even threatened to kill him.

The next morning, the house was unnaturally quiet. Nobody came to Consuelo's room. The telephone didn't ring. The governess seemed nervous. Finally Alva's great friend Mrs. Jay informed Consuelo that her mother had had a heart attack and that the sight of her refractory daughter could kill her. Consuelo relented. She had held out as long as circumstances let her. Finally, she had to let Win go.

Win Rutherfurd, the year before the Valiant *cruise. In her desperation to keep Consuelo apart from him, Alva told her there was madness in his family and that he couldn't have children.*

THE WAITING GAME

The last two weeks in August were the height of the season in Newport. Sunny arrived on the twenty-third, and now even Consuelo, who had been watched very carefully after the showdown with her mother, was allowed to take part in the whirl. The Vanderbilts and their noble guest went to a "Calico Ball" given by the R.T. Wilsons at the Country Club, where Sunny was amused by the quaint calico favors. They had dinner on John Jacob Astor's yacht. They drove to the Casino, and saw the polo, and did all the things one did in Newport. Alva watched Consuelo like a hawk and waited for a little announcement.

It had to come. Sunny had understood (hadn't he?) that his presence in Newport amounted to a declaration of intent. The English were rather unromantic about these things—he could hardly be waiting to fall in love—and certainly he had seen enough of Consuelo to be sure. Staying at Marble House, he would know from its grandeurs that Blenheim would pose no difficulties. Consuelo was used to formality, accustomed to a footman behind her chair and six forks at dinner. Her deportment never, under any circumstance, left anything to be desired. She would be the perfect wife for Sunny; she would make a marvelous duchess. So why didn't he propose?

The days crept on. More gorgeous sun and

DOING THE CONTINENTAL

Though British aristocrats were the husbands of choice, some American heiresses found Continental titles equally alluring. Florence Garner's two sisters married, respectively, a French marquis and a Danish count. Mrs. McKay's daughter won the Italian Prince Colonna. Winnaretta Singer, of the sewing-machine fortune, became, successively, Princesse de Scey-Montbéliard and Princesse de Polignac. And, in a well-publicized union that would ultimately contribute to American distrust of European husbands, Anna Gould wed Count Boni de Castellane.

A figure, literally, out of Proust (he is thought to be the model for the dandy Saint-Loup), De Castellane had been brought up at the Loire château of Rochecotte. His tastes were exquisite and expensive; his income, insufficient. Anna, daughter of the robber baron Jay Gould and orphaned by the time of her début, had been placed in the charge of her brother and his erstwhile-showgirl wife. They sent her off to Paris, where Boni fluttered round and succeeded in winning her hand.

His scheme was to transform his rather plain wife into a being acceptable to his tastes, and with the help of M. Worth he nearly succeeded. Other projects included building a pink marble house in the Bois de Boulogne, collecting art, and giving a fête on Anna's birthday for which he had 80,000 Venetian lamps hung in the trees. He ran through $1 million in less than a year.

Unfortunately, Boni could not bring himself to abandon his interest in other women, among them the notorious "belle Otéro." Prudently, Anna had refused to become a Catholic upon their marriage, and in 1906 she divorced him. Three years later, Boni was dangling (unsuccessfully) after J.P. Morgan's daughter Anne. As for Anna, she married Boni's cousin, the Prince de Sagan, in the end acquiring both a better husband and a better title.

On marrying De Castellane, Anna Gould wisely refused to convert to Catholicism, which would have ruled out a future divorce. The crowds of onlookers at her wedding were immense.

MARCH OF ANGLOMANIA
The Elms, the Newport home of the Berwinds, was patterned after a French château except for its three arched entrances, modeled after Buckingham Palace.

breezes. More drives under the elms and people whispering, as soon as the Vanderbilt carriage passed, how lovely Consuelo looked and what a lucky man Marlborough was. Would be. The night of Alva's party drew near. It was to be a Louis XIV ball, in Sunny's honor. If Alva's divorce had made her enemies, it didn't show, for Newport's Anglomaniacs couldn't pass up the chance to socialize with a duke. And there would probably be a significant announcement. One wouldn't want to miss that.

Naturally, it was a lovely party. Alva had brought $5,000 worth of favors over from Paris (one of her little secret tasks the previous spring); there were etchings, fans, mirrors and watchcases, each item marked with a medallion of Marble House. Exquisite taste, yes, of course—and the flowers, and the food, and the music, and Consuelo's satin dress trimmed with heirloom lace. But the announcement?

The announcement didn't come. Sunny had

The dark colors of the Gothic Room at Marble House moved Consuelo to describe its atmosphere as "propitious to sacrifice."

ANNUS MIRABILIS

Not counting marriages to Continental bridegrooms, the number of titled matches for American heiresses in the year 1895 was tallied at nine.

April 16: Maud Burke *m.* Sir Bache Cunard
April 22: Mary Leiter *m.* Hon. George Curzon
April 30: Josephine Chamberlain *m.* Talbot Leyland Scarisbrick (later 1st Baronet)
April 30: Lily, Duchess of Marlborough (the former Lily Hammersley), *m.* Lord William Beresford
October 21: Elizabeth LaRoche *m.* Sir Howland Roberts
October 23: Leonora Van Marter *m.* 7th Earl of Tankerville
November 6: Consuelo Vanderbilt *m.* 9th Duke of Marlborough
November 12: Pauline Whitney *m.* Almeric Paget (later 1st Baron Queenborough)
November 12: Cora Rogers *m.* Urban Hanlon Broughton (posthumously created Baron Fairhaven of Lode)

COMME IL FAUT
The conservatory, the library, any private place, is off-limits to a young lady and her partner at a ball.

evidently not proposed. The days rolled on. More balls, more walks, more drives. No announcement. The rumors started up again: the Duke had proposed to Willie's niece Gertrude (who was richer) and had been turned down. Word about Consuelo's preferred American suitor leaked out. It was September before Sunny took Consuelo into the Gothic Room at Marble House and asked her to be his wife. "I was content," Consuelo later wrote, "with his pious hope that he would make me a good husband and ran up to my mother with word of our engagement."

The next day, Alva made the news public. For her there could be no underestimating the triumph. The unremitting attention to every detail of Consuelo's upbringing had paid off. The Duke was paying the most extravagant compliment in his vocabulary by considering Consuelo suitable to be his duchess and mistress of Blenheim. Alva appreciated the full measure of her future son-in-law's compliment; it was a salute to her as much as to her daughter.

"I imagine our English cousins of the gentler sex must feel somewhat disgruntled that their American rivals should so easily secure the Marlborough plum twice in succession."
From *Metropolitan Magazine* (1895)

LET'S MAKE A DEAL

He is only marrying you for your money," said Consuelo's younger brother, Harold, upon learning of her engagement to the Duke of Marlborough. But it wasn't true. Sunny could not have betrayed his meticulous standards by bringing Blenheim an unworthy duchess. It *was* true, however, that without Consuelo's money, the match would not have been made.

While the women fussed over wedding plans, the Duke's solicitor, Sir George Lewis, arrived from London to look after the all-important settlements. More than one marriage had foundered

on this issue: Minnie Paget had lost a potential husband when his man of business discovered that her dowry was less than advertised. And, of course, the match between Jennie Jerome and Lord Randolph Churchill barely survived the financial haggling.

The scale of the Vanderbilt/Marlborough negotiations was much greater than the Jerome/Churchill proceedings. A basic feature of the progress from Buccaneer to Self-Made Girl to American Aristocrat was inflation of the sums changing hands. Naturally, they reached a peak with the American Aristocrats—money was the foundation of the American aristocracy, after all. It was to be expected that Consuelo Vanderbilt's dowry would eclipse that of any other American heiress.

The negotiations, in this case, went smoothly, and the ingenious result was a princely settlement on the Duke of $2,500,000 (or £500,000 at the then current exchange) in Beech Creek Railway stock, with a guaranteed

A Puck *cartoon, captioned: "A New International Interest. The American Gold Fields for Impecunious Noblemen."*

minimum yield of 4 percent (or £20,000) annually. That was only the beginning: the Marlboroughs had constant recourse to Vanderbilt dollars, which they put to use in building a £500,000 town house on Curzon Street. All in all (repairs and improvements to Blenheim included), the Vanderbilt contribution to the Marlboroughs is reckoned at $15 million.

As American fathers became familiar with the price of a noble son-in-law, they also grew more sophisticated about safeguarding the welfare of their daughters. In England, a woman's dowry was traditionally absorbed into her husband's estate; he thus controlled the capital she brought to the marriage, while she was paid an allowance, or "pin money." American fathers didn't like relinquishing control of large sums of money, particularly when their beloved daughters' welfare might depend on the investment savvy (and good will) of a son-in-law—hence Leonard Jerome's eagerness to provide Jennie with an independent allowance. By 1895 the Vanderbilts' lawyers were wise enough to the pitfalls of the international match to keep Consuelo's dowry in reliable railroad stock. Equally, the English had become accustomed to the American insistence on financial security for the brides and acquiesced in arrangements that would have been unacceptable to, for example, Lord Randolph Churchill's lawyers. In 1903, when Alice Thaw married the Earl of Yarmouth, her family advisers were extremely cautious: the income of $50,000 a year that would go to the Earl derived from money settled on Alice for life. It was not the traditional English way, but those were the terms of the deal. If English grooms wanted the pot of dollars, that was the form it came in. Take it or leave it. Usually, they took.

DOLLARS & PENCE

The press and the populace were fascinated by the phenomenon of transatlantic marriages, and from time to time lists were printed showing the amounts of money that had changed hands. Here, from *The New York Times* and London's *Tatler,* is a list of the putative amounts paid in dowries. A pound equaled five dollars in that era, and a general rule of thumb by which to reckon inflation is to multiply by 33.

Mrs. John Adair (née Cornelia Wadsworth, sister of Mrs. Arthur Post, later Lady Barrymore): $300,000
Minna, Marchioness of Anglesey (née King): $200,000
Mrs. George Cavendish-Bentinck (née Elizabeth Livingston): $1,500,000
Lady Arthur Butler (later Marchioness of Ormonde, née Ellen Stager): $1,000,000
Mrs. Ernest Beckett (née Lucy Lee): $500,000
Countess of Craven (née Cornelia Martin): £200,000
Lady Curzon (née Mary Leiter): £1,500,000
Countess of Donoughmore (née Elena Grace): £100,000
Lady Harcourt (née Elizabeth Motley): $200,000
Lady Fermor-Hesketh (née Flora Sharon): $2,000,000
Duchess of Manchester (née Consuelo Yznaga): £200,000
Duchess of Manchester (née Helena Zimmerman): £400,000
Duchess of Marlborough (formerly Lily Hammersley): £800,000
Mrs. Arthur Paget (née Minnie Stevens): $100,000
Duchess of Roxburghe (née May Goelet): £2,000,000
Cora, Countess of Strafford (formerly Cora Colgate): £200,000
Lady Vernon (née Frances Lawrance): $1,000,000
Lady Wolseley (née Anita Murphy): $2,000,000
Countess of Yarmouth (née Alice Thaw): £200,000

SHE IS NOW A DUCHESS

While his solicitor and the Vanderbilt lawyers hammered out the marriage settlements, Sunny, the Duke of Marlborough, left town to get in some hunting. He came back from the mountains and bracing air of the West to find that New York was feverishly excited about his wedding, though not exactly excited about him. It didn't help his case that his father had so recently wooed and won the Hammersley dollars. Furthermore, the publicity in 1888 had made it all too clear that the Marlboroughs needed money. They had had some American money, used it all up, and here they were again—back at the well.

The publicity about Alva's divorce heightened the interest, as did gossip about the spurned suitor, Win Rutherfurd. Alva began to assume the proportions of a gorgon. Information about intrafamily strife was leaked to both New York and London society by Maude Lorillard Tailer, who owned the house on 72nd Street where Alva and Consuelo were living in the fall of 1895 (and who would later marry the Honourable Cecil Baring, once betrothed to Grace Wilson). The story took on some of the aspects of a virgin sacrifice as the supposedly shy and gentle Consuelo submitted to her wicked mother's ambition. Sunny's behavior didn't help. First he told *The New York Times* that the engagement had been "arranged by Miss Vanderbilt's friends and those of the Duke of Marlborough." It seemed fine to him; that was how the aristocracy did things. America, however, for all its aristocratic pretensions, disapproved of arranged marriages. Where was romance in all of this?

Baby Cornelius Vanderbilt and his sister Gladys: the photographer's studio thoughtfully provided a small-scale wrought-iron gate of the sort the Vanderbilts were used to.

Everything Sunny did in the days before the marriage caused offense. He was stopped by the police for "coasting" his bicycle in Central Park. He had nothing complimentary to say about America. No one in his family was coming to the wedding. He stayed away from the rehearsal (but of course wouldn't miss signing the documents that were going to make him rich). And he was only five feet six inches tall. His height, finally, was a metaphor for the whole ugly phenomenon: an effete member of a dissolute family, coldly marrying a fresh, innocent American girl for her dollars rather than for her charm.

Naturally, anyone who could read knew how tall the Duke was, and a great deal more besides. By 1895, the American heiress marrying a European aristocrat was a familiar and thrilling phenomenon in the press. For weeks beforehand, newspapers would lash their readers into a frenzy of interest. Genealogies of noble husbands were illustrated with coats of arms, portraits, and woodcuts of the stately home. Glowing descriptions of the bride-to-be's beauty, refinement and charm usually included flattering misinformation about her dowry and her family's ancestry.

The acorn in the Vanderbilt coat of arms was supposed to remind viewers that "tall oaks from little acorns grow."

A Life *cartoon by Charles Dana Gibson. The fair bride and her puny husband are kneeling on Cupid's casket.*

Though a duchess is referred to formally and by servants as "Her Grace," in conversation she is addressed as "Duchess" (e.g., "More tea, Duchess?"). Among her social equals, however, she (or any titled lady) is referred to by her first name and her title, as in "Consuelo Marlborough," and she also signs her name that way.

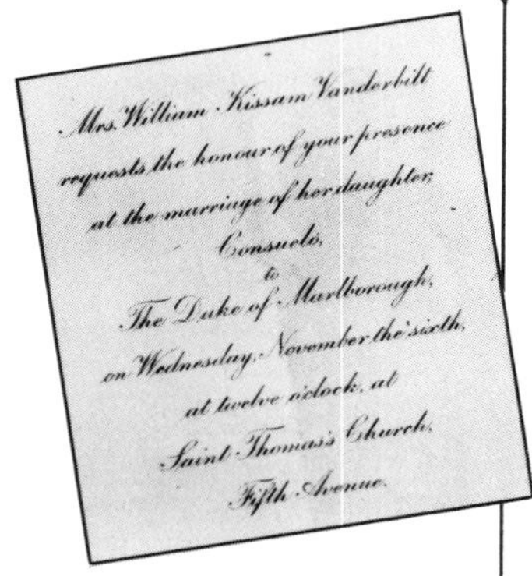

Mrs. William Kissam Vanderbilt
requests the honour of your presence
at the marriage of her daughter
Consuelo,
to
The Duke of Marlborough,
on Wednesday, November the sixth,
at twelve o'clock, at
Saint Thomas's Church,
Fifth Avenue.

Ordering 4,000 wedding invitations from the engraver must have given Alva deep satisfaction.

Mrs. George Gould invited some sneers by employing a press agent for the wedding of her sister-in-law Anna to the French Count Boni de Castellane. The Goulds were not in society and Mrs. Gould had been an actress, so such a *faux pas* was, if not forgivable, at least understandable. Yet the sheer volume of information available on Consuelo's marriage indicates that someone in the Vanderbilt *ménage* was also dealing with reporters. Moreover, some of the columns bore the stamp of a publicist. *The New York Times,* discussing the wedding preparations, noted that the pews were to be decorated with floral torches that would "recall the flambeaux on the old residences in London"—hardly an image to leap to the mind of the average New York journalist.

So great was the hunger for information that families who failed to cooperate with the press by periodically releasing innocuous news (the names of the officiating clergy, a description of the bridesmaids' dresses, statistics on floral decorations) ran the risk of seeing falsehoods or, worse, private matters in print. Consuelo Vanderbilt's trousseau was described and illustrated in *Vogue,* a project that must have required some cooperation from Alva. But to Consuelo's chagrin, the *Times* ran a one-and-a-half-column piece describing her lingerie, illustrated by a drawing of her white brocade bridal corset. "I read to my stupefaction that my garters had gold clasps studded with diamonds," she later wrote, "and wondered how I should live down such vulgarities."

In the end, most families played along with the papers to some extent. Edith Wharton describes, in *The House of Mirth,* "the 'simple country wedding'" where "the representatives of the press were threading their way, notebook in hand, through the labyrinth of wedding presents, and the agent of a cinematograph syndicate was setting up his apparatus at the church door." The wedding gifts were displayed with the cards of the donors, a custom that would have caused the Old New Yorkers to blanch but that gave a

In 1895, Lily, Duchess of Marlborough, three years a widow, married Lord William Beresford. Her stepson, Sunny, the 9th Duke of Marlborough, gave her away.

Any girl, not just a shy one heading for an arranged marriage, would detest having drawings of her lingerie published for thousands to read.

great deal of pleasure to the shopgirls who read the list of bridal spoils.

Indeed, the gifts were revealing. The assumption was that the groom's household was already equipped with priceless crystal, heirloom porcelain and all the other basics. By the time of Consuelo's marriage, even gifts of silver were considered superfluous—coals to Newcastle. Instead, something the bride could wear was preferable: a necklace, a bracelet, a hatpin, a brooch. And what item of jewelry would be most necessary for the American Aristocrat in her new life? A tiara, of course. Thus Consuelo's father presented her with a diamond tiara, tipped with large

THE HEIRESSES' NEWPORT

Richmond Barrett, in *Good Ol' Summer Days,* wrote that girls "made their formal débuts in New York coming-out parties and balls, but Newport was the display case for them." Nowhere was the concentration of American money more intense than in Newport, Rhode Island, where millionaires' houses lined the coastline for miles.

Above: Ochre Court, little used after Ogden Golet's death; his widow May often complained about what a bother it was.

Left: The Breakers, built after the first Breakers burned down. It is now open to the public, though Countess Szapary, a descendant of Cornelius Vanderbilt, maintains a private apartment there.

Right: Beechwood, the Italianate villa on Bellevue Avenue where Caroline Astor summered.

Above: Farther out Bellevue Avenue the elms gave way to wind-swept, rocky seashore, but that didn't prevent anyone from building massive houses there.

Right: Two of the old-fashioned wooden houses, with their porches and striped awnings. The rather modest one on the right belonged to Ogden Mills.

Above: Crossways, where the Stuyvesant Fishes ended the Newport season with their Harvest Ball

Right: Mid Cliff, illustrating the romantic gabled, many-chimneyed style that was largely supplanted by the châteaux.

The Cornelius Vanderbilts believed that Grace Wilson wanted more than anything to marry a Vanderbilt—any *Vanderbilt.*

THE WILSON FAMILY SCORECARD #4: GRACE & NEILY

The youngest of the "marrying Wilsons" had benefited greatly from the improved family fortunes. Grace was pretty, charming, well-dressed and sophisticated, but that was precisely the problem. She had her eye on Cornelius Vanderbilt III, and his parents (who, after all, met while teaching Sunday school) thought her much too sophisticated for twenty-two-year-old Neily. "There is *nothing* the girl would not do," Neily's sister Gertrude wrote in her diary. "She is at least 27 . . . has had unbounded experience. Been engaged several times. Tried hard to marry a rich man. Ran after Jack Astor to such an extent that all New York talked about it. Is so diplomatic that even the men are deadly afraid of her. There is nothing she would stop at." Among Grace's ex-fiancés, rumored and official, were Cecil Baring, son of Lord Revelstoke (who backed down when her dowry proved insufficient), and William Vanderbilt, Cornelius' deceased older brother.

Several newspapers received anonymous letters on Knickerbocker Club stationery stating that Grace was pregnant, but despite the opposition (Mrs. Vanderbilt told Gertrude that all of New York thought the Wilson woman's pursuit of Neily "the most dreadful thing of its kind that has ever happened in society") it was announced on June 10, 1896, that Grace and Neily would wed on June 18. Then word leaked out that Cornelius Vanderbilt, Sr., was threatening to disown his son if the marriage took place. June 18 came and went with no nuptials: Neily was ill with inflammatory rheumatism. A month or so later, immediately following a quarrelsome interview with his son during which Neily asserted his firm intention to marry Grace, Cornelius Sr. suffered a stroke—brought on, everyone believed, by his son's insubordination.

The pair were married nevertheless, on August 3, with no Vanderbilts present. When his father died shortly afterward, it was revealed that Neily had been cut off with a mere million dollars. Brother Alfred generously chipped in $6 million, and Grace went on to take her place among New York's leading society matrons, entertaining the crowned heads of Europe regularly and becoming particularly intimate with (some said the mistress of) Kaiser Wilhelm II.

pear-shaped stones, while Alva contributed a long string of immense pearls that once had belonged to Catherine the Great.

HERE COMES THE BRIDE

The day before the wedding, the estranged Vanderbilts, the affianced pair and their respective lawyers met at Alva's house on 72nd Street to sign the marriage contracts. It must have afforded Sunny deep satisfaction to think where those dollars would go. At last, a Duke of Marlborough would restore to the estate some of the glory that it deserved.

In fact, the whole wedding day was about glory, and pomp, and power, and wealth. By the 1890s any fashionable wedding—and particularly this one—was an opportunity for the plutocrats to reinforce their position of strength as well as to prove (however subliminally) to the titled son-in-law that he was marrying America's equivalent to himself. The church would be covered with thousands of flowers, preferably costly ones such as orchids and hothouse roses. The clergy would include at least one bishop. The bridesmaids would be numerous, and elegantly costumed. The wedding breakfast would be formal, lavish, and exquisitely served by multitudes of footmen. All the arrangements would speak more or less discreetly of thousands of dollars spent.

Though it was notionally a private event, the publicity leading up to an heiress's wedding guaranteed that the streets around the church would be thronged with curious onlookers. Thus the preparations included, along with ordering the wedding cake and choosing the music, arranging for enough security so that the bride could get to and from the church unmolested. To prevent a repetition of the disaster in 1893, when the unfortunate Cornelia Martin had been trapped in Grace Church by spectators bursting through the doors, on November 6 the streets between 72nd Street and St. Thomas' Church on Fifth

COMME IL FAUT
The horses hired to bring the bridal carriages to the church are traditionally matched grays, but some families purposely use bays or chestnuts to avoid attracting undue attention from passersby.

Avenue would be lined with policemen. Though the Vanderbilts traditionally attended St. Bartholomew's on Park Avenue, St. Thomas' was chosen for the wedding since its chancel had more room for the sixty-member choir Alva had enlisted.

The bride dressed at 72nd Street, assisted only by her maid. (Her wedding gown, naturally, was a Worth creation, ordered by her mother in Paris the previous spring, even before Sunny had proposed.) Alva had stated that Willie K. should appear at the 72nd Street house, take Consuelo to the church, give her away and then disappear. (The other members of the Vanderbilt family were ignored completely, and Consuelo even had to send back their gifts.)

Alva, stately in Worth's ice-blue satin trimmed with sable, had gone on to the church. She was thus treated to a heart-stopping twenty minutes when the ever dutiful, ever punctual Consuelo failed to materialize. The bride, whose face was puffy from crying at her nuptial fate, had been delayed by her efforts to sponge her eyes. At last the sexton signaled from the back of the church, and Dr. Walter Damrosch lifted his baton. The symphony orchestra launched into the "Wedding March," and eight bridesmaids, in white satin with blue sashes, paced down the aisle. Consuelo, in her satin and lace, followed. When the bishop said, "Who giveth this woman to be married to this man?" Willie K. relinquished her hand, which the bishop put in Sunny's. The pair said their vows and knelt on the cushions placed before them, Consuelo's dress billowing and glowing in the subdued light. They bowed their heads for the blessing. The bishop said, "Those whom God hath joined together let no man put asunder." They rose from their cushions, hand in slightly trembling hand. It was almost over. The bishop, pitching his voice to carry to the nave, proclaimed, "Forasmuch as Charles and Consuelo have consented together in holy wedlock . . . I pronounce that they be man and wife together." Another American woman had become a peeress.

The Duke of Marlborough and his new Duchess. The bouquet of orchids from Blenheim that she intended to carry arrived too late.

THE AMERICAN ARISTOCRAT'S WEDDING

"For richer, for poorer. . ."

When a girl from America's ruling class married a young man from England's ruling class, the nuptials had to be carried off with nearly oppressive pomp. As *Town Topics* said sardonically of Alva Vanderbilt in connection with Consuelo's wedding plans, she "has recognized that she does not live for herself alone. The very rich are the royal families of America." And their marriages were banner events. American heiresses were the celebrities of the day, and crowds gathered to watch them become peeresses.

It turned out there was a right and a wrong way to marry a duke. Consuelo's wedding had garnered so much negative press in 1895 that in 1903, when May Goelet wed the ninth Duke of Roxburghe, a great effort was made to present the match in an appealing way. The Duke was tall, which helped, and May no shy schoolgirl but a polished young lady who'd had plenty of time to make her choice. Most important, the Goelets saw to it that the (inaccurate) story was put about that the Duke had plenty of money of his own. "I am no fortune hunter," he obligingly told reporters. "I am merely an Englishman who thoroughly believes in American institutions!" The coup was that his mother crossed the Atlantic for the wedding, bringing a sister, Lady Isabel Innes-Ker, to be a bridesmaid and the Roxburghe emeralds to be worn at the wedding. She even gave an affable interview to reporters as she disembarked from the steamer that brought her from London.

THE VANDERBILT-WHITNEY SHOW

Consuelo Vanderbilt was not the only American heiress to wed an English noble at New York's St. Thomas' Church in November of 1895. As early as July, Pauline Whitney had announced her engagement to Almeric Paget, grandson of the Marquess of Anglesey and brother-in-law of Minnie Paget. The Whitney wedding, which took place at St. Thomas' on November 12, invited comparisons to the Vanderbilt wedding of the previous week.

VANDERBILT

- Three hundred police; thousands of onlookers
- Six ropes of flowers from dome, arches of bride roses across chancel; tall fence of lily of the valley and roses at altar rail; balcony hung with orchids; choir screened with palms, etc.
- Walter Damrosch and 50-piece orchestra; 60-voice choir
- Worth dress, five-yard train
- Mrs. Astor
- Five clergy, including Bishop Potter
- Bride weeping, nervous; half a head taller than groom
- None of Vanderbilt clan present

Above: Sherry's, the social restaurant of the 1890s, bedecked for the Vanderbilt-Marlborough reception. Right: Coachmen waiting outside St. Thomas' while Consuelo became a duchess. The awning was to protect her from the prying eyes of the populace.

Left: Some of Consuelo's bridesmaids, from left: Marie Winthrop, Miss Morton, Julia Jay, Katharine Duer and Daisy Post.

WHITNEY

- Two hundred fifty police; "matinée audience" of onlookers
- Four triple Gothic arches of orange leaves and mums, open gate of dahlias and mums; chancel banked with palms 35 feet high, columns twined with vines, mums, etc.
- Nathan Franko and smaller orchestra; opera stars Edouard de Reske and Lillian Nordica
- Worth dress, five-yard train
- Mrs. Astor
- Three clergy, including Bishop Potter
- Bride self-possessed; same height as groom
- Among guests: the George Cavendish-Bentincks, the Joseph Chamberlains, the George Curzons, the Michael Herberts, the Earl and Countess of Essex, and former Pres. Grover Cleveland

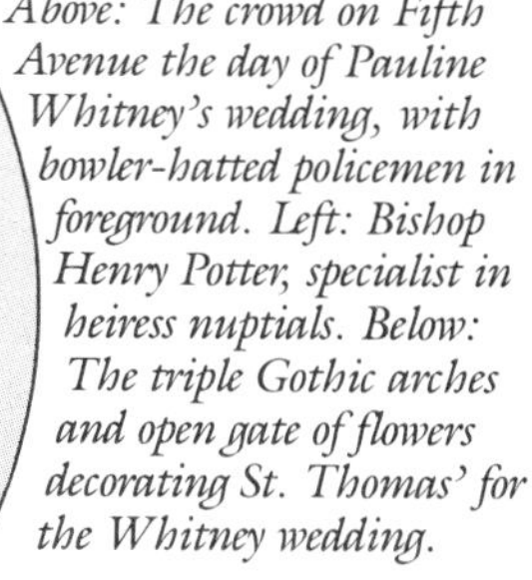

Above: The crowd on Fifth Avenue the day of Pauline Whitney's wedding, with bowler-hatted policemen in foreground. Left: Bishop Henry Potter, specialist in heiress nuptials. Below: The triple Gothic arches and open gate of flowers decorating St. Thomas' for the Whitney wedding.

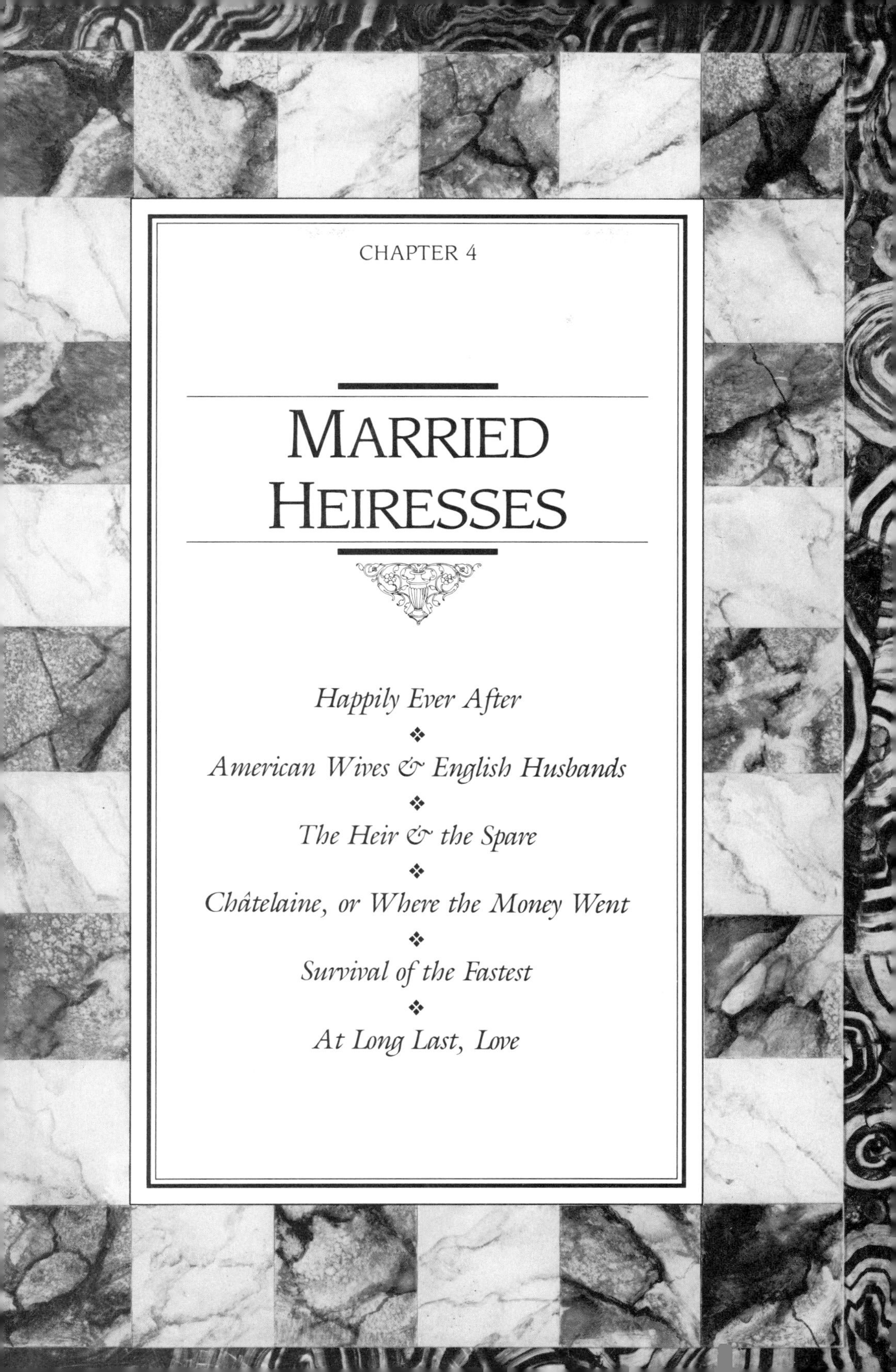

CHAPTER 4

MARRIED HEIRESSES

Happily Ever After

❖

American Wives & English Husbands

❖

The Heir & the Spare

❖

Châtelaine, or Where the Money Went

❖

Survival of the Fastest

❖

At Long Last, Love

HAPPILY EVER AFTER

From the moment she turned at the altar with her heirloom veil draped over the new tiara and swept back down the aisle on the arm of her new husband, the American heiress was starting life all over again. As she stood in the receiving line and heard old family friends archly address her by her new title, she began to feel apprehensive. Exactly what had she got herself into? Only a honeymoon—two weeks in Newport or Long Island, a few weeks more in the south of Europe—stood between her and England and a life she could only guess at.

The convention of the era held that new brides lie low for a while. So when the American heiress was taken back to England, her husband immediately stowed her away on the ancestral estate for a discreet period of adjustment. In other words, she moved in with her in-laws.

"As a rule, people looked upon her as a disagreeable and even dangerous person, to be very suspicious of, if not to be avoided altogether. Her dollars were her only recommendation, and all were credited with possession of them, otherwise what was her raison d'etre?"

LADY RANDOLPH CHURCHILL, on the American heiress

IN-LAW TROUBLE

The first sight of her husband's family, waiting on the great stone steps of the house, told her all was lost. London, the Set and the season were far, far away. She was on their territory now. Her mother-in-law came forward and dutifully kissed her on both cheeks, making sure their bodies did not otherwise touch. The father-in-law and her husband's sisters followed suit, murmuring "How do you do?" This gruff, polite greeting was so unlike the generous, gushing American one. Immediately, the heiress felt homesick and unhappy.

There was no fuss and bother, no excited chatter, no smiling interest in her needs. She was introduced to the staff and then handed over to them

The newly married heiress might find that her in-laws were nicer to their dogs than they were to people.

Bringing Home the Bride

The American bride's most striking indoctrination into her new status came when, once the intimacy of the honeymoon was over, she was brought to her husband's ancestral home. She might have enjoyed the pomp of her wedding, but the welcome extended to her by tenants and citizenry eclipsed any nuptial grandeur. To be sure, the wife of a younger son could simply slip into her new home with a handshake from her mother-in-law and a searching glance from the butler. But for the girl who had married a duke or an earl, the arrival at her new home would be unforgettable.

The train station closest to the house would be draped with flags and bunting and the inevitable close-clustered arches of flowers and leaves—as if for a national holiday. On the platform stood a welcoming committee of local dignitaries headed by the mayor or provost or corporation council, arrayed in the regalia of their rank. The bride, in turn, wore her furs, the regalia of *her* rank. (The Duke of Marlborough insisted that Consuelo wear her famous sables, even though it was March.) The dignitaries made speeches. A bouquet was presented. The bride smiled and perhaps said a few words of thanks. But it wasn't over yet. Outside the station, the crowds began: the townspeople and tenants and the merely curious, turned out to cheer and gawk. When Mary Leiter and George Curzon arrived at Derby after their honeymoon, some 35,000 onlookers thronged the streets and all the church

On the steps of Blenheim, Sunny thanks the tenants for their welcome. Decorations at Woodstock included a maypole in front of the town hall (inset, left) and numerous triumphal arches (bottom).

A pair of Northumberland newlyweds being hauled home by their loyal tenants.

bells pealed at once.

The town was decked as elaborately as the station. Schoolchildren and laborers had the day off, and tenants put on their best clothes to line the route and wave flags. There might be another stop, at a specially erected platform in town, for more speeches and more gawking and more cheering and more bouquets for the American bride. Inevitably, the horses were unharnessed and the young husband's own people drew the carriage to his ancestral home, causing a *frisson* of discomfort in the democratic breast. It was nice that these people were so happy—but must they abase themselves?

By now, the waving and smiling at the crowd might be a bit fatiguing. One might like a cup of tea, or wish to take off one's enormous hat. As the house drew into sight (always a heart-stopping moment), another crowd appeared: the servants and the family, lined up on the front steps, and more tenants down below. More speeches. The butler and the housekeeper, perhaps, wishing the couple well and avowing their service. Presentation of the wedding gift from the household, probably a massive piece of silver. A photograph, or more likely several, would be taken. More smiles and another speech from the bride, who by now was ready to drop from exhaustion.

Finally, in the privacy of her room, she could savor the grandeur and the glory. All those people, all that fuss! The Duke and Duchess of Roxburghe, arriving at Dunbar after their honeymoon, were preceded by pipers, drawn by coast guardsmen, followed by 100 torchbearers to what was, after all, only a subsidiary Roxburghe castle. There were even fireworks! The bridal pomp of the white dress and the "Wedding March" was nothing to it.

And yet, if she gave it any thought, the bride would discover a hard truth. The fuss was about her—but not about her *personally.* As she was to learn, her own identity as an American, as a rich man's daughter, as an individual, was swallowed up in the identity of her husband. "The young lord's wife"—that was what a girl was. His wife, and the potential mother of his heir. The public glee commemorated continuity above all.

> *We have just been staying . . . with Lord and Lady Mandeville—poor little thing, she is so delicate—so utterly helpless—and* most *charming. What a contrast to the Duchess. She cannot endure a country life and is quite miserable. . . .*
>
> MRS. ADAIR to Lady Waldegrave (1877)

Leonie Jerome Leslie might have been forgivably nonplussed by the dour façade of Castle Leslie in Ireland, her husband's ancestral home.

while the rest of the reception party disappeared down portrait-lined hallways and up carved-oak staircases. The new husband went off to see about his horses. Within minutes, there was silence. All was still. The household had returned to business as usual. When the maid closed the bedroom door behind her, the heiress felt quite alone.

LOCAL YOKELS

A day or two after their arrival, the newlyweds began the requisite tour of nearby family and friends. The heiress wore her best visiting dress, prepared by Worth for just this occasion: cut and uncut velvet and satin trimmed with silk and glass beads, topped off with a matching ostrich-plumed hat. A sable boa circled her neck, a sable muff warmed her hands. She was fit to meet the Queen.

Unfortunately, she was meeting "the County"—the area's other long-established, landowning families. These families were not necessarily listed in *Burke's Peerage*, nor were they likely to create much of a stir in London (if, indeed, they ever bothered to go up to London). But their high standing in the insular social order of the region gave them the right to expect to be introduced to the new bride.

Here, the heiress had the opportunity to meet

the fabled English eccentricity in all its glory. Consuelo Vanderbilt Marlborough, for example, was introduced to an uncle who took one look at her sable-lined coat and rang for the butler to fetch all his own furs so they could compare and see whose were better. Maud Cunard was greeted by a family friend seated in a wheelchair, white beard to his knees, top hat on his head, shrieking: "Take her away! Take her away!"

The ones who were not peculiar were haughty. The older women issued instructions on how to behave and the necessity of producing an heir. The younger ones were completely alien creatures—brisk, tweedy, toothy girls with hounds at their heels and keys jingling purposefully at their belted waists. The

Maud Cunard, a woman who always loved sophisticated social life, had trouble adjusting to rural Leicestershire from the very beginning.

The standard of a great house was that dinner for 100 could be given without hiring outside help or bringing in a single piece of china.

heiress couldn't imagine being friends with these girls. Nor could they imagine being friends with her. What sort of girl, after all, married away from home? They didn't for a moment question her desire to live in England. But they did question her ability to so easily dispose of parents and country. Among themselves, they shook their heads and assumed she was an adventuress with a heart of ice.

These were the same girls whom, only months earlier, the American heiress had so effortlessly, so gloatingly bested in the ballrooms of London. Now it was her turn to feel awkward and out of place, the girl standing off to one side, not quite included in the conversation and goings-on. She listened to their flutey tones and rising inflections. She observed their

The miscellany of an English house could be oppressive. Banners, chandeliers, urns and statues decorate the banqueting hall at Knebworth in Lancashire. Inset: an elaborate shell-shaped bed on a wave-patterned dais at Stonor Park, home of Mildred Sherman, Lady Camoys.

knee-high boots and tweed riding jackets with patches at the elbows. And she knew that everything about her was all wrong. Her dress was too showy. Her glance was too direct, her voice slow, unmodulated. Instead of delighted laughter, her funny American phrases drew raised eyebrows from these girls, or worse, furrowed brows and uncomprehending stares. To them, she was speaking a foreign language.

The American heiress realized, in a sudden, awful flash, that the county girl was what she was expected to become. Hers was the accent she must learn, the bearing she must assume, the values and the way of thinking she must make her own. By law she had, upon her marriage, lost her American citizenship. She was an Englishwoman now.

COMME IL FAUT
A lady never "paints." She may discreetly powder her nose in private, but makeup is reserved for the demimonde.

RUNNING HOT AND COLD

An Englishwoman was, first and foremost, a cold woman. The heiress found herself shivering in the middle of the day, *indoors*. Just to survive, she had to wrap herself in large, ugly shawls that ruined the effect of her delectable trousseau. Oh, the happy hours she had spent choosing every article of clothing. Who here would know about silk *ombré* roses and printed faille ribbon and buttercream duchesse satin? Who here cared? Newport heiress Mildred Sherman, as Lady Camoys, simply gave up going to dinner in other people's country houses because she couldn't withstand the arctic temperatures in an evening dress; at least at home she could huddle near the fire swathed in fur. If things got really bad, the heiress was forced to consult her sisters-in-law (of whom there were always plenty) on how to treat the painful sores on her hands and feet. They would explain to the weeping girl about chilblains and the proper way to bind them.

"From my window I overlooked a pond in which a former butler had drowned himself. As one gloomy day succeeded another I began to feel a deep sympathy for him."

CONSUELO VANDERBILT BALSAN, in *The Glitter and the Gold*

Maintaining her formerly impeccable toilette became a trial. Modern bathrooms had not yet penetrated to the interior of the great house. Instead, a tin

The grand corridor at Windsor Castle. Though even ducal homes were rarely as grand as Windsor, American brides had to get used to traveling immense distances indoors.

or copper tub was set before the fireplace in the heiress's bedroom, with the requisite mats and towels and jugs strewn in the vicinity. The heiress had had her own bathroom at home, and a porcelain tub with its very own tap for running hot water. This hauling of jugs of hot water from a kitchen that was yards, even miles of corridor away, by skinny servant girls in ill-fitting, by now somewhat damp uniforms, was just plain primitive. It also diminished the grandeur that was, to the heiress's way of thinking, her part of the marriage settlement.

Barely clean, the heiress emerged from her bedroom, her lavender satin day dress with the woven motif of golden flowers obliterated by a black wool shawl that was more like a blanket. Behind the closet door was the matching lavender parasol, trimmed with bobbin lace. (No point in dragging it with her; she'd only be laughed at.) She was making her daily trek to the library, which she knew to be the one room in the house with a blazing fire in the grate.

But first she had to traverse a vast stretch of dark, unheated, vacant rooms. She lit her way with a candle, for neither electric nor gas lighting had been installed in the great house. In these rooms, England's grandeur was all but defunct. The crusty drains and musty closets, drafty passages and leaking ceilings, frayed upholstery, bare floors, discolored damask, the faded, tarnished, blemished, warped and wobbling decrepitude dismayed her—and testified all too clearly to why she and her bags of American money were there.

The American heiress had known only the best in life. Her home had had the prettiest furniture, central heating and electric light, thick carpets and flush toilets. Everything was perfectly kept up and looked after, without a crack or spot anywhere. It unnerved her to find that behind all the polish of her husband's manner and dress existed such crudeness. She had had no idea that civilization could be so uncivilized.

FAMILY LIFE

Or so boring. London had been such an enchanting, entertaining city, so much more exciting than American cities. Life did not stop at 11 P.M. in London as it did in New York; there were always more parties to go to, more dances, more dinners. But she wasn't in London anymore. And here in the English outback life seemed to have stopped altogether. In the great house, the ticking of clocks could be heard all day long—there was no family noise to drown it out. The heiress had been raised in organized chaos. Her home had been alive with the uncoordinated comings and goings of family members. There was always an enthusiastic stream of guests bustling off to the next activity. And all the servants were at the beck and call of each and every clamoring family member.

Breakfast en famille: *another dull beginning to another endless day.*

In her husband's family home, ruled by an imperturbable, centuries-old routine, the servants were as mindful of hierarchy as their masters and mistresses. Each had specific, inflexible duties. The

COMME IL FAUT
Gentlemen eat oatmeal standing up.

Butlers ironed the newspapers, to set the ink.

A ROOM WITH A VIEW

❖

It all looks magnificent until one looks a little closer. The priceless (Louis XIV clock) and the ridiculous (Lady Anne's toleware urn) side by side, dwarfed on the massive mantel; the William and Mary firescreen next to the elephant-foot stool; the Louis XVI fauteuils facing the silly inlaid table Uncle Rupert brought back from Goa. Everywhere, relics of the family's grand past: battle standards, armor, portraits, a globe showing just where the 4th Earl was governor-general. Also everywhere, evidence of neglect: the massive Ming vase, chipped; the glorious plaster ceiling, water-damaged; the exquisite Aubusson carpet, stained by some dog—possibly the dog who has done the upholstery so little good. The heiress will be expected to right many of these wrongs, but she will not be permitted to remove the dog's bed.

George Curzon's father, Lord Scarsdale, whom Mary once referred to as "a despot from the thirteenth century."

heiress soon trained herself not to speak to the footman; she was supposed to ask the butler to ask the footman to bring in more coal for the fire. She could not pop down to the kitchen to ask Cook for a sandwich or request that the tea tray be brought up at two in the afternoon instead of four; at two, the serving girls were helping with dinner preparations or down in the laundry room or upstairs putting clean linen on the beds. The staff had its schedule, its list of tasks to be done at certain times on certain days, and were not to be blithely interrupted by impertinent Americans.

In order to fall in with these regulations, the husband's family moved as one through the day. Everyone got up at the same time each morning, ate at the same time, and sat together after dinner every night in the one room with a fire, waiting for one of the ticking clocks to strike eleven. Then, as a group, everyone climbed the stairs to bed.

HALF HORSE, HALF ALLIGATOR

At least in her bedroom the heiress didn't have to listen to any more absurd comments from her husband's provincial family. Consuelo Vanderbilt, Duchess of Marlborough, described how Lady Blandford, after blaming her failure to appear at her son's wedding on his refusal to pay her passage to America, made "a number of startling remarks, revealing that she thought we all lived on plantations with Negro slaves and that there were red Indians ready to scalp us just around the corner." Lord Scarsdale, Mary Leiter Curzon's father-in-law, made comments like "I suppose you don't know how to make mince pies in America" and "I suppose you don't have sea fish." Price Collier, the American journalist, maintained that there were people in provincial England who pictured the typical American as "half horse, half alligator, with a dash of earthquake." The heiress soon grew weary of trying to explain America to her English family, of trying to be simultaneously tactful and proud. She particularly loathed the moment when some sign of well-bred behavior on her part was rewarded with the backhanded compliment: "I should never have thought *you* an American."

When her in-laws weren't being mean, they were being weird. Eccentricity, the heiress discovered to her horror, might be found in her new family as well as in County neighbors. Mary Curzon claimed, for instance, that Lord Scarsdale was "very fond of examining his tongue in a mirror"; he also hated to hear his name and would turn his back on anyone who said it aloud. Calling him "the most tyrannical man I have ever met," Mary described how he mercilessly bullied his many daughters about getting married even though he refused to allow any young men to visit them at Kedleston. Lord Scarsdale, in his eccentric way, did try to extend kindnesses to Mary, but she was by that time too heartsick to accept them. "He wished me to call him Papa," she wrote to her parents, "but I have never brought my lips to it, for anyone less like my own beloved Papa I cannot imagine." Mary sounded so morose in her letters that her parents arranged alternating visits to England

"I cling like an old ivy leaf to my beloved family. I positively live for the posts when I sit here alone day in and day out."
MARY LEITER, LADY CURZON, in a letter to her parents

The south front of Kedleston (below left) and the marble hall. Robert Adam did some of his most superb work here, but it is hardly domestic.

throughout her early married life. "My dear Mother," she wrote to the woman who had once been such a liability, "you made the evening hours so sweet by sitting there with me before dinner. I love the chairs you sat on, and try to see you there, and my eyes fill with tears."

TO LOVE, CHERISH AND OBEY

The American heiress who looked for succor to the man she loved—or had married, anyway—was probably out of luck. Not at all like his American counterpart, the British husband did not want to hear about her little unhappinesses. He did not consider it his duty in life to be ever solicitous of her needs and whims. He also seemed to have expended his entire romantic repertoire on their courtship. The loss of Daddy meant she was deprived of the right to buy something new every day. This was bad enough. But lack of an American husband meant she was also robbed of the hugs and kisses, the daily I-love-yous, the repeated compliments on her appearance that were standard procedure in at least the early stages of American marriages.

Any intimacy the heiress had gained with her husband during their honeymoon was dispelled as he took up his former life. *He* didn't have to lie low. He went straight back to his clubs, to his sport, to playing cards and racing horses. He also returned to his mistress. Just because he was married was no reason to give her up; on the contrary, thanks to his new wife's money, he was now better able than ever to maintain a second household.

Comme il Faut
A lady must never look into the windows of gentlemen's clubs.

The heiress was only eighteen, perhaps twenty. She felt herself closed off from home and loved ones, surrounded by resentful dowagers, narrow-minded neighbors, haughty servants, soft-headed sisters-in-law and forbidding, unbending patriarchs. She was in a house that was too big, too old and, most of all, too, too cold. Things looked grim. Was life not going to be, as she had always been led to believe, fun?

AMERICAN WIVES & ENGLISH HUSBANDS

Sooner or later—and the sooner the better—the American heiress was released from her country-house prison. No more vast galleries of dark, glowering ancestral portraits, no more lonely midday rides, no more deadly drafts in the dining room. And no more in-laws. She moved to London. She got her own house. Depending on the level of Daddy's generosity, she now occupied a mansion in Grosvenor Square or a more modest dwelling in the still very fashionable side streets of Mayfair or Belgravia.

So far, so good. But the American heiress had a few more shocks in store. For one thing, she would actually have to run a household.

WIFE: "I thought you told me you were well off before you married me."

HUSBAND: "I am sure of it now, my dear!"

MANY AGAINST ONE

Running a household was something the American heiress did not know how to do. Too often her formative years had been spent in hotels and train stations. She was acquainted with houses mostly as a visitor. She hadn't any idea how the menu was arrived at, the clean linen produced, the dust made to disappear. This was the great gap in her otherwise superior education. The practical knowledge in household matters was "one of the triumphs of English education," wrote Lady Randolph Churchill, and armed the married woman "with the sinews of war." So the American heiress went into battle on the home front practically weaponless.

She remained the pure-minded, middle-class American princess, always expecting to be looked

The heiress who had so happily taken ship for London might be terribly homesick for the familiar streets of New York.

after, with no skills for looking after others. Florence Gordon-Cumming had read once in a novel, according to her daughter Elma, that "American women could always produce dainty little meals on chafing dishes. She was American; she bought a chafing dish; the only thing she omitted was learning to cook."

In 1897 New York's famous Patriarchs had to be disbanded because of too much pressure from outsiders.

This kind of ignorance inevitably led to a servant problem. The servants, as many as fourteen or fifteen in a London townhouse, recognized the heiress's inexperience immediately. And pounced on it. If they could, they would run the household. Mary Curzon had a terrible time of it. She was reduced to sending her plate back to the kitchen several times over in order to get enough food on it and, since she dared complain about the bills, to standing with the cook in the shopping queues in order to see for herself what the prices were.

As an American heiress, Mary was unaccustomed to command. Demand had always been her strong suit. She had no experience as the moral captain of the serving forces—what American servants did on their own time had always been their own business. But in England the American heiress found that she was supposed to oversee their personal conduct on and off the job, swiftly dismissing serving girls who came in late or footmen who gambled. So a good portion of the time she had expected to spend riding in the Row and changing her clothes was instead taken up with advertising for, interviewing, writing references for, training, supervising and dispensing with the services of servants.

"*English servants are* fiends. *They seem to plot among themselves. . . . I should like to hang a few and burn the rest at the stake.*"

MARY LEITER, LADY CURZON, to her mother

LADIES SECOND

And all this just to keep her *husband* happy. Because in England, horror of horrors, the domestic world revolved around the man of the house. "The home is not a playhouse for the women and their friends, nor a grown-up nursery for the mother and the children," American journalist Price Collier wrote of the English household, "but a place of rest and comfort in which the men may renew their strength."

The schedule of the house, the disposition of the furniture, the menus, the guest lists—all were overseen by the English husband. He was, unlike the American husband, a man of leisure with the time to consider the minutiae of daily living. Consuelo Vanderbilt, Duchess of Marlborough, wrote wearily that she and the Duke "seemed to spend hours discussing the merits of a dish or the bouquet of a vintage." Beneath her boredom is surprise: even a girl raised to be an aristocrat could not quite believe that a man should take an interest in such domestic trivialities.

Leonie Jerome and Jack Leslie the month before they were married. Unlike a hard-working American, the English husband would have all the time in the world for a midday ride.

The American heiress thus had to learn what the English wife took for granted: that she was there to produce heirs, run the household to her husband's pleasure, entertain as he deemed necessary and otherwise stay out of his way. She was not to interfere with his plans or make demands on his bank account. Somewhat akin to the servants and the hunting dogs, she was just another fixture in his congenial, convenient universe.

The domestic importance of the English husband and the relative diminution in power of his wife made it difficult for the American heiress to produce the one household effect for which she had received training: the "managed" husband, the most crucial and original invention of the American wife. This English aristocratic husband refused to become the obliging, confined figure so familiar in the American landscape, whose circumstances led American heiress husband Sir William Harcourt to comment that "the next great revolution in America will be the war for the emancipation of the American husband."

THE SILVER LINING

On the other hand, while the American husband had little say in the home, the American wife had no say outside it. Sure she ruled the roost—but that was all she ruled. She was sheltered, petted, adored, given her head, but she was also, essentially, shut out. American social rules were so restrictive that it was extremely dangerous for a society woman to assume any larger role. Public life, even philanthropy on anything but the most minor scale, was considered unseemly and therefore forbidden.

Lady Orford, née Louisa Corbin of New York. She shared her husband's passion for travel (they visited Japan, Ceylon and the West Indies), and together they once caught a 183-pound tarpon.

In England, the American heiress found to her delight, the wife was, in surprising ways, allowed into her husband's life. Finally the contrast between American and English married life began to work in her favor. All the trouble with in-laws and servants and uppity spouses began to pay off. The English aristocratic husband might have more to say in the domestic sphere, but she might have some say in his world, too. Lord and Lady Orford, for example, the instant her inheritance materialized, went together on a trip around the world; in Florida they both became tarpon-fishing aficionados, and upon returning to England they co-authored a book on the

Tea on the terrace at Parliament. The heiress who wed an aristocrat married into the governing class of England. Many women found this intimate exposure to politics thrilling.

> *"A girl, born and bred in the backwoods of some Western State, will adopt the manners and customs of her husband's country to such an extent that, after a few years, she might pass as of his nationality."*
>
> LADY RANDOLPH CHURCHILL

subject. George Montagu, somewhat to the dismay of his American mother-in-law, talked over with his wife Alberta what he planned to say at his next board meeting and pestered her to find out "whether the last chapter of the book he was writing on the history of locomotives had her approval."

This sharing, this overlapping of spheres of influence, was the saving grace of the international marriage. After all her girlhood freedom, marriage for the young woman who stayed in America offered very little more in the way of liberty than she already had and considerably more in the way of restrictions and responsibility. Her carefree days of social stardom ended. She was suddenly chaperone material. She must cede first place, in the matter of fun, to the next lot of pretty young heiresses. In London, however, where the unmarried girl was so restrained, so confined, so relentlessly supervised, the married woman came into her own.

Invitation to a ball given by the Corporation of the City of London for Victoria's Diamond Jubilee. Civic duties weren't all tedious.

BLESS MY SOUL! THAT YANKEE LADY

"There is no doubt that life in England is on much larger lines, and more full of occupation for the women of the leisured classes than that of any other country," wrote Jennie Churchill. "Everything is open to them if they have the ability." Jennie certainly had the ability, and she proved an invaluable ally in her husband's political career.

Randolph had become a controversial orator of renowned skill. The cry "Randy's up" in the corridors of the House of Commons would send members scuttling for their places. No one wanted to miss a blistering word, least of all Jennie. Long before it was fashionable she listened to Commons debates from the Speakers' Gallery, her interest all the keener since she helped Randolph prepare his diatribes—in fact was thought to have drafted some of them.

In the early 1880s, with the founding of the Primrose League, Jennie had a political career all her own. The League's purpose was to promote Conservative views among all classes of society. Jennie traveled throughout England, opening branches (called "habitations") and signing up recruits, and became an adept and popular speechmaker in her own right.

Such speechmaking from a society woman would not have been acceptable in America, where public speaking was for suffragettes and religious fanatics. Carrie Nation could make speeches; Caroline Astor could not. This was the most glaring instance of the different life of an English wife. Back home, politics and the upper class did not mix; in England, politics and the upper class were the same thing. New York society did not contaminate itself with the acquaintance of U.S. Senators. But in London it was possible to hear government discussed, the way Somerset Maugham swears he once did, as a matter between friends: "Jimmie can have India, Tom can have Ireland and Archie can have the Exchequer. . . ."

In 1885 Lord Randolph Churchill was ap-

Cartoonists continued to follow the American heiresses' activities in their new land. The legend on the balcony reads: "Reserved for American Wives of English Lords."

Jennie; the Ladies' Gallery at the House of Commons; a caricature of the Commons Lobby in 1886 (Lord Randolph, second from right in central group).

pointed secretary of state for India. Since he was too busy to campaign for reelection to his seat in the House of Commons, Jennie took over the job and canvassed the Woodstock constituency in her sister-in-law's wicker tandem, decorated with ribbons in brown and pink—Randolph's racing colors. Her success as a vote-getter inspired the opposition party's Sir Henry James to declare he would introduce "a new Corrupt Practices Act. Tandems must be put down; and certainly some alteration made in the means of ascent and descent therefrom. The graceful wave of a pocket handkerchief will be dealt with in committee." From New York, Leonard Jerome wrote his wife: "You have no idea how universally Jennie is talked about and how proud the Americans are of her."

By the general election of 1886, her reputation was such that the local press covered an appearance on behalf of another candidate with the reference "Lady Randolph, ably supported by Lord Salisbury's nephew, Mr. Balfour, M.P." That summer she and Randolph were in their heyday. Randolph became Chancellor of the Exchequer and Leader of the House of Commons. They were invited to stay with

"... *the fact is I* loathe *living here. It is not on account of its dullness,* that *I don't mind. . . . It is no use disguising it, the Duchess hates me simply for what I am—perhaps a little prettier and more attractive than her daughters.*"

JENNIE JEROME CHURCHILL, writing from Blenheim

JENNIE GETS PINNED

After vigorous work in promotion of medical aid to Indian women, Jennie Churchill hoped to be awarded the Insignia of the Order of the Crown of India. Randolph refused to speak on his wife's behalf, but the Prince put in a good word with his mother and Jennie was summoned to Windsor Castle. Her invitation included information on what train to take (the 1:10 from Paddington) and a note on what to wear (bonnet and morning dress, gray gloves) from a lady-in-waiting; a room would be made ready for her, presumably for tidying up lest a stray lock of hair disturb Her Majesty.

Received by the Queen, one of the Queen's daughters and a lady-in-waiting, Jennie made the correct curtsy without tripping or tipping over. Her dress, however, was so embroidered with jet that the Queen had difficulty affixing the pin and stuck it into Jennie's shoulder before placing it properly.

When, after curtsying, Jennie told the lady-in-waiting that she feared she'd been awkward, that lady said: "You need not be troubled. I know the Queen felt more shy than you did."

After meeting Jennie, the Queen wrote in her Journal: "Lady Randolph (an American) is very handsome and very dark."

The next day Jennie received a note, perhaps from the same lady:

My dear Lady Randolph,

I hope you got home quite comfortably yesterday, and took no cold. The Queen told me she thought you so handsome, and that it had all gone off so well.

Believe me ever,
Yours truly,
Jane Ely

Jennie's next move was a visit to M. Worth, who obtained a dress fabric that exactly matched the pale blue of the ribbon to which the pearl-and-turquoise cipher was attached. Clearly, there was no sense in getting pinned by the Queen if a new Worth gown was not part of the bargain.

the Queen at Windsor in early July. When Jennie drove through Hyde Park, her carriage was mobbed. She and Randolph were asked everywhere, the London season hummed with their names.

The sensation of popular worship, of social acclaim, of being near what in that era seemed to be the center of the universe, was heady indeed. Unfortunately for Jennie, her husband's irrational resignation from the Cabinet, just as he seemed on the brink of becoming England's next prime minister, brought that sensation to a sudden, heart-breaking end.

Jennie found out that Randolph had left the government when his letter of resignation was reprinted on the front page of *The Times*. It was the first she'd heard of it—they'd been to the theater the night before and he had whispered not a word. White with disbelief, she carried the paper into his room. Randolph looked up at her. "Quite a surprise for you," he said, and went back to his own paper. Their heyday was over.

"We are sorry Randy is in the muck," wrote *Town Topics*, expressing the general view, "less for his own account than for that of the gallant American girl he had the luck to marry. She had worked so hard to popularize him and forward his ends." Jennie's dream of becoming one of the most important women in the world was over.

Lord Randolph as Chancellor of the Exchequer. He was already very ill with syphilis, and his flashes of temper could be frightening.

LEITER OF INDIA

Jennie loved campaigning, loved public speaking, loved going about knocking on doors and exchanging words with the butcher and the brewer. But Mary Leiter Curzon loathed these tasks. She was the typical stoical political wife, smiling on the outside, cursing within. While an opposition newspaper noted that Curzon owed his 1895 electoral victory "far more to the winning smiles of his American wife than to his own speeches," Mary wrote home from Plymouth: "The people are an ungrateful lot of stupid cockneys,

Mary and George Curzon, early in their marriage. She had an even more difficult adjustment to face than most heiresses.

provincial to a degree, and very stupid." And, a few days later, "The people are an idle ignorant impossible lot of ruffians. I smile at them and look sweet because it would be the end of us if they knew all that I thought." Moreover, her father was paying for her misery: Levi Leiter picked up the tab for all George Curzon's campaign expenses.

When, having won, the Curzons went to London, Mary was rewarded for her suffering with a husband who thought only of work. George was not interested in going out in society, and Mary didn't dare keep him home once in a while for fear she would be accused, as Margot Asquith was, of hurting her husband's career. But Mary soon discovered that George's career and her sharing in it meant the ripen-

"*Oh! the ladyships! I feel like a ship in full sail on the high seas of dignity!*"
—MARY CURZON, on becoming a baroness after George's appointment as viceroy of India

ing of love. Her lonely, homesick years ended on August 11, 1898, when George was named viceroy of India, fulfilling his lifelong ambition.

It was in India, where the ever-driven George made her his chief confidant, that Mary came into her own. She'd always adored her husband—she once described how, when he came into a room, she felt "that the band is playing the Star Spangled Banner and that the room is glowing with pink lights and rills are running up and down [my] back with joy." Now he began to adore in return. If he had originally chosen Mary for a mixture of reasons—her beauty, her quiet grace, her wealth—in which there was little hint of genuine affection, he came during their time together in India to love her very much.

Her finest qualities flourished with his devotion. Though she suffered constantly from severe headaches after the birth of their first child, she never gave in to them. She pushed on with her duties as vicereine, as tough-spirited as any English colonial wife. When the political waters in England began to darken, she became George's envoy, returning to London all alone to give his side of the story, to size up the atmosphere, listen to the whispers and report back to him. He could trust her for that—she was the only person he did trust.

If Mary Curzon had a fault, it was that her devotion to George ("she had subordinated her personality to his," wrote Consuelo Marlborough, "to a degree I would have considered beyond an American woman's powers of self-abnegation") prevented her from criticizing him. His obstinate, self-righteous, uncompromising manner of ruling, brilliant though it may also have been, eventually ended in disaster for both of them. George was forced to resign in ignominy from his unprecedented, self-imposed second term as viceroy. But that didn't alter the fact that Mary's position as vicereine of India made her the highest-ranking American, man or woman, in the history of the British Empire.

George (now Lord) Curzon in his viceregal robes. He enjoyed the nearly oppressive splendor of the post.

DREAMS THAT MONEY CAN BUY

Lord Curzon in later life became Waldorf Astor's political patron, when Astor stood for Parliament in Plymouth just as Curzon once had. And, like Mary, Astor's American wife campaigned for her husband, though with considerably more enthusiasm. According to her biographer, Nancy Astor's campaigning "greatly strengthened her sense of the tie between her native and her adopted lands." It was a sentiment shared by most of the political heiresses.

And there were plenty of them. The pay of a member of the House of Commons was negligible, the outlay considerable. The American heiress wife bought fine horses, grand houses, and lots and lots of votes. She bought a twenty-four-carat setting for the diamond of her husband's talent. For the most part, the American money that did not go into renovating great country houses went into supporting Tory politicians. (It was almost always Tory politicians—American heiresses had not come to England to shake up the status quo.) It seems only fair, perhaps even predictable, that all the dollars and energy and verve contributed by American heiresses to British politics should result in Nancy Astor's becoming, in 1918, the first woman to take a seat in the House of Commons. And then in Winston Churchill's finally avenging his father's name and his mother's disappointment by becoming, in 1940, "that half-breed American" prime minister of Great Britain.

Unlike Mary Curzon, Nancy Astor was a born campaigner, reveling in the rough-and-ready wisecracking of canvassing. With her elegance and her quick tongue, she entranced voters.

THE HEIR & THE SPARE

It was standard procedure for a new bride to become pregnant promptly. On this point, at least, American and English attitudes were in harmony. Children were an important part of a marriage, and all but the most ignorant of girls would expect to be expecting in short order. (Poor Florence Garner was in for a shock. On her wedding night, Sir William Gordon-Cumming told her: "I won't come in to say good-night unless you want me to." In all innocence, she replied: "Oh, that would be nice." What followed astounded her.)

Americans were always surprised at the occasional crudeness of the English upper classes, however. And on the subject of providing an heir, they could be remarkably blunt. "Your first duty is to have a child," Consuelo Marlborough was told by the Duke's grandmother, "and it must be a son, because it would be intolerable to have that little upstart Winston become Duke. Are you in the family way?" Constant reference would be made, pressure exerted. The blushing bride must realize that married life offered upper-class Englishmen few advantages over a bachelor existence. They married because it was time to beget an heir.

Continuity, again, was the goal. The noble families had not survived revolutions and plagues and capricious monarchs only to die out, at the peak of Empire, from inanition. They hadn't cleverly preserved their estates just to see them pass into the hands of some South African mining millionaire. The system of entail, legal bedrock, was based on the solid expectation that a family would have male heirs. (This

Consuelo Marlborough was seven months pregnant when she laced herself into this costume for the Devonshire House Ball. A lady needn't retire from society until her "interesting condition" could no longer be hidden.

expectation persists in England, and aristocratic young brides like Diana, Princess of Wales, are usually pregnant within a year of their marriage.)

Custom, needless to say, played a huge part in this most central of family events. When Helena Zimmerman, wife of the ninth Duke of Manchester, was pregnant for the first time, the family seat had been rented out. Manchester tradition dictated that heirs be born under Kimbolton's roof, so the tenant obligingly vacated for the birth. Unfortunately, Helena produced a girl.

Stressing the relative importance of the eldest son, Sargent placed the Marquess of Blandford (holding his father's sword) at the center of his portrait of the Marlboroughs; his younger brother stands off to one side.

“*The trouble with you is that you have the worst blood of two continents in your veins!*”
LADY ASTOR, to Winston Churchill

BOYS, BOYS, BOYS

It was a pity, but a girl wasn't good enough. Jarring though it might be to the fine flower of American girlhood, the point was to have a boy—an "heir male of the body" to carry on the name, the title, the family glory. A girl was simply another mouth to feed, a liability to be dressed and dowered. Elma Gordon-Cumming wrote that her parents went to Italy when she was six weeks old, "presumably to recover from the shock of my being a girl." (Her mother's ignorance of physical matters had extended to childbearing; until the moment of Elma's birth, she expected the baby to emerge from her navel.) The Italian voyage was haunted, for Florence, by the knowledge that she'd have to endure the whole appalling ordeal again.

Minnie Paget, with great efficiency, had twin boys: Arthur George and Wyndham Reginald.

And possibly again and again. Many Englishwomen had suffered uncomplainingly through multiple pregnancies in order to produce the requisite heir, particularly in the early Victorian era of high infant mortality. Lord Randolph Churchill's mother bore eleven children. Six were girls; three sons died in infancy, leaving Randolph and his older brother Blandford (the eighth Duke of Marlborough). Having done her duty so spectacularly and stoically, it was no wonder she insisted that Consuelo follow suit.

The alternative scarcely bore contemplation. A younger son or his younger son would inherit. That was hardly the point of being a duke. May Goelet's slowness to produce a son caused all kinds of disturbance in the Innes-Ker family. Four years after her marriage, the Duke's younger brother, Lord Alastair, married his own American heiress, Anna Breese, and it was widely assumed that the Roxburghes' heirlessness added to Lord Alastair's attractions. The Duchess finally consulted a gynecological specialist in Vienna, to whom, rumor had it, the Duke paid £1,000, with another £1,000 to come if a male baby

Nanny occupied an elevated position in the servants' hierarchy, ruling over her own staff of nursery maids and subsidiary baby-nurses, ordering all the nursery meals, and deeply resenting maternal interference.

was born. In the event, May turned up trumps and produced the Marquess of Bowmont in 1913, ten years after her marriage. (The specialist's contribution, evidently, was to eliminate sugar from her diet.) The *Daily Sketch* reproduced a large photograph of Lady Alastair Innes-Ker framed in black with the superscription "Our sympathies." She was quoted as saying, "The Goelets might as well have the title as they've got the dough, too."

Starting so late, May failed to provide the backup younger son, but it was usual to try for at least two boys—"the heir and the spare," as Consuelo Marlborough phrased it. Thus the title wouldn't fall into the hands of some distant cousin in the Colonies or (heaven forbid) die out altogether. "You are a little brick!" said her mother-in-law when Consuelo gave birth to Lord Ivor (the spare). "American women seem to have boys more easily than we do!"

Producing an heir made everyone happy. When the little Marquess of Bowmont was born in London, the Roxburghe tenants lit bonfires, rang bells and made merry all over the Borders of Scotland. More inhibited but no less sincere was the rejoicing on the part of parents and grandparents. When a son was born to Alberta Sturges, Mrs. George Montagu (later Countess of Sandwich), her mother wrote to her stepfather: "A stream of carriages has been here all day. *All* the Montagus came to lunch. Lady Agneta writing from here to the Queen, Princess Christian and the Queen of Greece. It is touching to see their joy. It is a very great event for them all. When we telephoned Agneta to notify her she wept aloud through the telephone saying: 'Dear Berta how grateful we are for a boy, it is so like her!'"

NANNY DEAREST

Once the nursery was well populated, the pressure was off, yet the satisfaction of being a mother might be diminished by the English system of childrearing.

Mary Curzon with the Hon. Cynthia Blanche (in her lap) and the Hon. Mary Irene. She had another daughter, the Hon. Alexandra Naldera, in 1904.

"My sister and I were brought up like European royalty."
CORNELIUS VANDERBILT IV. in *Queen of the Gilded Age*

America, with its emphasis on youth and its constant awareness of children as the hope of the future, made much of its offspring. Alva Vanderbilt's elaborate involvement in her children's education was not unusual. In contrast, Consuelo remarks wistfully about her sons that "what between the governess, the head nurse, and the groom with whom they rode their ponies, there seemed little time left for mother." Her children were swept up into the English system. The nursery wing, in a separate corner of the house, was an independent establishment run by Nanny. (How different from her own bedroom at 660 Fifth Avenue, separated from her mother's only by a spiral staircase.)

Nanny ordered the nursery meals, bossed the nursery maid, and periodically delivered the children, on their best behavior, for parental inspection. "Chil-

Alva Vanderbilt's idea of a ducal cradle was a gilded baroque specimen that she'd seen in an Italian palazzo; she had it copied for Consuelo's offspring.

Jennie and Winston, whom many considered spoiled by his mother's American liberalism. Inset: Jennie with both sons (Jack is at left).

dren in my early days," remembers George Cornwallis-West, Jennie Jerome's second husband, "were looked upon partly as a nuisance and partly as a kind of animate toy, to be shown, if they were sufficiently attractive, to callers." The young rarely accompanied their parents to London for the season, and never on country-house visits. They stayed at home with Nanny. Children were taught their letters and their numbers; more important, they would learn to ride (Sir William Gordon-Cumming's children had their first full-size horses at age five) and shoot. The heir might be gradually introduced to the ways of the estate that would be his one day: the ninth Duke of Manchester had to earn his allowance by working for the estate mason, carpenter and stud-groom.

Further training inculcated further values—sportsmanship, chivalry, self-control. Individuality was sacrificed to teamwork, intellectual curiosity to physical prowess. For boys, these processes frequently took place on the playing fields of Eton or Harrow, where they were sent as early as age six. Here they spent twenty hours a week at games like cricket and football, sparing scanty attention to the large doses of Latin and Greek that dominated the curriculum. (George Curzon, whose bad back exempted him from games, was one of the rare few who actually developed intellectual discipline.)

"To have a grandson heir to a dukedom is considered a greater distinction than to be President of the United States."
JUVENAL

SPARE THE ROD

But American mothers didn't necessarily want English children with English values. They didn't want their daughters turning into those unfashionable, tongue-tied sticks whom they'd bested in the marriage stakes. They didn't want their boys, for that matter, to be just like their husbands. They *loved* their children, and the remoteness—or worse—of the English upbringing seemed criminal. Mrs. Goelet, lunching with the architect Edwin Lutyens, was "shocked" by a discussion of spanking boys at school. Though Jennie Churchill has often been accused of neglecting Winston, she was, from the English point of view, a hugely indulgent mother. Daisy, Countess of Warwick, relates with some surprise how Jennie, "true to her American training . . . did not check Winston when he asked questions or argued with her."

Americans, in fact, were thought to spoil their children. Sir Michael Culme-Seymour, Alberta Sturges' son-in-law, remembers the American Lady Hood visiting her son Alexander at school. She would swoop down on him, all warm hats and extra

Leonie Leslie's first photographic effort produced a portrait of Jack Churchill's posterior.

blankets and pressing concern about his health. When she left, the other boys would taunt him: "Oh, darling Alexander, oh, darling, darling..." Seymour Leslie writes how his mother (née Leonie Jerome) would greet him: "Why you *Dear Thing*! How perfectly *lovely* to see you back from school! I can't *wait* to hear your news of it! Tell me all about it, sit on the sofa there and don't leave anything out!" Leslie, to be fair, characterizes this as a "Jerome impulsive demonstration" and adds that his mother would instantly return to her correspondence.

"I Baptize Thee Albert Edward"

Having produced a child, one had to have him or her baptized with due pomp. Ostensibly religious occasions, baptisms also provided an opportunity to confirm some temporal ties. In the Anglican Church, children customarily have at least three godparents, who promise to take responsibility for their spiritual upbringing. In effect, they act as auxiliary parents, so marshaling an impressive group at the baptismal font is wholly desirable.

In England, of course, nothing was more desirable than having royalty in that lineup. And though it was an honor one would never dare request, His Royal Highness (later His Majesty) quite enjoyed being a godparent and tendered this signal favor to a number of Anglo-American offspring.

Viscount Mandeville, son of Helena Zimmerman and the 9th Duke of Manchester.

This was often a peak experience for the American parents of the bride: to think of being so intimately linked with royalty! For the heiresses, their husbands, their parents both English and American, the baptism might be their finest hour. The American wife's money and charm had, more often than not, secured this mark of royal esteem; her American health and vitality had produced the much wanted baby boy. The heiress might never be more popular or happier than at that very moment when her duty was done. In fact, the only fly in the ointment was that, if Edward was a godfather, one had to name the child after him, which

Some mothers, like the widowed Belle Wilson Herbert, took such exception to the English child-rearing practices that they had their children raised in the States. Belle's twin boys were much admired at Newport for their looks and their polished "English" manners. Another pair of twins, the Burke-Roche boys, were also brought up in the States, at the wish of their grandfather, Frank Work. Indeed, their American education was a term of his will: their mother, Frances Burke-Roche, would inherit none of Work's money if the children even visited England.

It was the fashion for London matrons to bring a child along for the afternoon drive, but only one—and only if he or she was extremely presentable.

meant (until 1901, when he dropped it) calling the child Albert. The 10th Duke of Marlborough went through life as "Bert."

ROYAL GODCHILDREN

Albert Edward Stanley Paget, *b.* 1879 to Minnie Stevens and Capt. Arthur Paget; godson of Edward VII.

Albert Edward Naylor-Leyland, *b.* 1890 to Jeannie Chamberlain and Capt. Herbert Naylor-Leyland; godson of Edward VII.

George Vyvyan Naylor-Leyland, *b.* 1892 to same parents; godson of George V.

Albert Edward William John Spencer-Churchill, 10th Duke of Marlborough, *b.* 1897 to Consuelo Vanderbilt and 9th Duke of Marlborough; godson of Edward VII.

Alexander George Francis Drogo Montagu, 10th Duke of Manchester, *b.* 1902 to Helena Zimmerman and 9th Duke of Manchester; godson of Queen Alexandra.

Lord Edward Eugene Fernando Montagu, *b.* 1906 to same parents; godson of Edward VII.

The Chapel Royal in St. James's Palace, venue of truly privileged christenings.

Lady Alexandra Naldera Curzon, *b.* 1904 to Mary Leiter and 1st Lord Curzon; goddaughter of Queen Alexandra.

Alexander Victor Edward Paulet Montagu, *b.* 1906 to Alberta Sturges and George Montagu (later 9th Earl of Sandwich); godson of Queen Alexandra.

William Edward Harcourt, 2nd Viscount Harcourt, *b.* 1908 to Mary Ethel Burns and 1st Viscount Harcourt; godson of Edward VII.

Edward John Sutton Ward, *b.* 1909 to Jean Reid and Hon. John Ward; godson of Edward VII.

George Victor Robert John Innes-Ker, 9th Duke of Roxburghe, *b.* 1913 to May Goelet and 8th Duke of Roxburghe; godson of George V and Queen Mary.

CHÂTELAINE, OR WHERE THE MONEY WENT

We had an Indian tent set up under the cedars on the lawn where I used to sit with our guests. We always brought out the *Times* and the *Morning Post* and a book or two, but the papers were soon discarded for conversation. . . . Sometimes we played tennis or rowed on the lake, and in the afternoon the household played cricket on the lawn. The tea table was set up under the trees. It was a lovely sight, with masses of luscious apricots and peaches to adorn it. There were also pyramids of strawberries and raspberries; bowls brimful of Devonshire cream; pitchers of iced coffee; scones to be eaten with various jams, and cakes with sugared icing." And, because the writer is Consuelo Vanderbilt, Duchess of Marlborough, the table was set with porcelain and silver and heavy monogrammed damask. White-wigged footmen in knee breeches stood at a discreet distance, waiting for a command, and the golden stone of Blenheim Palace loomed like a fantastic overscaled backdrop. Blenheim Palace, seven acres under one roof, the only non-royal palace in England, seat of the dukes of Marlborough. Whose châtelaine, in 1896, was a nineteen-year-old American heiress.

The Marlborough coat of arms, various parts of which appeared on household objects from the silver to the horse blankets in the stable.

Consuelo, having married a man who had come into his title, was spared the strain (to be blunt) of waiting for a papa-in-law to die. For the girl who wed the heir to a peerage, rather than a peer, marriage offered a curiously hybrid state. She was called Lady Acheson, for example, but was not a peeress since the title she bore was a courtesy title on loan, as it were,

Blenheim's west front, with the two levels of water terraces installed under Sunny's discerning eye.

from her father-in-law's selection of titles. If her husband was in Parliament, he was in the House of Commons (to which he had to be elected, not always a simple matter). And though she might go to the family's seat in the country, it was only as a guest.

But eventually Papa-in-law died. And suddenly the world opened up for the heiress. She was no longer the understudy, learning the role by observation; now she was the principal! It wasn't just the title, or remembering to sign oneself, for example, "Consuelo Manchester" instead of "Consuelo Mandeville." Moving up in rank, the heiress got to see a whole new group of faces at the dinner table. She would get her hands on the coronation robes; she would get her hands on the family jewels. And the keys of the house, finally, would be hers.

"There are uses for American heiresses and their money after all."
Lord "M" to Lord and Lady "G," on approaching Blenheim Palace through its renovated park, in Consuelo Vanderbilt Balsan's *The Glitter and the Gold*

WHO'S THE BOSS?

Not that taking possession was always easy. Even if the heiress married a man in possession of his title, somebody had already been keeping house for him. Somebody (a sister, an aunt) had been hostess for his parties, had given the servants their orders. And that somebody might not like being displaced. Consuelo Marlborough recalled a tussle she had with her husband's aunt, Lady Sarah Wilson, who had acted as Sunny's hostess during his bachelorhood. At one of the first dinner parties given by the young couple,

Marriage to a duke did give Consuelo a measure of self-possession.

Lady Sarah Wilson, Sunny's aunt and Consuelo's nemesis, was bested with a few soft words.

Lady Sarah, as had been her custom, gave the other ladies at the table the signal to rise and leave the gentlemen to their port. Consuelo's neighbor, Lord Chesterfield, exclaimed, "Never have I seen anything so rude; don't move!" But Consuelo gently put Lady Sarah in her place, by asking if she were ill—"There surely was no other excuse for your hasty exit." After that genteel but public rebuke, Consuelo had no more trouble from Lady Sarah.

Along with establishing social dominance, a young peeress had to establish her command over the servants, over the atmosphere—even, in a way, over the past and generations of predecessors. In Edith Wharton's *The Buccaneers,* the young Duchess of Tintagel has a daunting mother-in-law who quietly but deeply resents her relegation to dowager status. And "she had the awful gift of omnipresence, of exercising her influence from a distance; so that while the old family friends and visitors at Longlands said: 'It's wonderful, how tactful Blanche is—how she keeps out of the young people's way,' every member of the house-hold, from its master to the last boots and scullion and gardener's boy, knew that her Grace's eye was on them all, and the machinery of the tremendous establishment still moving in obedience to the pace and pattern she had set."

The cost of Sunny's costume for the Devonshire House ball appalled even Worth, but the Duke knew exactly what he wanted and insisted on it—to the last stitch of embroidery. As a poor bachelor, he could never have afforded it.

But what if the old pace and pattern were distasteful or, more likely, simply too slow for the American châtelaine? What if she wanted her dinners served in an hour instead of in two? What if she wanted to have luncheon in the Sèvres Room when only she and her husband were at home? What if she wanted to ride before breakfast? "Her Ladyship"—meaning her mother-in-law—"always rode in the afternoon" might well be the answer. And one would have to stare down the relevant servant and say, "Just so. But *I* will ride in the morning."

Some of the struggles for the upper hand were fueled by inertia or the English habit of adherence to routine. The Dowager Duchess of Tintagel, in *The*

> "*They have their pride, their rules of precedence, their code; they are fixed, immovable, unconcerned about other careers, undisturbed by hazy ambitions, and insistent upon their privileges, as are all other Englishmen. . . . To the average American these distinctions may be merely laughable. Let him come to England and keep house for a year and he will find them adamant.*"
>
> PRICE COLLIER, on English servants

Buccaneers, is deeply disturbed by her daughter-in-law's habit of "asking the reason of things that have nothing to do with reasons—such as why the housekeeper doesn't take her meals with the upper servants but only comes in for dessert. What would happen next, as I said to her, in a house where the housekeeper *did* take her meals with the upper servants?"

That was just the kind of practice so deeply mystifying to Americans and so deeply ingrained in the English. And it was one manifestation of a fact that the heiress, if she was going to be a successful châtelaine, must grasp: English servants had a culture all their own. As a young bride running her London house, an American heiress had skirmished with the phenomenon of the English servant. But the staff assembled to manage a town house was only an adumbration of the large, loyal staff required in a noble family's country seat.

THROUGH GREEN BAIZE DOORS

The great country houses, indeed any of the prosperous houses in England, were split in two. The front of

The servants at Hinchingbrooke, home of the Earl of Sandwich, a year after Alberta Sturges married his heir. Twenty-one people was not a large indoor staff.

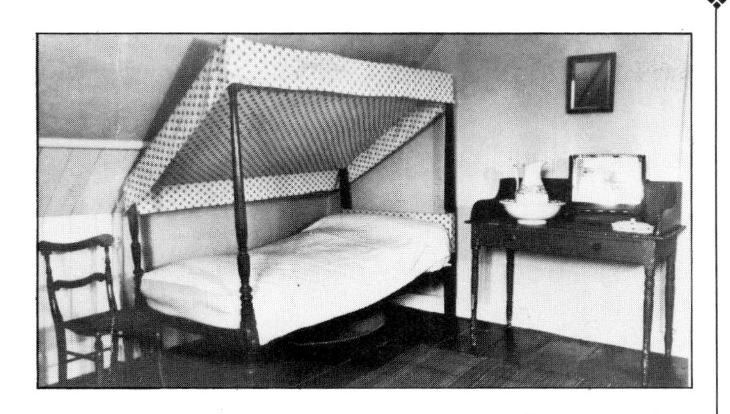

Servants' quarters, with fourposter designed to fit under the eaves.

the house, all high ceilings and lustrous silver, a profusion of flowers and a well-bred hush, brocade and Turkey carpets, ironed newspapers, and out the window a splendid view, was occupied by the master and his family. They were like the actors on a stage. At the ends of corridors, in a corner by the dining room, up near the fifth-best bedroom, were swing doors covered with green baize or felt and studded with upholstery nails. These were the doors to the backstage area, the servants' quarters.

The servants' sector mirrored the front of the house, but with complications. There were more rooms for special purposes, separate cells for brushing boots and pressing coats, cleaning knives and decanting wine, storing china and polishing silver. Extra twists and turns were built into the warren of narrow, low-ceilinged corridors to prevent food smells from drifting out to the front of the house. And the whole backstage area was a swarm of activity, a carefully regulated and intricately structured machine.

Just as the servants' area was a baroque variation on the family's living quarters, so was the servants' hierarchy a more complex version of the family structure. It had to be more complex, since there were usually three or four servants for each family member. Thirty or forty indoor servants would be usual in a grand house, with as many more working outdoors.

The chef at Blenheim, whenever he wanted to show his displeasure with Consuelo, would serve ortolans to her guests for breakfast because he knew she considered this mortifyingly nouveau riche.

UPSTAIRS, DOWNSTAIRS

One of the shocks for the new American bride was having to deal with English servants. She must always be aware of the hierarchy—and of its principal members.

THE BUTLER

In charge of the front of the house. Too elevated for menial tasks (decanting wine was the most physical he got), the butler oversaw the menservants and the silver.

THE HOUSEKEEPER

In charge of the bedrooms and the servants' quarters. Matters of cleaning and household maintenance (linens, inventories) and the housemaids' morals were the housekeeper's bailiwick, a huge ring of keys her badge of office.

THE CHEF

In pretentious houses, always French and paid outrageously. He was often locked in a vendetta with the housekeeper.

FOOTMEN

Responsible for all the actual lifting and carrying in the front of the house:

A lady's beast of burden.

calling cards on silver salvers, a tray of tea, newspapers for the gentlemen. Footmen also waited at table, accompanied Milady on errands to carry her packages, and stood around wearing livery and looking decorative on formal occasions. The best ones were easy to look at.

The master interviews his housekeeper, in an 1882 cartoon.

MILADY'S MAID

Entrusted with washing and arranging Milady's hair, mending and refurbishing and cleaning her clothes, and helping her in and out of them. She also took care of the jewels and accompanied Milady on visits.

THE HOUSEMAIDS

Numberless faceless creatures who did all the cleaning and dusting in the front of the house (at the crack of dawn before the gentry were awake) and in the bedrooms (when their occupants were down at meals).

THE VALET

Responsible for keeping Milady's husband neat. Besides laying out and caring for his clothes, the valet made travel arrangements, loaded his guns at shoots and boasted about him in the servants' quarters.

As a group, they were an alien race to Americans. Nobody could provide silent, self-effacing comfort like the English servant, it was true. Service was, in England, a perfectly respectable profession, and the largest single occupation in the country. In America, an Irish maid might be energetic, pert, and gone in a week in search of greener pastures; waiting on somebody else, in a democracy, was strictly an interim occupation. But in England one's footman might be the son of a butler, had probably begun service as a hall-boy at the age of twelve, and confidently looked forward to being a butler himself someday. As American observer Price Collier put it, English servants "have their pride, their rules of precedence, their code; they are fixed, immovable, unconcerned about other careers, undisturbed by hazy ambitions, and insistent upon their privileges, as are all other Englishmen."

"I am not enjoying myself as I have spent the entire week answering advertisements and looking for nurses and I haven't found one, and I am awfully cross."
BELLE WILSON HERBERT, to her sister Grace Wilson

When cars became fashionable, the coachman (in top hat) had to learn to drive. Next to him is Mrs. Bradley Martin. Behind them, in uniform, is the Earl of Craven with his wife Cornelia.

Helene Beckwith, as Lady Leigh, was a discreet châtelaine who made only those changes she felt utterly necessary.

Today Stoneleigh contains a red velvet sofa reputedly given to Helene Leigh by Louis Napoleon, whom she had met as a débutante at the Imperial Court in Paris.

A WOMAN'S HOME IS HER CASTLE

The American châtelaine had to accustom herself to this powerful backstairs culture. Efficiency must be jettisoned in favor of convention—the usual American concession in England. But she no longer had to resign herself to discomfort. The moment she got the chance, she tackled bringing the family seat up to American standards. Helene Beckwith, a New Yorker married to the third Lord Leigh at the advanced age of forty-three, had a large closet at Stoneleigh Abbey converted to hold a bathtub so she wouldn't have to traipse down the hall to her bath, clad only in a wrapper, under the servants' gaze. Mrs. Bradley Martin, mother of the young Countess of Craven, was responsible for installing bathrooms at Hamstead Marshall, while Flora Sharon's alterations at Easton Neston included new plumbing. (Her great-grandson has had some of the taps gilded, which would surely have pleased Flora.) The Honourable Mrs. Charles Coventry, while renting Lord Camoys' Stonor Park (as Lily Whitehouse of Newport, she had been a childhood friend of his wife, Mildred Sherman), reportedly installed an oil heater from a steamship.

Lady Camoys, exhibiting the usual American concern about hygiene, later had all the posts cut off Stonor's fourposter beds and the hangings removed because she thought they were germy.

Once the plumbing had been improved, the American châtelaine could do some cosmetic work. Occasionally, this fell into the category of wishful thinking, as in the case of Flora Sharon's medievalization of Easton Neston. Lady Camoys put a porch on red-brick, medieval and Elizabethan Stonor. Having grown up in the multi-porched Newport house that H.H. Richardson designed for her father, William Watts Sherman, she may have had visions of long, sunny afternoons spent drinking lemonade in the beech-bound valley of the Chiltern hills near Oxford. The family took meals on the porch when the weather permitted, but there was little to remind anyone of Newport. Vivien Gould's husband, Lord Decies, bought the medieval (with eighteenth-century modifications) Leixlip Castle after their marriage; Vivien installed Tudor mullions in place of the Georgian Gothic windows and paneled several rooms in oak. Women who had married "the tone of time" wanted their homes to look properly old.

In some cases, this return to the old style took place outdoors, and with no small sophistication. At Blenheim, for instance, the formal setting planned by the architect Vanbrugh had been swept away by Capability Brown in the eighteenth century. Though Brown's landscaping (including the celebated "drowned bridge") was lovely, taste had changed by 1895 and his destruction of the formal gardens seemed tragic. After replanting a *grande allée* of

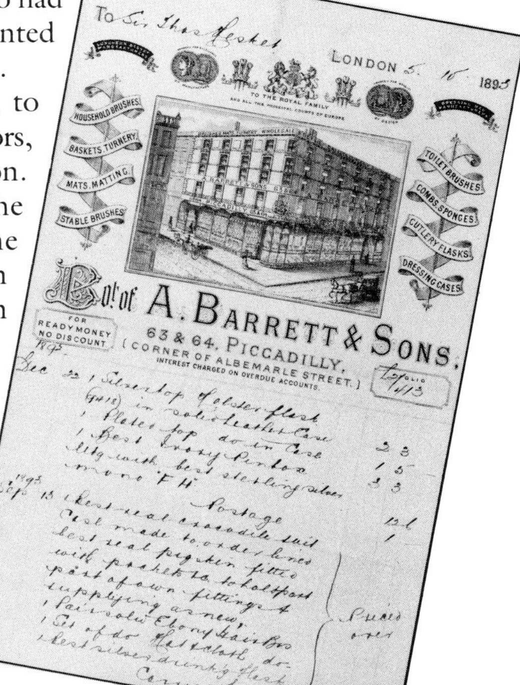
To Sir Thos Hesketh

LONDON 5. 10 1893

TO THE ROYAL FAMILY AND ALL THE PRINCIPAL COURTS OF EUROPE

HOUSEHOLD BRUSHES
BASKETS, TURNERY
MATS, MATTING
STABLE BRUSHES
TOILET BRUSHES
COMBS, SPONGES
CUTLERY, FLASKS
DRESSING CASES

Bo^t of A. BARRETT & SONS,
63 & 64, PICCADILLY,
(CORNER OF ALBEMARLE STREET.)
INTEREST CHARGED ON OVERDUE ACCOUNTS.

FOR READY MONEY NO DISCOUNT

FOLIO 413

1892 Dec 22
Postage
1893 Sep 13 1 Best real crocodile suit case made to order lined best real pigskin
1 Best silver drinking flask
Carried forward

A bill to Sir Thomas Fermor-Hesketh for, among other items, a "best real crocodile suitcase made to order lined best real pigskin." The bill, dated October 1893, includes items carried over from December of 1892. Gentry seldom paid promptly.

A Place for Everyone

Not belonging to any class could be an advantage in England—unless the English chose to rub one's nose in it, which they did every day when they lined up in order of rank to go in to dinner. Precedence, in England, was a legal right, and violation of this right was actionable. Of course, it never came to that, but tales abounded of huffy peeresses elbowing each other at doorways. The highest-ranking man went first, matched with the highest-ranking lady who wasn't his wife, and so on down from duke to baronet's younger son.

Should there be two guests of the same rank at dinner, the one whose title was older (say, an earldom from 1630 as opposed to 1765) would go first, or "take precedence." The same was true of their wives. Thus American heiress Beatrice Mills, married to the 8th Earl of Granard, would take precedence of fellow American Eloise Breese, whose husand was only the 2nd Earl of Ancaster. But Eloise would go before her sister Anna, Lady Alastair Innes-Ker, whose husband was only the younger brother of a duke.

It seemed odd to Consuelo Marlborough that she, a mere girl of nineteen, should precede older, wiser and more beautiful women. But the strict rules of precedence produced much odder situations: fathers taking their daughters in to dinner since the girls were the highest-ranking women there; young boys called down from the schoolroom to sit at the head of the table; a general yielding place to his aide-de-camp because the latter was a lord. At a country-house party, one had the same dinner partners for the duration of the stay, no matter how dull or odious they might be. Only new arrivals with new ranks would cause a musical-chairs shift at the dinner table.

Unfortunately, Americans had no rank unless it was diplomatic or acquired through marriage. No matter what their position at home (in the States, seating usually went according to "consequence," which tended to mean income), they would go at the end of the line and sit at the bottom of the table.

A party going down to dinner, two by two.

elms to the north of the palace, Sunny set about restoring the gardens. With French architect Achille Duchêne, he planned an Italian garden with symmetrical beds of dwarf box on the east side of the palace. The supreme labor, however, was the water garden constructed on the west front, where the land sloped steeply to the lake. Two terraces, each with pools and statuary, led the eye gently down to the lake below in a logical and beautiful sequence. While the look of the alterations at Blenheim depended in large part on Sunny's aesthetic judgment, which was unusually refined, Cornelia Craven relied rather on her subconscious in planning her "Dream Garden" at Hamstead Marshall. It literally came to her in her sleep. The next morning she gathered her gardeners together and had them follow her, marking her steps in whitewash to outline the beds she had dreamed of.

All the American money in the world couldn't make Gordonstoun cheerful.

The most typical alterations by the American heiress châtelaine involved transporting the Louis fixation to the English countryside. Appalled by the dinginess and dilapidation of her new home, many an heiress spent thousands of dollars to make it splendid. Poor, unhappy Florence Gordon-Cumming tried to console herself by tarting up the two Gordon-Cumming houses: the vast, gloomy Gordonstoun (which, according to Florence's elder daughter, was full of *oubliettes* and dungeons, and which has now been turned into a school whose most famous alumni are Prince Philip and Prince Charles) and the far more cheerful Altyre. In the former, she installed electric light, the requisite bathrooms, an Italian garden, new paneling and, since she was very religious, a reredos in the chapel. Altyre she rebuilt and redecorated almost completely—twice. New gunrooms, nurseries and schoolrooms were constructed, as well as an elevator, a chapel, and stables so large that later one barn was turned into a squash court. The bathrooms and corridors were paved with mosaic, her bedroom filled with Florentine furniture, all cherubs and putti. The dining room had parquet floors, red walls and a white

When he finally inherited Kedleston in 1916, George Curzon embarked on a renovation program that included installing bathrooms. With characteristic attention to detail, he lay down in all the bathtubs (first lining them with newspaper) to make sure they were long enough.

Left: Duchess of Roxburghe May Goelet, painted by Edward Hughes. Above: Floors Castle, the Innes-Ker family seat, where some of May's coroneted bed and table linens are still in use.

scrolled ceiling. Sir William's sister was so horrified by these changes that she never went back to Altyre. And, as pointed out by Florence's daughter, the redecoration, done "in the richest style . . . has all lasted."

The same is true at Floors Castle, which the Duchess of Roxburghe, May Goelet, completely transformed. The red damask with which she covered the walls of the Needle Room, the pale pink brocade upholstery in the main salon, the gilding, paneling and, most important, Brussels tapestries that her mother had carted to Ochre Court every summer—these remain as luxurious-looking as ever.

Sometimes the decorating techniques employed by the American aristocrats—scavenging from the Old World to furnish the New—were put to good use by American heiress châtelaines. Mary Smith, niece and heiress of the famous financier "Chicago" Smith, married, in 1887, a solicitor from Scotland named George Cooper and lived quietly enough in Elgin until she inherited £4 million. The Coopers then bought a town house in Grosvenor Square and Hursley Park in Hampshire, which they proceeded to enlarge and renovate. In the ballroom, the *boiseries* (French wall carvings) came from art dealer Joseph Duveen and framed the inevitable set of Boucher tapestries. The Inner Hall was paneled with woodwork from the chapel at Winchester College (since returned to Winchester), while the boudoir paneling came from a house in Yorkshire. The drawing room was all white and gold, with cornices and columns and pilasters, mirrored doors and brocade armchairs, chandeliers and a few pieces of priceless porcelain. It could have been the drawing room of any *nouveau riche* in the United States or in England. In the end, the American heiress with sufficient worldly goods was able to refashion her surroundings. She could achieve a truce with the servants and physical comfort, perhaps even elegance in the family home. But all the piped-in hot water in the world might not make her happy as an English noblewoman. That, the most important adjustment, depended entirely on her inner resources.

"The Triumphs of the Gods": late seventeenth-century tapestries at Floors, where Bacchus, Flora, Neptune, Venus and Apollo gambol all over the walls.

Although the 8th Duke of Roxburghe had been portrayed to New York's press as a wealthy man, his home required considerable sprucing up.

A hefty percentage of much of this home-improvement expenditure found its way into the pockets of art dealer Joseph Duveen.

COSTUME CHANGES

Bearing in mind the exigencies of one costume change, the fact that three or more were required daily accounts in one swoop for what Victorian ladies did with their time. A lady of high fashion might dress as follows during the London season.

EARLY MORNING

Skin-tight riding habit (black, navy blue, dark green) from Busvine; gloves, boots, hat, veil, riding crop, knot of flowers in buttonhole.

LATE MORNING

"Modest" dress for interviewing housekeeper, shopping, writing letters. Relatively plain, merino or serge, subdued color, neat but not gaudy; sleeves always long, to emphasize that one is above household chores.

LUNCHEON

Visiting dress. Silk, grosgrain, sometimes brocade; trimmings more elaborate than for morning dresses, from upholstery-look bobbles and chenille of the '80s to delicate chiffon ruffles fashionable twenty years later. Bonnet or hat, skewered to elaborate coiffure often augmented by someone else's hair. Parasol, reticule, mantle, gloves, etc.

Above: Jennie Churchill, stunning in a riding costume. Left: Flora Fermor-Hesketh, in sporting attire; Below: Daisy Warwick, with son Maynard, in a simple morning dress.

Cornelia Craven, shortly after her marriage, in an afternoon dress.

AFTERNOON

For paying calls, visiting dress as above; same for strolling in Hyde Park. For garden parties, Henley, Ascot, cricket at Lord's, polo at Ranelagh, lighter fabrics (silk, chiffon, the famous Edwardian laces), more frivolous bonnet trimming. For yachting, the strictest of tailor-mades, with ornament limited to buttons and braid.

DINNER

Neckline cut down but still modest (known as a "half-high bodice"); sleeves at least to the elbow. Fabrics dressy (satin, chiffon) but not grand.

RECEPTIONS

High-necked, long-sleeved but formal dress, possibly with a train; luxurious fabrics. A Worth reception dress from 1892 was bright blue with black stripes, trimmed with lace and jet. Dignity the keynote.

THEATER

Demure attire. Black or dark blue, with high neck and long sleeves, to discourage attention from the public at large. If a ball was on the evening's schedule, so was a change of clothes.

OPERA

Velvets and brocades, pearl trimmings, antique lace, and (in the 1900s) glittery appliqués. Safe in their boxes, society women pulled out all stops. *Décolletage*, often dramatic (*"commence trop tard"* was a censorious phrase used of necklines in the '90s). Long gloves. Jewels for matrons. Flowers in hair. Fur wraps.

BALLS

As above, but fuller skirt and perhaps showier lining to train (which one picked up for dancing). Gold lace rather than white; metallic threads and jewel trimmings; richer colors such as imperial purple. If royalty were to be present, a married lady wore her tiara. (One's maid waited in the dressing room to reposition one's headdress or tend to a torn frill.) The splendor reached its apogee at court balls, where women had to compete with men in uniform (all that gold braid). They managed.

Lady Grey-Egerton, née May Cuyler, ready for a ball with gloves, fan and train.

SURVIVAL OF THE FASTEST

A loving husband might smooth her way, but by and large the success of an American heiress in aristocratic England depended on her character and her expectations. Some girls moved easily from heiress to peeress. Others found the transition a great, ultimately unsuccessful struggle. The key to success was the individual heiress's mix of audacity and innocence. The American peeress would need her audacity to take on a life for which she had not been trained, to assume her place in society without undue commotion but nevertheless with confidence, to maintain the freshness and vitality, pluck and common sense that had got her there in the first place. But the innocence that was an element in her freshness often contained the seeds of her eventual disappointment.

MARCH OF ANGLOMANIA
Henry Poole & Co., the Prince of Wales' tailor, also made clothes for William Collins Whitney, J.P. Morgan and William K. Vanderbilt. Poole accepted new customers only by letter of introduction from an old customer.

INNOCENTS ABROAD

Most of the American heiresses, no matter how extravagantly rich their families, were raised on solid bourgeois values. The self-appointed American aristocracy was actually nothing more than an ornate version of the middle class. Men worked for a living; women took care of the home and family. Inherited money, in America, would always be tainted. To inherit one's money was to cheat in the great American game of self-determination.

A rustling, elaborate but *clean* prosperity was the American goal. Bizarre behavior and unconventional liaisons were not countenanced by the American aristocracy. Sons were not expected to take mistresses

Charles Dana Gibson captures the sadder side of the comedy he was so adroit at depicting.

when they came of age. They were supposed to enter the family business or in some other way make themselves useful. Marriages were not dynastic alliances but respectable romances. Of course, the American aristocrats, like the English middle class, had hopes of seeming aristocratic, of acquiring the aristocratic manner. But they wanted nothing to do with the accompanying mores.

In her book on Rosa Lewis, proprietress of the Cavendish Hotel, Edwardian daughter Daphne Fielding points out that it was "particularly fascinating that she knew who really were the fathers of one's friends." Which, no doubt, it was. But that sort of attitude, let alone that particular circumstance, was inconceivable to the American, even the American in high society. The lightheartedness of the statement, as well as the practice it implied, was anathema to the American social code. Discreet illegitimacy, in the land of the free, was unthinkable.

"England is all right for splendor, but dead slow for fun."

CONSUELO YZNAGA, DUCHESS OF MANCHESTER

CALIFORNIA GIRL

Nonetheless, it was a situation the American peeress would almost certainly come across, not only in the families of her friends, but in her own. Her capacity to recognize and tolerate such fuzzy—at least by middle-class standards—moral boundaries might very well be the final, crucial feature in her much vaunted adaptability.

There was a streak of Old World ease in the way Flora Sharon took to the looser morals of aristocratic England.

There were heiresses who seemed to be natural aristocrats, who married into the Marlborough House Set and quickly, gladly, adopted its manners and mores. They seemed born to the life of the hunt and the house party. They were not frightened by *louche* old ladies with too much makeup and middle-aged men who made passes. They adored gossip and flirting, were amused by rakes and dandies, wanted life to be a carnival and eventually, naturally, fell into deep, complicated extramarital love affairs.

Flora Sharon, for instance, married to Sir Thomas Fermor-Hesketh, was an uninhibited California girl who loved to hunt and was much admired for her style in the saddle. Her Anglomania was of the most primitive sort, expressing itself in her conversion of the drawing room of her husband's lovely Nicholas Hawksmoor house (c.1700) to an Olde English extravaganza. Her concept of her new country had to do with stuffed bears, King Arthur, suits of armor and exposed beams. Baroque elegance she spurned. Her decorating scheme was exactly what could be expected of the daughter of a disreputable U.S. Senator who had at one time been accused of murder. It was also exactly the sort of ignorant philistinism for which the English aristocracy has been so deservedly renowned.

When her husband began to bore her (his main interest remained extensive, expensive sailing

In the end Flora preferred independence from Fermor-Hesketh (inset) and Easton Neston, choosing instead to live at picturesque Rufford Old Hall.

Hawksmoor's plans for Easton Neston probably included symmetrical wings like those at Blenheim, but the Fermor-Hesketbs ran out of money and consequently owned a manageable house.

expeditions like the one he'd met her on), Flora launched herself on a series of affairs. The Prince of Wales, for instance, was a frequent visitor at Easton Neston, giving rise to all kinds of flattering rumors. Eventually Flora preferred to live apart from her husband, leaving Hawksmoor's stern symmetry for Rufford Old Hall, another family property, which, with its medieval Great Hall and hammer-beam roof, was much more her kind of house anyway.

SEPARATE BUT EQUAL

Flora Sharon had discovered the other great benefit of married life in aristocratic England. Married couples could share spheres of activity to a degree not possible back home. Conversely, if they so chose, husband and wife could lead quite separate lives. They could each pursue their own interests with their own friends according to their own schedules.

IN THE PUBLIC DOMAIN

he American heiress, caricatured, drawn, described and discussed with increasing frequency in the popular press, finally became a stock figure of fictional romance.

Notable among the drawing-room comedies and operettas centered around the heiress were American playwright Winston Churchill's *Title-Mart* and Abel Hermant's *Les Transatlantiques,* though these were outshone by the Victor Herbert operetta *Miss Dolly Dollars* and George Edwardes' 1909 *The Dollar Princess,* which was also produced in Berlin. (*Die Dollarprinzessin,* an Austrian production, and *El Imperio del Dollar,* the Spanish version, were probably related.)

Though Henry James and Edith Wharton both gave the American heiress careful literary consideration, lesser lights were also intrigued by her. Mrs. M.E.W. Sherwood, an etiquette writer, had the first crack at the phenomenon in her book *A Transplanted Rose* (1882), which is full of useful tips such as how to dispose one's train neatly over the feet upon sitting down. *Altiora Peto* (1883), by Lawrence Oliphant, features characters such as Mrs. Clymer and

The Dollar Princess *ran for two seasons in New York.*

Lord Swansdowne; Altiora herself is the untamed American. *Miss Bayle's Romance* (1887) and its sequel, *An American Duchess* (1891), by W.F. Rae, are based on the story of Jeannie Chamberlain. Society novelist Mrs. Burton Harrison's *Anglomaniacs* (1890) is the wittiest of the genre. *An American Girl in London* (1891), by Sara Cotes, features a Chicago girl traveling alone in England and is really a guidebook with a skeleton of a plot. Gertrude Atherton, a Californian, wrote several novels on the theme, among them *American Wives and English Husbands* (1898), which deals with a California girl's disillusionment in England, and *His Fortunate Grace* (1897), a cynical tale of a poor duke and a plain Chicago heiress.

Finally, in the 1910s, Charles and Alice Williamson made a cottage industry of the American heiress, publishing a series of light romances in which rich and beautiful American girls motor all over Europe and after many adventures marry handsome English lords. False identities, tourism and adventure add to the social appeal; *Lord John in New York* (1918) was even made into a movie, bringing the American heiress to the silver screen.

Thus Jennie Churchill could travel in a party with the Prince of Wales to shoot at an estate in Hungary with Randolph nowhere in sight. Or Randolph might take off for Africa with a group of male friends while Jennie made the round of country houses. They would write to each other, of course, and confer on matters of mutual concern—Winston's education, importunate tradesmen, politics. But at some point that was mutually, wordlessly arrived at in so many aristocratic marriages, they would go their separate ways. They were, in the English view, severing no bonds. They were merely making the alliance more flexible.

In some instances, the turning point was reached rather quickly. Although *Burke's Peerage* covered Katharine McVickar's tracks in later years, its 1880 and 1881 editions are frank in their unembellished recording of embarrassing dates. Katharine, from a good New York family, initially married Charles Grantley Norton but apparently, upon arriving in England, felt she'd made a mistake. Charles' nephew John Richard Brinsley Norton, the fifth Baron Grantley, was not only the titleholder but much younger than her husband.

In November of 1879 Katharine was about to

COMME IL FAUT
Gentlemen do not smoke in a lady's presence unless invited to do so. A gentleman who is smoking while out for a walk must instantly jettison his cigar if he meets a lady along the way.

The 1909 Midsummer Fair Fete, benefiting a London children's hospital, and other charity events provided an outlet for some American women's energy.

give birth to a child, not by her husband but by Lord Grantley. Since the all-important question of succession was raised by this situation (if the child was male, would he be eligible to inherit the title?), the first marriage was swiftly annulled and a second arranged to take place shortly thereafter. Katharine became Lady Grantley only five days before having issue—alas, a girl. The early contretemps didn't unnerve her, and society eventually forgot about it. In later years, Lady Grantley enjoyed quite a success hostessing late-night parties from her rented house in Piccadilly, where high-stakes card games were the chief—but not the only—attraction.

NOT MAKING IT

Comme il Faut
When out driving with his mistress, a gentleman places her at his left hand so that everyone he meets will know she is not his wife.

Other heiresses were neither as hardy nor as worldly as Jennie Jerome or Flora Sharon or Katharine McVickar. These heiresses' disillusionment was all the more profound because their innocence was so genuine and their Anglomania so heartfelt. England was supposed to be gentle, regal, ancient and calm. And correct. Above all, correct and proper. There wasn't anything more correct and proper than England and the English.

Such heiresses had never heard of men having mistresses, hardly knew that such women existed. Consuelo Marlborough remembered discovering the existence of the *demimonde* on her honeymoon in Monte Carlo. She wondered who were the beautiful women at the Hôtel de Paris, accompanying acquaintances of her husband's, and only after repeated questioning learned that "these were ladies of easy virtue whose beauty and charm had their price." She must not appear to recognize the men, Sunny told her, "even though some of them had been my suitors a few months before." It was the sort of etiquette rule an aristocratic English girl, though she might not speak fluent French like Consuelo, already knew.

The unfortunate Florence Garner was emblem-

The house party for the Prince of Wales' visit to Blenheim in 1896. Mary Curzon sits on the left of the Prince (center); Jennie Churchill and Consuelo are at the far left.

atic of the American innocent abroad in a society she couldn't understand and a way of life she couldn't adjust to. She married the classic type of high-living clubman, Sir William Gordon-Cumming, once described by the *Sporting Times* as "Possibly the handsomest man in London, and certainly the rudest." The marriage was inauspicious right out of the starting gate—the wedding took place in June of 1891, just as Sir William was making a forced exit from English society.

Gordon-Cumming had been accused a year earlier, by his hosts at a house called Tranby Croft, of cheating at cards. The Prince of Wales was staying at the house and sitting in on the game. In order to avert a scandal—the hosts were livid, Sir William vehemently protested his innocence—Gordon-Cumming signed a paper admitting that he had cheated. In return, the other guests agreed to keep quiet about the supposed breach of honor. But someone (usually identified as Daisy, Countess of Warwick, or the Prince himself) couldn't resist spreading such a good story, and it was all over English society in a matter of three days. The outraged Gordon-Cumming insisted on clearing his

> *"Everyone is doing the same old thing—just flirting, and dining, and dawdling."*
>
> MARY LEITER, LADY CURZON, in London, writing to her husband George in India

After September of 1890, Tranby Croft was no longer the name of a house but the name of a scandal.

name by bringing the matter to court—breach of contract—which meant the Prince had to take the witness stand for the second time in his career. For dragging His Royal Highness into court, Gordon-Cumming was banished from society.

Florence Garner thought her Bill was innocent, and she was gullible enough to believe he wanted to marry her for love. So she stuck by him in his hour of darkness, though he came to her directly from the courtroom to try to release her from the engagement. She wouldn't be released, and on June 10, 1891, the workmen installing a new organ at Holy Trinity, Sloane Street, had to stop banging for half an hour while a small, subdued party stood at the altar. Florence, in a gray dress and black hat, had procured the special license. Sir William wore a frock coat, pearl-gray gloves and a gloomy expression. They were

Sir William Gordon-Cumming testifies in court, while His Royal Highness listens with displeasure.

married by the curate and then hurried away. Three days later, *The Times* recorded that "Major and Lt. Col. Sir William Gordon-Cumming, Bart., is removed from the army, her Majesty having no further occasion for his services."

Florence did her best. She made brave attempts at giving house parties in huge, gloomy Scottish Gordonstoun. But she couldn't get the hang of it. When a house guest tried to make love to her, she demanded that her husband order him out at once. Sir William, who had made a career out of making passes at young married women, only replied: "My dear child, don't be so silly. You must learn to take care of yourself."

Poor Florence. Eventually Sir William brought a pair of girls to stay at Gordonstoun as his mistresses. Florence's response was to turn to religion. She got very fat and stopped going into society. As daughter Elma later explained, Florence and her two sisters (Lita, married to the Marquis de Breteuil, and Edith, wife of the Danish Count von Moltke Huitfeld), owing to "fastidious prejudices over which they had no control, were totally unfitted to the milieu in which they lived."

THE INVALID OPTION

For some heiresses, the discovery of the naughtiness beneath the aristocratic hauteur was too much to bear. Alberta Sturges Montagu, always a little on the pure-minded side, took to her bed for fourteen years, leaving her husband to raise their children with the help of a domineering nurse who guarded Alberta's bedroom door and took her place at the foot of the dining room table. It was an act of retreat and disillusion that to this day her eldest son, a man in his eighties, bitterly holds against her.

Yet another example of the later, frailer breed was Florence Breckinridge, Flora Sharon's American daughter-in-law. Hers was an arranged marriage: she

"*Thank God!—the Army and Society are now well rid of such a damned blackguard. The crowning point of his infamy is that he, this morning, married an American young lady, Miss Garner (sister to Mme. de Breteuil), with money!*"

THE PRINCE OF WALES, referring to Sir William Gordon-Cumming in a letter to Prince George

THE GLITTER & THE GOLD

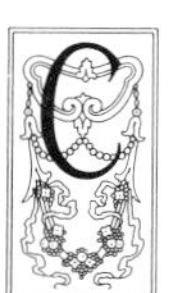

Consuelo Vanderbilt is the most familiar of the American heiresses, partly because her name is synonymous with the archetypal American fortune, partly because she married a duke from a famous family—and partly because she wrote a memoir, *The Glitter and the Gold,* published in 1952 and still considered one of the best accounts by anyone, English or American, of turn-of-the-century aristocratic life.

The memoir also gives Consuelo the last word on her marriage. She herself emerges as a gentle, long-suffering, heroine; Alva, her mother, as little more than an ogre; and Sunny, her husband, as an insufferable snob (even though their son, the 10th Duke, "blue-pencilled freely" when he read the manuscript). But another version of the story can be read between the lines. Despite her allegedly violent behavior, Alva never showed a sign of coldness toward her daughter.

A somewhat more sardonic view of Consuelo.

Consuelo writes movingly of driving away from her wedding reception and glimpsing her mother at the window: "She was hiding behind the curtain, but I saw that she was in tears." Is this a woman with a heart of stone? When Consuelo had her first baby, Alva was there. When Consuelo separated from the Duke, Alva was there. And when Consuelo wanted a formal annulment of her first marriage so that her second marriage (to French flier Jacques Balsan) could be acknowledged by the Catholic Church, Alva testified. Knowing that coercion was the only ground acceptable, Alva stoutly told the Catholic court, "I forced my daughter to marry the Duke," and then said to reporters: "This is merely one of those adjustments."

It may, in fact, have been an adjustment of the truth. Though Alva cited adultery in her divorce from William K. Vanderbilt, it was believed at the time that the gentle Willie K. simply obliged Alva by providing proof. Having cooked up a story for the courts once, why not do so again, especially for a beloved daughter? Furthermore, one wonders if Consuelo hated being a duchess all that much. Certainly, when Sunny died, she was back at Blenheim in short order in the role of doting mother of the 10th Duke. And her will, to the family's surprise, directed that she be buried not in Florida, where she lived the last decades of her life, not in New York with the rest of the Vanderbilts, not even in France by the side of her much loved second husband—but in the Churchill plot at Bladon, a stone's throw from Blenheim Palace.

was a stepniece of Flora, who'd brought her over to England and cultivated her as a wife for her eldest son (created first Baron Hesketh in 1935). When her children were still quite young, she too suffered a nervous collapse and lived the rest of her years as an invalid.

Indeed, the high-strung or merely sensitive American heiresses often took refuge in their ailments. Mildred Sherman, Lady Camoys, became a virtual recluse at Stonor and complained about the trains shunting at Henley (five miles away), which she said kept her awake all night. Pauline Whitney, after moving to England with her husband, Almeric Paget, divided her time between bridge and spas, which were supposed to revive her weak heart. Ethel Field, after her marriage to David Beatty (later naval hero Earl Beatty), suffered black depressions during which she could neither eat nor sleep for days at a time. Indeed, so prevalent was ill health among the late crop of American heiresses that the *Tatler*, writing about Lady Donoughmore, remarked that "unlike most smart Americans, [she possesses] fine health and high spirits."

Of course, this sort of hysterical reaction was common among unhappy upper-class women at the turn of the century. Edith Wharton suffered similarly after her marriage and was revived only by her career as a novelist and her subsequent independence from her husband. Nancy Langhorne Shaw, married to Waldorf Astor in 1906, was also afflicted with a series of mysterious ailments in the early years of her marriage. But then she discovered Good Works and abandoned invalidism in favor of the robust, somewhat self-righteous manner for which she became famous.

Florence Breckinridge, English peeress in the making. It was not a successful role for her.

THE SERIOUS SIDE

Good Works turned out to be something American peeresses were terribly good at and the English aristocracy, particularly toward the turn of the century, terribly keen on. There were heiresses who made a success of life in England by rarely rising before noon, by exploiting their American thirst for fun and high adventure, by applying all their cleverness to entertaining the Prince of Wales. But there were other heiresses who rose early, had little to do with the Prince of Wales and exploited their middle-class sense of duty and propriety for their success. These heiresses, converting an American democratic sympathy for those down on their luck to an aristocratic concern for the lower orders, fit seamlessly into the English upper-class pattern. Eloise Breese, the New York girl who became Countess of Ancaster, was appointed a justice of the peace and eventually earned membership in the Order of the British Empire for her service. Virginia Bonynge, Viscountess Deerhurst (from a none too savory California background),

On a visit to the States, Consuelo made a much publicized stop at the New York prison called the Tombs.

After a decade with Sunny, Consuelo Marlborough turned to philanthropy and social reform. Here, she supervises the weighing of a baby at a Mothers' and Babies' Welfare Centre.

worked with Princess Christian to further the cause of the Royal School of Embroidery. New Yorker Elizabeth French, Lady Cheylesmore, started a scheme in Ireland for less than prosperous local women to make and sell dolls that were caricatures of well-known personalities.

These American peeresses proved they could do more than live in the grand style; they were capable of shouldering the burdens as well as the benefits of nobility. The feudal system that permitted the endless deference accorded the nobility was, at the end of the century, still a two-way street. Along with penning the dinner menus and placating a temperamental cook, being a châtelaine meant seeing that the left-overs went to the needy or interviewing the candidates to teach at the village school.

Florence Gordon-Cumming, for all her other failings, was, according to her daughter, a "domineering" châtelaine. She kept close control of the school on the estate, set up model cottages for the tenants, browbeat them for their own good. May Goelet, growing carnations and playing bridge at Floors, was also very popular with the tenants for her evident concern with their lot. And though Sunny Marlborough deprecated her "Lady Bountiful" activities, such as reading aloud to blind villagers, Consuelo was a credit to him, and a credit to Blenheim.

Such peeresses nobly ignored their husbands' indiscretions and never considered indulging in any of their own. They became better Tories than their husbands and treated their visiting American brothers with an adopted English deference, according them a respect that the startled boys could never have hoped for back home. To one such American peeress went the ultimate accolade: "She does not bear the distinguishing marks of her nationality in the way many of her countrywomen do," claimed the *Tatler* of Ellen Stager, Lady Arthur Butler, "and she is often mistaken for English-born." What higher praise could the American heiress hope for?

Consuelo sold flowers in the street to benefit Queen Alexandra's charities. Her civic career climaxed with her election to the London County Council.

"Philanthropist, Patriotic Yank, Beauty, the used wife, what else!!!"

The 9th Duke of Marlborough, about his ex-wife Consuelo

PORTRAIT OF A LADY: SITTING TO SARGENT

Along with the "international" stories of Henry James, as well as Richard Morris Hunt's Newport mansions, the portraits of John Singer Sargent (who, naturally, painted portraits also of Hunt and James) are the most lasting memorials to the American heiresses and their era.

Sargent and James were, in fact, the best of friends: the round, balding writer and the lanky, ruddy painter were known in London drawing rooms of their day as "the inseparables." James, an early admirer and champion of Sargent, wrote glowing appreciations of his work for *Harper's* and saw that the artist was introduced to potential clients and invited to the interesting dinner parties. The two had much in common, with each other and also with the heiresses: the early years vagabonding about Europe with their parents, the dissatisfaction with society and culture in America; later years in Rome and Paris,

Sargent in his studio with the famous "Madame X."

learning to love the life of the *beau monde*; the crucial year or two in Newport, considered by Sargent the turning point of his career. (It was a point James had a hand in shaping, for just as the painter appeared in Newport, one of James' essays on Sargent appeared in print.)

By the turn of the century, Sargent was well-established as the premier society portrait painter, able to pick and choose his clients, painting only those whose faces he found interesting. Royalty he steadfastly refused to depict, and in 1902 he turned down Edward's invitation to paint the official coronation portrait.

His daily routine was fixed and immutable. Sitters would be shown up the red-carpeted stairs at 31-33 Tite Street by Nicolo, his Italian manservant. Usually a friend came along to "assist," as Sargent put it, by conversing with the sitter; this kept the sitter's expression alive, he believed, and left him free to concentrate on painting. The studio itself would be empty of anything but the smell of paint, a few tapestries, the canvases Sargent was working on, and the portrait props: a chair, some fabric for a backdrop, a table or two. A single portrait might take as few as fifteen or as many as forty sittings. Dressed in his regulation blue serge, Sargent would move about a great deal (he once estimated he logged four miles a day in the studio), smoking a quantity of cigarettes and from time to time joining in the conversation, amusing client and friend with expert imitations of people they all knew. The first official viewing of the portrait might come on the first Sunday in

April, known as "Picture Sunday," when all the London painters lined their studios with their selections for the Royal Academy's exhibition. Lady Randolph Churchill was usually present at these affairs, as was Henry James, though he "loathed the general practice."

Always considered a little daring and modern, Sargent was accused of "caricature" and "cleverness" in what seemed an informal, loose style of painting. Critics faulted him for failing to idealize his subjects (Sargent himself claimed he could feel the women pleading with their eyes to make them beautiful), but the fact was that English society's stately image was being traded in for one with an emphasis on dash and verve, on liveliness and spirit, on fun. Certainly Sargent's long, attenuated line, his exaggeration of height and slenderness, were perfectly in tune with Edwardian ideas of grace and elegance.

Three years before his death in 1907, King Edward would earn a snub from Sargent by recommending him ("the most distinguished portrait painter in England") for a knighthood. The King had forgotten that although Sargent was in England, he was not actually English. "I deeply appreciate your willingness to propose my name for the higher honour to which you refer," Sargent wrote the prime minister, "but I hold it is one to which I have no right to aspire as I am not one of His Majesty's Subjects but an American Citizen. Believe me, with very great respect, John S. Sargent."

Below left: Mary Endicott Chamberlain, in 1902. Below right: Daisy Leiter, later Countess of Suffolk. Sargent was a wizard when it came to drapery.

Far left: Though noted for his posed portraits, Sargent relished working outdoors. Left: Nancy Astor (1906). Sargent also made several drawings of her.

AT LONG LAST, LOVE

If the heiress had been married for her American money, if she had gone to the altar flushed with Anglomania rather than *amour,* all was not necessarily lost. After a decent interval, romance could yet be hers. The social code of her class and era permitted seeking a soulmate outside the boundaries of marriage. Should

The Hon. Mrs. George Keppel, model of an aristocratic mistress—beautiful, intelligent and discreet.

The public, of course, never saw the shadow of a rift between the Prince and his Princess.

she be willing to cast aside her middle-class prejudices against such behavior and play by the rules, she could find, at long last, love.

The tone in extramarital affairs (as in every social realm) was set by H.R.H. the Prince of Wales, whose amorous intrigues were legion and expertly managed. Although there were some very close calls, only one affair erupted into a major scandal. And even his wife, the enchanting Alexandra, seemed not to mind—the Prince's ladies were often invited for four-day stays at Sandringham. (There were those who thought the Princess would have minded if only she'd known; they contended that her unruffled accommodation was a result of her deafness, which she was too vain to correct and which thus ensured her never hearing whatever was being whispered about.)

The longstanding affair between Louisa, Duchess of Manchester, and the Duke of Devonshire was common knowledge in society.

In any case, there was never any appreciable diminution of affection between the pair: Alexandra was reported to have said, "But I was the one he loved best." Despite his Paris stays *en garçon,* when the pudgy royal body followed the lasciviously wandering royal eye, they were absolutely loyal to each other. In every crisis, they presented a united front. Her gesture, at the King's deathbed, of summoning *maîtresse en titre* Mrs. Keppel to his side remains one of the great kind acts and places her in history as a singularly caring wife.

THE GROUND RULES

If members of the Marlborough House Set were expected to follow the Prince's pattern in conducting an affair, they were also expected to adhere to his example in maintaining a marriage.

1. Don't make a fuss. Never, never, never go public. No one really questioned the need to relieve the tedium of a life of leisure with romantic dalliance, but the details were not to go beyond the safe confines of ballroom gossip. Almost anything was tolerated in private, but ruthless ostracism awaited any lover who "let down the side" by allowing an affair to reach the newspapers and the courts. The instant the rule was broken, social disaster ensued—witness the case of the affair between the Countess of Aylesford and the Marquess of Blandford (later the eighth Duke of Marlborough). It was possible, in contrast, to maintain forever an affair that was handled with dignity. Louisa, Duchess of Manchester (mother-in-law of Buccaneer Consuelo Yznaga), was for thirty years the mistress of the Duke of Devonshire. When her husband finally died, she married Devonshire, earning herself the sobriquet "Double Duchess."

One of Jennie Churchill's longtime lovers was the Austrian Count Charles Kinsky, a gifted diplomat, musician and womanizer.

Lillie Langtry at the races. She would not have qualified for the King's attentions without the existence of a dim but verifiable husband.

Easton Lodge, Daisy Warwick's home.

House parties at Easton Lodge were always tactfully arranged to make extramarital romance convenient. At this shooting lunch, Daisy sits in a white hat below the Prince of Wales (center) with her complaisant husband (in mustache and cap) at her feet.

*2. **Married ladies only.*** Mrs. Langtry, the Countess of Warwick, Mrs. Keppel—these ladies were eligible mistresses. The Prince did not fool around with débutantes. He flirted, he teased, he admired, but he did not bed the unwed. Nor was any nobleman expected to so indulge himself. (Servant girls were a separate issue.) A single woman who let down her guard in this respect, even if she did not become pregnant, could expect her marital prospects to dim unto darkness. She would find herself hurriedly bundled up the aisle with someone no one else had heard of—if she was lucky. Love affairs were a reward for, not a prelude to, getting married.

*3. **Keep the nursery well stocked.*** A woman's first duty to her husband was providing a son and heir. Jennie Churchill, who always played by the rules when it counted, waited until her sons were toddlers and she'd been married six years before embarking on her romantic escapades. At that point, still only in her mid-twenties, she was considered fair game by any interested friends of her husband. A woman who had not yet had children, or had produced only daughters (one of Lady Aylesford's big mistakes), had no business entertaining other men—and other men, if they knew what was good for them, would not consent to be entertained. Before making a single extramarital move, Edwardians made sure there were some lusty male babies bawling in their third-story bassinets.

*4. **Be an obliging mate.*** Did Lord Brooke (later the Earl of Warwick) know that his wife Daisy was carrying on with the Prince of Wales? Of course he did. But that did not prevent him from being the perfect host when the Prince came to Easton Lodge, or from accompanying his wife to every great house in England when the Prince was also conveniently expected. A wife should be similarly helpful to her philandering husband. Lord and Lady Elcho accommodated each other's love affairs for years, often inviting their respective partners down for the same weekend. Liking each other, as Edward and Alexandra did, made everything so much easier. Lord Londonderry was thought to be guilty of overreacting when, after being apprised of his wife's infidelity, he refused to address another word to her outside of certain essential public exchanges, until the day he died thirty years later.

COMME IL FAUT
A husband and wife in the fashionable set need not go to the same parties in the evening.

*5. **Never comment on a likeness.*** This was supposedly the only word of advice from Lady Moncrieffe to her daughters as they left Scotland for their first London season. The wisdom behind these words was considerable—it was possible for a last child to appear in the nursery of a nice house a good decade after his brothers and sisters. (Daisy Warwick, for instance, managed to be seven months pregnant on the occasion of her daughter's marriage, and not a soul at the wedding thought Lord Warwick responsible for her condition.) It was just as well, therefore, to pretend that the last arrival looked like his half-siblings even if he didn't. No need to embarrass host and hostess with a thoughtless remark about blue eyes when everyone else's were brown. As long as the husband had a son to call his own, he mustn't be so indiscreet as to disown some later production of his wife's. Accidents do happen. In a neat reversal of this credo, Daisy Warwick was known to have been furious with Lord Charles Beresford when his wife had a baby that looked just like him. How disloyal! He was supposed to be having an affair with *her.*

WHERE THERE'S A WILL...

Conducting an affair was an arduous business. Reputations and the virtues of one's servants had to be protected, and to this end the Edwardians did their level best to prevent situations in which women would find themselves in potentially compromising situations.

1. Afternoon tea. A lady could never be alone with a man who wasn't her husband—unless she was on or near her horse, or if, for some odd convenient reason, the man happened to drop by for tea. To indicate that he had in fact just dropped by, unexpectedly, he left his hat and walking stick on the floor next to his chair. (Surrendering them to the butler would mean he intended to stay.) It was possible, but only rarely, for the mistress of the house, if she and her caller were alone, to then ask the footman who was serving tea to remove himself belowstairs and tell his fellow servants she didn't wish any further interruption. Suspicious servants were a pain—there was no better way to get a good rumor going—and Edwardian ladies considered themselves responsible for setting an example.

A parlormaid answers the door to an afternoon caller. However discreet a mistress might be, her servants probably knew everything.

An additional barrier was provided by the lady's attire. All the layers of clothing, the lines upon lines of hooks and buttons, meant that a lady was not capable of undressing herself. It also meant that any activity while dressed was bound to be awkward as well as noisy. Corsets creaked. (Jennie Churchill, more daring than most of her contemporaries, solved this problem by wearing, in her boudoir, long, loose, free-flowing Japanese kimonos.) Yet another problem was presented by the gentleman's carriage, which, if it remained waiting outside the house for any amount of time, would let everyone in town know what was up. Afternoon tea, particularly since husbands were customarily at their clubs, provided an opportunity for fanning the flames but not for going "all the way." Glances, kisses, a little petting on the sofa was about

A WEALTH OF STYLE

Worth made the construction of fashion an art, removing it forever from the hands of the local seamstress. He produced between six and seven thousand dresses and four thousand outer garments a year, employing a thousand or more people at his atelier in the rue de la Paix. Just some of the Worth hallmarks are outlined here.

FABRIC

Almost inevitably heavy silk, used in combination with one or two other fabrics. Worth revived, almost singlehandedly, the French silk-weaving industry in Lyons, by persuading Empress Eugénie to wear exclusively dresses made from Lyons silk. (Initially, she thought they looked like curtains.) The fabric was frequently embroidered or brocaded in a large, lavish pattern; roses were favored, as were voided velvet and appliqués. Mills always submitted their patterns to Worth and waited for his orders before weaving; many of the patterns were copyrighted.

COLORS

Often rich and brilliant, sometimes subtle, always original, in combinations such as coral and silver, chestnut and bronze-green, black and midnight blue, or fuchsia and royal blue. The Worth forte: combinations of colors in the nougat/shell pink/cream/pale yellow range, especially in rich silks and brocades that caught the light.

A lesser artist would have centered the embroidered sunburst.

ASYMMETRY

Bodice draped to one side, train draped to one side, roses pinned to left shoulder, puffs of tulle on right side of skirt. A dress never looked the same from every angle.

This kind of large-patterned brocade was one of Worth's specialties.

Gathering yards of fabric into a graceful bustle took great technical skill.

SILHOUETTE

Always the cutting edge of fashion; always flattering. Worth took credit for having invented the crinoline, a light, cage-like hoopskirt, to replace the layers of hot, heavy petticoats. He brought it to the height of fashion, then dropped it when skirts became smooth in front and gathered into a bustle at the back. The bust was always emphasized, as bodices remained snug for close to sixty years.

TRIMMINGS

Tulle, netting, chiffon, silk flowers; contrasting fabrics such as cream lining on blush-pink grosgrain. Lace was very important —especially machine lace, which rivaled the look of handmade lace and was much less costly. Other machine-made trimmings included *passementerie*, tassels, chenille fringe, braid, paillettes, *galon d'argent* and glass pearls. On occasion, real jewels were sewn onto a dress the day of a ball, then cut off and put back into the vault.

HISTORICAL MOTIFS

Dresses in the style of Titian or Rembrandt or Jan van Eyck; stand-up collars à la Medici, Renaissance-patterned brocade, long, pointed basques. Having studied painting extensively, Worth enjoyed purloining from the past (he once commissioned a Lyons mill to weave a brocade patterned with eyes and ears, after a famous portrait of Elizabeth I) and could be relied upon to produce accurate reproductions of historical costumes for fancy-dress balls. He frequently made use of old materials, as in recutting an eighteenth-century embroidered man's jacket to be worn over a bustle or draping heirloom lace over the skirt of a red silk ball gown.

Left: A Worth pregnancy dress, designed for Mrs. Stanford White.

Right: Minnie Paget's Cleopatra dress required careful research.

all that time and clothing and discretion permitted. Of course, on select occasions, the many drawbacks could be, and were, overcome.

*2. **Helpful hostesses.*** In town, thoughtful hostesses arranged their drawing rooms into "favorable corners" so that lovers were seen to have been brought together not by their passion but by the furniture. At country-house parties, the hostess made certain that her guests would find their current *amours* not only present but accessible. The corridors of country houses could be long and chilly, their navigation a chore. Bedroom doors all look alike. If sleeping arrangements were not crystal clear, confusion—even pneumonia—could result. (One famous error involved an eager visitor leaping into bed with a cry of "Cock-a-doodle-do!" only to find that he had interrupted the virtuous slumber of the Bishop of Bath and Wells.) Some hostesses had brass card-holders placed at every door so that the identity of current inhabitants could be readily ascertained. Others discreetly informed concerned parties how to get from one room to another without running into servants or other guests, while in some establishments a warning bell rang an hour before morning tea was scheduled to be brought in by the servants. Nocturnal itinerants would thus have a chance to get back where they were supposed to be by the time the maid or

"*Silly little fool! All the young wives try me!*"
SIR WILLIAM GORDON-CUMMING to Leonie Jerome Leslie, when she wouldn't let him kiss her

A 1910 photograph of the King abroad with a lady whose identity has been carefully obscured so as not to give her away.

footman came in. Of course, there was no guarding against the unexpected, except by abstaining, and people did occasionally cross paths late at night. The polite thing, at such a juncture, was an anonymous salutation, followed immediately by total amnesia.

3. A letter to my love. Edwardians were mad letter-writers. When lovers couldn't manage to be together, they were busy scribbling notes to each other. Every day. Any serious set of lovers was duty-bound to start up a heated correspondence. In fact, it seems likely that some affairs were consummated on the page rather than between the sheets. Certainly a great deal of passion was expended there. Packets of compromising letters, usually tied up with pink or blue ribbon, thus became the centerpieces of a number of liaisons. It was such a packet that a malicious noblewoman had delivered to Lord Londonderry—letters written by his wife to the great Edwardian cuckolder Harry Cust. It was with such a packet (letters from the Prince to Lady Aylesford) that Lord Randolph Churchill tried to blackmail H.R.H. into easing up on his brother Blandford. In any case, if it was a long time between house parties, it was only polite to flatter a lady, or pour out one's heart to a gentleman, with regularity and gusto. And just hope it didn't come back to haunt one.

4. Sentimental keepsakes. Edwardian love affairs were often similar to the romances of the very young, filled with sentimental gestures, the regular exchange of darling little gifts, the celebration of secret anniversaries. Couples were capable of thinking of their affair as a marriage and wearing the lover's "wedding ring." Sex without sentiment was for the serving classes, the reason morality had been invented in the first place—to channel their animal spirits. The aristocracy need not bother itself with such concerns, enlightened as their baser instincts always were by elevated emotions. The prevailing theory seemed to be that as long as you were being faithful to *someone,* it didn't really matter whether you were married to that someone or not.

COMME IL FAUT
A gentleman receives letters from his mistress at his club. They are brought to him on a silver salver, address-side down, so no one else may see a possibly familiar handwriting.

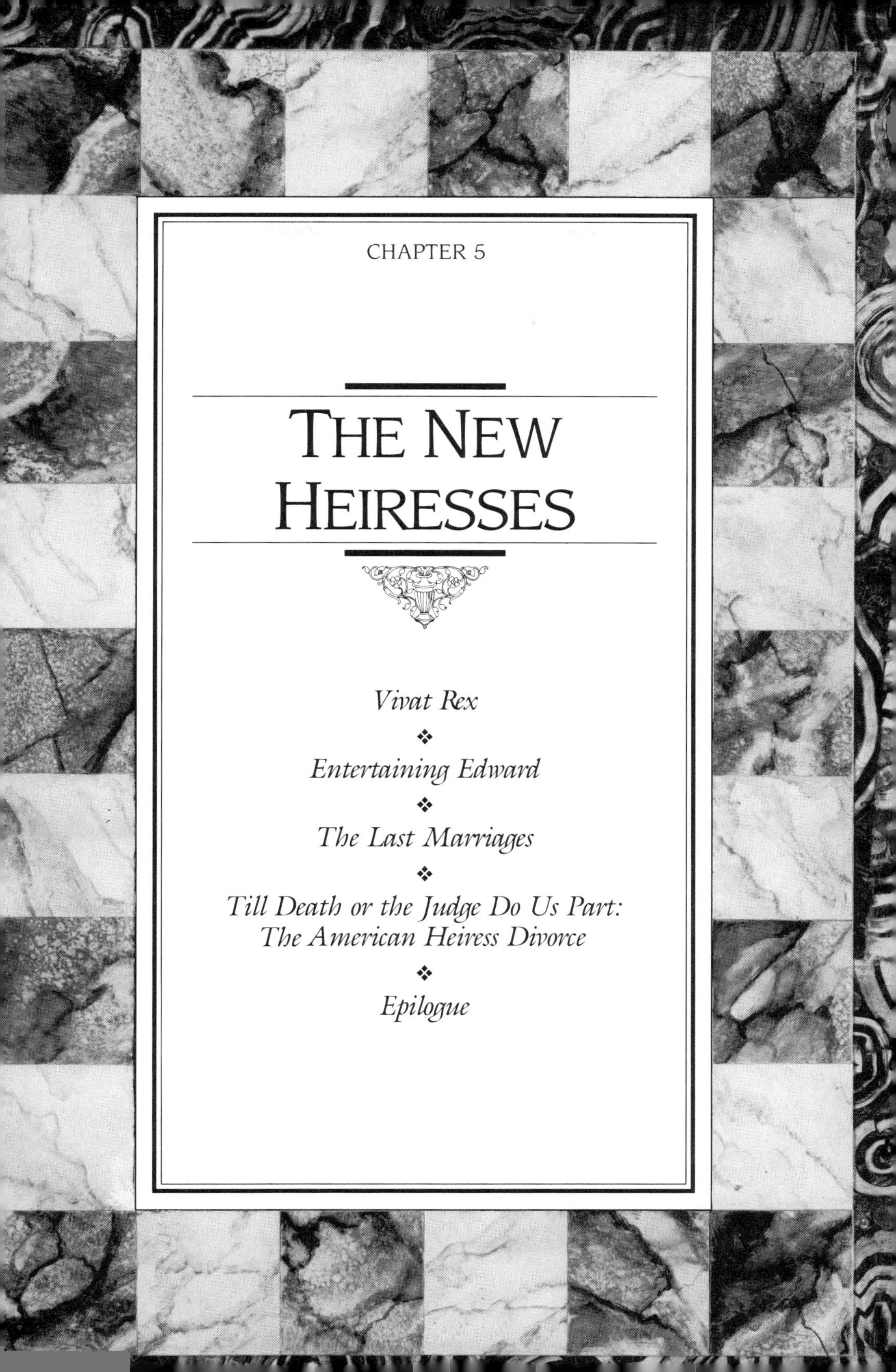

CHAPTER 5

THE NEW HEIRESSES

VIVAT REX

On January 22, 1901, Winston Churchill was in Winnipeg on a lecture tour. Far as Winnipeg was from England, it was still part of the British Empire, and when word of Queen Victoria's death arrived, flags were hoisted to half-mast and black bunting appeared on the cold gray buildings. Winston, in a letter to his mother, called the Queen's death "a great and solemn event." But he was also curious about its effect on Edward: "Will it entirely revolutionise his way of life? Will he sell his horses. . . . Will he become desperately serious? . . . Will the Keppel [*maîtresse en titre* Alice Keppel] be appointed first lady of the Bedchamber? . . . Will he continue to be friendly to you?"

Winston was not alone in his curiosity. What kind of king was Albert Edward going to make? Would he reform utterly? Would he be a sober monarch like his mother? Or would he remain loyal to his friends? Would his love of fun transform court ritual into a glittering fantasy? Was England, with a "corpulent voluptuary" (in Kipling's phrase) on the throne, to become the Promised Land for rich socialites?

The service book for the funeral, specially bound in purple velvet. The Queen, a connoisseur of mourning, would have been gratified by the public display of grief at her death.

Queen Victoria's funeral took place on a suitably mournful day in February. Many of the Empire's denizens had known no other monarch.

"This having to keep en evidence *all year! We society women simply drop down in harness!"*
MRS. JOHN R. DREXEL

NEW YORK ON PARADE

American women, particularly the ambitious variety, had never been in greater need of a Promised Land. Even in New York's most captious moments (as when pretty, well-dressed Mrs. John Mackay, with her newly minted silver-mining fortune, was cut dead at a musicale given by Mrs. Paran Stevens), both *parvenus* and Old New Yorkers had acted out of conviction. The gatekeepers knew that guarding the purity of New York society was crucial, and aspirants such as Mrs. Mackay knew that New York was worth assaulting. But by the turn of the century, their conviction had failed. Mrs. Astor, though still in New York, had retired from her throne. She'd gone mad, in a singularly appropriate fashion: gowned and jeweled as if for one of her balls, she wandered around her great house, graciously greeting a crowd of imaginary guests.

The Fifth Avenue Easter Parade typified New York society's aimlessness. New Yorkers were perpetually all dressed up with nowhere to go.

It took three women to replace Caroline Astor. Society was ruled now by "the Great Triumvirate": the acid-tongued Mrs. Stuyvesant Fish; Mrs. Hermann Oelrichs, whose father had been a rough-and-tumble miner in the Comstock Lode; and, inevitably, the indomitable Alva, who had become Mrs. Oliver H.P. Belmont shortly after Consuelo's wedding. These women cared less about keeping society pure than about keeping society entertained, and the result was a great deal of silliness. There was the famous "Dogs' Dinner," at which canine guests in their best collars ate pâté. There was the episode of Prince del Drago, a guest of Mrs. Fish, for whom a lavish party was given—and enjoyed, even though the Prince turned out to be a monkey. There was the Servants' Ball, to which all the guests came dressed as their own

Mamie Fish, Alva Belmont and Tessie Oelrichs, the Great Triumvirate, made amusement their top priority.

maids, footmen and cooks. There was the Belmonts' famous Automobile Parade, for which the novel "motors" were decked with flowers and drivers had to negotiate a course set with obstacles such as the dummy of a nursemaid with a carriage. As Betty Leggett, an exiled New York matron, wrote to her husband, "There seems no dignified social leadership in New York at all."

Betty had not "taken" in New York, so there was an element of sour grapes in her comparison. But she was not alone in noticing the emptiness of American social life. Henry James, visiting the States after a long absence, complained that there was nothing, in the evenings, to "go on to"—no state balls, no political receptions, just another evening of dressing up and eating too much and toddling home again. Ralph Pulitzer, in his sardonic *New York Society on Parade,* describes a typical conversation in an opera box, opening with a lady's remark to a young man that "she sees his grandmother is wearing her Pearls tonight. He professes surprise, as he had understood the Pearls were being cleaned at the jeweller's, and had therefore taken for granted that she would wear the Sapphires. They then remark with interest which of their jewels several other women are wearing. For hostesses and their social clients . . . are very much more familiar with their friends' gems than with their children, and take a deep and affectionate interest in their families of precious stones."

MARCH OF ANGLOMANIA
Mrs. Stuyvesant Fish had a famous English butler named Morton, who frequently set her on the right path by saying: "Just as you wish, Madam. But I can only assure you it is not done in the best English households . . ."

THE BRADLEY MARTINS GO TOO FAR

At the same time that American society was becoming both ostentatious and empty, the lower orders were becoming uppity. It was a restless period of labor disputes and discontent, which occasionally, as in the episode of the Bradley Martin Ball, punctured even the complacency of the rich. The Bradley Martins, having married their daughter Cornelia so advantageously to the Earl of Craven, had a fine position in London. Yet they still, in the late 1890s, maintained ties to New York. Cornelia had been married from New York, greatly to everyone's inconvenience but as a matter of principle.

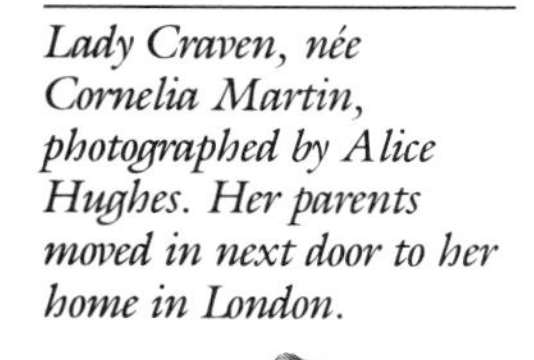

Lady Craven, née Cornelia Martin, photographed by Alice Hughes. Her parents moved in next door to her home in London.

Then in the winter of 1897—a particularly hard winter, when unemployment in New York was very high—the Bradley Martins gave a costume ball at the Waldorf-Astoria to stimulate the economy. Creating work for hairdressers, florists, costumiers, catererers, waiters and jewelers might not have done much for the destitute, but it attracted enormous attention of the nastiest nature. Anarchists, it was said, tried to blow up the Bradley Martin house a few days before the ball, and the windows

The ill-fated Bradley Martin Ball, depicted in Harper's Weekly. *The fair hostess is shown at top left of drawing.*

of the hotel were boarded up, either to prevent the hoi polloi from throwing bombs or simply to keep them from peeking in and seeing their betters at play.

The ball matched Alva Vanderbilt's 1883 costume ball in splendor. Mrs. Bradley Martin again went as Mary, Queen of Scots, this time wearing a cluster of diamond grapes, formerly Louis XIV's. Oliver Belmont wore a $10,000 suit of armor inlaid with gold, Anne Morgan was costumed as Pocahontas, and one Infanta of Spain had to dress at the hotel because her dress wouldn't fit through the door of her house. The difference, however, between Alva's ball and the Bradley Martin Ball was that Alva got away with hers. The Bradley Martin festivities were accompanied by hundreds of column-inches of newsprint and followed by denunciations from editorialists and clerics all over the city. The party was estimated to have cost $370,000 and, according to the rector of St. George's Church (J.P. Morgan's place of worship), would increase discontent among the poor.

The Bradley Martins, shocked by such harsh judgments and reassessed by the tax collectors, left New York for good. They may have remarked with chagrin that the Devonshire House costume ball, an even more lavish affair held in London less than six months later, was not the least bit controversial.

It is no wonder, then, that turn-of-the-century American social life, even for those at its very peak, seemed somewhat less than all-absorbing. Mrs. Ogden Goelet complained to her sisters about opening Ochre Court in Newport for the summer: "It will mean such a lot of trouble and endless domestic worries, running that big establishment—just a housekeeper for the 27 servants, the 8 coachmen and grooms and 12 gardeners. . . ." In fact, more and more people like Grace Wilson Vanderbilt (and like the Bradley Martins before their debacle) routinely spent the winter season in New York and the summer season in London. The "Steamer Set," the early version of the jet set, had come into being.

MARCH OF ANGLOMANIA
In 1887, when Mr. and Mrs. Bradley Martin returned to New York after three months in London, their name was suddenly spelled Bradley-Martin.

"*'I like to lead a well-rounded life,' was an expression Mother used all the time. By this she meant she liked to be in various parts of the world when the social season was on.*"
CORNELIUS VANDERBILT IV, in *The Queen of the Golden Age*

ROYAL CIRCLES

In the spring of 1901, American women crossed the Atlantic more eagerly than ever. The Prince of Wales, their chief patron in England, would soon be crowned king. With the rest of the international set, they waited for signs that Bertie's version of court life would prove as sumptuous and grand as his mother's had been austere and sober. A heartening signal came right away. On January 23, the day after Victoria's death, His Majesty announced to his Privy Council that he intended to be called "Edward, a name carried by six of our ancestors." He was dropping "Albert," his father's name, the name his mother had tried to insist on for all of her grandchildren. Whether or not he actually commanded his sisters to "Get this morgue cleaned up!" when he first visited Buckingham Palace as king, major alterations were soon underway: modern plumbing, an extended telephone system, garages for His Majesty's motors. His father's rooms, left intact since Albert's death, were turned out, and cartloads of photographs and bric-a-brac hauled away.

King Edward's sitting room at Buckingham Palace. His Majesty was swift to put his stamp on his new residence.

For the State Opening of Parliament, Edward decreed that the peers wear full state robes, and the procession to Westminster glittered as it hadn't done for years. The Drawing Rooms, where presentations to the Queen took place, were moved from the middle of the afternoon to the evening, and dance music was played afterward in the Palace. No longer did one arrive home from court at five in the afternoon, all dressed up with no place to go; one stayed and danced in the presence of the monarch. In royal residences, smoking was allowed, the conversation at dinner became general (as opposed to the Queen's system of individual inquisitions) and guests were permitted to sit in the presence of Their Majesties. Bridge tables appeared at the Palace, and the King even tried to end the men's custom of sitting at the

Edward and Alexandra at the State Opening of the first Parliament under his reign. Alexandra, in deep mourning, was nonetheless covered in diamonds.

Edward wearing St. Edward's Crown, which had been made for King Charles II. During the coronation, owing to his ill health, he was actually crowned with the lighter Imperial State Crown, made for Queen Victoria.

table drinking port and talking politics for half an hour after dinner. (Force of habit defeated him on this point.)

The new reign held great promise. The King had not become desperately serious. And although he was definitely making changes, they were all delightful ones. The Queen had written to him in 1868, "If you ever become King you will find all these friends *most* inconvenient, and you will have to break with them *all.*" Thirty-three years later he was king, he still had all these friends, and he was not finding them inconvenient in the least. Loyalty, after all, was one of Edward's strongest characteristics.

The "American Bar" at a coronation bazaar. From left: Mrs. Choate, Lady Dufferin, Mrs. Hall Walker and Lady Craven

ANGLO-AMERICAN ALLIANCE

Edward's loyalty to his old friends—most particularly to the Americans—was the source of satisfaction to a large and by now powerful contingent in English society. The Buccaneers, the Self-Made Girls, the American Aristocrats had taken root. Married to some of the most prominent men in the land, they wielded no small influence themselves. This cabal was remarked upon in 1895, when America and Great Britain came very close to war over a border dispute in Venezuela. George Curzon for example, was Under-Secretary for Foreign Affairs; Michael Herbert was British agent at the Tribunal of Arbitration. And, as the New York *Journal* put it, "There are in England's heart . . . ten American women, true daughters of the United States who are working quietly and mightily to prevent war between the two countries."

This genuine hostility turned to an inordinate fondness in 1898, when Britain sided with America in the Spanish-American War. The enthusiasm for an "Anglo-American alliance" was running high that year, and Joseph Chamberlain (who had an American wife), in a much publicized speech in Birmingham, called for "permanent amity with our kinsmen across the Atlantic." Sir William Harcourt, leader of the Opposition in 1898 (and married to an American), stated that his "foremost object has been the cultivation of good relations with the United States."

Daisy, Countess of Warwick, got on the bandwagon and arranged a tea party for the Prince of Wales and the American wives of English aristocrats, to urge his support for the cause. She even flew the Stars and Stripes from the flagpole at Warwick Castle to make the Americans feel at home.

> *"The most astonishing feature of the present time is the sudden transition of this country from Anglophobia to the most exuberant affection for England and 'Britishers' in general."*
>
> SIR JULIAN PAUNCEFOTE, former British ambassador, to Prime Minister Lord Salisbury (1898)

REMEMBERING THE *MAINE*

Though little of substance emerged from Daisy's plots, American energy and organization benefited England when a group of American women met in

October of 1899 to plan for a hospital ship to be sent to South Africa, where the British were fighting the Boer War. The ship, the nurses and the financing were to be American. Dashing widow Jennie Churchill (Randolph had died in 1895) was chairman, Mrs. Adair (née Cornelia Wadsworth of Geneseo, New York) and Fanny Ronalds were on her committee. There were fund-raising concerts starring American performers. An American shipping millionaire offered the ship—called the *Maine* after the boat sunk in the Spanish-American War. Mrs. Whitelaw Reid, whose husband would shortly be appointed American ambassador to the Court of St. James, supplied the medical staff from the Mills School of Nursing

Above: Jennie Churchill, shown with her son Jack, found that uniforms were becoming to ladies. Right: Winston, aged twenty-five, persuaded the Morning Post *to send him to South Africa as a war correspondent.*

THOROUGHLY MODERN JENNIE

When the *Maine* left England in December 1899, Jennie was on board, ostensibly to keep peace between various warring factions on the staff. That she was useful in an executive position, no one doubted. She certainly looked smashing in her nurse's cap and cape. But she was also trying to keep an eye on Winston, who was in South Africa as a war correspondent. And, gossip had it, she wanted to be near her new love, George Cornwallis-West, called "the handsomest young man in England."

He was indeed handsome. And young—half Jennie's age, a mere two weeks older than Winston. Jennie had met George, the only son of rival professional beauty Patsy Cornwallis-West, at a Warwick Castle garden party in 1898. The two had fallen in love. Which would have been fine if George, swept away by Jennie's lush, kimono-clad figure, had not wanted to marry her.

Jennie was free to marry, if not exactly eager. Lord Randolph Churchill had succumbed to syphilis three years earlier. Shortly before his death, Count Charles Andreas Kinsky, Jennie's lover of many years, had finally despaired of ever getting her to divorce Randolph and married instead an Austrian countess. Jennie liked life as a widow. She was publisher and editor-in-chief of a lavish literary magazine called *The Anglo-Saxon Review.* She was Winston's literary agent, hostess and political mentor. And she continued to have lovers. But none was as persistent or devoted as George. He was eligible for the hand of the noblest, wealthiest young women in England—and as such was irresistible to the forty-five-year-old ex-American heiress.

When the idea was put about that the two might actually marry, George's parents were aghast. The match was unflattering to Patsy and unpromising for the Cornwallis-West family fortunes. Jennie would be providing no dowry and,

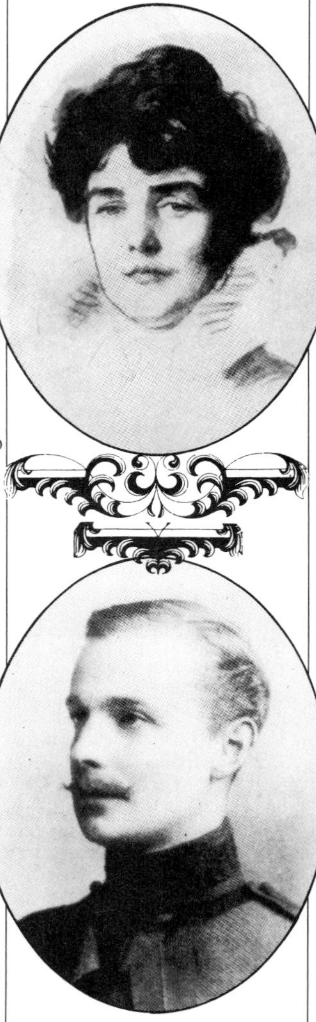

Jennie and George: even Sargent, in his charcoal sketch, couldn't hide the fact that she was no ingenue, but perhaps that was what George loved about her.

at her age, no heirs. Nevertheless, during Cowes Week—the same week Jennie and Lord Randolph had become secretly engaged a quarter-century earlier—Jennie and George announced their engagement. *The New York Times* headline declared, "British Society Astonished."

In fact, it was livid. Immediately pressure was applied from all sides to dissuade the two. George was summoned to the *Britannia,* where the Prince of Wales lectured him on the difference in ages. Bertie clearly objected to having Jennie taken out of circulation. Jennie's sons expressed their apprehension. Then George's commanding officer, Col. Arthur Paget, husband of Minnie and long-time friend of the Prince, asked for what George described as "a verbal understanding that I would not marry or become engaged before leaving for South Africa." He agreed. *The New York Times* printed a cheerful retraction from Winston, and George went off to fight in South Africa.

But by June 1900 George was back in England, the *Maine* had returned from service in Durban, and the engagement was on again. George's commanding officer again interfered. This time George gave up his army career rather than Jennie, and the pair were married in July at St. Paul's, Knightsbridge. George's family stayed away, but much of London did not. There were no restrictions on entering the church to watch the service, and such was the public interest that police were required to control the rush for seats.

Sunny, Duke of Marlborough, gave Jennie away. As Winston later wrote to his brother Jack, "The whole of the Churchill family, from Sunny downwards, was drawn in a solid phalanx, and their approval ratified the business." The Prince signaled his consent by sending Jennie a jeweled gold pig as a wedding gift (she collected pigs) and suggesting George talk to the royal financial adviser, Sir Ernest Cassel, about the thorny problem of making a living. Jennie's friends chipped in and bought her a pearl-and-diamond tiara. From Kinsky she received nought but a black-bordered card with the message *Toujours en deuil* ("Always in mourning").

The rest of English society, though not in mourning, continued to be unhappy about the match. The general air was conveyed by Lady Dorothy Nevill: when asked what she was up to as she strolled among the children in Hyde Park, the eighty-year-old grande dame replied, "Well, if you want to know, my dear, I am searching in the perambulators for *my* future husband."

THE
ANGLO-SAXON
REVIEW
A QUARTERLY MISCELLANY
EDITED BY
LADY RANDOLPH SPENCER CHURCHILL
(MRS. GEORGE CORNWALLIS-WEST)

Elaborate bindings were standard for Jennie's magazine.

"What her ultimate influence on English life will be it is difficult to estimate at present; but there can be no doubt that, of all the factors that have contributed to the social revolution of London, there are few more important, and none more delightful, than the American Invasion."
OSCAR WILDE, in *The Pilgrim Daughters*

(founded by her father). It took only two weeks for the committee to assemble the staff and £15,000 in funds. There was even a benefit tea in New York, organized by Lillie Langtry, where the Earl of Yarmouth (not yet married to Alice Thaw), pursuing an acting career on Broadway, served as bartender and made no bones about accepting generous tips. The Earl was quoted by *The New York Times* as saying that his tending bar "may make a bit of a stench here, but it will do me a lot of good with the Prince."

The crisis of the Boer War brought out the organizational tendencies of Jennie's friends as well. Minnie Paget, who by now had a reputation as a formidable fund-raiser, masterminded a society theatrical benefit called *The Masque of Peace and War.* Theatrical producer Beerbohm Tree lent a theater, and all of society paid enormously high prices to see their friends onstage, singing music composed just for the occasion by Sir Arthur Sullivan. The *Masque* made over £6,000 for the widows and orphans of men killed in South Africa.

AMERICANS IN LONDON

The strong American presence in London was felt in less obvious ways as well. In 1899, for example, America's diplomatic mission in Britain was upgraded to a full embassy, and New York lawyer Joseph Choate was appointed first U.S. ambassador to the Court of St. James. Queen Alexandra, who was rather deaf, took lip-reading lessons with Consuelo, Duchess of Marlborough. American accents—for the clever women always kept their accents—could be heard cutting through the din at any ball or political reception. Upon the retirement of Sir Julian Pauncefote, long-time ambassador to the United States, every high-ranking diplomat considered to replace him had an American wife. (Sir Michael Herbert, Belle Wilson's husband, was chosen because he was a friend of Theodore Roosevelt.)

EARNING A TITLE

Some of Edward's earliest acts as king were to reward his loyal subjects for their service when he was Prince of Wales. Col. Arthur Paget, for instance, was elevated to a knighthood in recognition of his military deeds (although the one who had truly earned the reward was the indefatigable Minnie, Edward's favorite hostess). Titles, from lowly, noninheritable knighthoods to full-fledged peerages, were usually conferred for outstanding political, military or diplomatic service, but Edward recognized other kinds of duty as well: financier Ernest Cassel, for example, who had lent him money, and Luke Fildes, who was responsible for the official coronation portrait, became Sir Ernest and Sir Luke.

A large proportion of the husbands of American heiresses received honors for reasons that are difficult to discern from *Burke's Peerage*.

Minnie Paget, finally titled like her fellow Buccaneers after her husband was knighted by King Edward.

George Cooper was a Scottish solicitor who had married, in 1887, one Mary Emma Smith from Chicago. They lived rather quietly in Scotland until, on the death of her uncle, Mary Cooper inherited some £4 million. The Coopers promptly showed up in London, bought a house on Grosvenor Square and a country house in Oxfordshire, and spent thousands enlarging and decorating and subsequently entertaining. On King Edward's Birthday List of honors in 1905, George Cooper was created a baronet.

In the end, an American heiress who had not managed to marry a titled Briton could often rectify that omission. Her money, her charm, and her skill at keeping her sovereign entertained could make her a Lady after all.

MARCH OF ANGLOMANIA
American newspaper coverage of U.S. participation in the coronation was comprehensive.

The importance of the American community in London was also marked by commercial venture, when an enterprising publisher began producing *Bancroft's Guide to Americans in London.* The 1901 edition devoted nineteen pages to a residential directory. Most entries gave little biographies, and a separate section listed titled American women. The introduction to the 1902 edition (for Mr. Bancroft's directory was profitable enough to warrant annual revisions) claimed to give "the names, addresses, and titles of those men and women who constitute what may be called American Society in London."

CORONATION FEVER

The coronation was scheduled for the summer of 1902. Mourning for Queen Victoria was finished, and by late spring the London season was shaping up to be the most glamorous ever. Of course, those Americans who were married to Englishmen would be entertaining. So would the handful of wealthy American families who had moved to England. Waldorf Astor, owner of the *Pall Mall Gazette,* would

A large New York contingent set out on the Kronprinz Wilhelm, *while a larger New York contingent said goodbye from the pier.*

have house parties at Cliveden. The Michael Graces, with their three lovely daughters, would no doubt be eager to host fellow Americans at historic Battle Abbey in Sussex. (Grace, originally from Ireland, had done very well with his brother William in Peru, and while William occupied himself with New York politics, Michael oversaw the English side of the Grace shipping empire.) Then the Anthony J. Drexels, of the Philadelphia banking family, had become deeply entrenched in English life: their son went to Eton, their yacht was moored mostly in English waters, and during the season they entertained brilliantly at their vast house off Grosvenor Square.

The resident contingent was augmented, in the 1902 season, by every ambitious American who could organize a steamer ticket and a place to stay. The *Tatler,* England's society magazine, stated as early as August of 1901 that "preparations are already being made for next season among the army of Americans who propose to storm these shores during that period. The characteristic transatlantic desire to be 'on the spot' for the coronation festivities and ceremonials is rising to fever heat."

By June of 1902 the *Tatler*'s predictions had been borne out. The Savoy, the Berkeley, the Carlton and Claridge's hotels were full, with names like Widener, Schwab, Elkins, De Young and Yerkes on the registers. The W.K. Vanderbilt Jrs., the Alfred Vanderbilts, the Peabody Wetmores, the Lorillards were all in town. Mrs. Mackay, once snubbed by New York, had achieved such a position in London that her musicale at Carlton House Terrace (Caruso and Emma Calvé performed) was one of the high points of the season. The Drawing Rooms were packed with American débutantes in their Worth presentation gowns, and American papers breathlessly covered the London engagements of visitors like the Whitelaw Reids, who were scheduled to dine with the Prince of Wales (later King George V), the King and Queen, Lord Pembroke and Princess Christian of Schleswig-

The Tatler *got in on the act with its own timely features. From the top: Lady Newborough, the Marchioness of Dufferin and Lady Lister-Kaye.*

Holstein, and who were also to go to Blenheim for a weekend. It was noted that Oliver and Alva Belmont were the only Americans present at a dinner given by Lord and Lady Rothschild for the King and Queen. Much was made of the fact that Queen Alexandra's coronation gown was to be made of fabric embroidered in India and chosen by Lady Curzon.

London was full of exotics: not merely Americans but Indian princes, a delegation of Japanese, and monarchs from all over Europe who had come to see their relative crowned. As it had been sixty-five years since the previous coronation, no one remembered quite what the ceremonial was, but the Duke of Norfolk, England's hereditary Earl Marshal, had come up with something that was suitably hierarchic, dignified and colorful. Then the King fell ill and, two days before the coronation, had an emergency operation for peritonitis. The coronation had to be postponed. The bunting was taken down, food for the celebratory banquet was given to the poor, and the exotics left without having had a chance to wear their coronation finery.

Consuelo Marlborough in her coronation robes. In her memoir she smugly recalled her foresight in ordering a new, small coronet that would fit neatly inside her tiara.

THE CROWNED KING

On August 9, in a shortened but nonetheless glorious ceremony, Edward was finally crowned. True, the foreign monarchs had all gone home, but everyone said that made it a more profoundly *English* event. The Abbey was filled with peers and peeresses, diplomats from all over the world, English politicians. The American women among the peeresses were, as at most London gatherings, the handsomest, best-dressed and most impressively bejeweled ladies present. Consuelo Marlborough, one of the four tall, beautiful duchesses carrying Alexandra's canopy, was singled out for her grave charm. What impressed the King most was the moment when, after the coronation of Queen Alexandra, each of the

The cover of a coronation souvenir booklet, featuring flags from all over the Empire.

peeresses put on her own coronet. The simultaneous movement of those hundreds of white arms, the rustling of robes, the flashing of the jewels made him think of a scene from a ballet.

The King's sensitivity to feminine beauty, as well as his famous loyalty, was evident in the composition of his private guest list for the coronation. In a gallery overlooking the transept were seated a number of women who, not of the peerage, would normally have been absent from the ceremony. All of Edward's old friends were there: Minnie Paget, Mrs. Cavendish-Bentinck, Lady Naylor-Leyland and Mrs. Adair; Jennie with her new mother-in-law, Mrs. Cornwallis-West, and her sister-in-law, the Princess of Pless. These women joined Mrs. Keppel, Sarah Bernhardt and Baroness de Meyer as the occupants of what was dubbed "the King's Loose Box."

Of course, there were a few mishaps. Cora, Countess of Strafford (formerly Mrs. Colgate of the soap-manufacturing family), put on her coronet crooked and sat with it at a tipsy angle for the rest of the ceremony. The Marchioness of Londonderry dropped her massive tiara into the sole toilet provided for the peeresses; the only way to extricate it without damage was with gynecological forceps, and a long

Edward wasn't too busy being crowned to take a moment to appreciate the beauty of his loyal peeresses as they donned their coronets.

THE GREAT DURBAR

In April of 1902, in honor of Edward's coronation, a durbar was held in Delhi. All the Indian princes and nawabs and rajahs—and a good many British socialites—gathered to pay homage to the new king-emperor. As vicereine, Mary Curzon presided over it all.

Above: The viceregal lodge at Simla, the hill resort where the English spent the hot Indian summers. Right: George and Mary, with their prey.

Mary riding in the procession.

The King and Queen in full coronation regalia, including velvet robes and scepters.

Minnie Paget, as a commoner, could not have attended except as Edward's guest.

line of ladies in white satin dresses and red velvet robes queued restively while the forceps were found. After the Royal Procession finally left the Abbey, one elderly Duchess was so anxious to reach the facilities that she literally knocked down another peeress.

The net result of the coronation, however, was a burst of pride in English hearts—and in American hearts as well, for the American ladies at the coronation had made a very impressive contingent, one with obvious influence. Surely, under King Edward's reign, an American woman in London was to be a favored creature.

The unfortunate Cora, Countess of Strafford, who wore her coronet crooked.

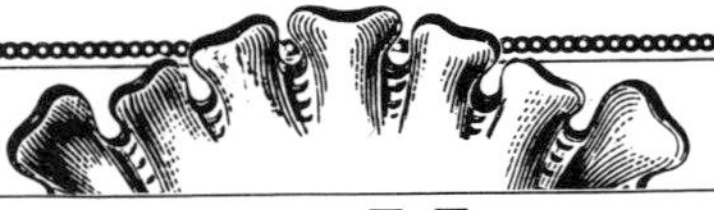

DEVONSHIRE HOUSE BALL

If the crowning event of Victoria's reign was her Diamond Jubilee in 1897, the social pinnacle of that celebratory summer was the costume ball held at Devonshire House on July 2. The Duke and Duchess's 700 guests, in "allegorical or historical costume before 1815," represented eminent figures from the courts of Elizabeth I, Catherine the Great of Russia, Maria Theresa of Austria, King Arthur, various Oriental potentates and, naturally, Louis XV and XVI.

Many of the guests, incapacitated by their elaborate costumes, could not actually dance. The Countess of Westmoreland, as Hebe, wore a stuffed eagle on her shoulder; Lord Rodney stalked around in full armor as King Arthur. Capt. Arthur Paget, as the Black Prince, was covered in chain mail down to his fingers. His wife Minnie, as Cleopatra, was only one of the many American women, costumed by Worth and brilliantly jeweled, who were remarkable even in that extraordinary company.

Consuelo Marlborough, seven months pregnant and laced to disguise it, was a lady of Catherine the Great's court, while Sunny wore a lavish, jewel-embroidered eighteenth-century costume that astonished even its maker, Worth. Mary Curzon was Valentina Visconti of Milan, and Fanny Ronalds, still a social figure to reckon with, represented Euterpe, the muse of music, with an electrically lit lyre on her head.

Jennie Churchill (left) as Empress Theodora by Worth, with emeralds and diamonds hanging from her headdress. Below: May Goelet, as Scheherazade, in gold gauze embroidered with precious stones.

Devonshire House, designed in 1733 by William Kent. Inset: The Duke, as the Holy Roman Emperor Charles V. Left: The Duchess, as Zenobia, Queen of Palmyra, entered the ballroom in a palanquin. Below: The Prince of Wales, as Grand Master of the Order of St. John of Jerusalem.

The King and Queen arrive for a country visit with their considerable retinue.

ENTERTAINING EDWARD

Entertaining was more important than ever during the Edwardian years. As Kim, the ninth Duke of Manchester, put it, "When one came to London for the season then, one came prepared for an orgy of parties, and ivory cards fell like snowflakes. One could count on being two or three deep every evening in balls." Keeping the King amused was still an essential task, but eliciting his pleased purr of "Yes, yes, yes" at a dinner party or musicale became more difficult. His thirst for novelty was unending, yet a substantial break with tradition was unthinkable. The Servants' Ball, so screamingly funny in Newport, would never do in Buckingham Palace. There was a narrow margin between convention and the constant threat of tedium.

Opulence, doing things on a grander and grander, but still correct scale was the only answer. And that suited the American contingent right down

A country-house party to meet the King (center, back row), including Alice Keppel and Consuelo Manchester (fourth and fifth from left, front row) and Jennie Cornwallis-West (far right).

to the ground. The American hostesses, as *Vanity Fair* remarked, entertained "with a splendid disregard for money, which our sadly handicapped aristocracy cannot afford to imitate." Somehow they kept providing something new enough to be charming, without straying into danger.

Mrs. Mackay, for instance, would hire to perform, on one evening, not only the Russian Choir Singers but Coquelin, Blanche Pierson and Réjane as well. Her house itself, 6 Carlton House Terrace, could only belong to an American. It had a new carriageway built from the curb to the stairs, lined in scarlet silk—no Englishwoman would have bothered. It also featured a marble entrance hall and a fifty-foot ballroom opening onto a terrace, while the furnishings included a massive and ornate table service of over fifteen hundred pieces, made by Tiffany of silver from the Comstock Lode. And Mrs. Mackay was hardly alone in her penchant for luxury. About the Bradley Martins, vilified in New York, the *Tatler* stated: "Indeed, in the extravagance of their entertainments they have completely outshone the functions of the wealthiest leaders of English society."

It was thus entirely appropriate that Whitelaw Reid, upon his appointment as ambassador to the Court of St. James, should install his family in the finest house in London. Built less than fifty years earlier, Dorchester House featured a grand staircase (crucial for parties in London, where the ballroom and drawing rooms were usually on the second floor) that rose in an immense three-story hall surrounded by a wide arched gallery. The saloon, or ballroom, had one wall pierced with similar arches that enabled dancers to look out on the arcaded gallery and allowed guests ascending the stairs to glimpse the figures twirling on the parquet floor. It was a splendid showcase of a house, and its occupation by the Reids spelled out very clearly the new American posture in English society, what the *Tatler* was calling "the American Invasion."

COMME IL FAUT
A royal "request" or invitation may never be refused.

Whitelaw Reid started life as a farmer's son, but journalistic brilliance (and marriage to California banker Darius Mills' daughter) catapulted him into the highest social spheres.

Tradition has it that painter Sir Edwin Landseer suggested piercing the walls between the saloon and staircase hall at Dorchester House. Largely finished by 1860, the house had been built by a rich Gloucestershire squire and was the most dramatic mansion in London.

The grand staircase at Dorchester House.

ONWARD & UPWARD

The invasion brought to London the American devotion to gilding and marble and brilliant little table decorations. And American social competitiveness. With Edward's coronation, the rivalries and anxieties that buzzed through the New York and Newport seasons had been transferred to London wholesale. As *Vanity Fair* commented, "It has happened that members of that exclusive body, the 'Four Hundred,' have been dreadfully shocked to find some compatriot who is taboo on the other side of the water received with open arms in Mayfair and Belgravia." In this regard, not much had changed since the Buccaneers' days. Except that in the 1870s London society could not have cared less about the Four Hundred.

"I don't know what it is you are all *after,*" Mrs.

Cavendish-Bentinck remarked about the striving in New York society. As a former New Yorker, she did, of course, know, but certainly in London the goal was so much clearer. What everyone was *after* was the favor of the King, signaled to all of society by His Majesty's presence under one's roof.

Lesser lights settled for lesser royalty. Elizabeth French, Lady Cheylesmore, according to the *Tatler*, "never reached the innermost circle of smart society"; she had entertained the Connaughts and other minor royalty, but never the big hitters. Still, the Cheylesmores were not socially ambitious, living as they did in un-smart Prince's Gate, forgoing bridge games and balls, and Cheylesmore was a new title as well, the family having made lots of money in importing silk.

Lady Leigh, a somewhat old-fashioned hostess, would not tolerate gambling or fast behavior at Stoneleigh.

Plebeian, plebeian. As the *Tatler* said, "'Onward and upward' is the American motto," and most heiresses would not have been satisfied with second-rank royalty and a house in Prince's Gate. If they chose to play the game at all, they wanted to win the prizes, and entertaining the King was the brass ring. It wasn't so much that one would enjoy herself; the onus of keeping His restless Majesty continually beguiled was too great for mere pleasure. But the cachet! The respect! And the publicity! *The Illustrated London News,* for example, frequently carried picture-spreads of houses visited by the King, with biographies and photographs of the host and hostess. The *Journal* pointed out, on the occasion of Edward's visit to Kylemore, that "for the fashionable classes of America who had never considered the Duchess of Manchester as being quite as important as the other conspicuous American heiresses, this event will show them that they have made a mistake." The privilege of housing and feeding the King was the supreme vindication for any social slights.

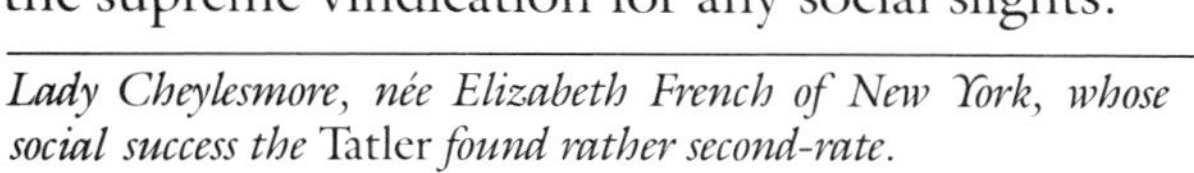

Lady Cheylesmore, née Elizabeth French of New York, whose social success the Tatler *found rather second-rate.*

In Edward's era, "bubbly" replaced claret as the tipple of choice. H.M. preferred Charles Heidsieck's product.

THE ROYAL VISIT

The King invited himself, of course, for no subject would dare presume. Either in person or through an equerry, he would express the wish to visit Blenheim or the Hesketh's' Easton Neston or the Harcourts' Nuneham Park. Of course, one agreed with alacrity. A tentative list of guests went to His Majesty, and to Queen Alexandra as well if she was joining her husband. One would have taken care to list people His Majesty liked, including his official mistress Mrs. Keppel. He often eliminated the names of those he didn't want to meet, or added new favorites.

At the same time, a rapid building and redecoration program would be launched. For a simple summer dinner, Lady Paget added an extension to her country house at Coombe Warren and erected a marquee in the gardens. For the royal visit to Kylemore, the railroad station was enlarged and elaborately decorated with red carpets and the usual masses of flowers; the castle itself was done over (with special attention to the royal suites), and commemorative presents for the King and Queen were purchased. One had to lay in the very best of food and drink; His Majesty was fond of such esoterica as ptarmigan pie and always had lobster salad with his tea. If there were

Kylemore Abbey in Ireland was built by a rich Liverpudlian in the 1860s. The Manchesters sold it to an order of nuns after World War I.

entertainments, special programs had to be printed; at Floors Castle, a church leaflet commemorates the visit of the Prince and Princess of Wales (later King George V and Queen Mary) to the Duke and American Duchess of Roxburghe.

An additional logistical burden was imposed by the royal staff. His Majesty traveled with two equerries (each with a valet), his own valet, a "sergeant footman," a brusher, two loaders for shooting weekends, two grooms (or two chauffeurs), and possibly gentlemen-in-waiting, telephonists, more footmen, and an Arab boy who made his coffee. The Queen, if she were present, had her staff as well, though she usually limited herself to one lady-in-waiting.

Even kings and queens are human: the Wolferton Royal Railway Station near Sandringham had special plumbing installed for the royal travelers (above, King Edward's; below, the Queen's).

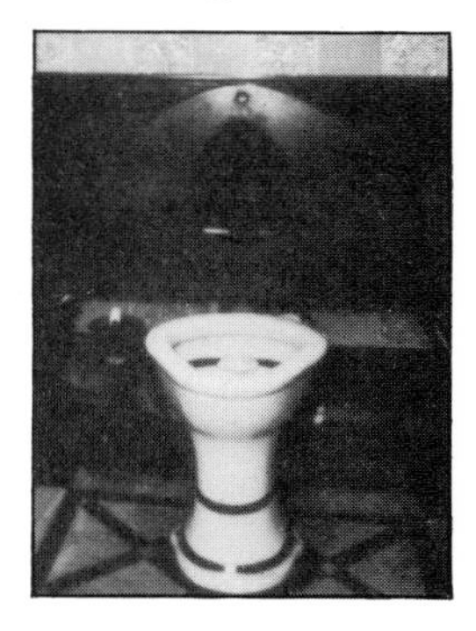

Entertaining the King was thus a fearfully expensive project. Daisy Warwick, in her autobiography, says: "I could tell stories of men and women who had to economize for a whole year, or, alternatively, got into debt, that they might entertain Royalty for one weekend!" When the Manchesters were honored by Edward's presence in 1904, newspapers estimated that the cost of the visit was $150,000, paid of course by the Duchess's papa, Mr. Zimmerman, who had bought Kylemore for Duchess Helena.

Part of the cost was dressing the part. The King, for a week's stay, would be bringing forty suits or uniforms and at least twenty pairs of shoes and boots, and costumes were expected to be splendid in his presence. Consuelo Marlborough remembers at least four changes of clothes: an elegant silk costume for breakfast in the dining room, a tweed suit for lunch with the "guns" (the men who were shooting), a tea gown, and the most formal brocade or velvet evening dress with the grandest jewels possible (always including a tiara) for dinner. One could not wear the same ensemble twice, and what reasonable woman would not want completely new outfits for such a momentous occasion? Sixteen new ensembles (four dresses for each of four days) from, say, Worth would substantially increase the cost of a royal visit.

TAKING THE MEASURE

In a formal, highly civilized society like England's there were, naturally, a thousand ways to display rank and wealth. Many of these were for the benefit of the hoi polloi, leftover traditions or habits that impressed upon underlings the power of their feudal overlords. Some, however, were so finely calibrated that the underlings couldn't possibly grasp their significance. They were quiet signals, from one tribal chief to another: "Just between us, I'm richer."

A GIRL'S BEST FRIENDS

The ideal was jewels so large they could safely be disparaged, as in "the family fender" (the enormous Londonderry tiara) or the Royal Family's modern version, "Granny's chips" (Queen Mary's imposing stones from the giant Cullinan diamond). There was a reverse chic that Americans would never understand in the old, heavy, dingy, ugly settings.

Queen Alexandra in a Russian-style tiara encrusted with 488 diamonds. Inset: The Cullinan III and IV diamonds, cut from the immense stone given to Edward VII by the South African government.

The King (second from right) inspects the day's bag.

DEAD BIRDS

In an agricultural economy, it took a certain panache to turn acres of cropland into a sanctuary for doomed birds. To provide really good shooting, birds had to be raised and fed, and keepers and beaters trained to expertise. At Wilton, the Earl of Pembroke's seat, such was the beaters' skill that the birds could be sent flying over the "guns" high, medium or low. On a shooting weekend at Eaton, the Duke of Westminster's place, the beaters had orders to start sending the birds over the day's stand, whether or not a single "gun" was present. A very good day's bag might number 2,000 dead birds.

THE SIX-FOOT FOOTMAN

Only the grandest families kept servants in livery. Nothing was more conspicuous than a tall, handsome young man, dressed in canary yellow with green plush breeches, trailing behind a woman in the Burlington Arcade to carry her packages. Footmen were paid extra for every inch of height over six feet, so a row of towering young men along the stairs at a ball was a clear signal of superiority.

Sunderland House, the Marlboroughs' new home in Mayfair, with its windows right on the street.

OUTER SPACE

By the turn of the century, London real estate was hugely expensive. Thus the supreme status of dwellings like Lansdowne House in Berkeley Square and Devonshire House in Piccadilly, whose gardens backed onto each other, and the prestige of forecourts where carriages could drop off passengers without blocking city traffic.

LIVELY HORSES

All horses (known in deprecatory masculine slang as "cattle") should be fine, not just Thoroughbreds but hunters and carriage horses as well. True grandiosity would insist that all horses also be the same color. (Sunny, 9th Duke of Marlborough, tolerated only grays.) A complete wardrobe of carriages ranged from the enormous town chariot (drawn by a team of four horses, two ridden by postilions) to the light, fast, low-slung curricle.

Mary Burns, Lady Harcourt, made the gardens of Nuneham Park, Oxford, into a splendid showplace.

Comme il Faut
Menu cards, listing the dishes that footmen will offer for each course, are placed on the dinner table between every two guests. The polite guest will choose only one.

DETAILS, DETAILS

Once the guests had responded and the building program was underway, rooms must be assigned. Bachelors were easy enough—they could be tucked into the second-best bedrooms or put in the bachelor wing if the house had one. But a duchess, an ambassador, a bishop would expect one of the best bedrooms. Furthermore, in the King's set, couples with an extramarital understanding would expect to be placed near each other. (Keeping up with the gossip was an essential part of a hostess's duty.)

Menus also had to be invented for the duration of the party, whether it was Saturday-to-Monday (never "the weekend," which implied one had to be back at "a job of work") or a full week. The chef must be interviewed. Could turtles be obtained for turtle soup? If salmon was served on Saturday, what would Sunday's fish course be? The old Duchess was very fond of the prune soufflé, they must have that one evening. And were there enough lobsters on hand for His Majesty's teatime treats? Although the houses that maintained good chefs were few—Blenheim, of course, was one—the sheer amount of food devoured was fantastic. The hostess, moreover, had to write out menus for every meal. These menus, placed between each pair of guests, were swiftly examined before service began, as it was not always possible to tell precisely what it was the footman was proffering. And one couldn't ask.

A strategic session with the housekeeper followed the planning with the chef. How many bedrooms would be made up? Did Milady remember that the chimney in the Tapestry Room smoked? And that the last time Lord Robert was put in the Tower Room, he complained that the bed was too short? There would be twenty for tea on Saturday, the same on Sunday, so the stillroom maid should make seedcake.

Finally, consultation with the butler: the big

THE CROWNING TOUCH

Even in New York, where the trappings of court seemed faintly silly, every woman with aspirations to a grand social life owned a tiara (though she couldn't wear it unless she was married). And woe betide the Edwardian lady who chose to go without. "The Princess has taken the trouble to wear a tiara," the Prince of Wales once scolded Consuelo Marlborough. "Why have you not done so?"

Wearing a tiara could be troublesome indeed, since they were always diamonds—with, perhaps, another precious gem—set in gold or platinum and the bigger the better. An air of *superbia,* a carriage that yielded not a millimeter to the weight of the stones, was crucial. Helena Zimmerman, Duchess of Manchester, wore the family tiara (with heart-shaped scrollwork, roughly four inches high all the way round) with a look of misgiving, while Queen Alexandra could support even a massive Russian-style diadem with aplomb. "I've seen women turn actually grey under the weight of their tiaras," says Lady Barnstaple in Gertrude Atherton's *American Wives and English Husbands.* "Still, unless you blaze at a great party, you simply are not seen."

The Manchester tiara, worn by Consuelo.

It was out of the question for an American woman not to be seen. So Jean Reid, at her marriage to John Ward, was given a diamond tiara containing over 100 stones, some a quarter-inch across; the headpiece was butterfly-shaped, and measured eight by three inches at the widest and highest points! And Nancy Shaw's wedding gift from Waldorf Astor was a tiara containing the Sancy diamond, weighing in at fifty-three and a half carats.

Nancy Astor's tiara, centered with the Sancy diamond.

Around 1905, a new style emerged. The very richest American matrons had their tiaras reset as copies of European crowns. Mrs. Charley Yerkes' tiara duplicated a Spanish crown; Mrs. Howard Gould had a tiara patterned after one owned by Queen Elena of Italy. Mrs. Bradley Martin's was the twin of Empress Josephine's. And Mrs. John Jacob Astor and Mrs. Clarence Mackay both wore replicas of English crowns. There was no mistaking the message: America's queens of society felt they were taking, at last, their rightful place among the royalty of Europe.

The King and Queen on the royal yacht at Cowes in 1909. They both look younger than their years: unretouched photographs of them were rarely made public.

épergnes for Sunday, filled with orchids, and the Meissen dinner service; so on Saturday the Sèvres, with the Bohemian crystal goblets, and white lilac. The four-ten and the five-ten and the six-thirty trains should all be met on Saturday, with wagons for servants and luggage, carriages for the guests.

Before the guests arrived, the hostess went round the rooms to ensure that everything was as it should be: plenty of coal in the grate, fresh ribbons threaded through the hems of sheets, clean blotting paper, new pens, a full ink bottle and various sizes of writing paper at the desk; fresh flowers, perhaps corsages for the ladies (a specialty at the Sackvilles' Knole) and reading matter gauged to the occupants' tastes. Consuelo Marlborough went down to

The 9th Duke of Marlborough hired a small black boy to act as page to Consuelo, and he followed her around Blenheim wearing an Oriental costume topped off by a turban.

Blenheim on Saturday morning to make these rounds, before the guests arrived in the afternoon.

After her executive session in the morning, the hostess must be ready in the drawing room for Edward's arrival, all nerves, rehearsing again and again the details of arrangements for his comfort. She would have coached the children: Leonie Jerome Leslie's children remembered their mother issuing "paralyzing instructions to us boys 'Never sit down while THEY stand, never start the conversation, never change the subject, never ask a question—and don't touch the Bar-le-Duc jam!'" All of those instructions (save the one about the Bar-le-Duc) applied equally to adults, and though they were second nature to court habitués, a slip would bring that freezing look of annoyance into the royal gray eyes.

COMME IL FAUT
The King and Queen enter a room when all the guests are assembled, and they are the first to leave.

A HOSTESS'S DUTIES

After tea and a stroll on the lawn on a fine evening, the guests returned to their rooms to change for dinner. In her boudoir, the American hostess took one more look at the guest placement. A leather pad, with slots cut in an oblong and cards with names inserted into the slots, showed who would sit where. The lady of highest rank at her husband's right hand;

Racing always entertained the King. Here, he leads home his Derby winner, Persimmon, in 1896.

The ladies joining the "guns" at Lord Craven's house, Coombe Abbey. Jennie, at the far right, keeps her profile to the camera.

The King was a fine shot, and the sport at Sandringham was some of the best in the country. An average of 30,000 birds a year were bagged there.

the gentleman of highest rank at the hostess's right hand. Everyone else followed according to rank. This was so important that *Debrett's Peerage* assigned a number for each peer, peer's wife, and children, right down through the hundreds of baronets. One need only consult this convenient Table of Precedence.

Watching the service during dinner, making sure the footmen kept the glasses filled, noting that the sauce on the partridges was curiously bitter, the hostess still had to keep conversation going. During the first course, one addressed the person on one's right. As the second course was served, it was up to the hostess to "turn the table" by addressing herself to the gentleman on her left. And when dinner was over, when the last fruit knife had been laid at the side of a plate, the hostess rose and took the lady guests with her to the drawing room, leaving the gentlemen to enjoy their port and cigars while they discussed the ruling of the country or the results of the Derby (more likely the latter in the King's presence). Afterwards a band, shipped down from London, might provide music for dancing, or amateur theatricals, assiduously rehearsed for several days beforehand, might be presented. A ball at a neighboring country house might be the weekend's peg, in which case the entire house party would bundle off into carriages to drive to a similar house where a similar house party was already in progress.

On a shooting weekend, the entire group was expected at breakfast, though ladies never went out with the "guns." Otherwise, mornings were quiet. While His Majesty was safely in his rooms reading official papers, his hostess reviewed her troops. The chef: what had been wrong with the partridges? The housekeeper: Lord Robert put his foot through the sheet. The butler: Lady Angela would like to ride at eleven, so a horse should be saddled for her, and was it fine enough for luncheon outside?

The quiet was not always a blessing, however. "Sundays were interminably long," wrote Consuelo Marlborough, "for a hostess who had no games wherewith to entertain her guests. Golf and tennis had not yet become the vogue nor would they have been played on the Lord's Day." Instead, at Blenheim, entertainment included two church services, morning and evening. (His Majesty often read the lesson.) "Promenades were the fashionable pastime, and the number of tête-à-tête walks she could crowd into an afternoon became the criterion of a woman's social success. . . . Sometimes I had to find a recalcitrant swain to accompany a fair lady. One never knew where one's duties as a hostess would end."

THE ROYAL GUEST

When the King was one's guest, those duties never ended at all. His lightest whim, of course, was a command. Thus when an equerry sought out the American hostess to suggest that His Majesty might enjoy a slice of rare roast beef before retiring, the roast beef would materialize even if the servants went hungry. The *Tatler*, in 1909, listed some of his likes and dislikes. He rose early, and had coffee and a roll in his room, then went for a walk

Always fond of novelty, the King loved motoring. Here, he poses in a 1900 Daimler.

OUT OF THE PAST

Shut out in New York, Mrs. John Mackay had become an important London hostess by the end of the '80s. But, eagerly as she took advantage of that city's social tolerance, she didn't like to see it applied indiscriminately. In particular, she didn't like seeing it applied to Charles Bonynge, who had returned to England with his pretty daughter and stepdaughter (eventually Lady Maxwell and Viscountess Deerhurst). It was his American career as a broker of mining stocks that offended Louise Mackay; in the rudimentary social pecking order of her hometown, Virginia City, Nevada, a stockbroker was beneath the notice of a miner's wife.

Mrs. Mackay had not forgotten that distinction. She entertained widely in London, but Charles Bonynge she ignored. During the season of 1889, the American minister Phelps remonstrated, suggesting that Mrs. Mackay put aside her prejudice for the unity of the tight-knit American community, but still she refused. There was no reason, she maintained, to "invite a C Street broker to my house."

Though Louise had successfully translated herself since her Virginia City days, when she gave piano lessons and took in sewing to make a living, her past had followed her to London. Nasty little stories were often leaked to the British press, claiming that she'd run a boarding house or been a washerwoman, and that John Mackay had been one of her customers. Who in London had known her in Virginia City? Charles Bonynge. And she was sure he was behind some of those nasty tales.

A little feud born in the dusty hills of Nevada couldn't block her ambition for long, of course, and soon Mrs. Mackay had achieved her goal. The morning after a party at her home, attended by the Prince of Wales, all the guests received newspaper clippings and an ill-spelt pamphlet repeating the washerwoman story. A successful lawsuit stopped the publication of further gossip, but Bonynge himself could not be chastened until the day he met John Mackay unexpectedly in a banker's office. Mackay punched him in the eye, knocking him down, and later told reporters with satisfaction how Bonynge's blood "poured all over my trousers." The Wild West vendetta that carried over into English court circles had finally been settled—frontier style.

John Mackay wasn't afraid to use his hands to defend his wife's honor.

with his host, who should be sure to be available for this event.

After breakfast in his room and an hour or so spent on state duties, His Majesty was ready for relaxation. He was an avid racegoer and a keen shot (though he didn't hunt). Out shooting, he liked to have the ladies join the "guns" for lunch, but he didn't like them around when the shooting resumed. Bad weather could be disastrous. One might take the King motoring, or get up a rubber of bridge, but as the *Tatler* reminded its readers, Edward possessed "a very restless nature" and looked for "constant amusements when staying with any of his subjects."

By 1902, Edward VII's chest and waist both measured forty-eight inches.

In the evening he liked cards and music; he also liked formality. One of the Blenheim servants remembered the sight of the dinner table when the then Prince visited the Marlboroughs: "I think the first thing that struck me was the flashing headgear of the ladies. The Blue Hungarian [band] was playing and there was the Prince himself looking really royal and magnificent in military uniform. The table was laid of course with the silver-gilt service . . . and the royal footmen waiting side by side with our own." That dinner followed a torchlight parade in the park. On the last night of the royal visit, the Marlboroughs had a concert to which they invited some of the prominent county families, and Consuelo describes how "the royal procession wound its way through the throng of bejeweled women and men in knee breeches and uniforms and stopped here and there for a word of greeting."

Edward leaving Blenheim after a visit in the late 1890s. Consuelo stands on the steps, on the red carpet laid down for the royal visitor.

She was vastly relieved when the royal party left, as, in all probability, were most hostesses. The King would affably give autographs and always signed the visitors' book (taking up almost a page with his signature), so there it was, in writing, proof of his royal condescension—"the accolade," as Nancy Astor's biographer said, "of fashionability." *That* would show them back in New York!

"I thought everyone must know that a short jacket is always worn with a silk hat at a private view in the morning."

What Edward wore, other men soon copied. When he arrived at Marienbad to take the cure, tailors from all over Europe recorded any new crease, or collar on the royal person. If he appeared at Longchamps Races in a strangely shaped hat, the boulevards of Paris were soon full of men sporting similar hats.

No one was exempt from a royal rebuke on the subject of what he was wearing. "Trousers are always worn on board ship!" Edward said to a minister who appeared on the *Victoria and Albert* in knee breeches. And, to a groom-in-waiting: "Is it possible you are thinking of going to a *wedding* in a black waistcoat?" On one occasion, he spied medals arrayed in the wrong order on the chest of the Swedish ambassador. "Hunt and Roskill, 148 Piccadilly," he quickly whispered, apparently feeling that only a personal visit to the court jewelers would set this miscreant straight.

Edward's own sartorial subtlety knew no bounds. Once, when approaching the coast of Scotland, he requested that his valet put out something "a little more Scottish" for the next day—not completely Scottish, mind you, since he wasn't yet *in* Scotland. So much did he care about the correct outfit, be it ceremonial or sporting or something in between, that he changed what he was wearing at least half a dozen times a day. He traveled with two val-

Edward the trend-setter, dressed for town and country.

ets, while another two stayed behind to tend the royal closets, where costumes were stored for every variation of climate and occasion in every corner of the world.

Clockwise from top: The Admiralty effect, with Garter insignia; a Scottish sporran for the accessory-lover; the original "Prince of Wales" plaid; full Masonic regalia.

FASHIONS BY EDWARD

Dinner Jacket. Born on a trip to India, when Edward replaced the traditional swallowtail coat with a short dark blue jacket over black trousers, with a black bow tie.

Creased Trousers. Edward tried on a pair that had been lying folded and liked the slimming effect. He took it one step further and tried trousers folded across to disguise his bandy legs, but this look never caught on.

Hats. Owner of over 100 different hats, Edward introduced the black Homburg and lent his approval to the Tyrolean. He detested the Panama and anybody who wore one.

Unbuttoned Button. Dressing hurriedly for dinner, Edward neglected to do up the bottom button of his waistcoat. (Still the correct—and, for larger men, more comfortable—way to wear a waistcoat.)

Norfolk Jacket. Flattered the royal figure—and those of stout men everywhere.

Tweed at Goodwood. When Edward substituted a tweed suit for his usual frock coat at the season's last race meeting, everyone, according to Winston Churchill, "followed the King's sensible example." And still does.

"For richer, for poorer. . ."

The Last Marriages

During the decade following the *annus mirabilis* of 1895, the year that saw so many notable Anglo-American matches, the pace tapered off. Daisy Leiter's marriage to the Earl of Suffolk was one of the few notable matches of 1904; there were none in 1905. The American Aristocrats were staying home. But there were still Americans in London, and several of them had daughters. These girls were heiresses of yet another new breed.

Helen Post, for example, had lived for years as an English girl; her mother had come to London as the widowed Mrs. Arthur Post and in 1889 had married Lord Barrymore. Margaretta Drexel's parents were well established in London, with one of the largest town houses and one of the most famous chefs in London. Jean Reid was the ambassador's daughter, living in splendor at Dorchester House, and Mildred Carter's father was secretary of the embassy. All these girls had London débuts; in fact, when John Carter was recalled to the United States, Mildred was sent back to London for the season and chaperoned by Mrs. Reid.

The new heiresses had English friends, English educations, even English accents. They were cosmopolitan, and there was never any sense about them that being American required an apology. The *Tatler*, describing Jean Reid, stated that she "in common with most of her heiress compatriots might have been born in the very midst of the purple for all she shows of her yeoman descent." Only thirty-five years had passed since the Marlboroughs thought Jennie Jerome nearly savage. The United States had grown up in the world, and its daughters now took their place with confidence and command. Daisy Miller, with her audacity and innocence, had been superseded by a thoroughly sophisticated young lady.

> *"As may be guessed this début was attended by a fine flourish of trumpets, for where can the free-born American be found who does not know the art of self-advertisement?"*
> Open letter to Hon. Mrs. John Ward, formerly Miss Jean Reid, in the *Tatler* (1909)

CLEVER AND CULTURED AMERICANS

These daughters of the international set were more or less bound to make English marriages, since their very lives were thoroughly English. They were considered perfectly eligible, moreover, for the English were finally becoming familiar with the signposts of American social life. Of Beatrice Mills (who married the Earl of Granard in 1909), the *Tatler* noted that "her mother, who was a Livingstone, belongs to the ancienne noblesse of the United States." In a paragraph on Alice Blight, a beautiful Philadelphian who had married Englishman Gerard Lowther, the *Tatler* referred to "the millionaire Mills-Astor circle" and knowingly called the new Mrs. Lowther "as cultivated as any Bostonian."

The Countess of Granard (at right), née Beatrice Mills. Mrs. Cavendish-Bentinck was her aunt, Jean Reid her cousin, and Amy Phipps her sister-in-law.

Of course, the traditional American attractions had not faded. Mentioning a dinner given by the Marchioness of Granby, *Town Topics* remarked that "it was easy to pick out the American girls. They dress so well and know exactly how to put on their clothes." And American girls were still richer than anyone else.

So they married their Englishmen. The weddings did not have the same triumphant aura that peaked in the Vanderbilt and Whitney weddings of 1895. When Beatrice Mills married the Earl of Granard in 1909, the comparatively modest cere-

COURT CURTSY

One of the crucial rituals of the American Invasion was being presented at court. Though traditionally a recent bride wore her wedding dress, other ladies ordered splendid new gowns. By court ruling, one's dress must have a low neck and short sleeves. (Even elderly women wore *décolletage* unless they'd sent a doctor's certificate ahead of time to the Lord Chamberlain's office.) Any unmarried woman under sixty dressed in white, while the matronly *grandes dames* appeared in rich purple, crimson or even black.

Once dressed for court (it took a good two hours), one got into a town-chariot and proceeded to the Mall leading to Buckingham Palace. During Victoria's reign, women left the house at nine A.M. because the Drawing Rooms at which they were presented began at eleven, and one could expect to be stuck in Palace-bound traffic for two hours. The wait was the grueling part. Highly vocal onlookers amused themselves by commenting on the women's clothes and jewels, while the court hairdresser hopped from carriage to carriage putting finishing touches on coiffures and feathers. Even at the Palace, the waiting continued. Here the women were herded, with their trains over

Buckingham Palace, c.1895. On Drawing Room days, a traffic jam extended down Pall Mall. Right: Rosalind Secor Chetwynd, dressed for presentation at court.

their arms like bundles of laundry, through a succession of rooms known as "the pens."

The actual moment of presentation was very brief. At the door to the audience chamber, a lady's train was lifted from her arm and spread out by a gentleman-in-waiting. A card giving her full name was handed to a lord-in-waiting, who passed it on to the Lord Chamberlain, who in turn announced the name. The presentee walked forward and curtsied to the King (he had long ago taken Victoria's place at Drawing Rooms, as she hated public appearances while he relished the chance to look over each fresh crop of women) and any other royals present. The court curtsy was very deep, with the head nearly touching the floor, and required extensive rehearsal. The trickiest part was inching out of the royal presence, since one may not turn one's back on royalty. A lady held out her arm for her train, which was tossed to her by a page (there were dreadful rumors about pages throwing trains over ladies' heads, or purposely crossing their trains to trip them), and tried to walk smoothly backward without glancing over her shoulder. English girls were drilled in the procedure. Elma Gordon-Cumming, daughter of the American Florence Garner, recalled: "Every dancing class I ever attended, even at the age of nine, included rehearsals of court curtsies."

In Victoria's time, neither food nor drink was served; afterward, one could only go home, wildly overdressed for the midafternoon. But when Edward became king, receptions were tacked on after the evening courts, or one could take off one's veil and feathers and go to a dance in one's glorious dress, and everybody would know one had been to court.

Right: The process allowed all too much time for final adjustments. Below: The first court under the new king, March 14, 1901. Presentees were required to wear three ostrich plumes, affixed to the back of the head "so they can be clearly seen on approaching the Presence."

mony took place at home in New York, with no fanfare about guest lists and gifts. And many of the girls simply married in England. The effort of coming home to marry off a daughter on her native soil was no longer seen as necessary. The new heiresses' families and friends were in England. Frequently their bridesmaids were English. (They had often been bridesmaids in English weddings.) Why even bother with New York, when one could join a long line of society brides who had been wed at St. George's Hanover Square or St. Margaret's Westminster?

ROYAL FAVOR

There was still competition. Some American features are not as easily eradicated as an accent, and what better opportunity to compete than a wedding? Worth wedding dresses in white satin were still *de rigueur*; elaborate flowers, Mendelssohn and Wagner on the organ were essential. The American diplomatic community must always be represented. (Ambassador Reid went to so many weddings that it's hard to know how he got any work done.) Other London features were numerous titled guests, especially American heiresses of previous vintages, and the presence in force of the groom's delighted family.

Jean Reid was the ruling belle of the American community in London, and her wedding was signally marked by royal favor.

But the crucial distinction was the interest—or lack thereof—that Their Majesties showed in these marriages. On one level were royal wedding presents. Usually the newspaper listings of gifts featured the offering from the Palace: a clock, a piece of jewelry, some fine lace. On an entirely loftier plane was actual royal attendance; since the King and Queen seldom went to weddings, even of the English *haute noblesse,* their presence was considered a real coup. In this category, Jean Reid came out miles ahead. Her father was Whitelaw Reid, ambassador to the Court of St. James,

Margaretta Drexel and her fiancé, Lord Maidstone, at a race meeting shortly before their marriage.

from a country whose position in the world was growing steadily more important; her fiancé, the Honourable John Ward, was the Earl of Dudley's brother and His Majesty's favorite equerry. Royal condescension at her wedding was almost crushing. Not only did the ceremony take place at the Chapel Royal in St. James's Palace, in the royal presence (along with that of the Prince and Princess of Wales, the Duke and Duchess of Connaught, Princess Patricia of Connaught, Prince and Princess Alexander of Teck, Prince and Princess Francis of Teck, and Grand Duke Michael of Russia), but on her wrist the bride wore the personal royal wedding presents: matching diamond snake bracelets with jeweled eyes, ruby from the Queen and cat's-eye from the King. After the ceremony the Queen kissed the bride, and the King slapped the groom on the back as he said, "Well done, Johnny!"

END OF THE WORLD

The season of 1910 was slated to produce a bumper crop of new heiress brides. Margaretta Drexel would marry, in early June, Lord Maidstone, heir of the Earl of Winchilsea (who had declared bankruptcy in the 1870s); the reception would take place at the Drexels' house. Mildred Carter and Helen Post, two of Margaretta's bridesmaids, were to marry later in

Among Margaretta's bridesmaids was Mildred Carter (third from left). The bouquets included daisies, also known as "marguerites."

"Are there any more like you at home?"

Jennie, Clara and Leonie Jerome: sisters who always stood by each other in financial and romantic crises.

Like any pioneers in a new land, the American wives in England got themselves settled, looked around—and sent for the rest of the family. In particular, they sent for their unmarried sisters. As young matrons in fashionable English society, they found themselves in an unparalleled position to provide what every young girl in that era wanted to find: an eligible bachelor.

Sisters wouldn't have to fight for social sponsorship or forge alliances on their own; owing to the close-knit nature of English society, the weight of their brother-in-laws' families would back them up. Furthermore, American sisters married to Englishmen would form their own power block in society. So the sisters came to London. They were charming and pretty and rich. They were something of a given quantity. In no time at all, they were married.

In addition, not a few American mothers, having successfully placed their daughters and somehow become single again, settled down for the second time with Englishmen of their own.

THE SISTER ACTS

The Bonynges: Louisa (*m.* Major General Sir John Maxwell) and her stepsister Virginia (*m.* Viscount Deerhurst).

The Breeses: Eloise (*m.* Lord Willoughby de Eresby, later Earl of Ancaster) and Anna (*m.* Lord Alastair Innes-Ker, younger brother of 8th Duke of Roxburghe, who married May Goelet).

The Carrs: Alys, "the lovely young widow Mrs. Chauncey" (*m.* Sir Cecil Bingham), and Grace (*m.* Lord Newborough).

The Chamberlains: Jeannie (*m.* Herbert Naylor-Leyland, later Sir

Herbert) and Josephine (*m.* T.T.L. Scarisbrick of Lancashire).

THE FROSTS: Jane (*m.* Sir Lewis Molesworth), Evelyn (*m.* Philip Beresford-Hope) and Louisa (*m.* Hon. William F.C. Vernon).

THE GRACES: Elena (*m.* Lord Donoughmore) and Elisa (*m.* Hon. Hubert Beaumont).

THE JEROMES: Jennie "the Beautiful" (*m.* Earl of Randolph Churchill), Clara "the Good" (*m.* Moreton Frewen) and Leonie "the Witty" (*m.* Sir John Leslie).

THE LEITERS: Mary (*m.* Hon. George Curzon, later Lord Curzon), Marguerite (Daisy) (*m.* Earl of Suffolk) and Nancy (*m.* Major Colin Campbell).

THE RANDOLPH/WHITNEY STEPSISTERS: Adelaide Randolph (*m.* Hon. Lionel Lambart) and Pauline Whitney (*m.* Almeric Paget, later Lord Queenborough).

THE WADSWORTHS: Widow Cornelia Wadsworth Ritchie (*m.* John Adair of County Rathdaire, Ireland) and her widowed sister Elizabeth Wadsworth Post (*m.* Arthur Barry, later Lord Barrymore).

THE YZNAGAS: Consuelo (*m.* Viscount Mandeville, later Duke of Manchester) and Natica (*m.* Sir John Lister-Kaye).

MOTHER-DAUGHTER DUOS

LADY BARRYMORE (née Elizabeth Wadsworth) and **Helen Post** (*m.* Hon. Montague Eliot, later Earl of St. Germans).

WIDOW MRS. EDWARD PADELFORD (*m.* Ernest Cunard) and **Florence** (*m.* Hon. Robert Grosvenor, later Lord Ebury).

The Three Graces: Elisa, Elena and Margarita, who married Amy Phipps' brother John. Insets: Mary Leiter (left) disapproved when Daisy (right) married Suffolk, thinking it was merely an ambitious match.

"For my part I do not think that common justice is done by writers and journalists to that wondrous thing, American womanhood. After all, the best class of women from the New World have done much to change the face of London society. In a word, they brought the grit and 'go' of a new race to bear on our rusty if cherished institutions. They have made us more modern in our ways and more up-to-date in our opinions; they have taught us how to manage the mere man, and how to rule our own houses and keep our own money. In a word, they opened our eyes to women's rights long before we ever heard of a Suffragette demonstration. We were a weaker, more backward, and certainly poorer people before the seventies and eighties brought us the first of our now well-known Anglo-American alliances."

Open letter to the Countess of Donoughmore, formerly Miss Elena Grace of New York, in the *Tatler* (1910)

the month. Mildred's fiancé was Viscount Acheson, eldest son of the Earl of Gosford, and she was to be married from Dorchester House since her family no longer lived in London. Helen Post was engaged to the Honourable Montague Eliot, second son of the Earl of St. Germans. Each of these weddings would be held at St. George's Hanover Square. The church would be packed with Anglo-American nobility, and displayed among the gifts would be a memento sent with best wishes from Buckingham Palace.

Mildred Carter and her fiancé, Viscount Acheson. Acheson's father had sold the contents of the family home to pay his debts.

Then, in May, the King died. His reign had been less than one-sixth the length of his mother's, but he was no less deeply mourned. When the funeral procession wound through London, with the King's dog Caesar following the coffin, the onlookers' tears were sincere. Edward's death, particularly for Americans in London, seemed the end of the world.

The Drexel, Carter and Post marriages took place as scheduled. Despite messages from the Palace that court mourning should not interfere with the celebrations, most of the guests at all three weddings were dressed in black. It was considered notable that Mrs. Anthony Drexel, Margaretta's mother, chose to put aside mourning for the day and wear peach. It was hard to be festive when so much had changed.

TILL DEATH OR THE JUDGE DO US PART: THE AMERICAN HEIRESS DIVORCE

Marrying an English aristocrat meant that the American heiress had to make enormous cultural transitions. But what if she simply gave up? Decided she hated her husband? Wanted to be American again? In the early years of the transatlantic match, the heiress who regretted her choice of husband was out of luck. Divorce, in England, was almost unheard of. Grounds for the proceeding were few (adultery, insanity, previous marriage) and shameful. A divorcée like the ninth Duke of Marlborough's mother automatically disappeared from society. So women like Consuelo Yznaga (tied forever to the reprehensible eighth Duke of Manchester) had to make the best of matters by availing themselves of the aristocratic, Marlborough House Set leniency toward adultery.

In the United States, the prevailing attitude toward divorce was very different. With a characteristic combination of idealism (Americans expected marriages to work) and pragmatism (if it's not working, throw it away), individual states had thrashed out divorce laws that suited them. It was usually possible for an unhappy couple to find some haven (most often a western city) for a parting in which no one lost face. Grounds could be as innocuous as desertion. Frances Burke-Roche, having suffered through a con-

Alva took credit later in life for helping to make divorce socially acceptable. She considered this one of her great achievements.

Jacques Balsan had been present at Consuelo's Paris début and was an occasional visitor to Blenheim. He and Consuelo were married in the Episcopal church in 1921.

Like mother, like daughter: Consuelo, after her separation from Marlborough, with her father.

tested divorce proceeding in London, returned to the States and succeeded in obtaining a Delaware divorce in 1891. (The outraged Burke-Roche subsequently sued *Burke's Peerage* for noting the divorce in his listing.) And once Alva Vanderbilt faced down society with her New York state divorce from Willie K., more and more women followed suit.

One of them was her daughter. In 1906, after eleven unhappy years, Consuelo moved out of Blenheim and into the newly built Sunderland House in London. Here, she began a new life, pledging herself to politics and Good Works while Sunny devoted his time to the lovely Bostonian Gladys Deacon—who had also been a warm friend of his wife's. (Some sources alleged that both Marlboroughs had strayed before the separation, although Consuelo would always play the injured party.) Their estrangement infuriated Edward VII, who refused to meet either of the pair socially. In 1920, the divorce became final; a year afterward, Sunny married Gladys. Then, in 1926, Consuelo asked the Catholic Rota to annul her first marriage so that she could marry Frenchman Jacques Balsan in the Catholic Church. The Marlborough union, which had resulted in two sons, was declared void because it had been entered into under duress; the sons would not, however, have to suffer the taint of illegitimacy.

In 1928, Mildred Carter divorced the Earl of Gosford for adultery and desertion. (Telling Mildred that he'd be back in four months' time, the Earl had left for China in 1919 and stayed there for three years.) American women married to Englishmen were finding they couldn't completely shed their American-ness. As the twentieth century advanced, and "American" took on more legitimate and less outlandish connotations in Europe, they were more willing to claim the rights their nationality gave them. One of these was "the pursuit of happiness," and that had nothing to do with being yoked for life to an incompatible husband.

EPILOGUE

By the turn of the century, trusting Americans were finally realizing that noble blood was no guarantee of noble character. Reporting on Virginia Bonynge's engagement to Viscount Deerhurst, New York's *Town Topics* gloomily stated that the heiress could hardly be congratulated and reminded its readers that Deerhurst's father, the Earl of Coventry, "practically disowned his son after the latter had dissipated to such an extent that all efforts to induce him to reform appeared fruitless. Lord Deerhurst, finding that his father at length refused to pay his debts, promptly became bankrupt and then proceeded to Australia where *strange* tales of his proceeding were reported." The concept of decadence had come alive—a titled cad could exist.

"Now I do not often complain—but few men have been plagued with such a woman as C—— truly her life is spent in doing harm to the family whose name she bears."

THE 9th DUKE OF MARLBOROUGH, about his ex-wife Consuelo

A DAWNING DOUBT

One of the messiest of the mercenary matches was that between Alice Thaw and the Earl of Yarmouth (he of the bartending skills). Yarmouth, eldest son of the Marquess of Hertford, was a very handsome young man whose thespian aspirations had brought him to New York, where he joined a stock company under the name Eric Hope and penned some articles for the *World* on the art of being a lady. He met Harry K. Thaw, the young heir to a Pittsburgh railroad fortune, at a dinner party and before long found himself aboard the same train that was carrying Harry's sister Alice and Mrs. Thaw to Palm Beach. Alice was a serious girl, devoted to her church and charity work, but she fell for Lord Yarmouth and the date for their marriage was set.

Alice Thaw, whose brother Harry found her a husband just as inappropriate as his wife Evelyn Nesbit would be.

Unfortunately, on the morning of the wedding, Yarmouth was arrested for three hundred pounds'

"*A Hanging Offense*"

Frank Work, father of Frances Burke-Roche, put his disapproval of foreign marriages quite baldly. During an interview quoted in his obituary, which appeared in the New York *Tribune* in 1911, he stated: "It's time this international marrying came to a stop for our American girls are ruining our own country by it. As fast as our honorable, hard working men can earn this money their daughters take it and toss it across the ocean. And for what? For the purpose of a title and the privilege of paying the debts of so-called noblemen! If I had anything to say about it, I'd make an international marriage a hanging offense."

Strong as these words were, Work reinforced them in the terms of his will, which turned out to feature fifteen codicils that mirrored Frances' marital career. In 1901, she was to be left $70,000 per year if she had nothing else to do with her ex-husband. The fifth codicil forbade her to have anything to do with the National Horse Show and horse trainers—she was rumored at the time to be getting too intimate with a Hungarian trainer. The sixth codicil cut her allowance to $12,000 if she had anything to do with her former husband; the seventh increased her allowance to $80,000. A twelfth codicil stated that if she married the Hungarian trainer, Aurel Batonyi, she would forfeit her interest in her father's estate. Frances married Batonyi, and was cut out of the will by the thirteenth codicil.

Frances Burke-Roche: later, much against her father's will, Frances Batonyi.

In a fourteenth codicil, Work was prepared to make an allowance if Frances would separate from Batonyi. She eventually did divorce the man (very messily; he countersued, accusing her of adultery, and she was publicly cut dead at the Newport Casino by all her old friends), and after her father's death she and her sister shared the estate.

The Thaw wedding party at Calvary Church in Pittsburgh.

The Earl of Yarmouth. After his marriage, he was caricatured in the New York Journal *as a female impersonator powdering his nose.*

worth of outstanding London debts. He took the opportunity to renegotiate the settlements, achieving a total rumored to exceed a million dollars, and delayed the marriage for forty-five minutes until the papers were signed. The bride, left waiting at the church, would have done well to use those minutes to reconsider. *The New York Times* printed the story that her favorite dog jumped up on Yarmouth at the wedding reception and was violently thrown against a wall. Within ten months, when the Yarmouths visited the United States, he was staying alone in New York while she went to Palm Beach and Pittsburgh.

It didn't help when brother Harry shot and killed architect Stanford White over the affections of actress Evelyn Nesbit. Returning to the States for the trial, Alice was not accompanied by a supportive husband. Yarmouth had gone to Monte Carlo. Rumors of separation were rife, and no one was surprised when a suit to annul the marriage was entered in a

Harry K. Thaw. When he shot Stanford White, Yarmouth's family worried about tainting the family line with insanity. Their concern, it turned out, was misplaced.

London divorce court. "The Earl's companions and his manner of living," wrote *The New York Times*, "were such that he could not give his wife the position in society that she had a right to expect. She supplied immense sums to defray her husband's extravagances. . . ." The only grounds for annulment in England were insanity prior to marriage, an already existing marriage, or nonconsummation. On the last of these, the marriage was annulled: the Earl and Countess had never "lived together as man and wife." Yarmouth's lawyer, as a parting shot, pointed out that at least there were no grounds for divorce.

Most important, Lord Yarmouth got no money. The Thaws had carefully tied up Alice's settlements in trusts. Her husband's income of $50,000 per year derived from money settled on her for life—money he had no access to after they parted. By 1903, the year of the Thaw/Yarmouth marriage, American estate lawyers had learned something about protecting the interests of their clients who married English peers.

THE MILLIONS BELONG IN AMERICA

The backlash had actually begun in the 1890s. When Gertrude Vanderbilt married Harry Payne Whitney, literally the boy next door, journalists had a field day. The New York *Journal* blared, "Money will marry money next Tuesday. Broad acres will be wed to broad acres. . . . But it will be an American wedding. There will be no foreign nobleman in this—no purchased titles. The millions all belong in America and they will all remain here." Bandleader Nathan Franko, in a paroxysm of patriotism, could not restrain himself from playing *The Star-Spangled Banner* at the reception.

The mercenary matches, by then, were adding up. It was impossible to forget the Hammersley/Marlborough courtship. And there was Mrs. Burke-Roche, a fixture of New York society, every inch the wronged woman. The Vanderbilt/Marlborough

Gertrude Vanderbilt and Harry Payne Whitney, the all-American couple.

Anthony J. Drexel, Jr. (with his sister Margaretta) and Marjorie Gould (inset), daughter of George Gould.

When Anthony and Marjorie married, the Tatler *coverage included the headline: "Dukes at a Discount."*

match also looked ugly. As the century turned, the sentiment against Anglo-American matches grew stronger until an Englishman's marriage proposal seemed less a compliment than a calculation. While women like Betty Leggett were rushing off to England to establish themselves in the new social capital, their husbands were thinking things over. It was all very well for the ladies if it kept them entertained, but really, America was a very fine place and what good was a title anyway? "A good social position I can agree with you is most desirable," Frank Leggett wrote to Betty, "if one is endowed with all the qualities and attainments to fill it with dignity and credit." But he was writing about Alberta's engagement to George Montagu, heir presumptive to the Earl of Sandwich, and he found it difficult to muster enthusiasm. "I shall try to show as much pride in the connection as you and Alberta must feel, but above all hope that happiness will prove the dominant feature of the whole affair. For happiness is worth more than millions of money and the most exalted positions."

"Those who are always carping at the tendency on the part of our young peers to take unto themselves wives from among the heiresses of America will be glad to hear that there is a suggestion in the United States that a graduated tax, increasing according to the size of the lady's fortune, should be levied on all rich American brides who marry titled foreigners."

"Round and About Notes," the *Tatler* (1908)

> *"The King dines alone."*
> EDWARD VII's last diary entry (May 4, 1910)

END OF THE WALTZ

It wasn't merely the risk of marrying a reprobate that lessened the attraction to the English aristocrat. The breed was losing some of its otherworldly patina. In the first years of the twentieth century, it became commonplace for peers to serve on the boards of various businesses. Viscount Maidstone, for example, after marrying Margaretta Drexel, went into the City every day to work in a brokerage firm. If an American girl wanted to marry a stockbroker, she might just as well stay home.

Another important factor in the waning of the transatlantic match was America itself. In the 1870s, the still-new republic was just recovering from a civil war, just forging a national identity and a national culture. By 1910 it was the imperial republic that had annexed the Philippines and built a navy to rival Germany's. America's international stature was indisputable. This held true on the social as well as miliary fronts. Expatriates who cut a swathe in English society—Grace Wilson Vanderbilt on the Kaiser's yacht at Kiel, Consuelo Vanderbilt Marlborough visiting the Imperial Court at St. Petersburg—need not apologize for being American.

The Royal Ascot race meeting the month after Edward's death was nicknamed "Black Ascot" because society, out of respect for His late Majesty, wore black to the race course. The Royal Box was deserted since the late King's family naturally could not attend while mourning him.

Society in America became more sure of itself. Social climbers no longer needed titles for legitimacy; America could provide its own distinctions. By 1910 New York was not a backwater but an important stop on the international social circuit, along with London, Paris, Newport and emerging pleasure spots such as Palm Beach and the French Riviera.

The whole world, in fact, was changing. The pleasantly ample curves and pastel palette of the Edwardian era (equally charming in women, furniture and paintings) were giving way to modernity. Picasso was creating strange, ugly gray pictures. The tuneful waltzes of Strauss were dissolving into the spiky atonalities of Berg. And Charles Frederick Worth's son was designing dresses that ended above ladies' ankles.

THE PARTY'S OVER

Perhaps the final, irrevocable blow to the era of Anglo-American matches came with the death of "that arch vulgarian," King Edward VII, in 1910. George and Mary, the instant they assumed the throne, indicated that things were going to be different. When they chose their courtiers, two of Edward's grooms-in-waiting, Sir John Lister-Kaye and the Honourable Montague Eliot, were not reappointed. Since both men had married American heiresses, the point was made: George and Mary did not like Americans. After forty years of love from the top, American women were no longer in favor at court.

Not that it was a court they would have had much liking for. George V and Queen Mary were as different from Edward and Alexandra as the latter pair had been from Victoria and Albert. George was his grandmother all over again, minus the brains: hardworking, thrifty (if not downright cheap), dignified, disdainful of frivolity. He did not have his father's appetites or robust appreciation of beautiful women. Mary had no passion for clothes or parties. The massive tiaras, the houses stuffed with treasures, the elaborate entertainments, the Worth dresses—those were Bertie's style. George and Mary represented the England that hated having dollars thrown in its face. They reigned within their means and according to their mediocre taste. Bridge games were out (cards equaled gambling equaled sin), as were the lavish balls and free-flowing champagne. This was a sober, respectable court, in bed by eleven; hardly a court worth crossing an ocean for. And so the heyday of the American heiress and her countrymen in London became a thing of the past—at least until another fun-loving, high-living Prince of Wales came along to welcome them once again.

The King at his last Derby, in 1909, won by his colt Minoru. The next year, his dog Caesar, below, followed his casket in the funeral procession.

"It was a period when many of the daughters of America elected to marry and identify their lives with Europeans and notably Englishmen—They exchanged the home life of America for that of England, and the new angles of vision with which they perceived the old world enabled them to leave an imprint on the customs of a society which hitherto had grown up sheltered in its insular tradition.

"This period of social intercourse, this period of international relation is not likely to recur because Europe and its traditions no longer appeal with the same force and vigour to the American feminine mind as they did in the closing years of the Victorian era."

—9TH DUKE OF MARLBOROUGH

AN AMERICAN HEIRESS DIRECTORY

Register of American Heiresses

❖

Walking Tour of the American Heiresses' London

❖

Bibliography/Selected Reading

❖

Index

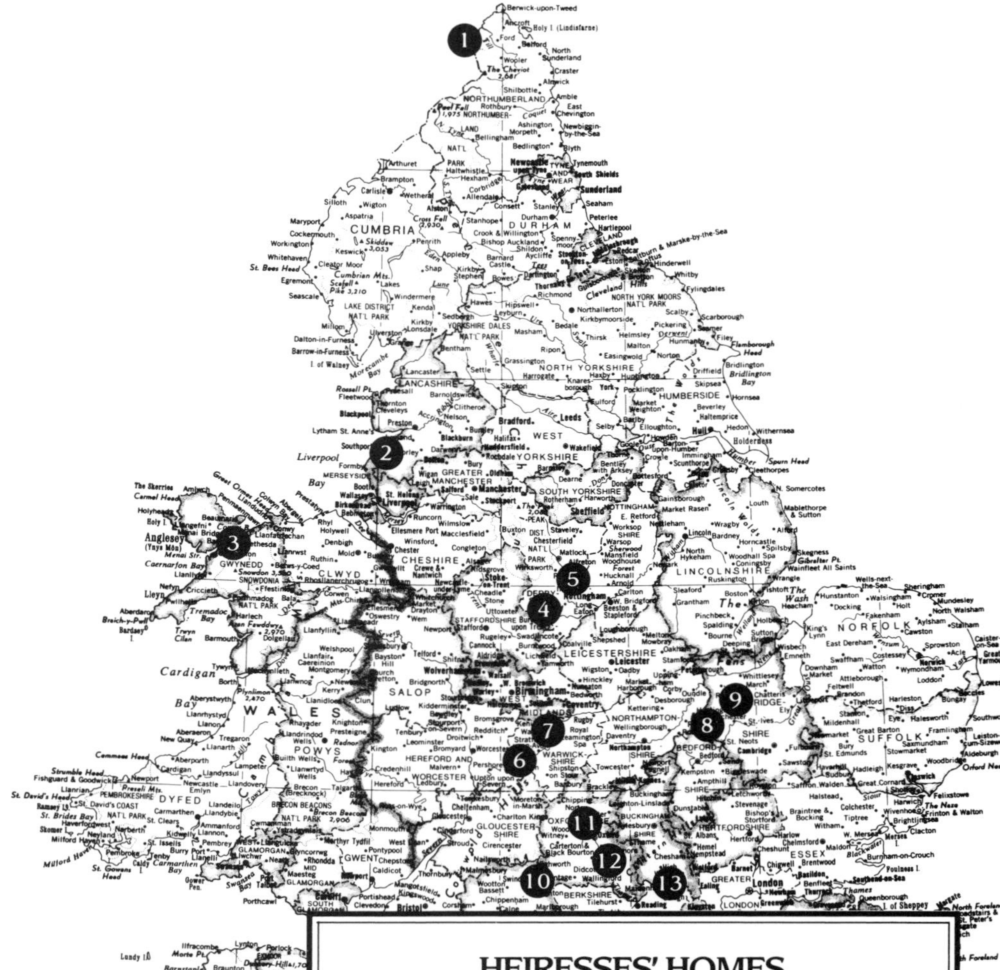

HEIRESSES' HOMES OPEN TO THE PUBLIC

1 **Floors Castle**, Kelso, Roxburghshire, Scotland
2 **Rufford Old Hall**, Rufford, Lancashire
3 **Pencarrow House**, Washaway, Bodmin, Cornwall
4 **Sudbury Hall**, Sudbury, Derbyshire
5 **Kedleston Hall**, Kedleston, Derbyshire
6 **Ragley Hall**, Alcester, Warwickshire
7 **Stoneleigh Abbey**, Kenilworth, Warwickshire
8 **Kimbolton Castle**, Huntingdon, Cambridgeshire
9 **Hinchingbrooke House**, Huntingdon, Cambridgeshire
10 **Ashdown House**, Ashbury, Oxfordshire
11 **Blenheim Palace**, Woodstock, Oxfordshire
12 **Stonor Park**, Henley-on-Thames, Oxfordshire
13 **Cliveden**, Maidenhead, Buckinghamshire
14 **Plas Newydd**, Isle of Anglesey, Gwynedd, Wales

(Not shown: **Kilkenny Castle**, Co. Kilkenny, Ireland)

REGISTER OF AMERICAN HEIRESSES

BECKWITH, FRANCES HELENE FORBES

Daughter of Nelson Beckwith of New York
Married November 29, 1890
To: the Hon. Francis Dudley Leigh, later 3rd Baron Leigh
*Seat: *Stoneleigh Abbey, Kenilworth, Warwickshire*

Helene's engagement to Leigh, whom she met while visiting Mrs. Bradley Martin in Scotland, surprised New York. Having been a belle at Napoleon III's court, Helene was a bit long in the tooth—eight years older than her thirty-five-year-old fiancé. She was a conservative châtelaine, said not to tolerate the "rapid set" at Stoneleigh house parties. After her death in 1909, Leigh married Marie Campbell, also an American.

BLIGHT, ALICE

Daughter of Atherton Blight of Philadelphia
Married February 28, 1908
To: Gerard Augustus Lowther, later 1st (and last) Baronet

A great beauty, Alice had traveled in Europe fairly extensively by the time she married Lowther (nephew of the 3rd Earl of Lonsdale). His diplomatic career took them to Constantinople for five years and earned his baronetcy.

BONYNGE, LOUISA

Daughter of Charles William Bonynge of London
Married 1892
To: Sir John Grenfell Maxwell, KCB, CVO, CMG, DSO

The English-born Bonynge began his American career as a San Francisco landscape gardener, then flourished as a broker in the boom years; when he moved back to London with Louisa and Virginia [q.v.], their presentation at court aroused a fuss about lowered social standards. Maxwell, a soldier who distinguished himself in the Imperial wars, was later disgraced for ordering the execution of Irish rebels at Kilmainham Gaol during the Easter Rising of 1916.

**Open to the public.*

"In the art of amusing men they are adepts, both by nature and education, and can actually tell a story without forgetting the point—an accomplishment that is extremely rare among the women of other countries."
OSCAR WILDE, in *The Pilgrim Daughters*

Despite her dubious antecedents, Virginia Bonynge was a bosom friend of Queen Victoria's daughter Helena, Princess Christian of Schleswig-Holstein.

BONYNGE, VIRGINIA

Stepdaughter of Charles William Bonynge of London
Married March 10, 1894
To: George William Coventry, Viscount Deerhurst, eldest son of 9th Earl of Coventry
Seat: Earls Croome Court, Earls Croome, Worchestershire

Virginia's real father, William Daniel, had committed murder in the Wild West, but the bankrupt Deerhurst was himself no marital bargain. Deerhurst died before succeeding to the earldom; two younger brothers married Americans, Lily Whitehouse and Edith Kip (McCreery) [q.v.]. A tapestry-hung salon from Croome Court is in New York's Metropolitan Museum of Art.

BRECKINRIDGE, FLORENCE

Daughter of John Breckinridge of San Francisco
Married September 8, 1909
To: Thomas Fermor-Hesketh, 8th Baronet, later created 1st Baron Hesketh
Seat: Easton Neston, Towcester, Northamptonshire

Florence, stepdaughter of Frederick W. Sharon, thus stepniece of Flora Sharon [q.v.], was taken to England as wife material for Flora's son, keeping the Comstock Lode dollars in the family. She found the adjustment difficult and took to her bed in reaction.

BREESE, ANNA

Daughter of William L. Breese of New York
Married October 10, 1907
To: Lord Alastair Robert Innes-Ker

Lord Alastair, younger brother of the 8th Duke of Roxburghe (husband of May Goelet [q.v.]), gained stature when the Duke seemed unable to produce an heir; Anna was widely assumed to be heartbroken when the Roxburghes finally had a son in 1913.

BREESE, ELOISE

Daughter of William L. Breese of New York
Married December 6, 1905
To: Gilbert Heathcote-Drummond-Willoughby, Lord Willoughby de Eresby, later 3rd Earl of Ancaster
Seats: Grimsthorpe, Bourne, Lincolnshire; Drummond Castle, Crieff, Perthshire, Scotland

Stepdaughter of Englishman Harry V. Higgins, impresario of the Covent Garden Opera, Eloise was lively and very "American"—a good match for the reticent Willoughby de Eresby. Their eldest son married the Hon. Phyllis Astor, daughter of the 2nd Viscount and Nancy Langhorne [q.v.].

BROWN, ELIZABETH TRIMBLE

Daughter of Judge James Trimble Brown of Nashville
Married February 17, 1897
To: the Hon. Archibald John Marjoribanks, 4th son of 1st Baron Tweedmouth

Elizabeth's grandfather was Neil P. Brown, former governor of Tennessee and U.S. minister to Russia. Archibald's brother Edward, the 2nd Baron Tweedmouth, caused a furor in 1908 when, as first Lord of the Admiralty, he allegedly disclosed British naval estimates to the German emperor.

BURBANK, LILLA

Daughter of John Burbank of Boston
Married 1884
To: Sir Arthur Augustus Boswell Eliott, 9th Baronet

The Scottish Sir Arthur was descended from Boswell, biographer of Samuel Johnson. His and Lilla's son and two daughters married Americans.

BURKE, MAUD

Daughter of E.F. Burke of San Francisco
Married April 16, 1895
To: Sir Bache Cunard, 3rd Baronet
Seat: Nevill Holt, Market Harborough, Leicester

Maud's father figure (and putative source of her dowry) was California real-estate magnate Horace Carpentier. Jilted by Prince Poniatowski and in need of a husband as cover for her warm friendship with playwright George Moore, Maud married the man at hand. Sir Bache (of the steamship line) was a hunting squire; Maud, a bright-lights, big-city girl who filled his drawing rooms with bohemians. She changed her name to Emerald (she hated the fact that there was no final "e" in her real name) and ran a London salon. She was a great champion of Wallis Simpson's cause and reportedly wailed, when Edward VIII abdicated, "How *could* he do this to me?"

BURNS, MARY ETHEL

Daughter of Walter Hayes Burns of New York and North Mymms Park, Hatfield, Hertfordshire
Married July 1, 1899
To: Lewis Harcourt, later Sir Lewis, created Viscount Harcourt 1917
Seat: Nuneham Park, Oxford

Burns was manager of J.S. Morgan & Co. of London and son-in-law of J.P. Morgan. Harcourt's father was Sir William Harcourt, famous politician and husband of Elizabeth Motley (Ives) [q.v.]. Nuneham's gardens gained renown under Lady Harcourt.

Mary Burns Harcourt and her husband's political agent, going over voter lists. Mary was one of the few heiresses to marry a Liberal.

Grace Carr and her husband shared a taste for travel; they had met in Egypt, and honeymooned in Ceylon.

BURROWS, MARY

Daughter of Ogden Hoffman Burrows of New York and Newport
Married July 22, 1891
To: Somerset Frederick Gough-Calthorpe, later 8th Baron Calthorpe
Seat: Perry Hall, Birmingham

The Calthorpe family had developed Edgbaston, a posh suburb of Birmingham, earlier in the century.

CAMERON, MARTHA

Daughter of Sen. James Donald Cameron of Harrisburg, Pennsylvania
Married March 18, 1909
To: the Hon. Ronald Charles Lindsay, 5th son of 26th Earl of Crawford

Cameron followed in his father's footsteps as U.S. senator and secretary of war, but was also a banker and railroad investor; his wife, twenty-four years younger, was a celebrated Washington hostess. Lindsay had a distinguished diplomatic career, culminating in the post of ambassador to the U.S. (1930–39).

CARR, ALYS (Mrs. Chauncey)

Daughter of Col. Henry Mongtomerie Carr of Louisville
Married 1911
To: Sir Cecil Bingham

Before her marriage to Bingham, Alice was well known in London as a lovely young widow. Nothing is known about Chauncey.

CARR, GRACE BRUCE

Daughter of Col. Henry Montgomerie Carr of Louisville
Married November 7, 1900
To: William Charles Wynn, 4th Baron Newborough
Seat: Bryn Llewellyn, Rhug, Corwen, Clywd, Wales

Grace and Newborough met in Egypt. They were married at the Savoy Chapel, where the bride was given away by U.S. Ambassador Choate. Newborough owned some 28,000 acres, mostly in Wales; he died on active service in World War I.

CARTER, MILDRED

Daughter of John Ridgely Carter of Baltimore
Married June 21, 1910
To: Archibald Charles Montague Brabazon Acheson, Viscount Acheson, later 5th Earl of Gosford
Seat: Gosford Castle, Markethill, Co. Armagh, Ireland

Mildred, whose handsome father was first secretary at the U.S. embassy, had a lavish London début in 1909. (The money came from her mother's side of the family.) Acheson's father was a courtier and friend of Edward VII; a spendthrift, he sold off the family estate library to pay racing debts and later sold the entire contents of his gloomy neo-Norman mansion in Ireland. After serving in the Boer War, Acheson worked for the Rothschild Bank. He and Mildred were divorced in 1928; his second wife was also an American.

The Carter-Acheson match was unhappy. Acheson spent three years in China in the early '20s and did not contest the divorce charges of adultery and desertion.

CHAMBERLAIN, JEANNIE

Daughter of William Selah Chamberlain of Cleveland
Married September 5, 1889
To: Capt. Herbert Naylor-Leyland, later 1st Baronet
The original Self-Made Girl and a great beauty, Jeannie entranced the Prince of Wales (Princess Alexandra reportedly referred to her as "Miss Chamberpots") and was rumored to have been his mistress after her marriage to Naylor-Leyland. She entertained lavishly at Hyde Park House in London and was the model for the popular novel *Miss Bayle's Romance*. Kings Edward VII and George V were godfathers to her sons.

COLGATE, CORA

Widow of Samuel Colgate
Married December 6, 1898
To: Henry William John Byng, 4th Earl of Strafford
Seat: Wrotham Park, Barnet
Cora's first father-in-law, English-born William Colgate, founded the soap-manufacturing company. Strafford, aged sixty-seven, had been equerry to the Prince of Wales for twenty-five years. He died five months after his marriage to Cora, and Wrotham Park (into which she had poured money) passed to his nephew. Cora was remarried (to another Englishman) in 1903.

OTHER DISTINGUISHED 19TH-CENTURY ENGLISHMEN WITH AMERICAN WIVES

Sir Thomas Beecham, Sir Anthony Hope Hawkins, Rudyard Kipling, Alfred Noyes, E. Phillips Oppenheim, Bertrand Russell (3d Earl Russell), Robert Louis Stevenson.

CORBIN, LOUISE

Daughter of Daniel Corbin of New York
Married May 17, 1888
To: Capt. Robert Horace Walpole, later 5th Earl of Orford
Seat: Wolterton Hall, Erpingham, Norwich

Corbin was an important investor in western railroads. Orford, descended from England's first prime minister, was a sportsman; he and Louise enjoyed tarpon fishing together.

CUYLER, MAY CAMPBELL

Daughter of Maj. James Wayne Cuyler of Morristown, New Jersey
Married January 4, 1893
To: Sir Philip Henry Brian Grey-Egerton, 12th Baronet

Cuyler, son of an army surgeon, had a distinguished career in the Army Corps of Engineers. May's wedding, which took place in London before this was the general rule, received extensive New York newspaper coverage featuring lists of the jewels received as gifts (including a diamond tiara from Sir Philip's tenants). The marriage ended in divorce in 1906; both sons, who were twins, died in action in World War I.

Clandeboye, the Dufferins' Irish home, was full of curiosities collected by the 1st Marquess, among them a stuffed grizzly bear and a mummy case.

DAVIS, FLORENCE ("FLORA")

Daughter of John H. Davis of New York
Married October 16, 1893
To: Lord Terence Temple-Blackwood, later 2nd Marquess of Dufferin and Ava
Seat: Clandeboye, Co. Down, Ireland

Davis was a New York banker; Lord Terence's father was governor-general of Canada and viceroy of India. The marriage took place at the British embassy in Paris, where Lord Terence was posted as secretary. When Terence's elder brother died in the Boer War, Flora became marchioness and châtelaine of Clandeboye. A year after her husband's death, in 1918, she married the 4th Earl Howe, whose previous wife was a sister of Randolph Churchill and sister-in-law of Jennie Jerome [q.v.].

DOLAN, MARIE ELIZABETH

Daughter of [?] of New York
Married March 13, 1906
To: Sidney Augustus Paget

Paget's brother Arthur married Minnie Stevens [q.v.]; his brother Almeric married Pauline Whitney [q.v.].

DONNELLY, FRANCES EMILY

Daughter of James C. Donnelly of New York
Married February 19, 1906
To: Francis Denzil Edward Baring, 5th Baron Ashburton

Ashburton, a member of the Baring banking family, was

succeeded by his son Alexander from a previous marriage. In 1924, Alexander married the Hon. Doris Harcourt, daughter of Viscount Harcourt and Mary Burns [q.v.].

DOVE, LAURA *(Mrs. John Adams Blanchard)*

Daughter of John Dove of Andover, Massachusetts
Married February 4, 1884
To: George Alexander Philip Haldane Duncan, later 4th Earl of Camperdown

Duncan was heir presumptive to the earldom when he married the widowed Laura. He ran a marine engine business, and they lived in Boston. Laura died in 1910, eight years before Duncan succeeded to the earldom. He diverted most of his inheritance to younger members of the family and remained in Boston, where he had many pet charities.

DREXEL, MARGARETTA

Daughter of Anthony J. Drexel of Philadelphia, Newport and London
Married June 8, 1910
To: Guy Montagu George Finch-Hatton, Viscount Maidstone, later 14th Earl of Winchilsea and Nottingham

There were so many gifts to display at Margaretta Drexel's wedding that they filled the ballroom of her parents' house.

Margaretta's father, of the banking Drexels, also held interests in real estate; her brother Anthony later married Marjorie Gould, sister of Vivien Gould [q.v.]. After her 1907 début, under the aegis of the Duchess of Connaught (Queen Victoria's daughter-in-law), Margaretta was the catch of her era, with rumored engagements to numerous impoverished Continental princes. Maidstone's family was old and poor (Uncle Denys Finch-Hatton achieved fame as a white hunter and also as a lover of Baroness Blixen, a.k.a. Isak Dinesen). The wedding was grand, with ten bridesmaids (including Mildred Carter and Nellie Post [q.v.]) and two thousand guests at the huge Drexel mansion on Grosvenor Square. The newlyweds lived with the Drexels, and Maidstone went back to his job on the Stock Exchange; he later earned medals for active service in World War I.

DUDLEY, HELEN MAY

Daughter of James Garrard Dudley of Frankfort, Kentucky
Married May 14, 1890
To: the Hon. Amyas Stafford Northcote

Helen's family claimed to be descended from the Earls of Dudley. Northcote was the seventh son of statesman Sir Stafford, 1st Earl of Iddesleigh. Married in Kentucky, the couple lived in Chicago, where Northcote was business manager of an English real-estate investment syndicate. His brother Oliver married Edith Fish [q.v.].

EAMES, FRANCES CAMPBELL

Daughter of Charles Eames
Married April 25, 1877
To: Alexander Penrose Gordon-Cumming

Frances' father was former U.S. minister to Venezuela; Gordon-Cumming's older brother was Sir William, husband of Florence Garner [q.v.]. After their marriage in Washington, he became an American citizen.

ELLISON, PATRICIA BURNLEY

Daughter of Andrew Ellison of Louisville
Married November 19, 1901
To: Sir Charles Henry Augustus Frederick Ross, 9th Baronet
Seat: Balnagowan, Parkhill, Ross-shire, Scotland

Patricia was married at home in Kentucky by a New York minister. (Ross had been previously married.) August Belmont lent the newlyweds his private railroad car for their honeymoon.

ENDICOTT, MARY

Daughter of William C. Endicott of Massachusetts
Married November 16, 1888
To: Rt. Hon. Joseph Chamberlain, M.P., P.C.

Endicott was secretary of war (1885–89). Chamberlain, a self-made millionaire from Birmingham known as "Radical Joe," wore a monocle and always dressed elegantly with an orchid in his buttonhole; he retired from business at age thirty-eight, became mayor of Birmingham, was elected to Parliament at age forty and eventually was head of the Liberal party. Posted to Washington as ambassador extraordinary, he fell in love with Mary, thirty years his junior. Their small wedding in Washington was attended by President Cleveland. Mary was painted by Sargent.

The Chamberlains at a society wedding. After Joseph's death Mary married Canon William Carnegie, Chaplain of the House of Commons.

FIELD, ETHEL

Daughter of Marshall Field of Chicago
Married May 22, 1901
To: Capt. David Beatty of the Royal Navy, later 1st Earl Beatty

Lovely, high-strung and very spoiled, Ethel was the classic rich man's daughter. Her first husband was Arthur Tree, an American by whom she had three children (of which only one survived); they lived in England, entertaining lavishly, until Tree moved out with their son Ronnie (who later married a niece of Nancy Langhorne [q.v.]). Promptly after their divorce, Ethel married Beatty, the youngest admiral in the Royal Navy and later aide-de-camp to Edward VII (1908–10). He was created Earl Beatty for his brilliance in the World War I naval Battle of Jutland. Ethel became more and more unstable, and their marriage was not happy. Their eldest son married Americans three times.

FISH, EDITH

Daughter of Hamilton Fish of New York
Married June 6, 1883
To: the Hon. Hugh Oliver Northcote, 5th son of 1st Earl of Iddesleigh

Edith's father, an heir (through his mother) to the great Stuyvesant real-estate fortune, was governor of New York, U.S. senator, and secretary of state under Grant. Northcote's brother Amyas would marry Helen Dudley [q.v.]. The Northcotes lived in New York; they had a son and a daughter. Edith died in 1887.

FITZGERALD, CAROLINE

Daughter of William J. Fitzgerald, Litchfield, Connecticut
Married November 23, 1889
To: Lord Edmond George Petty Fitzmaurice, later 1st Baron Fitzmaurice

Caroline, whose mother was heiress to a New York real estate fortune, had spent a year abroad, studied Sanskrit with a Yale professor, and published a book of poems while living in London. Fitzmaurice, younger son of the 4th Marquess of Lansdowne, was a Liberal M.P. and barrister. Their marriage was annulled in 1894 in England.

FRENCH, ELIZABETH RICHARDSON

Daughter of Francis Ormonde French of New York and Newport
Married July 14, 1892
To: the Hon. Herbert Francis Eaton, later 3rd Baron Cheylesmore

Elizabeth and Eaton met when his Grenadier Guards regiment was stationed at Bermuda, where she was vacationing. They married in London, at the Guards' Chapel, with Flora Davis and Antoinette Pinchot [q.v.] as bridesmaids. Eaton's family had made money in the silk trade; their title was new, and they were not very fashionable. Elizabeth left England during World War II (Cheylesmore had died in 1925) and died in Newport.

FROST, JANE GRAHAM

Daughter of Gen. Daniel Marsh Frost of St. Louis
Married June 3, 1875
To: Sir Lewis William Molesworth, 11th Baronet
*Seat: *Pencarrow, Washaway, Bodmin, Cornwall*

Jane's sister, Louisa Frost [q.v.], married the Hon. William Vernon. Jane was known to be a good conversationalist, clever dresser, and "among our smart married women."

Having left Ronnie Tree for the handsome and heroic Beatty, Ethel was nevertheless unfaithful to her second husband. She was also subject to deep depressions.

BROTHERS WHO MARRIED HEIRESSES

Hon. Charles Coventry *m.* Lily Whitehouse; Hon. Henry Coventry *m.* Edith Kip McCreery
Alexander Gordon-Cumming *m.* Florence Garner; Sir William Gordon-Cumming *m.* Frances Eames
3rd Lord Leigh *m.* Frances Helene Beckwith; Hon. Rowland Leigh *m.* Mabel Gordon
8th Duke of Marlborough *m.* Lily Hammersley; Lord Randolph Churchill *m.* Jennie Jerome
Hon. Amyas Northcote *m.* Helen Dudley; Hon. Hugh Northcote *m.* Edith Fish
Almeric Paget *m.* Pauline Whitney; Arthur Paget *m.* Minnie Stevens; Sidney Paget *m.* Marie Dolan
8th Duke of Roxburghe *m.* May Goelet; Lord Alastair Innes-Ker *m.* Anna Breese
7th Baron Vernon *m.* Frances Lawrance; Hon. William Vernon *m.* Louisa Frost

"Why, money isn't everything to an Englishman. There are other considerations when he marries, for instance, fondness for the girl."
THE DOWAGER DUCHESS OF ROXBURGHE, on arriving in New York for her son's wedding

FROST, LOUISA

Daughter of Gen. Daniel Marsh Frost of St. Louis
Married April 17, 1884
To: the Hon. William Frederick Cuthbert Vernon, 2nd son of 6th Baron Vernon

William's brother, the 7th Baron, married Fanny Lawrance [q.v.]; his cousin Sir William Harcourt married Elizabeth Motley (Ives) [q.v.].

GAMMELL, HELEN LOUISE

Daughter of Prof. William Gammell of Providence
Married 1892
To: Arthur James Herbert, knighted 1904

Herbert was British minister to Norway.

GARNER, FLORENCE

Daughter of William T. Garner of New York
Married June 10, 1891
To: Sir William Gordon-Cumming, 4th Baronet
Seats: Altyre, Forres, Morayshire, Scotland; Gordonstoun, Elgin, Morayshire

Garner, one of the biggest producers of printed cotton in the world, owned mills in New York that brought in as much as $2 million a year. In 1876 he and his wife died in a freak sailing accident off Staten Island, leaving Florence and her two sisters in the care of their aunt, Mrs. Francis Lawrance (who married off her own daughter, Fanny Lawrance [q.v.], to Lord Vernon in 1885). Florence's sisters married French and Danish nobles. The handsome, arrogant Gordon-Cumming, twenty-three years older than Florence, was a brilliant soldier and sportsman; a friend of the Prince of Wales, he owned some 40,000 acres in Scotland. After his engagement to Florence, he became embroiled in a scandal over cheating at cards and was dismissed from the army. He tried to release Florence from their engagement, but she refused; they lived quietly and very unhappily on two Scottish estates, ostracized from the society that he had loved.

When the Duke of Roxburghe came to America for his wedding to May Goelet, the Goelets reportedly hired ten extra servants for him, three of them valets.

GARRISON, MARTHA

Daughter of William R. Garrison of New York
Married May 28, 1885
To: the Hon. Charles Ramsay, 4th son of 12th Earl of Dalhousie
Martha's grandfather was mayor of San Francisco and had founded a bank there; her father took over the bank, then expanded into railroad interests including New York City elevated railways. The 10th Earl of Dalhousie had distinguished himself as governor general of India (1847–56).

GOELET, MAY

Daughter of Ogden Goelet of New York and Newport
Married November 10, 1903
To: Henry John Innes-Ker, 8th Duke of Roxburghe
*Seats: *Floors Castle, Kelso, Roxburghshire, Scotland; Broxmouth Castle, Dunbar, Lothian, Scotland*
Goelet, heir to a New York real-estate fortune, had married May Wilson (sister of Belle Wilson [q.v.] and Grace Wilson, who married Cornelius Vanderbilt, cousin of Consuelo Vanderbilt [q.v.]). The Goelets lived much abroad and on their yacht, but summered in Newport. May was a great catch, and at one point the reprobate 9th Duke of Manchester announced his engagement to her as a way of calming his creditors. Roxburghe was a fitting match for May; a cousin of the 9th Duke of Marlborough (husband of Consuelo Vanderbilt [q.v.]), he carried Queen Alexandra's crown at the coronation. They lived mostly in Scotland; she redecorated Floors, where the current Duke and Duchess of York became engaged, in the style that largely remains. An heir was finally born in 1913 (to the putative disappointment of Anna Breese [q.v.], married to the younger brother Lord Alastair Innes-Ker). Having inherited her mother's box in the Diamond Horseshoe at the Metropolitan Opera House, May often visited New York after the Duke's death in 1932.

Consuelo Marlborough thought May Goelet repressed too much of her American personality in her marriage with Roxburghe, but May was happy to play the Scottish châtelaine.

Vivien Gould in her wedding finery. She unfortunately inherited the swarthy Gould looks instead of her mother's opulent beauty.

GORDON, MABEL

Daughter of Gen. William Washington Gordon of Georgia
Married October 31, 1898
To: the Hon. Rowland Charles Frederick Leigh, 4th son of 2nd Baron Leigh

Mabel's father had been a captain in the Confederate Army and a general in the Spanish-American War; her grandfather, a Savannah lawyer, had helped build important southern railways. Leigh was a barrister; his older brother, the 3rd Baron Leigh, married Helene Beckwith [q.v.].

GOULD, HELEN VIVIEN

Daughter of George Jay Gould of New York
Married February 7, 1911
To: John Graham Hope de la Poer Beresford, 5th Baron Decies

Gould, son of the unscrupulous railroad baron Jay Gould, had married actress Edith Kingdon. The Goulds were never really of New York society (although Vivien's sister Marjorie married Anthony Drexel, Jr., brother of Margaretta Drexel [q.v.]). Vivien and Beresford met in Switzerland, but he was considered ineligible until his older brother died and he came into the title. They bought medieval Leixlip Castle in Co. Kildare, Ireland, and installed Tudor-style windows and oak paneling. After Vivien died in 1931, Beresford married another American, Elizabeth Drexel, widow of Henry Symes Lehr.

GRACE, ELENA

Daughter of Michael P. Grace of London
Married December 21, 1901
To: Richard Walter John Hely-Hutchinson, 6th Earl of Donoughmore
Seat: Knocklofty Grange, Clonmel, Co. Tipperary, Ireland

Elena's uncle was the Irish-born W.R. Grace, who founded the shipping firm and later became the first Catholic mayor of New York. Her father managed the Grace interests in London; one of his business partners was the 5th Lord Donoughmore (father of his son-in-law), and among his friends was Moreton Frewen (husband of Clara Jerome [q.v.]). Elena was one of three lovely daughters, inevitably known as "the Three Graces." Her sister Margarita married John S. Phipps, brother of Amy Phipps [q.v.]. Donoughmore had a distinguished political career.

GRACE, ELISA

Daughter of Michael P. Grace of London
Married 1900
To: the Hon. Hubert Beaumont, 3rd son of 1st Baron Allendale

Elisa's father-in-law was Wentworth Beaumont, a Liberal party stalwart who was created Baron in 1906. In 1917 Elisa was drowned in a lake in Italy, where she had gone with the Red Cross while her husband was at the front.

The London headquarters of W.R. Grace & Co., India House, Hanover Square.

GRACE, OLIVE *(Mrs. Henry Kerr)*

Daughter of John W. Grace of New York
Married November 24, 1909
To: Capt. the Hon. Charles Beresford Fulke Greville, later 3rd Baron Greville

Olive was a niece of Michael and W.R. Grace, and thus a cousin of Elena and Elisa Grace [q.v.]. She was said to have inherited $1 million outright when her first husband died. Greville was rumored to own some 20,000 acres; he had been ADC to the governor of Bombay and military secretary to the governor-general of Australia. They married in London, with a large reception at the Carlton House Terrace home of Mrs. Frederick Guest (Amy Phipps [q.v.]), which they had rented for a year.

GRAHAM, MARION ALICE *(Mrs. Henry Cabot Knapp)*

Daughter of James Jeffrey Graham of New York
Married July 23, 1904
To: William Spencer Bateman Hanbury, Lord Bateman
Seat: Shobden Court, Shobden, Hereford

The widowed Alice had no children by Bateman; the title is extinct.

As Countess of Essex, Adele was a fixture at all the Anglo-American weddings in London.

GRANT, ADELE

Daughter of David Beach Grant of New York
Married December 14, 1893
To: George Devereux de Vere Capell, 7th Earl of Essex
Seat: Cassiobury Park, Watford, Hertfordshire

Adele, having once been engaged to the Earl of Cairns (who left for Genoa to buy her a boatload of camellias but ended up marrying someone else), married the widower Essex in a huge, splashy London wedding for which Sir Arthur Sullivan played the organ. They led a fashionable life as members of the smart racing set, despite which Adele was rumored to run a laundry business in the London suburbs. Essex died in 1916, succeeded by his son from his first marriage. Cassiobury Park was torn down in 1922; its Grinling Gibbons staircase is in New York's Metropolitan Museum of Art.

GREEN, AMY

Daughter of William Arthur Green of San Francisco
Married August 30, 1892
To: Sir James Home-Spiers, 11th Baronet
Amy and Sir James, formerly of the Royal Highlanders, had a big London wedding, covered in *The New York Times.*

HALE, JOSEPHINE

Daughter of Joseph P. Hale of San Francisco
Married April 30, 1890
To: the Hon. Robert John Lascelles Boyle, later 11th Earl of Cork and Orrery
Seat: Castle Martyr, County Cork, Ireland
Boyle was the second son of the 9th Earl; he succeeded to the title after his brother's death in 1925.

HAMILTON, MARGARET

Daughter of William Hamilton of Napa, California
Married March 28, 1882
To: Sir Sidney Hedley Waterlow, 1st Baronet
Margaret was twenty-two when she married the widowed, sixty-year-old Sir Sidney, former Lord Mayor of London and M.P. (1872–80). He died in 1906, having given Waterlow Park, Highgate, to the London County Council in 1889.

HAMMERSLEY, LILIAN PRICE

Daughter of Comm. Cicero Price of Troy, New York
Married June 29, 1888
To: George Charles Spencer-Churchill, 8th Duke of Marlborough
*Seat: *Blenheim Palace, Woodstock, Oxfordshire*
Lilian, beautiful widow of wealthy New York merchant Louis Hammersley, always wore white and was famous for covering her opera box entirely in orchids. Her marriage to Marlborough, divorced by his first wife over a flagrant love affair, was widely regarded as a cynical trade of money for title. (Marlborough's philandering continued; he had another flagrant affair with Lady Colin Campbell.) The Hammersley money re-roofed Blenheim, built an organ in the Long Library and supplied a laboratory for Marlborough's science experiments. Marlborough died in 1892, and in 1895 Lily married Lord William de la Poer Beresford, third son of the 4th Marquess of Waterford.

Lord William was elated at his luck in winning Lily. Her stepson Sunny gave her away at their merry, very social wedding.

HOWARD, HANNAH SARA

Daughter of Hiram Edward Howard of Buffalo, New York
Married October 15, 1878

To: the Hon. Octavius Henry Lambart, 5th son of 8th Earl of Cavan

Sara and Lambert lived in Canada. His nephew, the Hon. Lionel Lambart, married Adelaide Randolph [q.v.].

HOWELL, KATE

Daughter of Warwick Howell of South Carolina
Married 1881
To: Augustus Arthur Perceval, later 8th Earl of Egmont
Seat: Cowdray Park, Midhurst, Sussex

Kate, according to *The New York Times,* was a waitress; Perceval, born in New Zealand, had run away from his Royal Navy training ship to become a common sailor. A year after they married, he joined the fire brigade of Southwark, and by 1887 he was working as a janitor at the town hall. He later worked in salt mines in Chesire, then in South Africa, borrowing against his expectations of inheriting the title and 12,000-acre estate. He succeeded to the title in 1897.

JEROME, CLARA

Daughter of Leonard Jerome of New York
Married June 22, 1881
To: Moreton Frewen

Clara's father was one of the first generation of nineteenth-century stock speculators. Frewen, of a good Sussex family, was a handsome visionary, full of brilliant ideas that never made money; among these were a cattle-ranching venture in Wyoming and forestry in Africa. Clara's life with him was hand-to-mouth but fashionable.

Jennie Jerome, one of the few "beauties" of the era who still looks beautiful to modern eyes.

JEROME, JENNIE

Daughter of Leonard Jerome of New York
Married April 15, 1874
To: Lord Randolph Churchill, 2nd son of 7th Duke of Marlborough

A pioneering Anglo-American match: Jennie, a true beauty, and the brilliant, aristocratic Randolph. A riveting speaker in Parliament, Randolph rose to Chancellor of the Exchequer and Leader of the House of Commons. He was widely expected to become prime minister but resigned from government suddenly; he suffered from syphilis, which drove him mad and eventually killed him in 1895. Jennie was rumored to have had affairs with, among others, the Prince of Wales and the Austrian Count Kinski. She wrote plays, founded the *Anglo-Saxon Review* and promoted the political career of her son Winston. In 1900, she married George Cornwallis-West (Winston's age); divorcing him in 1913, she married again (Montagu Porch, younger still) in 1918.

Lady Leonie Leslie, costumed as Brünhilde for the Devonshire House Ball. Like many of the guests, she must have found it difficult to dance with her props.

JEROME, LEONIE

Daughter of Leonard Jerome of New York
Married October 3, 1884
To: Sir John Leslie, 2nd Baronet
Seat: Castle Leslie, Glaslough, Co. Monaghan, Ireland

Leonie was youngest of the three lovely Jerome sisters. Leslie's family, who disapproved of her, had plenty of money and land in Ireland. Once Leslie succeeded to the title, they entertained frequently at Castle Leslie. Their eldest son was the writer Shane Leslie.

KING, MARY SANDS ("MINNA")

Daughter of J.P. King of Sandhills, Georgia
Married June 25, 1872
To: the Hon. Henry Wodehouse, younger brother of 3rd Baron (later 1st Earl) Wodehouse, died 1873
Remarried June 26, 1880
To: Henry Paget, 4th Marquess of Anglesey
*Seat: *Plas Newydd, Llanfair P.G., Isle of Anglesey, Gwynedd, Wales*

The widowed Minna was Anglesey's third wife. Anglesey died in 1898 and was succeeded by his son, "the Dancing Marquess," who spent a fortune on jewels that he wore himself.

KIP, EDITH (Mrs. Richard McCreery)

Daughter of Col. Lawrence Kip of New York
Married December 3, 1907
To: the Hon. Henry Thomas Coventry, 3rd son of 9th Earl of Coventry

Edith, a niece of Pierre Lorillard and thus a cousin of Maude Lorillard [q.v.], was left a widow by McCreery. Coventry's brother, Viscount Deerhurst, married Virginia Bonynge [q.v.]; another brother, the Hon. Charles Coventry, married Lily Whitehouse [q.v.].

LANGHORNE, NANCY (Mrs. Robert Shaw)

Daughter of Chiswell Dabney Langhorne of Virginia
Married May 3, 1906
To: William Waldorf Astor, later 2nd Viscount Astor
*Seat: *Cliveden, near Maidenhead, Bucks*

The Langhornes, though prosperous (Chiswell was worth about $1 million at his death), were not hugely rich; Nancy, one of three lovely sisters, had divorced the alcoholic Shaw. Astor's father (of the rich American Astor clan) had migrated to England, where young William was covered with glory at both Eton and Oxford. Nancy met William on a steamer, en route to the season's foxhunting. Astor *père* gave them Cliveden (now a luxury hotel) and presented her with a tiara set with the fifty-three-plus-carat Sancy diamond. Astor became an M.P. in 1910; when his father (created 1st Viscount) died, he had to go into the House of Lords. Nancy won his seat and became the first woman ever to sit in Parliament. Renowned for her sharp tongue, she was a rabid Christian Scientist and staunch teetotaler. She was painted and sketched several times by Sargent; a portrait still hangs at Cliveden.

Nancy Langhorne Astor in late middle age, when her beauty had been hardened by a kind of steely resolve.

LAROCHE, ELIZABETH MARIE

Daughter of William Tell LaRoche of Harrington Park, New Jersey
Married October 21, 1895
To: Sir Howland Roberts, 5th Baronet

LaRoche was a doctor and president of the College of Dentistry in New York; his wife was one of the Old New York Quackenbushes. The Robertses had two children.

LAWRANCE, FRANCES ("FANNY")

Daughter of Francis Lawrance of New York
Married July 14, 1885
To: George William Henry Vernon, 7th Baron Vernon
*Seat: *Sudbury Hall, Derbyshire*

Fanny was a cousin of Florence Garner [q.v.] through her mother, Frances Garner Lawrance, sister of Thomas Garner. Vernon's brother, the Hon. William Vernon, married Louisa Frost [q.v.]; his cousin, Viscount Harcourt, married Mary Ethel Burns [q.v.]. Sudbury, the Vernons' seventeenth-century house with Grinling Gibbons carvings, is now owned by the National Trust.

LAWRENCE, AIMEE MARIE SUZANNE

Daughter of John Lawrence of New York
Married November 28, 1899
To: Douglas Walter Campbell, nephew of 9th Duke of Argyll

The 9th Duke had married Princess Louise, one of Queen Victoria's daughters. Douglas and Aimee's son Ian became the 11th Duke of Argyll in 1949 and had a stormy, well-publicized marital history.

LEE, LUCY TRACY

Daughter of William P. Lee of New York
Married October 4, 1883
To: Ernest Beckett, later 2nd Baron Grimthorpe
Seat: Westow Hall, York

Lucy, a very pretty woman, was painted with her two daughters by Edward Hughes, the conservative alternative to Sargent. Beckett was an M.P. and banker in Yorkshire. Lucy died in 1891.

Daisy Leiter, cover girl.

The 20th Earl of Suffolk, Daisy Leiter's son, worked in the famous Unexploded Bomb Squad in World War II, accompanied by his lady secretary and elderly chauffeur. Known as "the Holy Trinity," the trio dismantled thirty-four bombs before, in 1941, the thirty-fifth killed them.

LEITER, MARGUERITE HYDE ("DAISY")

Daughter of Levi Leiter of Washington, D.C.
Married December 26, 1904
To: Henry Molyneux Paget Howard, 19th Earl of Suffolk and 12th Earl of Berkshire
Seat: Charlton Park, Malmesbury, Wiltshire

Leiter, partner of Marshall Field, made a fortune in Chicago real estate and moved to Washington, D.C., for superior social opportunities. Daisy visited her sister Mary Curzon (then vicereine) in India and afterward never really reentered social life in the States. Suffolk, an aide-de-camp to Lord Curzon, was notoriously broke; reporting on his engagement to Daisy, *The New York Times* noted that "his estate . . . in Wiltshire will be restored to the glory of its former days." Daisy was painted by Sargent. Suffolk was killed in action in 1917; their eldest son was killed in action in 1941.

LEITER, MARY

Daughter of Levi Leiter of Washington, D.C.
Married April 22, 1895
To: the Hon. George Nathaniel Curzon, 1st Baron, then 1st Marquess Curzon of Kedleston
Seat: Kedleston

Mary, whose charms made the Leiter girls popular despite their vulgar mother, was a belle of Washington, D.C.; attention from the Prince of Wales led to equal social success in London. After a long-distance romance and secret two-year engagement, she married Curzon, eldest son of Viscount Scarsdale. He was intelligent and ambitious; three years after the marriage, he was appointed viceroy of India, a post he filled brilliantly. Mary, as vicereine, was the second-highest-ranking woman in the British Empire (after the Queen). She grew ill in India and died in 1906. Curzon's second wife, Grace Duggan, was also American.

LEWIS, MARGUERITE

Daughter of William Lewis of New York
Married November 21, 1906
To: Maj. the Hon. Murrough O'Brien, 2nd son of 14th Baron Inchiquin

O'Brien had a distinguished military career, earning several medals.

LIVINGSTON, ELIZABETH

Daughter of Maturin Livingston of New York and Newport
Married August 12, 1880
To: George Cavendish-Bentinck, grandson of 3rd Duke of Portland

Livingston, from a very Old New York family with extensive Hudson River landholdings, was one of the original Patriarchs. Elizabeth's twin sister married Ogden Mills, father of Beatrice Mills [q.v.]. Cavendish-Bentinck's mother was Prudence Penelope Leslie, of the Leslie family into which Leonie Jerome [q.v.] married. (Elizabeth told the family, when Leonie's engagement to Sir John was announced, that Leonard Jerome was a New York garbage collector.) One of the Cavendish-Bentinck daughters married Walter Burns, brother of Mary Ethel Burns [q.v.]. Elizabeth was one of the principal London contacts for American heiresses.

LORILLARD, MAUDE (Mrs. T. Suffern Tailer)

Daughter of Pierre Lorillard of Tuxedo Park, New York and Newport
Married November 8, 1902
To: the Hon. Cecil Baring, later 3rd Baron Revelstoke

Pierre Lorillard, of the tobacco fortune, was the first American ever to win the English Derby (with Iroquois, entered in the race through the courtesy of the Prince of Wales). Maude divorced Tailer, a fashionable sportsman, in 1902 in South Dakota. Cecil was a member of the Baring banking family. (His older brother John was in love with Nancy Langhorne [q.v.]; kinsman Francis Baring, later Baron Ashburton, married Frances Donnelly [q.v.]). Maude and Cecil bought Lambay Island, off the Dublin coast, and hired Edwin Lutyens to rebuild a little fort on the island into Lambay Castle. Their son Rupert married the Hon. Flora Fermor-Hesketh, daughter of the 1st Baron Hesketh and Florence Breckinridge [q.v.].

MARTIN, CORNELIA

Daughter of Bradley Martin of New York
Married April 18, 1893
To: William George Robert Craven, 4th Earl of Craven
*Seats: Hamstead House, Hamstead Marshall, Newbury, Berkshire; *Ashdown House, Ashbury, Oxfordshire; Coombe Abbey, Coventry, West Midlands*

The socially ambitious Martins, from upstate New York, rented Balmaccaan on Loch Ness beginning in 1881. Cornelia's mother, known as something of a bully, was credited with introducing Helene Beckwith [q.v.] to Lord Leigh. The Cravens had a reputation for dissolution, based in part on the 3rd Earl's relationship with the famous courtesan "Skittles" Walters. The 4th Earl was a cousin of Viscount Deerhurst and the Coventry brothers, who married Virginia Bonynge, Edith Kip (McCreery) and Lily Whitehouse [q.v.]. He and Cornelia met at Balmaccaan, married in New York when Cornelia was seventeen and lived in London. They had one son, who was painted by Boldini. The Earl died in 1921, of drowning; Cornelia lived until 1961.

The Earl and Countess of Craven—the child bride matured into a woman of great poise.

"Nearly all the attachés of the various embassies at Washington are captured, before their term of office expires, by American beauties and American heiresses."
THE MARQUESS OF DUFFERIN AND AVA (1897)

MAY, LILIAN

Daughter of Henry May of Baltimore
Married July 25, 1903
To: William Bagot, 4th Baron Bagot
Seats: Blithfield, Rugeley, Staffordshire; Pool Park, Ruthin, Wales
May was a lawyer and member of Congress. The pretty Lilian had been traveling on the Continent for a number of years when she met Bagot, a courtier and sportsman. Thought to be a hardened bachelor, he was forty-six when they married.

MCVICKAR, KATHARINE

Daughter of William Henry McVickar of New York
Married November 5, 1879
To: John Richard Brinsley Norton, 5th Baron Grantley
Katharine was married first to Grantley's nephew, Charles Grantley Norton. The marriage was dissolved, and she married Grantley, giving birth to his daughter five days after the wedding. She died in 1897. The Grantleys' son, the 6th Baron, was secretary to Almeric Paget, M.P. (husband of Pauline Whitney [q.v.]).

MEIGGS, HELEN CORNELL

Daughter of John Gilbert Meiggs of New York
Married October 30, 1890
To: Sir James Rhoceric Duff M'Grigor, 3rd Baronet
M'Grigor was a banker and army agent.

MILLER, FLORENCE

Daughter of Gardner L. Miller of Providence
Married June 17, 1901
To: the Hon. William Arthur de la Poer Horsley Beresford, youngest son of 3rd Baron Decies
Florence's father was a doctor; William's older brother was Jack, 5th Baron Decies, who married Vivien Gould [q.v.]. The Beresfords lived in Providence and had five children. They were divorced in 1919.

"Newport is the most English of all towns out of England. It has its daily fog, the houses remind one of an English town built a century or two since. The best people, the dwellers in the cottages, imitate the English airs, teams, turnouts, flunkies and manners. . . . If there is a British lord in the country he naturally finds his way to Newport and is more at home there than anywhere else on this continent. No sensible American will object to all this."
D.G. CROSBY, in *The Hour*

MILLS, BEATRICE

Daughter of Ogden Mills of New York, Staatsburgh and Newport
Married January 14, 1909
To: Bernard Arthur William Patrick Hastings Forbes, 8th Earl of Granard
Seat: Castle Forbes, Newtown Forbes, Co. Longford, Ireland
Ogden Mills' father, Darius, made a fortune in California banking; his sister Elisabeth married Whitelaw Reid, father of Jean Reid [q.v.]. Beatrice, whose mother was a sister of Elizabeth Livingston [q.v.], was a twin; her sister married Henry Carnegie Phipps, brother of Amy Phipps [q.v.].

Granard was Deputy Speaker of the House of Lords, a lord-in-waiting to Edward VII, Master of the Horse for both Edward VII and George V, and a member of the Senate of the Irish Free State (1922–34). He and Beatrice rented Dartmouth House on Charles Street (now the home of the English-Speaking Union), where they gave big (reputedly dull) political receptions and entertained Edward VII during Derby Week.

MOKE, JULIA NORRIE

Daughter of George L.A. Moke of New York and London
Married July 19, 1883
To: John Rahere Paget, later 2nd Baronet

Julia's parents had houses in London and New York. Paget's father was created Baronet for services as Sergeant Surgeon to Queen Victoria.

MOTLEY, ELIZABETH CABOT (Mrs. Thomas Ives)

Daughter of John Lothrop Motley
Married December 2, 1876
To: Sir William George Greville Venables Vernon Harcourt, knighted 1873

Motley, U.S. minister to The Hague and to England, wrote a famous history of the Netherlands. Elizabeth was the widow of Mr. Ives of Rhode Island. Harcourt, a widower, was an M.P. and Chancellor of the Exchequer; his son Lewis, by his first marriage, married Mary Ethel Burns [q.v.] and became the 1st Viscount Harcourt.

MURPHY, ANITA THERESA

Daughter of Daniel T. Murphy of San Francisco
Married July 17, 1883
To: Sir Charles Michael Wolseley, 9th Baronet
Seat: Wolseley Hall, Stafford

Wolseley claimed direct descent from Anglo-Saxon Lords of Wisele. He and Anita had two sons.

COUSINS WHO MARRIED HEIRESSES

2nd Baron Ashburton *m.* Frances Donnelly; 3rd Lord Revelstoke *m.* Maude Lorillard
Sir John Leslie *m.* Leonie Jerome; George Cavendish-Bentinck *m.* Elizabeth Livingston
9th Duke of Marlborough *m.* Consuelo Vanderbilt; 8th Duke of Roxburghe *m.* May Goelet

At one New York dinner party, the cigarettes were rolled in $100 bills stamped with the host's monogram in gold.

Padelford, Florence

Daughter of Edward M. Padelford of Savannah and Baltimore
Married February 1, 1903
To: the Hon. Robert Victor Grosvenor, later 3rd Baron Ebury
Florence's mother later married Ernest Cunard, son of William Cunard of 95 Eaton Square, London. Ebury died in 1921; Florence, in 1927.

Parks, Alice Margarita

Daughter of Rev. Leighton Parks of New York
Married November 18, 1902
To: John Nicholson Barran, later 2nd Baronet
Alice's father was rector of St. Bartholomew's on Park Avenue; Barran's father had founded John Barran & Sons, merchants in Leeds, and had been an M.P. for nearly twenty years. Barran was Parliamentary Private Secretary to Asquith and M.P. (1909–18).

Mrs. Charles Pfizer, her daughter Helen, and son Gustav in Stuttgart in 1870. The family always maintained strong European ties.

Pfizer, Helen Julia

Daughter of Charles D. Pfizer of Brooklyn and Newport
Married May 22, 1888
To: Frederick William Duncan, later 2nd Baronet
Pfizer immigrated from Germany in the early 1840s and founded the Pfizer chemical firm, which he headed for fifty-one years before handing it over to his son, Charles Jr.

Phipps, Amy

Daughter of Henry Phipps of Pittsburgh
Married June 28, 1905
To: Capt. the Hon. Frederick Edward Guest, 3rd son of 1st Baron Wimborne
Henry Phipps, a cobbler's son from Philadelphia, was a lifelong business associate of Andrew Carnegie in iron and steel; when Carnegie sold to Morgan in 1901, Phipps received $50 million in stock. Caricatured by Charles Dana Gibson as "Mr. Pip," he rented estates in England and Scotland, where he kept a piper to play bagpipes at breakfast. Amy's brother John married Margarita Grace, sister of Elena and Elisa Grace [q.v.]; her sister Helen married Bradley Martin, Jr., brother of Cornelia Martin [q.v.]. The 1st Baron Wimborne was Ivor Guest, husband of Lady Cornelia Churchill (Lord Randolph Churchill's sister, sister-in-law of Jennie Jerome [q.v.]). The Guests' money was from ironworks in Wales; the Wimborne town house at 22 Arlington Street would be Evelyn Waugh's model for Marchmain House in *Brideshead Revisited*. After a London wedding (the Phippses had taken Brook House in Park Lane), Amy and Frederick lived in London (Carlton House Terrace) and then Palm Beach. She became a Christian

Scientist; he was an M.P. and at one time treasurer for George V's household. Amy backed Amelia Earhart's transatlantic flight and wanted to go along, but was prevented by her family.

PINCHOT, ANTOINETTE

Daughter of James W. Pinchot of New York and Washington, D.C.
Married December 21, 1892
To: the Hon. Alan Vanden Bempde Johnstone, later knighted
The Pinchots were an Old New York family, with a house in Gramercy Park. Antoinette's brother Gifford was first chief of the Forestry Bureau and one of the architects of the national parks system. The Johnstone wedding was attended by Mrs. Grover Cleveland, the Reids and the Vanderbilts. Johnstone was secretary to Her Majesty's legation in Copenhagen.

POST, HELEN AGNES

Daughter of Arthur Post of New York
Married June 22, 1910
To: the Hon. Montague Charles Eliot, later 8th Earl of St. Germans
Helen was brought up largely in England, after her mother, Elizabeth Wadsworth (Post) [q.v.], married Arthur Barry, Lord Barrymore. Clare Frewen, daughter of Clara Jerome [q.v.], was a bridesmaid at her wedding; Nancy Cunard, daughter of Maud Burke [q.v.], was a flower girl. Eliot was Gentleman Usher to Edward VII (1901–08) and Groom-in-Waiting (1908–10). His court appointment was not renewed under George V, possibly because the royal couple disliked Americans.

At Adelaide Randolph's coming-out party, the climax of the cotillion was the "automobile figure" in which a car loaded with favors was driven onto the ballroom floor.

POTTER, CLARA LUCILE

Daughter of Frederick G. Potter of New York
Married November 24, 1906
To: Robert Henry Green-Price, later 3rd Baronet
Clara's father was a Yale graduate, lawyer and banker. Green-Price became High Sheriff of Radnorshire in 1930.

RANDOLPH, ADELAIDE

Daughter of [?] Randolph of New York
Married May 8, 1904
To: the Hon. Lionel Lambart, younger brother and heir presumptive of 10th Earl of Cavan
Adelaide's mother, née Edith May of Baltimore, took as her second husband William Collins Whitney, father of Pauline Whitney [q.v.]. Lambart's brother, the 10th Earl, was commander of all British troops in Italy in World War I and received the Legion of Honour as well as the Croix de Guerre.

READE, MARY

Daughter of Robert Reade of New York
Married September 25, 1879
To: Col. Byron Plantagenet Cary Falkland, later 12th Viscount Falkland

The Falklands were a very old family, long broke. Mary, who did some philanthropic work, was made a Lady of Grace of the Order of St. John of Jerusalem.

Whitelaw Reid, whose great wealth and status as American Ambassador gave his daughter, Jean, an enviable position among the American heiresses in London.

REID, JEAN

Daughter of Whitelaw Reid of New York and London
Married June 22, 1908
To: the Hon. John Hubert Ward, later knighted; 2nd son of 1st Earl of Dudley

Reid, a farmer's son from Ohio, was a brilliant journalist at the New York *Tribune*, where he was made managing editor before age thirty-five; becoming involved in politics (especially after his marriage to Elisabeth, daughter of Ogden Mills and aunt of Beatrice Mills [q.v.]), he was appointed special ambassador to the Court of St. James for the coronation in 1902 and ambassador in 1905. The Reids took Dorchester House, the most splendid house in London. Ward was Equerry to Edward VII and a great favorite at court; rumor had it that Edward had engineered his marriage to Jean. They lived at Dudley House in Carlton House Terrace; after Edward VII's death, Ward stayed on as Equerry to Queen Alexandra. Jean did distinguished philanthropic work during World War II and was made Commander of the British Empire. At Elizabeth II's coronation in June 1953, the Wards' son Col. Edward (godson of Edward VII) was Commander of Household Cavalry & Silver Stick in Waiting; that same month, Lady Ward gave a débutante party for her granddaughter Elizabeth, which was attended by Queen Elizabeth II.

ROBINSON, AUGUSTA BEVERLY

Daughter of E. Randolph Robinson
Married January 17, 1903
To: Commander Louis Wentworth Chetwynd, Royal Navy

Augusta was a granddaughter of John Jay; her husband was a grandson of 6th Viscount Chetwynd.

ROBINSON, GEORGIANA ("ANNA")

Daughter of George Robinson of Minneapolis
Married March 20, 1905
To: James Francis Harry St. Clair-Erskine, 5th Earl of Rosslyn

Georgiana is listed in *Debrett's Peerage* as "a member of the dramatic profession." St. Clair-Erskine, who had obtained a Scottish divorce from his first wife in 1902, was a half-brother of Daisy, the famous Countess of Warwick; he had also been engaged to another American, Beatrice Irwin. Anna was granted an Edinburgh divorce from him in 1907.

ROGERS, CORA LELAND

Daughter of Henry Huttleston Rogers of New York and Fairhaven, Massachusetts

Married November 12, 1895

To: Urban Hanlon Broughton, posthumously created Baron Fairhaven of Lode

Rogers, who had left Fairhaven for Pennsylvania oilfields at age twenty-one, was responsible for crucial inventions such as oil pipelines; he was director of Standard Oil, with extensive industrial interests, and a great admirer (and eventually business manager) of Mark Twain. Cora's sister was Millicent Rogers, a famous fashion plate. Broughton, an engineer, had worked on a project in Fairhaven. After marriage, he was an M.P. (1915–18), a major contributor to the Conservative party (to which he donated the estate of Ashridge) and director of many U.S. industrial companies. He died before he could be elevated to the peerage; Cora was given the right to the title "Lady Fairhaven," though not precedence. In 1929 she and her sons bought Runnymede, in danger of falling to developers, and donated it to the National Trust. Anglesey Abbey, where her son (effectively the 1st Baron Fairhaven) lived, is now National Trust property.

A lady's maid's responsibilities included keeping track of furs and jewelry, down to the number of pearls on each string.

RUSSELL, EDITH

Daughter of Samuel Hammond Russell of Boston

Married October 3, 1878

To: Sir Lyon Playfair, later 1st Baron Playfair

Edith was one of the few Boston girls to marry an Englishman. Playfair, a prominent Liberal M.P., was Deputy Speaker of the House and Lord-in-Waiting to Queen Victoria.

FATHER-SON DUOS

Sir William Harcourt *m.* Elizabeth Motley Ives; 1st Viscount Harcourt *m.* Mary Burns

Sir Thomas Fermor-Hesketh *m.* Flora Sharon; 1st Baron Hesketh *m.* Florence Breckinridge

8th Duke of Manchester *m.* Consuelo Yznaga; 9th Duke of Manchester *m.* Helena Zimmerman

8th Duke of Marlborough *m.* Lily Hammersley; 9th Duke of Marlborough *m.* Consuelo Vanderbilt

7th Baron Vernon *m.* Frances Lawrance; 8th Baron Vernon *m.* Helen Traer

Flora Sharon and Sir Thomas Fermor-Hesketh, by San Francisco photographers.

SALISBURY, MARY WOOD

Daughter of Joseph L.R. Wood of New York
Married April 28, 1905
To: the Hon. Ernest Victor Gibson, 4th son of 1st Baron Ashbourne

Mary died in September of 1905. Gibson's second wife was also a New Yorker.

SANDS, MAY EMILY

Daughter of Benjamin Aymar Sands of New York and Southampton
Married September 19, 1908
To: the Hon. Hugh Melville Howard, 3rd son of 6th Earl of Wicklow

May's father, son of banker Samuel Sands, was a lawyer and active in Republican politics; a trustee of Columbia University, he was also a director of a number of banks and a Fellow of the Metropolitan Museum.

SCHLEY, VIRGINIA

Daughter of Adm. Winfield Scott Schley
Married January 22, 1891
To: the Hon. Ralph Granville Montagu-Stuart-Wortley, younger brother of 2nd Earl of Wharncliffe

Virginia was from an old Maryland family, in the United States since 1739; her father had served in the Civil War and Spanish-American War, and taught at the Naval Academy. She made her début in Washington, D.C. Wortley was vice-president of the Atlantic & Danville railroad. Their children lived in America; a great-grandson, a contractor in Maine, is 5th Earl.

SECOR, ROSALIND

Daughter of William Holt Secor of New York
Married January 5, 1902
To: Sir Guy Chetwynd, 5th Baronet

Rosalind's father was a lawyer; her grandfather, Charles A. Secor, a shipbuilder. Chetwynd's mother was half-sister of the 4th Marquess of Anglesey, who married Mary Sands King [q.v.]. Divorced from Chetwynd in 1909, Rosalind embarked on an acting career, calling herself "Rosa Lynd"; she was actress-manager of the Comedy Theatre. Chetwynd's sister Lilian was married, unhappily and briefly, to the 5th ("Dancing") Marquess of Anglesey, her cousin.

SHARON, FLORENCE EMILY ("FLORA")

Daughter of Sen. William Sharon of San Francisco and Nevada
Married December 23, 1880

To: Sir Thomas George Fermor-Hesketh, 7th Baronet
*Seats: Easton Neston, Towcester, Northamptonshire; *Rufford Old Hall, Rufford, Lancashire*

Sharon, who made a fortune as the Bank of California's Comstock Lode representative as well as in railroads and real estate, owned the magnificent Palace Hotel in San Francisco. Flora, convent-educated, spent her winters in Washington, D.C.; she met Hesketh during his around-the-world voyage on the yacht *Lancashire Witch.* He was from an old, respectable Lancashire family. They lived in England, where Flora installed bathrooms and Tudor-look paneling in Hawksmoor-designed Easton Neston; she was rumored to have been the Prince of Wales' mistress. Hesketh continued his yachting, and eventually Flora moved into Rufford Old Hall (now run by the National Trust). She imported her brother's stepdaughter, Florence Breckinridge [q.v.], to groom as wife material for their son.

SHERMAN, MILDRED

Daughter of William Watts Sherman of New York and Newport
Married November 25, 1911
To: Ralph Francis Julian Stonor, 5th Baron Camoys
*Seat: *Stonor Park, Henley-on-Thames, Oxfordshire*

Sherman, who married two very prominent Rhode Island women (first a Wetmore, then a Brown), was a banker and treasurer of the Newport Casino. The Stonors had lived at Stonor Park since the twelfth century. Mildred and Stonor were married quietly in New York (Sherman was very ill), after which their lives were disrupted by World War I. Mildred, very sensitive, suffered from the cold of English houses; she was never presented at court and rarely even dined out. She'd been so cossetted that on her honeymoon, when she bent down to unfasten her shoes (without her maid's help), she fainted.

Stonor Park, home of the Stonor family since the twelfth century, and a far cry from Mildred Sherman's New York and Newport homes.

SMITH, MARY EMMA

Daughter of George S. Smith of Evanston, Illinois
Married April 2, 1887
To: George Alexander Cooper, later 1st Baronet

Smith's brother, the financier known as "Chicago" Smith, left a fortune to Mary and her brother (called "Silent" Smith). After she inherited (some £4 million), she and Cooper, a solicitor in Elgin, Scotland, moved to a huge house on Grosvenor Square; they also bought a house in Hampshire, which they decorated and enlarged. They were big Duveen customers. He was created Baronet in 1905, after his apotheosis as a rich man.

The famous sphinx in Blenheim's Water Terrace Garden. It sports Gladys Deacon's features.

ONCE IS NOT ENOUGH!

For a number of English husbands, the family fuss over their first marriage to an American had little bearing on their choice of a second wife. In fact, for the second go-round, more heiresses' husbands married Americans than reverted to their own nationality. It was as if, having tried the liveliness and exoticism (not to mention financial ease) of living with an American, they couldn't be content with the less colorful company of an Englishwoman.

THE 1ST BARON CURZON OF KEDLESTON, bereft after the death of his lovely wife Mary Leiter in 1906, married the immensely wealthy American widow Grace Duggan in 1917. It was quite clear, however, that Mary was his true love. The elaborate memorial in the chapel at Kedleston bears the touching inscription: "She was mourned in three continents / And by her dearest will be / For ever unforgotten."

THE 5TH BARON DECIES' wife Vivien Gould died in 1931, and five years later Elizabeth Drexel Lehr became his second wife. One of the banking Drexels, Elizabeth was the widow of Harry Lehr, the acid-tongued jester to Mrs. Stuyvesant Fish, who had told her on their wedding day that he'd only married her for her money.

THE 5TH EARL OF GOSFORD, divorced from Mildred Carter in 1928 (on grounds of desertion and adultery, uncontested), married Beatrice Claflin Breese, ex-wife of Robert P. Breese of New York. He continued to live in the States, running a wine shop in Manhattan, and at age sixty-five joined the New York City police force.

THE 3RD BARON OF LEIGH, having married the older Frances Helene Beckwith, was not unexpectedly widowed after nineteen years. In 1923 he married another New Yorker, Marie Campbell, whose tenure at Stoneleigh Abbey would be somewhat marred by the continuing presence of her husband's maiden aunts.

THE 9TH DUKE OF MANCHESTER was divorced in 1931 from the long-suffering Helena Zimmerman. His second wife, Kathleen Dawes, couldn't rehabilitate him, and in 1935 he was sentenced to nine months in Wormwood Scrubs prison for trying to pawn some jewelry that belonged to his trustees. (After serving a month's time, his sentence was overturned in a court of appeals and he left prison looking healthier than when he'd gone in.)

ALMERIC PAGET, later 1st Baron Queenborough, became a widower when Pauline Whitney (never robust) died in 1916. He consoled himself five years later with the thirty-year-old Florence Miller of New York.

THE 9TH DUKE OF MARLBOROUGH already had a second string to his bow when his divorce from Consuelo became final. The beautiful, intelligent (and wild) Bostonian Gladys Deacon had been Sunny's lover for ten years before their 1921 marriage. By 1931 their relationship had deteriorated into open hostility, though they never divorced.

Kilkenny Castle, where Ellen Stager became châtelaine, was damaged in 1922 during Ireland's Troubles.

STAGER, ELLEN

Daughter of Gen. Anson Stager of New York and Chicago
Married March 8, 1887
To: Lord James Arthur Wellington Foley Butler, later 4th Marquess of Ormonde
*Seat: *Kilkenny Castle, Co. Kilkenny, Ireland*

Anson Stager, an early pioneer in use of the telegraph, was chief of U.S. Military Telegraph in the Civil War and later involved with Western Union as well as Vanderbilt business interests in the West. Ellen, known as the prettiest girl in Chicago, moved to New York in the mid-'80s after her parents died. Lord Arthur, from an old and powerful Irish family, succeeded his brother as 4th Marquess in 1919.

STEVENS, MARY FISKE ("MINNIE")

Daughter of Paran Stevens of New York and Newport
Married July 27, 1878
To: Col. Arthur Paget, later knighted

Paran Stevens ran New York's Fifth Avenue Hotel; his wife Marietta was a grocer's daughter from Lowell, Massachusetts. The provenance of the Stevens fortune was too pragmatic for New York, hence the Stevens women's departure for Europe. The pretty, green-eyed Minnie shopped around extensively (with exaggerated reports of her dowry) before finally settling on Arthur Paget, son of Gen. Lord Alfred Paget, grandson of the 1st Marquess of Anglesey, and brother of Sidney (who married Marie Dolan [q.v.]) and Almeric Paget (husband of Pauline Whitney [q.v.]. They enjoyed much royal attention; the Prince of Wales was godfather to their eldest son, who died in action in World War I. Minnie was a great London hostess, a brilliant fund-raiser, and a crucial contact for American heiresses on the prowl.

Minnie Stevens Paget, in a very uncomfortable-looking medieval costume.

STOKES, SARAH

Daughter of Anson Phelps Stokes of New York and Lenox
Married February 11, 1890
To: Hugh Colin Gustave Halkett, Baron Halkett of Hanover

Stokes, a merchant, banker and real estate investor as well as an official of the Ansonia (Conn.) Clock Co., was a founder of the Metropolitan Museum and vice-commodore of the New York Yacht Club. (His brother developed the Ansonia Hotel in New York.) Sarah's brother, Isaac Newton Phelps Stokes, is portrayed in the famous Sargent double portrait now at the Metropolitan. Halkett of Hanover was a foreign title borne by a British subject. The marriage was not a success. In 1900, the pair was living in Lenox; Sarah obtained a divorce in 1903, discarded the title, and wrote and illustrated children's books.

Stone, Romaine (Mrs. Lawrence Turnure, Jr.)

Daughter of Gen. Roy Stone of Washington, D.C.
Married July 1, 1903
To: Augustus Debonnaire John Monson, 9th Baron Monson
Seat: Burton Hall, near Lincoln

Stone, an engineer originally from Morristown, New Jersey, had fought at Gettysburg and in the Spanish-American War. Turnure, Romaine's first husband, was from an Old New York banking family descended from the Huguenots. Monson was private secretary to his uncle, Sir Edward Monson, the British ambassador in Paris; his family had long been struggling financially. He and Romaine were married in Paris, after which she lived a very social life in New York and London. Their son married an American; a grandson was the author of *Nouveaux Pauvres*, a lifestyle manual for poverty-stricken aristocrats.

Sturges, Alberta

Daughter of William Sturges of New York
Married July 25, 1905
To: George Charles Montagu, later 9th Earl of Sandwich
**Seat: Hinchingbrooke House, Huntingdon, Cambridgeshire*

Alberta's mother, the widow Sturges, married New York wholesale grocer Frank Leggett and pursued a social career in London. Alberta had a splashy début in 1901 but showed little interest in the social world. Montagu was an earnest young M.P. and heir presumptive to his uncle when he married Alberta. Their son Victor disclaimed the title for life in order to serve in the House of Commons. Hinchingbrooke is now a school.

Alice Thaw was as innocent as Americans could come. Her marriage provided a disillusioning education in the ways of the world.

Thaw, Alice Cornelia

Daughter of William Thaw of Pittsburgh
Married April 27, 1903
To: George Francis Alexander Seymour, Earl of Yarmouth, later 7th Marquess of Hertford
*Seat: *Ragley Hall, Alcester, Warwickshire*

The Thaw money was from coal and the Pennsylvania Railroad. Alice's brother Harry, assassin of Stanford White, met Yarmouth while the latter was pursing a stage career in New York. The 4th Marquess had left all unentailed property, including a fabulous art collection, to his illegitimate son, Sir Richard Wallace, so Yarmouth was deep in debt at the time of his marriage to Alice. (He was also rumored to have proposed first to Alice's niece by her father's first marriage.) Alice's petition for an annulment was granted in 1908 on the ground of nonconsummation; Yarmouth was denied any part of the annual $50,000 settled on him at marriage.

TOUZALIN, ELLEN (Mrs. George Nickerson)

Daughter of A.E. Touzalin
Married January 19, 1910
To: The Hon. Horace Lambert Hood, younger brother of 5th Viscount Hood

Hood was aide-de-camp to Edward VII in 1912; he was knighted posthumously after his death in the Battle of Jutland (1916), and Ellen was granted the style ("Lady Hood") of a knight's wife. Their son Samuel succeeded as 6th Viscount.

TUCKER, ETHEL

Daughter of William Austin Tucker of Boston
Married January 31, 1900
To: the Hon. Archibald Lionel Lindesay-Bethune, later 13th Earl of Lindsay

Ethel's father founded the Tucker, Anthony banking house of Boston and New York. The Lindsays were divorced in 1906, but then married each other again in 1921 and lived in Boston, where he contributed to the British war relief effort. Their son, the 14th Earl, attended Groton.

VANDERBILT, CONSUELO

Daughter of William K. Vanderbilt of New York and Newport
Married November 6, 1895
To: Charles Richard John Spencer-Churchill, 9th Duke of Marlborough
*Seat: *Blenheim Palace, Woodstock, Oxfordshire*

William K. was a grandson of Commodore Vanderbilt, founder of the great fortune. Consuelo, named for her mother Alva's best friend, Consuelo Yznaga [q.v.], was brought up in great splendor in the States and abroad. The proud Marlborough (stepson of Lily Hammersley [q.v.] and nephew of Jennie Jerome [q.v.]) was saddled with the immense Blenheim and very little income; both his father and his grandfather were spendthrifts. Minnie Stevens [q.v.], also a good friend of Alva, set up the first meeting between the Duke and Consuelo, whose objections to the match were overruled. The Marlboroughs entertained lavishly at Blenheim, where the Prince of Wales was a frequent guest, and played a highly visible part in Edward VII's coronation. They separated in 1906 and were divorced in 1920. In 1921 the Duke married Gladys Deacon of Boston (for several years his mistress). Consuelo married French airman Jacques Balsan; she died in 1964 and was buried at her request in the Churchill family plot.

"O dear me if I was only a little older I might 'catch' him yet! But Helas! I am too young . . . And I will have to give up all chance to ever get Marlborough."

GLADYS DEACON, writing in her diary at age 14, after she read about the 9th Duke's engagement to Consuelo Vanderbilt; she later became his 2nd Duchess

The Countess of Tankerville with her only son, Lord Ossulton. The Tankervilles made little splash in London society.

VAN MARTER, LEONORA SOPHIA

Daughter of James G. Van Marter of New York
Married October 23, 1895
To: George Montagu Ker Bennet, Lord Ossulton, later 7th Earl of Tankerville
Seat: Chillingham Castle, Alnwick, Northumberland

Ossulton, a sportsman, painter and fine tenor, had served in the Royal Navy and as aide-de-camp to one of the Lords-Lieutenant of Ireland. Leonora was also musical and had studied Latin and Greek. They had a son and two daughters.

WADSWORTH, CORNELIA (Mrs. Montgomery Ritchie)

Daughter of Gen. James Wadsworth of Geneseo, New York
Married 1869
To: John Adair of Rathdaire, Ireland

The Wadsworths, with vast holdings in Geneseo, were prominent in many fields (e.g., Hartford's Wadsworth Atheneum). Cornelia was an aunt of Helen Post [q.v.]; her first husband died in the Civil War. Adair, though untitled, was a big landowner in Ireland (he had bought widely after the potato famine) and had a tract in Texas rumored to produce £40,000 a year. After he died, Cornelia was rumored to be engaged to the Duke of Marlborough in 1887. She attended the 1903 Durbar in India with her own chef and acted as Kitchener's hostess; she was also a marriage broker.

The redoubtable Mrs. Adair was a highly influential hostess, credited with pioneering the use of several small round tables for dinner (thus freeing hostesses from the rigors of precedence).

WADSWORTH, ELIZABETH (Mrs. Arthur Post)

Daughter of Gen. James Wadsworth of Geneseo, New York
Married February 28, 1889
To: Arthur Barry, later created 1st Baron Barrymore
Seat: Fota Island, Co. Cork, Ireland

Elizabeth was the beautiful widow of Arthur Post; her daughter was Helen Post [q.v.]. Barry had been widowed in 1884. Together they added the Long Gallery to Fota Island and continued the program of planting rare specimens in the famous arboretum there.

WALKER, MARGUERITE

Daughter of Judge Samuel J. Walker of Chicago and Frankfort, Kentucky
Married April 1897
To: the Hon. Oliver Henry Wallop, later 8th Earl of Portsmouth
Seat: Farleigh Wallop, near Basingstoke, Hampshire

Marguerite and Oliver lived a long time in Wyoming, where he was among the best-known residents, then moved to England when he succeeded to the title in 1925. They had two sons, the younger of whom stayed in Wyoming as a rancher; their grandson Malcolm is a U.S. senator from Wyoming.

WHITEHOUSE, LILY

Daughter of William Fitzhugh Whitehouse of New York and Newport
Married January 16, 1900
To: Col. the Hon. Charles John Coventry, 2nd son of 9th Earl of Coventry

Whitehouse, originally a Chicago lawyer, became director of the Louisville & Nashville Railroad and traveled in Europe to educate his six children. One of Lily's brothers was private secretary to Ambassador Whitelaw Reid, father of Jean Reid [q.v.]. Coventry's older brother, Viscount Deerhurst, married Virginia Bonynge [q.v.]; his younger brother married Edith Kip [q.v.]. He and Lily rented Stonor Park and, according to the daughter of Mildred Sherman [q.v.], put in a hot-water heater taken from a steamship.

Mrs. Astor owned a gold dinner service rumored to be worth $75,000. The gold dinner services belonging to Mrs. Whitelaw Reid and William Collins Whitney included plates, candelabra, épergnes and serving dishes as well as cutlery.

WHITNEY, PAULINE

Daughter of William Collins Whitney of New York, Lenox, Long Island, the Adirondacks
Married November 12, 1895
To: Almeric Paget, later 1st Baron Queenborough

Whitney, a lawyer and politician turned businessman, earned $40 million in just over five years as a founder of Metropolitan Transit. After the death of Pauline's mother (née Flora Payne) in 1892, he married Edith May Randolph, mother of Adelaide Randolph [q.v.]; she died in 1899, and it was rumored that Frances Work (Burke-Roche) [q.v.] was a candidate for his third wife. Pauline's mother was a great friend of Mrs. Paran Stevens, mother of Minnie Stevens (Paget) [q.v.] and Almeric's sister-in-law. Almeric had made money in Minnesota real estate; after his marriage to Pauline (the wedding was overshadowed by that of Consuelo Vanderbilt [q.v.] a week earlier), he worked for Whitney in New York. In 1902 the Pagets moved to England, where they had homes in London and Suffolk. She was socially ambitious and an inveterate card player; he became an M.P. and High Sheriff of Suffolk, and was created Baron for political service.

WILSON, BELLE

Daughter of Richard T. Wilson of New York and Newport
Married November 27, 1988
To: the Hon. Michael Henry Herbert, later knighted; younger brother of 13th Earl of Pembroke

Wilson, a New York banker with investments in railroads, was originally from Georgia and had served as commissary-general in the Confederate Army. Belle's sister May was the mother of May Goelet [q.v.]; her sister Grace married Cornelius Vander-

"P.S. Will you send us another letter of credit for £2,000 made out to Hon. Michael Herbert and Mrs. L.B. Herbert?"
THE HON. MICHAEL HERBERT, to his Wilson in-laws

bilt, cousin of Consuelo Vanderbilt [q.v.]. Belle was one of Charles Worth's most famous success stories. Herbert, secretary at the British legation in Washington, was later posted to Constantinople; he was appointed British ambassador to Washington in 1902 and died the following year.

WORK, FRANCES

Daughter of Frank Work of New York and Newport
Married September 22, 1880
To: the Hon. James Boothby Burke-Roche, later 3rd Baron Fermoy

Frances' father was a stockbroker for Cornelius Vanderbilt. Burke-Roche was a handsome sporting type who looked like poor husband material, but the headstrong Frances insisted on marrying him. They lived in New York a few years (Work had to pay Burke-Roche's $50,000 gambling debts), then in England. Frances divorced him in 1891, winning custody of their twin sons. She lived stylishly in New York until her short marriage to (and scandalous divorce from) Hungarian horse trainer Aurel Batonyi; this episode caused her to be disinherited by her father and ostracized by society.

"*We have just been staying up at Tandragee [the Manchesters' place in Ireland] with Lord and Lady Mandeville—poor little thing, she is so delicate—so utterly helpless—and* most *charming. What a contrast to the Duchess. She cannot endure a country life and is quite miserable. . . .*"

MRS. ADAIR to Lady Waldegrave (1877)

YZNAGA, CONSUELO

Daughter of Antonio Yznaga del Valle of New York and Newport
Married May 22, 1876
To: George Victor Drogo Montagu, Viscount Mandeville, later 8th Duke of Manchester
*Seats: *Kimbolton Castle, Kimbolton, Cambridgeshire; Tandragee Castle, Co. Armagh, Ireland*

Consuelo's father had been a well-to-do Cuban merchant in Natchez; her mother, a planter's daughter, brought the family to New York after the Civil War. Her brother Fernando married Alva Vanderbilt's sister. Consuelo met Mandeville at Saratoga; legend has it that he fell in love as she nursed him through a bout of typhoid. In England she was known for her easygoing, slightly wild ways and became the Prince of Wales' mistress. Mandeville, who left her at Tandragee while he squired a music-hall singer around London, was declared bankrupt in 1890. Always hard up for money, Consuelo reputedly accepted "gifts" for social introductions. Her son, the 9th Duke, married Helena Zimmerman [q.v.].

YZNAGA, NATICA

Daughter of Antonio Yznaga del Valle of New York and Newport
Married December 5, 1881
To: Sir John Pepys Lister-Kaye, Baronet

Natica and Consuelo were called "the Little Sisters of the Rich." Lister-Kaye, who claimed descent from Sir Kay of Arthurian legend, was a groom-in-waiting to Edward VII.

ZIMMERMAN, HELENA

Daughter of Eugene Zimmerman of Cincinnati
Married November 14, 1900
To: William Angus Drogo Montagu, 9th Duke of Manchester
*Seats: *Kimbolton Castle, Kimbolton, Cambridgeshire; Tandragee Castle, Co. Armagh, Ireland; Kylemore Castle, Letterfrack, Co. Galway, Ireland*

Helena's father was a stockholder in Standard Oil and railroad president. Kim (nicknamed for his childhood title, Lord Kimbolton) had been unsuccessful in trolling the States for a rich wife; he worked at the New York *Journal* as a reporter one summer. He was declared bankrupt just before his secret marriage to Helena, which appalled his mother, Consuelo Yznaga [q.v.]. Edward VII and Alexandra were their guests in 1904 at Kylemore Castle in Ireland (bought for them by Helena's father) on a much-publicized visit. The Manchesters divorced in 1931; the Duke remained improvident.

Helena Zimmerman as a young girl. Six years after her divorce from Manchester, she married an old friend, the 10th Earl of Kintore.

THE BRIDESMAID CONNECTION

BRIDES	BRIDESMAIDS
CONSUELO YZNAGA *(Duchess of Manchester)*	MINNIE STEVENS *(Lady Paget)*
ELLEN STAGER *(Marchioness of Ormonde)*	ROMAINE STONE *(Lady Monson)*
ELIZABETH FRENCH *(Lady Cheylesmore)*	ANTOINETTE PINCHOT *(Hon. Mrs. Alan Johnstone)*
	FLORA DAVIS *(Marchioness of Dufferin)*
FLORA DAVIS *(Marchioness of Dufferin)*	EDITH KIP MCCREERY *(Hon. Mrs. Henry Coventry)*
MARY LEITER *(Lady Curzon)*	DAISY LEITER *(Countess of Suffolk)*
	NANCY LEITER *(Mrs. Colin Campbell)*
CONSUELO VANDERBILT *(Duchess of Marlborough)*	MAY GOELET *(Duchess of Roxburghe)*
MAY GOELET *(Duchess of Roxburghe)*	BEATRICE MILLS *(Countess of Granard)*
MARGARETTA DREXEL *(Countess of Winchilsea)*	MILDRED CARTER *(Countess of Gosford)*
	NELLIE POST *(Countess of St. Germans)*

THE AMERICAN HEIRESSES' LONDON

❖

Like New York's Fifth Avenue, Mayfair and Belgravia were almost entirely residential before World War I. And like Fifth Avenue, Mayfair and Belgravia are now much changed. What has not been lost to the wrecker's ball has been given over to shops and offices. Still, some of the London of the American heiresses remains. Just squint your eyes as you walk the streets suggested on the following pages, and try to remember that the air was much more polluted, the streets much narrower and the champagne much, much more intoxicating.

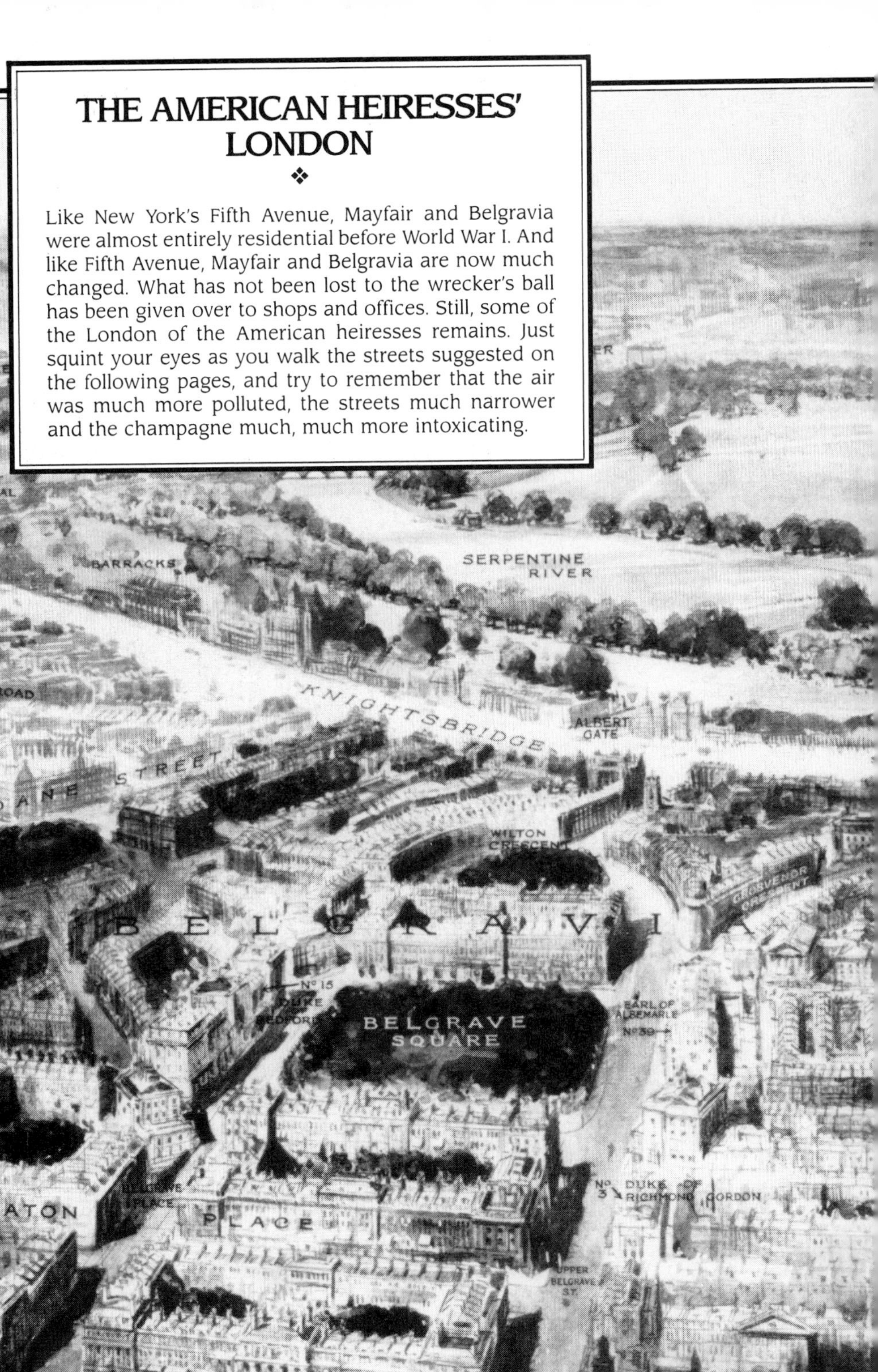

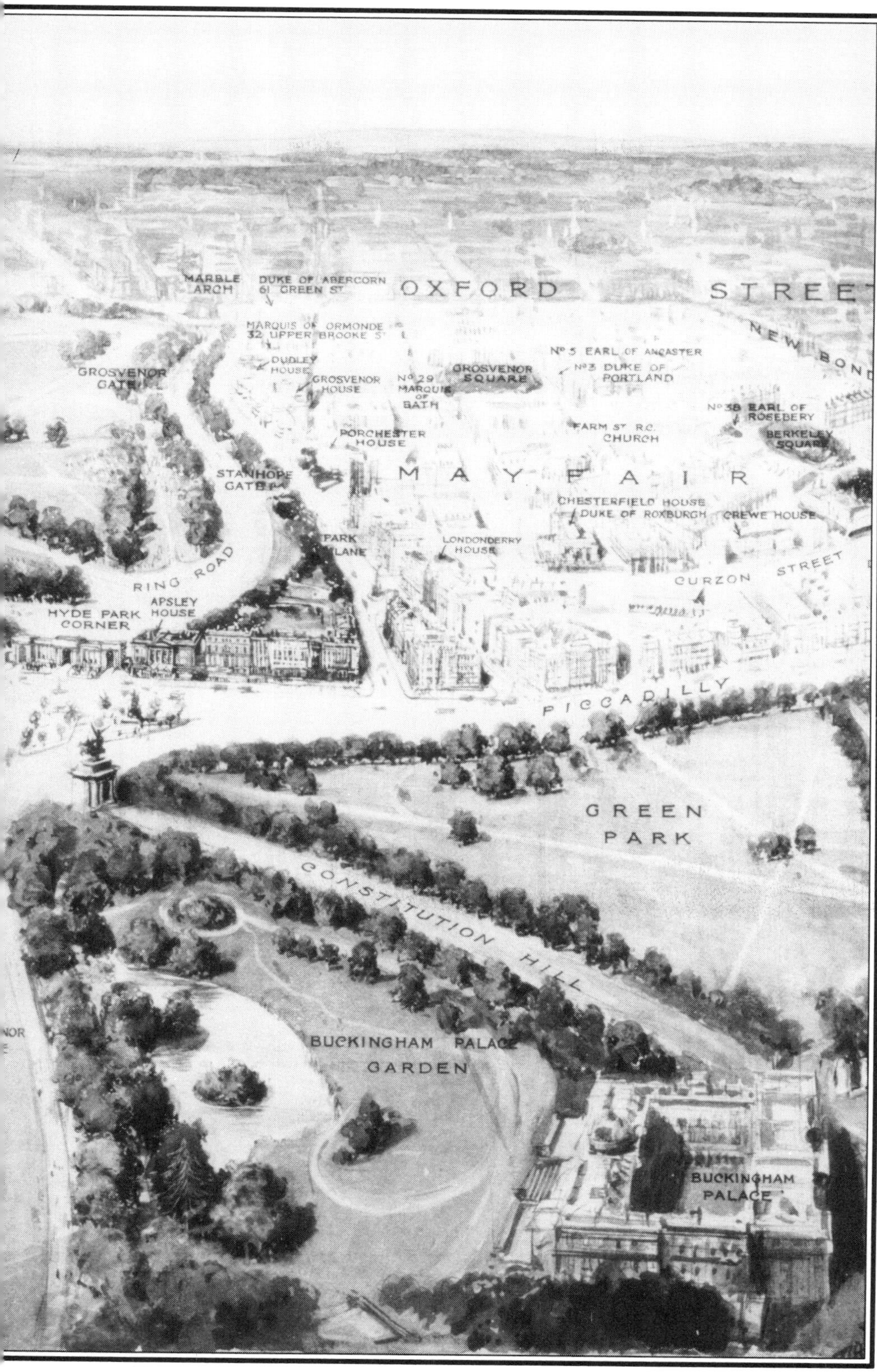

MARBLE ARCH
DUKE OF ABERCORN 61 GREEN ST
OXFORD STREET
NEW BOND
MARQUIS OF ORMONDE 32 UPPER BROOKE ST
Nº 5 EARL OF ANCASTER
Nº 3 DUKE OF PORTLAND
GROSVENOR GATE
DUDLEY HOUSE
GROSVENOR HOUSE
Nº 29 MARQUIS OF BATH
GROSVENOR SQUARE
Nº 38 EARL OF ROSEBERY
BERKELEY SQUARE
FARM ST R.C. CHURCH
PORCHESTER HOUSE
STANHOPE GATE
MAYFAIR
CHESTERFIELD HOUSE DUKE OF ROXBURGH
CREWE HOUSE
PARK LANE
LONDONDERRY HOUSE
RING ROAD
CURZON STREET
APSLEY HOUSE
HYDE PARK CORNER
PICCADILLY
GREEN PARK
CONSTITUTION HILL
BUCKINGHAM PALACE GARDEN
BUCKINGHAM PALACE

WALKING TOUR OF THE AMERICAN HEIRESSES' LONDON

In some country houses, a discreet bell rang at 6 A.M. to allow guests to return to their own beds before the servants were up and about.

ALBEMARLE STREET.

Brown's Hotel: "a dingy structure in a narrow street," according to Consuelo Vanderbilt, but then and always the hotel of choice for Americans in London. Tea at five. Dress appropriately and bring an appetite—the sweets are divine.

ALDFORD STREET.

No. 18: owned by Clara Frewen, eldest of the Jerome girls. Since her husband was regularly broke, Clara spent a good portion of her married life visiting relatives and kind friends.

AUDLEY SQUARE.

No. 6: at one time the town house of the Earl of Minto. By 1910 it was occupied by the 2nd Earl of Ancaster and American heiress Eloise Breese.

BELGRAVE SQUARE.

Now just a lot of embassies and zebra crossings, but once one of the prettiest and most chic of the London squares. *No. 15* (Royal Agricultural Society of England): occupied by Minnie Stevens when she and Arthur came into their own; Consuelo Vanderbilt was introduced to the Duke of Marlborough here. *No. 45:* residence of Michael P. Grace, Anglophile and Wall Street Father of American heiresses Elena, Countess of Donoughmore, and Elisa, wife of the Hon. Hubert Beaumont. Also in Belgrave Square was Herbert House, where the happily married Belle Wilson and Michael Herbert stayed when they were in London.

BERKELEY SQUARE.

Almost unrecognizable; only a strip of houses along the west side gives any hint of its former grandeur, which had faded even by the time of the heiresses. Still, it was exclusive enough for "avidly social" Pauline Whitney and Almeric Paget, who lived at *No. 38. No. 14* was the home of Mary Ethel Burns, the future Lady Harcourt. And *No. 45* was home to Lady Dorothy Nevill, whose Sunday afternoon teas were among the most fashionable in London.

BRUTON STREET.
A typical Mayfair side street. *No. 12* was lived in for some years by the ambitious Betty Leggett, wife of the New York wholesale grocer, mother of Alberta, Countess of Sandwich, and best friend of the even more ambitious Maud Cunard. American heiress Louise Corbin lived up the street at *No. 36.*

CADOGAN PLACE.
No. 7: home for years and years to Fanny Ronalds, one-time mistress of Leonard Jerome and August Belmont. In London, she was courted by the Duke of Edinburgh and fell in love with Sir Arthur Sullivan.

CADOGAN SQUARE.
No. 75 belonged to the former Florence Davis of New York, married to the 2nd Marquess of Dufferin and Ava. "The present marchioness is a pretty woman of many accomplishments and exquisite taste," claimed the *Tatler*, "the great white staircase and magnificent blue hall of her beautiful house in Cadogan Square being of her own design."

CARLTON HOUSE TERRACE.
The residence of choice for American heiresses. Why? Because it was practically in Marlborough House's back garden—about as close to Bertie as a non-royal could get. *No. 1:* bought by Levi Leiter for George and Mary Curzon. *No. 3:* lived in by Lily Hammersley after her 1895 marriage to Lord William Beresford. *No. 5* was once the residence of Maud Cunard. Next door, in gaudy magnificence, lived Mrs. John W. Mackay. New York wouldn't touch her—but London ate her up. *No. 7* was for a time the residence of Belle and Mungo Wilson (doubtless with Papa Wilson's money). *No. 18* belonged to W.W. Astor, one of Daisy Warwick's best friends until she converted to socialism. *No. 20* was lived in by Lady Parker, American wife of Sir Gilbert Parker, author and M.P. *No. 22* belonged to Amy Phipps Guest.

In London, silver had to be polished daily because it began to yellow after twenty-four hours in the dirty air.

CHARLES STREET.
No. 37 (English-Speaking Union) once belonged to the Baring family, of banking fame; the American heiress in residence was Maude Lorillard Baring. *No. 39:* home to the last Earl of Camperdown and his American wife, Laura Dove. *No. 40:* sometime home of the Earl of Cork and his California girl, Josephine Hale.

CHESHAM STREET.

No. 15: home of Mr. and Mrs. John Ridgely Carter. He was American minister in England; she provided the cash. Their daughter Mildred married, inevitably, an English lord: the 5th Earl of Gosford.

CHESHAM PLACE.

No. 29: home of Margaret Hamilton. Her husband, Sir Sidney Waterlow, was a former Lord Mayor of London and about three times her age.

CHESTERFIELD GARDENS.

Down on its luck, but not without atmosphere. The Duke of Roxburghe lived here before Goelet money took him to Chesterfield House. *No. 3* (now demolished) belonged to Cornelia Martin, Countess of Craven. Its walls were knocked through to connect with her mum, who had moved in next door at *No. 4*. *No. 5:* residence of Elena Grace, American Countess of Donoughmore. *No. 8:* home of Eloise Breese Drummond-Willoughby, the future Lady Ancaster.

CHESTERFIELD STREET.

No. 14: home of Jean Reid and the Hon. John Ward.

CONNAUGHT PLACE.

No. 2: occupied by Lord and Lady Randolph Churchill from 1888 to 1892. Randolph's amateur scientist brother Blandford installed a dynamo in the cellar, allowing Jennie to claim that hers was the first London house to be lit by electricity.

CURZON STREET.

No. 30: home of Mrs. Adair, reputed by the *Tatler* to have "silk-lined walls, some good pictures and any amount of costly French furniture." The ballroom had a minstrel gallery. *Crewe House*, across the street, was once leased by Henry Phipps, steel-magnate father of American heiress Amy Phipps Guest. Down the street is *Sunderland House*, built for Consuelo Vanderbilt Marlborough. "I can't stand the dining room," wrote Daisy, Princess of Pless, "it is not high enough and the windows have always to be covered with stuff as they are right on the ground floor and the people in the dirty little back street can look in." Consuelo lived here after she moved out of Blenheim; when she left England, Sunny sold the house.

In the summer of 1913, the 9th Duke of Marlborough was visiting the French resort of Beaulieu-sur-Mer when to his displeasure he ran into his cousin the Hon. Reginald Fellowes, second son of the Baron de Ramsey. Reginald was supposedly Consuelo Marlborough's lover (though eight years younger than she); his parents were said to be furious with Consuelo because they wanted him to marry and felt she was keeping him on a string.

EATON SQUARE.

St. Peter's Church (recently severely damaged by fire): site of Minnie Stevens' wedding to Arthur Paget, one of the events said to have started the transatlantic marriage stampede.

Great Cumberland Place.

No. 3: town house of the 11th Baronet Molesworth, married to American heiress Jane Frost. *No. 10* (now the Cumberland Hotel): long-time address of the popular Leonie Leslie, youngest Jerome sister. *No. 35:* town residence of Jennie Jerome and second, much younger husband George Cornwallis-West. *37A:* another home of the wandering Clara Jerome Frewen.

Grosvenor Square.

Maud "Emerald" Cunard's ashes were scattered here, and with good reason—she'd devoted her life to social climbing from this venue. In her early days in London, remembered a fellow heiress, Maud "never went away. Winter and summer, weekdays and Sundays she stayed on the job. In her beautiful house, always at home, concentrated on the matter at hand." *No. 15* was the long-time home of Consuelo Yznaga Manchester, who died there a year before her king; many an American heiress first met her man at a dinner or tea in this house. *No. 5* belonged to Helena Zimmerman, Consuelo's American heiress daughter-in-law. *No. 8:* residence of American heiress Edith Kip Coventry. *No. 22:* home of Anthony Drexel, Wall Street Father and Collector *par excellence*, and of his daughter and son-in-law, the Earl and Countess of Winchilsea and Nottingham. *No. 26* was bought by Mary Smith and Englishman George Cooper from some of the £4 million she inherited from her uncle. At *No. 50* Randolph Churchill succumbed to syphilis, only a month after returning to England from a trip round the world.

In a well-run house, servants changed the blotting paper in bedrooms daily.

Hanover Square.

St. George's Church: the church of choice for society weddings. Jeannie Chamberlain married Captain Herbert Naylor-Leyland here. Adele Grant, Countess of Essex, lived around the corner at 16 George Street.

Haymarket.

No. 5–6: home then as now of American Express.

Hertford Street.

No. 8, around the corner from Sunderland House: home of Helene Beckwith Leigh.

Hill Street.

No. 20: residence of Mrs. Arthur Post, the future Lady Barrymore. *No. 26:* residence of Baron Revelstoke, suitor of Nancy Shaw Astor and older brother of Cecil Baring, husband of American heiress Maude Lorillard.

HYDE PARK.

Hyde Park House, Albert Gate: famous for entertainments given by one-time H.R.H. protégée Jeannie Chamberlain, Lady Naylor-Leyland. Because the Frewens were again without a home, their daughter Clare was married from this house (now the French embassy). *Rotten Row:* scene of much stately cantering and of Sir William Gordon-Cumming's 1882 question to American heiress Leonie Jerome, "Over here husband-hunting?"

JERMYN STREET.

The proprietor of the *Cavendish Hotel* was Rosa Lewis, a cook who worked her way up in the world. Male patrons were particularly keen. She provided suites with private dining rooms (the King had one).

KNIGHTSBRIDGE.

St. Paul's Church, where Jennie Churchill married George Cornwallis-West to jam-packed pews. Here also, Alberta, Betty Leggett's daughter, married George Montagu, the future Earl of Sandwich.

MARLBOROUGH HOUSE.

The London home of the Prince of Wales until he became Edward VII.

PALL MALL.

Club row. No. 17: residence of Baron Bagot until 1903, when he married Baltimorean Lilian May. *30–35:* Junior Carlton. *52:* Marlborough Club, founded by Bertie. *70:* Guards'. *71:* Oxford and Cambridge. *94:* Carlton Club, the next most frequently listed club of husbands of American heiresses after Marlborough. *104:* Reform. *106:* Travellers'. *107:* Athenaeum.

PARK LANE.

Once a residential street of distinction (now an eight-lane highway lined with hotels). *Dorchester House*, the most splendid house in London, became the residence of Whitelaw Reid when he was appointed ambassador in 1905. His daughter Jean married the Hon. John Ward, second son of the 1st Earl Dudley, and moved to Dudley House. Ellen Stager, future American Marchioness of Ormonde, lived in Park Lane, as did Anna Robinson, actress wife of Earl Rosslyn. Also in Park Lane was *Londonderry House*, ruled over by Theresa Londonderry, the dominant political hostess of the day, and *Grosvenor House*, the Duke of Westminster's London home, where Mary Leiter first met George Curzon.

Rumors after Consuelo Marlborough's separation from Sunny had it that she was unfaithful first; one of her lovers, as early as 1907, was supposed to be Lord Castlereagh, the Londonderrys' eldest son.

PICCADILLY.

A small collection of houses near the Hyde Park end of Piccadilly gives an indication of what it looked like to the American heiresses. Lord and Lady Rothschild had their London residence at *No. 148*; the American Flora Sharon, at *No. 111*. At *No. 78*, where now stands an office block, was once the forecourt of *Devonshire House*, London home of the Duke of Devonshire. Opposite is the *Ritz*, whose management used to send the Jerome women *terrines de fois gras* "in recognition of their support," i.e., sending lots of filthy-rich American clients their way.

PORTLAND PLACE.

Below Regent's Park. *No. 3:* home of Grace Bruce Carr, Baroness Newborough after her marriage in 1900. *No. 8:* home of Maude Lorillard Baring until she moved to Bryanston Square.

PORTMAN SQUARE.

No. 8: home of Alberta Sturges, future Countess of Sandwich. *No. 15:* H.R.H.'s daughter Princess Louise and her husband, the Duke of Fife. *No. 30:* Mrs. George Keppel. *No. 45:* Consuelo, Duchess of Manchester.

PRINCE'S GATE.

No. 14: occupied by J. Pierpont Morgan. *No. 16:* Lord and Lady Cheylesmore, who, deigning to exist outside Mayfair, were credited by the *Tatler* for "a worthy keeping up of old traditions." *No. 42:* Charles Bonynge and his daughter and son-in-law, the Viscount and Viscountess Deerhurst.

RICHMOND TERRACE, WHITEHALL.

No. 4: for years the town address of Elizabeth Cavendish-Bentinck, one of the premier social godmothers and an Old New York girl to boot.

ST. JAMES'S SQUARE.

No. 4: the town residence of Nancy Astor. The Randolph Churchills, in their early married life, lived in nearby St. James's Street; next door was Sir Stafford Northcote, whose son married American Edith Livingston Fish. *Clubs. 28:* Boodles. *37:* White's. *69:* Carlton. *74:* Conservative.

SLOANE STREET.

No. 122: home of American heiress Rosalind Secor, Lady Chetwynd. Down the street, at Holy Trinity, Florence Garner married Sir William Gordon-Cumming.

In 1919 American social climber Mrs. William Leeds was looking forward to the big dinner she'd planned at the Ritz for Prince Christopher of Greece when Minnie Paget, who had been her social guide, died suddenly on the day of the party. Not wanting to disturb all her arrangements, Mrs. Leeds simply didn't announce the death and gave the dinner regardless. Five months later, Minnie's wardrobe was sold by auction in London; her famous Cleopatra costume, made by Worth, went for a little more than £9.

BIBLIOGRAPHY/SELECTED READING

FICTION

ATHERTON, GERTRUDE. *American Wives and English Husbands.* Service & Paton, 1898.

——. *Tower of Ivory.* John Murray, 1910.

HARRISON, CONSTANCE CARY. *Anglomaniacs.* Cassell, 1890.

JAMES, HENRY. *The Ambassadors.* Penguin, 1973.

——. *The American.* Penguin, 1981.

——. *The Europeans.* Penguin, 1964.

——. *The Golden Bowl.* Oxford, 1983.

——. *A London Life.* Scribner's, 1907.

——. *The Portrait of a Lady.* Penguin, 1984.

——. *The Reverberator.* Grove Press, 1885.

——. *Washington Square.* Signet, 1964.

——. *The Wings of the Dove.* Penguin, 1982. Short Stories: "A Bundle of Letters," "Crapy Cornelia," "Daisy Miller," "An International Episode," "Lady Barbarina," "Lord Beaupré," "Miss Gunton of Poughkeepsie," "Mrs. Medwin," "Pandora," "The Pension Beaurepas," "Point of View," "The Siege of London."

RAE, WILLIAM FRASER. *An American Duchess.* R. Bentley & Son, 1891.

——. *Miss Bayle's Romance.* H. Holt & Co., 1887.

SACKVILLE-WEST, VITA. *The Edwardians.* Avon, 1983.

SHERWOOD, MARY E. *A Transplanted Rose.* Harper & Bros., 1882.

TROLLOPE, ANTHONY. *The Duke's Children.* Oxford, 1954.

——. *The Way We Live Now.* Oxford, 1982.

WHARTON, EDITH. *The Age of Innocence.* Scribner's, 1970.

——. *The Buccaneers.* Appleton-Century, 1938.

——. *The Custom of the Country.* Scribner's, 1913.

——. *The House of Mirth,* Bantam, 1984. Short Stories: "Autres Temps," "Madame de Treymes."

NONFICTION

ALSOP, SUSAN MARY. *Lady Sackville.* Avon, 1978.

AMORY, CLEVELAND. *Who Killed Society?* Harper & Row, 1960.

ANDREWS, ALLEN. *The Splendid Pauper.* Harrap, 1968.

ASTOR, MICHAEL. *Tribal Feeling.* John Murray, 1963.

ATHERTON, GERTRUDE. *Adventures of a Novelist.* Jonathan Cape, 1932.

——. *Can Women Be Gentlemen?* Houghton Mifflin, 1938.

BAKER, PAUL. *Richard Morris Hunt.* M.I.T., 1980.

BALSAN, CONSUELO VANDERBILT. *The Glitter and the Gold.* Harper & Bros., 1952.

Bancroft's Americans' Guide to London. Bancroft, 1901–06.

BARRETT, RICHMOND. *Good Old Summer Days*. Appleton-Century, 1941.

BARROW, ANDREW. *Gossip*. Pan Books, 1978.

BATTISCOMBE, GEORGINA. *Life of Queen Alexandra*. Constable, 1969.

BEEBE, LUCIUS. *The Big Spenders*. Doubleday, 1966.

BEERBOHM, MAX. *Things Old and New*. Heinemann, 1923.

BERLIN, ELLIN. *Silver Platter*. Doubleday, 1957.

BLUNDEN, MARGARET. *The Countess of Warwick*. Cassell, 1967.

BOURGET, PAUL. *Outre-Mer*. Scribner's, 1895.

BRANDON, RUTH. *The Dollar Princesses*. Alfred A. Knopf, 1980.

BRIDGE, JAMES HOWARD (pseud. Harold Brydges). *Uncle Sam at Home*. H. Holt & Co., 1888.

BROWN, MARY MACDONALD. *Amazing New York*. Andrew Melrose, 1913.

BROUGH, JAMES. *Consuelo*. Coward, McCann & Geoghegan, 1979.

CABLE, MARY. *American Manners & Morals*. American Heritage, 1969.

——. *Top Drawer*. Atheneum, 1984.

CAMPBELL, CHARLES SUTTER. *Anglo-American Understanding, 1898–1903*. Johns Hopkins Press, 1957.

Catalog of Memorial Exhibition of the Works of John Singer Sargent. Museum of Fine Arts (Boston), 1925.

CHURCHILL, ALLEN. *The Splendor Seekers*. Grossett & Dunlap, 1947.

CHURCHILL, PEREGRINE, and JULIAN MITCHELL. *Jennie*. St. Martin's, 1974.

CHURCHILL, LADY RANDOLPH. *Small Talks on Big Subjects*. Pearson, 1916.

CHURCHILL, RANDOLPH. *Fifteen Famous English Homes*. Verschoyle, 1954.

CHURCHILL, WINSTON. *My Early Life*. Scribner's, 1930.

CLEWS, HENRY. *Twenty-Eight Years in Wall Street*. Sampson Low, Markson, Searle and Rivington, 1888.

COLLIER, PRICE. *England and the English*. Scribner's, 1914.

COOPER, NICHOLAS. *The Opulent Eye*. Architectural Press, 1976.

CORELLI, MARIE, with Lady Jeune, Flora Annie Steel, and Susan, Countess of Malmesbury. *The Modern Marriage Market*. Hutchinson, 1898.

CORNWALLIS-WEST, GEORGE. *Edwardian Heydays*. Putnam's, 1930.

COWLES, VIRGINIA. *The Astors*. Alfred A. Knopf, 1979.

——. *Edward VII and His Circle*. Hamish Hamilton, 1956.

CROWNINSHIELD, FRANK. "The House of Vanderbilt." *Vogue*, Nov. 15, 1941.

DEMARLY, DIANA. *History of Haute Couture*. Holmes & Meier, 1980.

DOWNES, WILLIAM HOWE. *John S. Sargent*. Butterworth, 1926.

DUMAURIER, GEORGE. *Society Pictures*. Bradbury, Agnew, 1891.

EDEL, LEON. "Henry James, Edith Wharton, and Newport." Redwood Library & Athenaeum (Newport), 1966.

——. *The Life of Henry James*. Penguin, 1977.

ELIOT, ELIZABETH. *Heiresses & Coronets*. McDowell, Obolensky, 1959.

ELLIOTT, MAUD HOWE. *This Was My Newport*. Mythology, 1944.

——. *Three Generations*. Little, Brown, 1923.

ESCOTT, THOMAS HAY SWEET. *King Edward & His Court*. Unwin, 1903.

——. *Society in London*. Chatto & Windus, 1885.

ENSOR, R.C.K. *England: 1870–1914*. Oxford, 1946.

FIELD, LESLIE. *The Queen's Jewels*. Harry N. Abrams, 1987.

FIELDING, DAPHNE. *Duchess of Jermyn Street*. Eyre & Spottiswode, 1964.

——. *Emerald and Nancy*. Eyre & Spottiswode, 1968.

FISKE, STEPHEN. *Offhand Portraits of Eminent New Yorkers*. Lockwood & Sons, 1884.

FLOWER, SYBILLA JANE, comp. *Debrett's Stately Homes of England*. Holt, Rinehart & Winston, 1982.

FRIEDMAN, BERNARD HARPER. *Gertrude Vanderbilt Whitney*. Doubleday, 1978.

GERNSHEIM, ALISON. *Victorian & Edwardian Fashion: A Photographic Survey*. Dover, 1981.

GREEN, DAVID. *The Churchills of Blenheim*. Constable, 1984.

GRISWOLD, FRANK GRAY. *Afterthoughts*. Harper & Bros., 1936.

HARRISON, CONSTANCE CARY. *Our Best Society*. Century, 1899.

HARRISON, ROSINA. *Rose: My Life in Service*. Viking, 1975.

HARTZELL, A.E., comp. *Titled Americans*. Street & Smith, 1890.

HIBBERT, CHRISTOPHER. *Edward VII: A Portrait*. Penguin, 1976.

HILLS, PATRICIA. *John Singer Sargent*. Whitney Museum, 1987.

HUGHES, ALICE. *My Father and I*. Butterworth, 1923.

JAMES, HENRY. *Portraits of Places*. James R. Osgood, 1884.

JAMES, ROBERT RHODES. *Lord Randolph Churchill*. A.S. Barnes, 1960.

JOSEPHSON, MATTHEW. *The Robber Barons*. Harcourt, Brace, 1934.

"JUVENAL." *An Englishman in New York*. Stephen Swift, 1911.

LAMBERT, ANGELA. *Unquiet Souls*. Harper & Row, 1984.

LANG, THEO. *The Darling Daisy Affair*. Atheneum, 1966.

LANGHORNE, ELIZABETH. *Nancy Astor and Her Friends*. Praeger, 1974.

LEGGETT, FRANCES. *Late & Soon*. Houghton Mifflin, 1968.

LEHR, ELIZABETH DREXEL. *King Lehr & the Gilded Age*. Lippincott, 1935.

——. *Turn of the World*. Lippincott, 1937.

LESLIE, ANITA. *Lady Randolph Churchill*. Scribner's, 1969.

——. *The Marlborough House Set*. Doubleday, 1973.

——. *The Remarkable Mr. Jerome*. Henry Holt, 1954.

LESLIE, SEYMOUR. *The Jerome Connection*. John Murray, 1964.

LESLIE, SHANE. *Studies in Sublime Failure*. Ernest Benn, 1932.

LEWIS, R.W.B. *Edith Wharton*. Harper & Row, 1975.

LONGFORD, ELIZABETH. *Louisa, Lady in Waiting*. Mayflower, 1981.

——. *Victoria R.I.* Weidenfeld & Nicolson, 1964.

MCALLISTER, WARD. *Society as I Have Found It*. Cassell, 1890.

MAGNUS, PHILIP. *Life of Edward VII*. Dutton, 1964.

MANCHESTER, WILLIAM ANGUS DROGO MONTAGU, 9th Duke. *My Candid Reflections*. Grayson & Grayson, 1932.

MARTIN, FREDERICK TOWNSEND. *Passing of the Idle Rich*. Doubleday Page, 1911.

——. *Things I Remember*. John Lane, 1913.

MARTIN, RALPH G. *Jennie: The Life of Lady Randolph Churchill*. Vol. I: *The Romantic Years*. Signet, 1969. Vol. 2: *The Dramatic Years*. Prentice-Hall, 1971.

MITFORD, NANCY. *Noblesse Oblige*. Futura, 1980.

MOONEY, MICHAEL. *Evelyn Nesbit & Stanford White*. Morrow, 1976.

MORRIS, LLOYD R. *Incredible New York*. Random House, 1951.

MURPHY, SOPHIA. *The Duchess of Devonshire's Ball*. Sidgwick & Jackson, 1984.

NAPIER, ELMA. *Youth Is a Blunder*. Jonathan Cape, 1948.

NICHOLLS, CHARLES WILBUR DE LYON. *The Ultra-fashionable Peerage of America*. Arno, 1976.

NICOLSON, NIGEL. *Mary Curzon*. Harper & Row, 1977.

O'CONNOR, RICHARD. *The Golden Summers*. Putnam's, 1974.

OLIAN, JOANNE. *The House of Worth: The Gilded Age, 1860-1918*. Museum of the City of New York, 1982.

PEACOCK, VIRGINIA. *Famous American Belles of the Nineteenth Century.* Lippincott, 1901.

PEARSON, HESKETH. *The Pilgrim Daughters.* Heinemann, 1961.

PLESS, DAISY, PRINCESS OF. *By Herself.* John Murray, 1928.

POIRET, PAUL. *My First Fifty Years.* Victor Gollancz, 1931.

PULITZER, RALPH. *New York Society on Parade.* Harper & Bros., 1920.

RATCLIFF, CARTER. *Sargent.* Abbeville, 1982.

ROSKILL, STEPHEN. *Admiral of the Fleet Earl Beatty: The Last Naval Hero.* Atheneum, 1981.

ST. HÉLIER, MARY JANE (Lady). *Memories of Fifty Years.* Edward Arnold, 1909.

SAUNDERS, EDITH. *The Age of Worth.* Indiana University, 1955.

SLADEN, DOUGLAS, and W. WIGMORE, eds. *Green Book of London Society.* J. Whitaker & Sons, 1910.

STEAD, W.T. *The Americanization of the World.* Horace Markley, 1901.

STERN, ROBERT A.M., GREGORY GILMARTIN and JOHN MASSENGALE. *New York 1900.* Rizzoli, 1983.

STONE, LAWRENCE and JEANNE C. *An Open Elite? England, 1540–1880.* Oxford, 1984.

SWANBERG, W.A. *Whitney Father, Whitney Heiress.* Scribner's, 1980.

SWEETSER, M.F., and SIMEON FORD. *How to Know New York City.* J.J. Little, 1890.

SYKES, CHRISTOPHER. *Four Studies in Loyalty.* Collins, 1946.

——. *Nancy: The Life of Nancy Astor.* Harper & Row, 1972.

THOMPSON, F.M.L. *English Landed Gentry in the Nineteenth Century.* Routledge & Kegan Paul, 1963.

VANDERBILT, CORNELIUS. *Queen of the Gilded Age.* McGraw-Hill, 1956.

——. *The Vanderbilt Feud.* Hutchinson, 1957.

VAN RENSSELAER, MAY KING. *Newport, Our Social Capital.* Lippincott, 1905.

VICKERS, HUGO. *Gladys, Duchess of Marlborough.* Holt, Rinehart & Winston, 1979.

WARWICK, FRANCES, COUNTESS OF. *Afterthoughts.* Cassell, 1931.

——. *Discretions.* Scribner's, 1931.

——. *Life's Ebb & Flow.* Hutchinson, 1929.

WECTER, DIXON. *The Saga of American Society.* Scribner's, 1937.

WHARTON, EDITH. *A Backward Glance.* Scribner's, 1933.

WILDE, OSCAR. *Impressions of America.* Keystone Press, 1906.

WORTH, JEAN PHILIPPE. *A Century of Fashion.* Little, Brown, 1928.

INDEX

(Page numbers in *italics* refer to illustrations. Page numbers in **boldface** refer to entries for individual heiresses in register.)

A

C

D

E

F

H

L

M

N

O

P

Q

R

S

T

V

W

Y

Z

PICTURE CREDITS

Wherever possible, we have made every effort to find and credit the original source for each picture.

Back cover photograph: Courtesy of Countess of Craven.

CONTENTS

P. V: Courtesy of Lord Hesketh. **P. VII:** Mary Evans Picture Library. **P. VIII:** Brown Brothers. **P. IX:** Courtesy of Countess of Craven. **P. X:** Illustrated London News Picture Library.

PROLOGUE

Pp. 1, 3 *(top right):* Bettmann Archive. **P. 2:** New York Historical Society. **P. 3** *(left):* Picture Collection, New York Public Library. **P. 3** *(bottom right):* Museum of the City of New York.

THE BUCCANEERS

Pp. 7 *(left),* **29** *(right),* **32:** Museum of the City of New York. **Pp. 7** *(right),* **8, 9, 12** *(bottom),* **14, 20, 21, 25** *(insets),* **35** *(top right & bottom),* **38** *(left),* **40** *(right),* **41** *(right),* **42:** Picture Collection, New York Public Library. **Pp. 12** *(top),* **13** *(top & bottom left),* **30, 34, 35** *(top left),* **43:** New York Historical Society. **P. 13** *(bottom right):* Mariner's Museum, Newport News, Va. **Pp. 15, 24** *(left),* **25** *(bottom):* Illustrated London News Picture Library. **P. 16** *(top left):* Costume Research Center, Bath. **Pp. 16** *(top right),* **17** *(top):* AP/Wide World Photos. **P. 16** *(bottom):* reproduced by permission of Kensington Palace State Apartments and Court Dress Collection, Crown Copyright. **Pp. 17** *(bottom),* **25** *(top):* British Tourist Authority. **Pp. 18, 37, 39, 42:** Bettmann Archive/Hulton Picture Company. **P. 23:** British Information Service. **Pp. 24** *(right),* **25** *(center):* Mary Evans Picture Library. **Pp. 26, 27** *(right),* **28** *(top right & bottom):* courtesy of Tarka King. **P. 27** *(left):* New York Life Insurance Company Archives. **P. 28** *(top left):* Culver Pictures. **P. 29** *(left): Plantation Life on the Mississippi* by Williams Edwards Clement, copyright 1952, Pelican Publishing Company. **P. 32** *(insets):* Beinecke Library, Yale University. **P. 36:** Courtesy of Lord Hesketh. **P. 38** *(right):* Beken of Cowes, Ltd. **P. 39** *(top):* Bettman Archive. **P. 40** *(left):* Public Record Office. London. **P. 41** *(left):* Newport Historical Society Collection. **P. 44:** Gernsheim Collection, Harry Ransom Humanities Research Center, University of Texas at Austin. **P. 45:** Brown Brothers. **P. 47:** Trustees of the Chatsworth Settlement.

THE FAIR INVADERS

P. 51 *(left):* W.K. Vanderbilt Historical Society. **P. 51** *(right):* Museum of the City of Mobile. **Pg. 52, 53, 57** *(top right),* **58, 59, 60, 61, 62, 63** *(top right & bottom right),* **81:** New York Historical Society. **P. 54:** Vanderbilt Museum, Centerport, N.Y. **Pp. 55** *(top),* **72, 92:** Brown Brothers. **Pp. 55** *(bottom),* **70** *(top right):* Culver Pictures. **P. 57** *(top left):* Metropolitan Museum of Art, Gift of Orme Wilson, 1956, (56.52). **Pp. 57** *(bottom),* **65, 68, 70** *(top left),* **71** *(top & bottom left),* **75** *(insets),* **80, 83, 86, 87** *(center),* **94** *(bottom),* **104, 107** *(right),* **110** *(left),* **113, 114, 115, 116:** Picture Collection, New York Public Library. **Pp. 63** *(top left),* **75** *(bottom):* Museum of the City of New York. **Pp. 63** *(bottom left),* **77, 78** *(left & center),* **79** *(left): Dictionary of American Portraits,* by Dover Publications, Inc., 1967. **P. 64:** Kit Barry, Brattleboro, Vt. **Pp. 66, 69, 84, 95, 102** *(bottom),* **112:** Bettman Archive/Hulton Picture Company. **P. 67:** Billy Rose Theater Collection, New York Public Library at Lincoln Center, Astor, Lennox and Tilden Foundations. **P. 70** *(bottom):* Brooklyn Museum (label on 64.124.3). **P. 71** *(bottom right):* Museum of London. **P. 73:** Harvard University Archives. **Pp. 74** *(top),* **78 & 79** *(border):* New York Stock Exchange Archives. **Pp. 74** *(bottom),* **78** *(right):* Nevada Historical Society. **P. 75** *(top):* Reprinted with permission of AT&T Bell Laboratories Archives. **P. 76:** Marshall Field. **P. 79** *(right):* Cincinnati Historical Society. **Pp. 82, 88:** Mary Evans Picture Library. **P. 85:** AP/Wide World Photos. **Pp. 87** *(left)*, **97:** Nastional Portrait Gallery, London. **Pp. 87** *(right)*, **101, 118:** Courtesy of Tarka King. **P. 89:** Trustees of the Chatsworth Settlement. **P. 93:** Department of the Environment, London. **P. 96:** New York Public Library. **Pp. 99** *(left)*, **103** *(bottom)*, **111:** Illustrated News Picture Library. **Pp. 99** *(right)*, **103** *(top)*, **105, 117:** Bettmann Archive. **P. 100:** Courtesy of Countess of Craven. **P. 102** *(top):* Brown's Hotel. **P. 106:** Northern Ireland Tourist Board. **P. 107** *(left):* Chicago Historical Society. **P. 110** *(right):* British Travel Association Photo. **P. 119** *(top):* Courtesy of Lord Hesketh. **P. 119** *(bottom):* Grace Church.

AMERICAN HEIRESSES: WHAT WILL YOU BID?

P. 123: Wyoming State Archives, Museums and Historical Department. **Pp. 124** *(top)*, **133, 163** *(inset):* New York Historical Society. **Pp. 124** *(bottom)*, **126** *(bottom)*, **128** *(top left)*, **129** *(left)*, **135, 136** *(top right)*, **137** *(top left)*, **147, 151** *(left)*, **160** *(bottom)*, **161** *(bottom)*, **166, 169** *(bottom)*, **178** *(top):* Picture Collection, New York Public Library. **Pp. 125, 126** *(top)*, **130, 149:** By kind permission of His Grace the Duke of Marlborough, J.P., D.L. **Pp. 128** *(top right)*, **151** *(center)*, **157** *(left):* British Tourist Authority. **P. 128** *(bottom):* Bettmann Archive/Hulton Picture Company. **Pp. 129** *(right)*, **176:** Culver Pictures. **P. 131:** Illustrated London News Picture Library. **Pp. 132** *(left)*, **146, 152:** Brown Brothers. **P. 132** *(right)*, **150** *(right):* AP/Wide World Photos. **Pp. 134** *(top)*, **136** *(bottom left)*, **137** *(bottom right):* Kit Barry, Brattleboro, Vt. **P. 134** *(bottom left & right):* De Golyer Library, SMU, Dallas, Tx. **P. 136** *(top left):* Bar Harbor Historical Society. **P. 136** *(bottom right):* Edison National Historic Site, West Orange, N.J. **P. 137** *(top right):* Architect of the Capitol. **P. 137** *(center left):* Notman Photographic Archives, McCord Museum of Canadian History. **P. 137** *(center right):* Valentine Museum, Richmond, Va. **Pp. 138, 141** *(bottom left)*, **142, 144** *(bottom)*, **145** *(center left)*, **161** *(top & center left)*, **172 & 173** *(all homes):* Newport Historical Society. **Pp. 139, 145** *(center right & bottom)*, **163** *(bottom)*, **170, 171, 178** *(center)*, **179** *(top & bottom):* Museum of the City of New York. **Pp. 140** *(top)*, **148, 169** *(top):* Vanderbilt Museum, Centerport, N.Y. **Pp. 140** *(bottom)*, **141** (top): Courtesy of Countess of Craven. **P. 141** *(bottom right):* Mattes Photography/ Tuxedo Park Library. **P. 144** *(top):* French Government Tourist Office. **Pp. 144** *(center)*, **145** *(top)*, **157** *(right)*, **164:** Preservation Society of Newport County. **Pp. 150** *(left)*, **156** *(top)*, **179** *(center): Dictionary of American Portraits,* Dover Publications, Inc., 1967. **Pp. 150** *(center)*, **159, 168, 174:** Bettmann Archive. **P. 151** *(right):* Grace & Co. **P. 153:** Royal Commission on the Historical Monuments of England. **P. 155:** Mary Evans Picture Library. **P. 156** *(bottom):* Mariner's Museum, Newport News, Va. **P. 158:** Mansell Collection Ltd. **Pp. 160** *(top)*, **161** *(center)*, **162:** International Tennis Hall of Fame. **P. 172** *(flower):* W. Atlee Burpee & Co. **P. 177:** Courtesy of Lord Hesketh. **P. 178:** New York Public Library.

MARRIED HEIRESSES

P. 183: Anne Robins. **Pp. 184, 200, 211, 213** *(top)*, **216, 233** *(bottom):* Illustrated London News Picture Library. **P. 185:** Courtesy of Miss M.V. Howey/Northumberland Record Office. **P. 186:** Irish Tourist Board. **Pp. 187, 219** *(bottom)*, **232** *(bottom)*, **250** *(right):* Bettmann Archive. **Pp. 188** *(inset)*, **219** *(top):* British Tourist Authority. **Pp. 188, 197, 198, 201** *(bottom)*, **202, 203** *(left)*, **208, 214** *(left)*, **217, 224, 231** *(bottom right)*, **232** *(top)*, **235, 242, 249** *(top right)*, **250** *(left)*, **252** *(right)*, **253, 255, 258:** Picture Collection, New York Public Library. **Pp. 190, 203** *(center)*, **239, 252** *(left)*, Bettmann Archive/Hulton Picture Library. **P. 191:** National Trust Photographic Library/ Jonathan Gibson. **P. 194:** National Trust, Kedleston; photograph, Courtauld Institute of Art. **P. 195** *(left)*, Mike Williams/ Royal Oak Foundation, Inc. **P. 195** *(right):* Andrew Halsam/Royal Oak Foundation, Inc. **Pp. 199, 215:** Courtesy of Tarka King. **Pp. 201** *(top)*, **207:** Mary Evans Picture Library. **P. 203** *(right):* Mansell Collection, Ltd. **Pp. 204, 249** *(bottom right):* Culver Pictures. **Pp. 205, 214** *(right):* AP/Wide World Photos. **P. 206:** Indian Office Library. **Pp. 209, 221, 251, 257** *(bottom right):* Trustees of the Chatsworth Settlement. **Pp. 210, 213** *(bottom)*, **218, 241:** By kind permission of His Grace, the Duke of Marlborough, J.P., D.L. **Pp. 220, 226** *(left):* Brown Brothers. **P. 222:** County Record Office, Huntington. **P. 223:** The National Trust, Erddig. **Pp. 225, 233** *(top):* Courtesy of Countess of Craven. **P. 226** *(right):* Stoneleigh Abbey Preservation Trust. **Pp. 227, 232** *(center)*, **236, 237** *(left)*, **245:** Courtesy of Lord Hesketh. **P. 228:** Copyright Reserved. Reproduced by gracious permission of Her Majesty Queen Elizabeth II. **P. 229:** Gordonstoun School. **Pp. 230** *(top)*, **231** *(top & bottom left):* Roxburghe Estates Office. **P. 230** *(bottom):* Pilgrim Press Ltd. **P. 237** *(center):* National Trust Photographic Library. **P. 237** *(right):* A.F. Kersting. **Pp. 238, 257** *(bottom left):* Museum of the City of New York. **Pp. 244, 246, 247:** Vanderbilt Museum, Centerport, N.Y. **P. 248:** Archives of American Art, Smithsonian Institution. **P. 249** *(top left):* National Gallery of Art, Washington, D.C. **P. 249** *(bottom left):* National Portrait Gallery, London/Collection Ormond Family. **P. 256** *(top):* Metropolitan Museum of Art, Gift of Orme Wilson and R. Thornton Wilson in memory of their mother, Mrs. Caroline Schermerhorn Astor Wilson, 1949, (49.3.28ab). **P. 256** *(bottom):* Brooklyn Museum, Cape, Worth, Gift of Princess Viggo. **P. 257** *(top):* Metropolitan Museum of Art, Costume Institute (CI 39.6.1ab).

THE NEW HEIRESSES

Pp. 263 *(left),* **268, 269** *(right),* **280** *(top),* **290** *(bottom),* **291** *(top),* **294, 296** *(left),* **297, 300, 301, 304** *(top):* Bettmann Archive/Hulton Picture Library. **Pp. 263, 271** *(left),* **272** *(top),* **279** *(bottom),* **288** *(top),* **295, 308, 309, 312** *(top):* Picture Collection, New York Public Library. **P. 264:** Museum of the City of New York. **Pp. 265** *(left),* **316** *(bottom):* Dictionary of American Portraits, Dover Publications, 1967. **Pp. 265** *(center),* **276, 281** *(bottom),* **311:** Vanderbilt Museum, Centerport, N.Y. **Pp. 265** *(right),* **275:** Brown Brothers. **Pp. 266** *(left),* **279** *(top):* Courtesy of Countess of Craven. **P. 266** *(right):* New York Historical Society. **Pp. 269** *(left),* **278, 291** *(bottom),* **312** *(bottom),* **319** *(left):* Bettmann Archive. **Pp. 270, 272** *(bottom),* **277, 280** *(left center & bottom),* **281** *(top left & top right),* **282** *(right),* **284** *(bottom),* **287, 293** *(top),* **296** *(right),* **303, 304** *(bottom),* **305** *(bottom),* **306, 307, 309** *(top & bottom right),* **310, 313, 315** *(top left),* **316** *(top),* **317, 318:** Illustrated London News Picture Library. **Pp. 271** *(right),* **285:** AP/Wide World Photo. **P. 273:** Winston Churchill Memorial & Library, Westminster College, Fulton, Mo. **Pp. 280** *(center right),* **319** *(right):* Mansell Collection Ltd. **Pp. 282** *(left),* **283:** Trustees of the Chatsworth Settlement. **P. 286:** Royal Commission on the Historical Monuments of England. **P. 288** *(bottom):* Irish Tourist Board. **P. 289:** Lucinda Lambton/Arcaid. **P. 290** *(top):* National Portrait Gallery, London. **P. 291:** Copyright reserved to Her Majesty Queen Elizabeth II. **P. 293:** Valentine Museum, Richmond, Va. **P. 298:** Nevada Historical Society. **P. 299:** By kind permission of His Grace the Duke of Marlborough, J.P., D.L. **Pp. 302, 348:** Courtesy of Lord Hesketh. **Pp. 284** *(top),* **305** *(top):* Mary Evans Picture Library. **P. 314:** Granger Collection. **P. 315** *(top right):* Carnegie Library of Pittsburgh. **P. 315** *(bottom):* Bettmann Newsphoto.

AN AMERICAN HEIRESS DIRECTORY

Pp. 324, 325, 326, 327, 328, 329, 331, 333, 336, 351 *(top),* **354** *(top),* **358 & 359:** Illustrated London News Picture Library. **Pp. 330, 334:** Brown Brothers. **P. 335** *(top):* W.R. Grace & Co. **P. 335** *(bottom):* Bettmann Archive/Hulton Picture Library. **P. 337:** Courtesy of Tarka King. **P. 338:** Trustees of the Chatsworth Settlement. **Pp. 339, 352:** Culver Pictures. **P. 340:** Chicago Historical Society. **P. 341:** Courtesy of Countess of Craven. **P. 344:** Pfizer, Inc. **P. 346:** AP/Wide World Photos. **P. 348:** Courtesy of Lord Hesketh. **P. 349:** Stonor Enterprises. **P. 350:** By kind permission of His Grace, the Duke of Marlborough, J.P., D.L. **P. 351** *(bottom):* Picture Collection, New York Public Library. **P. 354** *(bottom):* Panhandle-Plains Historical Museum, Canyon, Tx. **P. 357:** Cincinnati Historical Society.